THE UNITED NATIONS

Also by Geoff Simons and published by Macmillan

IRAQ: From Sumer to Saddam
LIBYA: The Struggle for Survival

The United Nations

A Chronology of Conflict

Geoff Simons

M
MACMILLAN

First published 1994 by
THE MACMILLAN PRESS LTD
Houndmills, Basingstoke, Hampshire RG21 2XS
and London
Companies and representatives
throughout the world

ISBN 0-333-59378-2

A catalogue record for this book is available
from the British Library

Printed in Great Britain by
Antony Rowe Ltd
Chippenham, Wiltshire

Contents

List of Tables

Preface

I have long thought that many types of non-fiction books are impossible to write – for reason of what logicians are happy to call the 'combinatorial explosion'. The writer takes a theme and then finds that research spins off in every direction: everything is pertinent to the task in hand. And if *everything* is relevant to the theme, how can *anything* be omitted from the finished book? Despite the ambitious scope of this volume I am painfully aware that within the confines of the permitted wordage there is much that is left out.

If some books are impossible to write, some are more impossible than others. The United Nations, unique among institutions, is universal in its scope and ambitions, embracing 184 Member States in early 1994 and striving to address all their areas of concern: peace, economic development, science and technology, morality and law, employment, ecology, education, health, human rights. . . . A *full* understanding of the United Nations would need a detailed knowledge of almost every nation on earth, an educated insight into almost every human discipline.

Anyone wishing to write a book about the United Nations can tackle the problem in various ways, most easily by selecting a particular aspect or theme. This approach, not open to the generalist, inevitably generates distortion: in particular, failing to do justice to the richness of the institution and its traditions.

There is another distortion, typical in academic books that purport to deal with social and political questions. There are facts, chronologies and analyses in abundance but somehow the people at the heart of the studies are absent. I am sensitive to an observation made by James Walvin (in his excellent *Black Ivory: A History of British Slavery*, 1992): 'We now know more about the slave trade than ever before. Oddly enough, in the process the slaves have disappeared from view.'

This is a malaise that afflicts many books about the United Nations. The institutions and procedures may be well delineated, the use of the veto nicely chronicled, the statistics assiduously collected; but somehow the people are left out. There is little mention of wounds, blood and death; of suffering humanity. But the desperate issues that confront people are at the heart of the human predicament. And these issues, nothing else, are the only legitimate reason for the United Nations.

GEOFF SIMONS

Acknowledgements

I am very grateful to staff of the United Nations Information Centre (20 Buckingham Gate, London SW1E 6LB), who always responded promptly and skilfully to my many enquiries: Alexandra McLeod, Elizabeth Lee and George Armstrong.

I appreciate also the efforts of staff, often in busy circumstances and with inadequate resources, in the Stockport and Manchester Central Libraries.

Christine Simons provided invaluable research and editorial support.

GEOFF SIMONS

Introduction

The United Nations is many things. At best it is a reservoir of selfless idealism, a symbol of the essential oneness of humankind. Here it enshrines the ageless dream of universal peace and justice, the yearning for a harmonious world. At worst it has come to represent bureaucracy and mismanagement, at once an ineffective busybody and a tool in the hands of powerful states.

How we view the United Nations derives in part from our political perspective, but also in part from the nature of the UN itself. The very complexity of the United Nations, taken together with its many associated institutions, means that it is quite incapable of functioning with a coherent identity. This has been shown many times over the history of the United Nations, but one example will suffice: after the 1991 Gulf War a range of UN aid agencies worked hard to counter the drastic effects of continuing UN sanctions on Iraq. Thus the United Nations – like many great religious texts – has multiple personalities, a definite boon for exegetes: you select a focus that serves your purposes and that becomes a defining principle.

The character of the United Nations, in its many manifestations, cannot be divorced from its historical roots. It was founded half a century ago but it sits squarely in a complex tradition that runs through all human history. Part I (Chapters 1–3) profiles some of the main contributing elements in that tradition and describes the main organs and institutions that came to define the United Nations. Chapter 1 shows how such elements as peace studies, human rights and international law came together in the tradition; it gives particular attention to the League of Nations, the forerunner of the United Nations. Chapter 2 describes the origins of the UN, emphasising the extent to which the UN and its linked bodies were shaped by the United States with an eye on its own strategic interests. The main UN organs and institutions are profiled in Chapter 3.

The main influence on the development of the United Nations in its early years was the Cold War – in which Washington was a principal player. With the collapse of the Soviet bloc the first major phase in the life of the United Nations was at an end. The United States no longer needed to exploit the UN, where possible, in an anti-Communist crusade, but there were still vital strategic interests to protect. After the disintegration of Soviet power, Washington's exploitation of the United Nations assumed a different character.

Part II (Chapters 4–7) profiles first (Chapter 4) some of the most significant features of the Cold War, the crucial framework that determined how the United Nations would confront political disputes over several decades. One of the inevitable consequences of the Cold War was that extremist attitudes to the United Nations were stimulated in both the major power blocs.

The Soviet Union seized the chance to spread propaganda via the United Nations to the Third World, well perceived by the Soviets as the exploited bulk of humanity; while some dissident Communist agitators wanted no truck with an international body clearly cast in the image of Wall Street. Washington for its part calculated that the United Nations, particularly its financial institutions, could be exploited to advance American interests; while a lead advocate of the American Right could still proclaim: 'When the UN finally topples, it will be the result of a ground swell of renewed patriotism and a rebirth of the American spirit of victory over tyranny – a return to the traditional American principles which made this country great.'[1]

In Chapter 5, profiles are given of the main issues that the United Nations was forced to confront through the period of the Cold War. Here brief background information is included to convey something of the character of the issues in question: it is always important to remember that the issues – and what they meant for individual human beings – are the primary matter. Chapter 6 highlights some of the main features of the East European collapse, the great conflux of events that was to launch the second macro phase of UN evolution and bring much ill-considered talk of a New World Order. Now the US hegemony was glaringly obvious. Throughout the period of the Cold War the United States had contrived in many different ways to manipulate the United Nations, but now Washington's dominance in the international body was transparent. Was the United Nations '*World voice or US puppet?*'[2] Events were soon to provide an answer. Chapter 7 describes the nature of the US-mediated UN involvement in various important disputes following the Communist collapse in Eastern Europe.

Part III (Chapter 8) gives a brief profile of questions being asked about reform of the United Nations. For many years there was little hope of substantial change, with the five Permanent Members of the Security Council deemed unlikely to welcome reforms that might dilute their power. Thus when British Foreign Secretary Douglas Hurd visited Tokyo in April 1993 he emphasised that the existing Permanent Members would remain on the Council, and that Japan should not hold out hopes of gaining a permanent seat.[3] Two months later, to evident British consternation, Madeleine Albright, the US ambassador to the United Nations, declared that Washington would work for permanent seats on the Council for Germany and Japan. It seemed, after all, that radical reform of the UN might be on the agenda.

It is important to remember that the high-profile manoeuvres of the Security Council represent only a small part of the lineaments of global power. A key focus of global control in the interest of world capitalism is the IMF/World Bank/GATT nexus, a crucial part of the UN structure. Here the main purpose is to expose the world to investment capital, irrespective of the (often) devastating impacts on local communities or national peoples: 'In Africa, mention the [World] Bank and the Fund [the IMF] and tempers rise, faces harden, voices are raised. They are the twin faces of an evil empire . . . The Bank was originally a development fund, but has become the West's policeman for economic policy in developing countries, particularly Africa.'[4] In the same vein, Mari Marcel Thekaekara, having worked for a decade with indigenous people in the Indian state of Tamil Nadu, comments (in *New Internationalist & Amnesty*, June 1993) on how the IMF and the World Bank impose their will 'through the process of *structural adjustment*, the newest obscenity in the development dictionary'. He adds:

> Open your markets, they decree. Cut public spending. Remove subsidies on health and food. (If people die in the process, population growth will be tamed; an added bonus, that.) Produce more goods for export. Do all these things without fail or we will order sanctions against you.

Under the terms of the new GATT agreement 'farmers would no longer have the right to replant their own seeds if these had been patented by multinationals'. Instead, the poor peasants, without funds or other resources, would be forced to purchase seeds from the global corporations or face the confiscation of their land: 'The plan is diabolical.'

Pierre Sané, the Director-General of Amnesty International, has emphasised the links between political repression and economic policy pursued at the behest of the banking institutions dominated by the West:

> The World Bank, through its economic programme, is imposing an economic order that means reducing social rights, by cutting health and education policies. Governments have to restructure their economies in order to pay back their debts and they use force in order to impose their views, and what can a weak government do in front of the IMF. We have seen food riots in many countries which governments explain were the results of policies they have implemented which were forced down their throats by the IMF.[5]

It seems obvious that the interests behind the powerful banking institutions will continue to derive financial benefits from patterns of world trade that are forcing much of the global population into destitution. It is hard to imagine how such patterns, protected by vast military and economic power, will not persist in the years ahead. At the same time we need to note the growing constraints on American power, caused largely by the burden of the US deficits complemented by the growing assertion of European and Japanese interests (which themselves profit from the IMF/World Bank/GATT nexus).

It is significant that Washington has so far been unable to persuade the rest of the Security Council to impose a mandatory ban on Libyan oil exports, in support of US strategic interests; that Europe has been prepared to dissent from Washington over the Yugoslavian chaos; and that the British Trade Secretary, Richard Needham, has been prepared to denounce Washington's illegal trade blockade of Cuba, an odious policy – in violation of UN General Assembly Resolutions 47/19 and 48/16 – that in 1993 contributed to neural eye disease in 50,000 people and malnutrition in many more. On 27 May 1993 Dr David Levinson, a San Francisco physician who visited Cuba, stated that the US embargo was causing a severe shortage of medicines and 'effectively holding the health of the Cuban people hostage . . . This is an inhumane, cruel policy which must be ended.'[6] On 26 October 1993 Alexander Watson, US Assistant Under-Secretary of State for Inter-American Affairs, declared in a keynote speech that the blockade of Cuba would continue. There would be no respite for 'a society trembling on the brink of famine and chaos' (*The Guardian*, 28 October 1993).

The embargo on Cuba is part of the developing global pattern, with powerful interests – sustained by UN-linked institutions – using their growing control over world food resources to impose their political will. This is the reality of global power that bears so heavily on the peoples of the world.

There are at the same time various signs of US military retrenchment, partly as a recognition of the collapse of the Communist threat and partly as an inevitable consequence of budgetary mismanagement through the Reagan–Bush years. In May 1993 Peter Tarnoff, Under-Secretary for Political Affairs in the Clinton Administration, commented that an American lead in international crises 'is going to be the case much less than it was before. We simply don't have the leverage. We don't have the influence, the inclination to use military force.'[7] The comments were discounted by White House spokeswoman Dee Dee Myers: 'Our responsibility of leadership is undiminished'; but then she offered the significant caveat that US leadership in the future would perhaps be 'a somewhat different leadership'. At the same time there were reports that American military planners had revised US contingency plans downwards: in future, we were told, the United States would be able to fight only one war at a time. Such considerations will progressively influence Washington's perception of its role in the world community in general and in the United Nations in particular.

The UN itself is currently entrapped in various massive disputes, unable to act with adequate resources or sufficient authority but unable to extricate itself in ways that would avoid immense loss of prestige and credibility. In such regions as Angola, Cambodia and the former Yugoslavia there were few reasons for optimism: in all these theatres the United Nations had made large commitments but had failed to achieve the intended objectives. Worse, in Somalia the UN forces – under precipitate American prompting – found themselves in direct military clashes with the Somali people. In June 1993 Washington, for reasons best known to American policy planners, authorised a series of air strikes against Somali targets. The bulk of the aid campaign ground to a halt; Somali casualties mounted; and there was a massive upsurge of popular feeling against the UN and US presence. All such matters were combining to make the future direction of the United Nations – some said its very existence – uncertain.

The League of Nations was ultimately defeated by disagreements among its members, by the enervating failure to reach consensus on the major issues of the day. It had long been obvious that a number of powerful League members were systematically violating both the spirit and the letter of the Covenant; and equally obvious that there was no way to construct a consensus that would preserve the authority of the League. In circumstances of deepening malaise the League of Nations, having suffered many minor wounds, was at last mortally impaled on the trident of Manchuria, Abyssinia and Spain. It remains to be seen whether the United Nations, suffering many minor setbacks, will at last be mortally impaled on the spikes of Angola, Cambodia, Somalia and the former Yugoslavia.

NOTES

1. G. Edward Griffin, *The Fearful Master: A Second Look at the United Nations* (Belmont, Mass.: Western Islands, 1972) p. 231.
2. Godfrey Hodgson, 'World voice or US puppet?', *The Independent* (London), 18 June 1991.
3. Kevin Rafferty, 'Hurd discourages Tokyo's UN hopes', *The Guardian* (London), 8 April 1993.
4. Richard Dowden, 'Inside this building the officials are deciding what's best for Africa', *The Independent on Sunday* (London), 28 March 1993. One estimate suggests that more than 100,000 foreign experts working in Africa consume a

major chunk of foreign aid (Tami Hultman, 'World Bank signals U-turn on African aid policy', *The Guardian* (London), 24 May 1993).
5. Leonard Doyle, 'Clinton wants UN to take on tyrannical rulers', *The Independent* (London), 14 June 1993.
6. Noll Scott, 'Havana to lose last trade lifeline', *The Guardian* (London), 28 May 1993.
7. David Usborne, 'White House in foreign policy row', *The Independent* (London), 27 May 1993.

Part I
Gestation and Birth

1 Roots

And he shall judge among the nations, and shall rebuke many people: and they shall beat their swords into plowshares, and their spears into pruning hooks: nation shall not lift up sword against nation, neither shall they learn war any more.

Isaiah 2:4

The words of Isaiah,* much quoted and finding resonances throughout all human history, symbolise the ubiquitous yearning for a peaceful world in which political differences are settled by talk and not by physical conflict. This vision of a harmonious international order was one of the motivating forces behind the creation of the League of Nations (and later of the United Nations). It was not the only factor. People also envisaged how human rights *within* states could be protected, how the benefits of medical science could be brought to all, how the global environment could be protected, and much else – all within the framework of international law.

It was perhaps inevitable that the practical fruits of such a multifaceted idealism would often be traduced and suborned by political pressures in the real world, where hegemonic powers were characteristically concerned more with interests than with ethics. But it would be too cynical to assume that all idealism necessarily perishes on the altar of *realpolitik*. The League was shaped – at least in part – by an idealistic dream of a better world, as is the United Nations. It is useful to recall some of the theoretical and practical contributions to the League/UN tradition.

TOWARDS THE LEAGUE

There have always been thoughts of an international order, established by military conquest, economic imperialism or spiritual and ethical commitment. Ancient conquerors were proud to extend their sway throughout the known world, and proselytisers of every hue have always been keen to unite humanity under their persuasion. The great Dutch humanist Erasmus (1466–1536) imagined 'kingdoms of moderate power united in a Christian league',

* In a different mood Isaiah was keen to celebrate the wrath of God: 'Thy men shall fall by the sword, and thy mighty in the war' (3:25).

though the fathers of the Roman Catholic Church, increasingly preoccupied with the fruits of mammon, had a different universal vision. Some men envisaged practical political arrangements whereby the threat of war would be removed. Thus Maximilien de Béthune, Duc de Sully (1560–1641), who became Henry IV's Chief Minister and trusted counsellor, gave details in his *Memoirs* of an ambitious Grand Design, a scheme that echoed in the Covenant of the Twentieth-Century League. Sully envisaged a Universal Christian Commonwealth of Europe, with a supreme Grand Council able to consider disputes that threatened the peace and built upon radical territorial adjustments framed to establish a stable order. He proposed that his own country, France, should renounce all territorial claims on other states, as a condition for more harmonious relations between the European nations.

At the same time the Dutch jurist and theologian Hugo Grotius (1583–1645) was working on his magisterial *De Jure Belli et Pacis* (On the Law of War and Peace), published in 1625, in which he sought to lay the basis for legal relations between states and so created the concept of international law. Grotius recognised that there may be circumstances in which war was just and lawful but protested against the prevailing view that powerful rulers could lawfully begin wars whenever they chose. His efforts to make legal distinctions between just and unjust wars were largely ignored in international law until the framing of the League Covenant nearly three centuries later.

In 1693 William Penn (1644–1718), the Quaker founder of Pennsylvania, published *An Essay Towards the Present and Future Peace of Europe*, in which he paid tribute to Sully's Grand Design and made his own practical proposals. There would be a 'Sovereign or Imperial Diet, Parliament, or State of Europe; before which . . . should be brought all differences depending between sovereign and another that cannot be made up by private embassies before the sessions begin. . . .' Any 'sovereignty' that refused to submit a dispute to the assembly would be compelled to comply by the other sovereignties, 'united as one strength'. Penn proposes a method of voting in the Diet, the majority required for a decision, how delegates should be sent there, and other details (showing in one instance nice regard for the importance of geometry: 'To avoid quarrel for precedency, the room may be round, and have divers doors to come in and go out by, to prevent exceptions'). In 1713 the Abbé de Saint-Pierre proposed a *Project for Settling Perpetual Peace in Europe*, which, along with Sully, stimulated the French political philosopher Jean Jacques Rousseau (1712–78) to publish in 1761 his *Judgement on a Plan for Perpetual Peace*. Now Russia was to be added to the ambitious scheme for a federal Europe, with rulers forced 'to be just and pacific'. The new arrangements would safeguard princes 'against the ambition of irresponsible and iniquitous Pretenders and the revolts of rebellious subjects' – a firm defence of the status quo that seems paradoxical in a thinker usually associated with revolutionary causes. There is reference also to the need for a Code of International Law.

Such ideas in turn influenced the German philosopher Immanuel Kant (1724–1804) who, in the essays *An Idea for a Universal History from a Cosmopolitan Point of View* (1784) and *Perpetual Peace* (1795), argued for an international league of constitutional democracies governed by the rule of law. In *Perpetual Peace* Kant declared:

> Nature will drive men with the scourge of war, with the extravagant and ever-growing burden of armaments, the weight of which must be felt in the end by every State even when at peace: she will compel them to make attempts, halting at first and incomplete, and then, after much desolation, destruction and revolution, to do what reason could have taught them at once without so many bitter experiences, namely to give up their lawless life of savages and enter a League of Nations, an organisation where every State, even the smallest, can expect security and peace, not from its own power or its own decision as to what is right in its own cause, but from this great Society of Nations.

Here there were principles rather than a detailed plan: states should be run by constitutional governments rather than by totalitarian despots; no state should interfere with another; standing armies should be gradually disbanded; foreign loans should be forbidden. The Kantian prescriptions served as an inspiration to activists in America and elsewhere seeking to create the League of Nations.

In 1816, following the efforts of the Quaker William Allen, the pacifist Peace Society was founded, followed by the monthly journal *Herald of Peace*, sent to public libraries, ministers of religion and Members of Parliament. A branch of the London-based Peace Society was formed in 1827 in Birmingham under the leadership of the Quaker Joseph Sturge. Quaker pacificism was often attacked by mainstream Christian writers. Thus an article in 1819 in the *Northumberland Monthly* declaims: 'Will holding out the idea that war is inconsistent with Christianity restrain the Turks, the pirates of Algiers, or the savage Indians of North America? Nothing could be more gratifying to Turkish and heathen nations than to hear that Christians had abolished war; in this case every European kingdom would soon be deluged with blood, and every Christian community exterminated.' The American Peace Society was founded in 1828 when William Ladd of New Hampshire welded together a number of local groups. Ladd himself advanced ideas that would later influence the shaping of the League of Nations and the United Nations. He proposed, for example, the development of international law and the creation of an international court:

> First – A congress of ambassadors from all those Christian and civilised nations who should choose to send them, for the purpose of settling the principles of international law by compact and agreement, of the nature of a mutual treaty, and also of devising and promoting plans for the preservation of peace, and meliorating the condition of man. Second – A court of nations, composed of the most able citizens in the world, to arbitrate or judge such cases as should be brought before it, by the mutual consent of two or more contending nations.

A General Peace Convention was held in London in 1843, with delegates from the United Kingdom, the United States, France and Switzerland. Quakers and Whig Members of Parliament were prominent at the Convention, which, according to *The Times*, was also attended by 'a few hundred less prominent Englishmen, and a scattering of not very influential foreigners'. Further Peace Conferences were held from 1848 to 1853, led by such committed activists as Henry Richard and Elihu Burritt. At the 1848 Congress the topic of disarmament was broached, to be supported by Charles Dickens in the *Daily News*. Activists such as Richard Cobden and John Bright urged free trade as a means of bringing nations together, with Bright denouncing the Crimean War while at the same time opposing the idealistic absolutism of the Peace Society. Now there were various themes – the pacific settlement of disputes, the growing importance of international law, agitation for free trade – coming together to prepare the ground for the creation of international bodies that would symbolise the community of nations. The idea of a League of Nations was born centuries before it came to practical fruition, and throughout the nineteenth century the idea was further refined and developed. It is interesting, for example, that Bertrand Russell reminds us (in *Which Way to Peace?*, 1936) that in 1871 his father, Lord Amberley, advocated a version of the League, 'with the whole apparatus of economic and military sanctions'.

The industrial developments of the nineteenth century encouraged a practical internationalism as a route to commerce and the pacific solution of disputes. It was increasingly recognised that states stood to benefit by observing international norms and rules, and by encouraging their (sometimes more powerful) neighbours to do the same. Various international organs were set up and granted powers over individual administrations: for example, the Danube Commission (established in 1856); the International

Telegraphic Union (1865); the Universal Postal Union (1874), the International Institute of Agriculture (1905); and the International Health Office (1907). By 1914 there were more than 30 such organisations. At the same time major inter- and extra-governmental bodies were working on the codification and development of international law: for example, the *Institut de Droit International*, founded in 1873 in Brussels. The nineteenth century also saw the development of the powerful Concert of Europe, the ill-defined institution that enabled the major European powers to settle a number of disputes, often against the interests of weaker nations, without resort to war. The Concert, gravely handicapped by the absence of a formal constitution, failed to prevent various military conflicts, not least the European conflagration that began in 1914.

On 24 August 1898 Tsar Nicholas II of Russia proposed a conference to achieve the purpose 'of insuring to all peoples the benefit of a real and durable peace, and, above all, of putting an end to the progressive developments of the present armaments'. Representative of 26 nations assembled on 18 May the following year at The Hague, the first international conference to have legislative features. At the 1899 Hague Conference (18 May–29 July) the question of arms limitation went unresolved but The Hague Tribunal (Permanent Court of Arbitration) was set up and a ban was imposed on poison gas, 'dumdum' (expanding) bullets, and aerial bombardment from balloons. Forty-four nations attended the second International Peace Conference at The Hague (15 June–18 October 1907). Again no agreement was reached on arms limitation, though agreement was reached on the rights of neutral shipping, general conventions on land and sea warfare, and on the banning of submarine mines. A third conference was cancelled because of the outbreak of the First World War, but now the basis had been laid for the creation of the League of Nations.

THE FOURTEEN POINTS

Thomas Woodrow Wilson (1856–1924), a university law professor and the twenty-eighth President of the United States, was one of the principal architects of the League of Nations. On 8 January 1918, in a message to the US Congress, he detailed the conditions of peace for the normalisation of international relations at the end of the Great War. The preamble to this speech includes the words: 'What we demand . . . is that the world be made fit and safe to live in; and particularly that it be made safe for every peace-loving nation which, like our own, wishes to live its own life, determine its own institutions, be assured of justice and fair dealing by the other peoples of the world as against force and selfish aggression.' There then follow the celebrated Fourteen Points variously urging open diplomacy (I), freedom of navigation on the seas (II), free trade (III), a reduction in armaments (IV), an adjustment of all colonial claims (V), and matters of territorial adjustment and sovereignty (VI–XIII). The final Point (XIV), the herald of the League, urged that:

> A general association of nations must be formed under specific covenants for the purpose of affording mutual guarantees of political independence and territorial integrity to great and small states alike.

With an undimmed commitment that frequently exasperated others, Woodrow Wilson worked first to establish the Covenant of the League as part of the Paris Peace agreement; and then to sell the spirit and letter of the League to a sceptical America. On 30 May 1919, in his Memorial Day speech at the American graveyard at Suresnes near Paris, he included the words:

> . . . it is our duty to take and maintain the safeguards which will see to it that the mothers of America and the mothers of France and England and Italy and Belgium and all the other suffering nations should never be called upon for this sacrifice again. This can be done. It must be done, and it will be done. The great thing that these men left us . . . is the great instrument of the League of Nations.

Wilson then placed a wreath, sent by the Boy Scouts of America, by the graves, and a Frenchwoman added her own flowers. Two months later, on 10 July, Wilson presented the Versailles Treaty (which includes the Covenant of the League of Nations) for the approval of the US Senate.

THE PEACE CONFERENCE

It was decided that the Conference would be held in France, not least as a gesture to Clemenceau's premiership and as a recognition that France was now the main Continental power. The delegates for the participating nations[1] were accompanied by vast numbers of permanent officials, technical advisors, secretaries and clerical assistants. For example, about a thousand staff were drafted in to support the British delegation in Paris, the Hotel

Majestic and the Hotel Astoria taken over in their entirety to serve as a little Whitehall. In an attempt to emulate the Vienna Congress of 1814–15 the various European aristocracies opened salons, held banquets and gave balls. Such events were duly reported, but in the more serious political areas the Allied Press, though expensively lodged, encountered problems from the outset.

In an ironic violation of Wilson's First Point ('diplomacy shall proceed always frankly and in the public view'), the Press was initially excluded from the sittings of the Congress, and the delegates themselves pledged not to communicate with the journalists. Pressure was brought to bear on President Wilson and Lloyd George and a compromise was achieved: 'representatives of the Press shall be admitted to the meetings of the Full Conference, but on necessary occasions the deliberations of the Conference may be held *in camera*'. In the event no full (or plenary) meetings were held, except to endorse the decisions arrived at secretly by the Great Powers.

The leading powers began informal discussions on 9 January 1919. On 12 January the Five-power Supreme War Council (comprising Britain, America, France, Italy and Japan) was established, to be joined by the Minor Powers only when matters concerning them were discussed. The Conference was formally inaugurated on 18 January at a plenary meeting at the French Foreign Office. Here Clemenceau, having been elected permanent president, declared that the programme of the Conference had already been laid out by President Wilson, and that now the aim was not just a Continental Peace but a peace of peoples. At this plenary session, observed by 200 journalists in an adjoining ante-room, it was decided that the second sitting should concern the central question of the League of Nations. On 25 January a resolution to establish the League, moved by President Wilson and seconded by Lloyd George, was passed in plenary session. The vote was unanimous and enthusiastic, though soon fresh tensions emerged. Belgium protested at being excluded from the real work of the Conference, now dominated by the self-constituted Supreme War Council. It was clear that the smaller states had gained little and that the Great Five could do as they pleased. Commissions were appointed, involving the smaller states, to investigate such matters as reparations, enemy violations of the laws of war, international labour legislation, and the international regime of ports, waterways and railways. But the Great Powers reserved to themselves the right to adjudicate over matters most directly affecting their interests.

The third plenary sitting was held on 14 February to discuss in detail the Covenant of the League of Nations, after which President Wilson returned to America for a short visit. On 19 February a French anarchist fired a shot at Clemenceau, wounding him in the shoulder. This event, coupled with Wilson's absence, suggested to the world that the Conference was losing momentum. The Armistice had been renewed but there appeared to be little progress towards a settled peace. The feeling was growing that Wilson was more interested in the League than in the local interests of Europe, a perception that began to generate a reaction against the League. When Wilson returned from America on 13 March he immediately streamlined the Council of Five, reducing the ten members (two from each of the Five) to four men (one from each of Britain, the United States, France and Italy). The revamped Council did little to remove the prevailing distrust and dissatisfaction. On 25 March Clemenceau himself was attacked in the French Chamber of Deputies, and two days later President Wilson found it necessary to issue a statement denying that the delay in establishing a European peace had anything to do with the institution of the League of Nations.

On 28 April 1919 the fifth plenary session settled and approved the draft of the Covenant of the League; on 5 May a further plenary approved the Treaty of Peace – without a vote but with dissent voiced only by small states that the Great Powers felt able to ignore (the new Council of Four was now one of Three, a dissatisfied Italy having withdrawn its delegates). Two days later, on the anniversary of the sinking of the *Lusitania*, the Treaty was delivered to the German delegacy at the Trianon Palace at Versailles. Clemenceau handed over the document, containing 440 separate articles in about 80,000 words, and declared: 'The time has come when we must settle our accounts. You have asked for peace. We are ready to give you peace. We shall present to you now a book which contains our conditions.' At first Germany demanded concessions from the Allies, but on 23 June her final submission was announced. Five days later, in the famous Hall of Mirrors at Versailles, Germany signed the Treaty of Peace. Clemenceau was at last able to declare: 'the signature of the conditions of peace between the Allied and Associated Powers and the German Republic is an accomplished fact. The session is adjourned.'

THE COVENANT

President Wilson was keen that the League Covenant be made part of the Peace Treaty: in this way the existence of the Covenant would be assured even if there was significant public and political movement against the idea of the League. In fact, Wilson managed to secure the Covenant as the first section of the fifteen-section Peace Treaty (the Treaty of Versailles). He had declared that he could not see 'how a treaty of peace could be drawn up or how both elasticity and security could be obtained save under a League of Nations'; the alternative was to maintain 'the idea of the Great Powers and of balance of power, and such an idea had always produced only aggression and war; the people are heartily sick of such a course and want the peace conference and the powers to take an entirely new course of action'. Some of the participants in the Peace Conference saw the presence of the Covenant as a means of ameliorating some of the harshness and errors in the rest of the Treaty. The Germans, perhaps predictably, resented the fact that the Covenant appeared as a section of the Treaty text. Thus Fritz Berber, Director of the Berlin-based Research Department, *Hochschule für Politik*, observed that arms had been laid down

> for the promise of a new world order in which there would be neither victims nor vanquished, neither annexations nor reparations . . . These hopes rapidly turned out to be a terrible illusion . . . It is not amazing that the German nation turned all its disillusion about Versailles at the same time against the League . . . the League in many instances was made the executor of Versailles . . . the most important regulations of the Covenant seemed to be meant for nothing else but for the maintenance of the unbearable Versailles *status quo* . . . The connection between Versailles and Geneva [the subsequent home of the League] did not lift up Versailles to the level of Geneva, but tended to drag down Geneva to the level of Versailles.

If such an interpretation were sound, how ironic that the League – designed as it was to secure a 'peace of the peoples' – merely paved the way for Adolf Hitler.

President Wilson may be regarded as a principal force behind the spirit of the League, but many individuals were involved in the drafting of the Covenant. Lord Robert Cecil, British Parliamentary Under-Secretary of State for Foreign Affairs, the third son of Lord Salisbury, Queen Victoria's last Prime Minister, drafted a peace memorandum, the first draft of which formed the basis of the League Covenant. The committee proposed by Cecil 'to inquire . . . into the various schemes for establishing by means of a League of Nations, or other device, some alternatives to war as a means of settling international disputes' was chaired by Lord Phillimore and the resulting report is generally known by his name. The French government had also established a committee under Léon Bourgeois, a former Prime Minister, to explore the League idea. To such efforts was added the famous pamphlet *The League of Nations: A Practical Suggestion*, produced by General Jan Christian Smuts, South African premier (1919–24, 1939–48).[2]

The League Covenant (Appendix I) contains a comprehensive scheme for the pacific settlement of international disputes.[3] It remains of interest because of its contrast with the Charter of the United Nations (Appendix II).

THE LEAGUE

The character of the League was determined in part by its structure and powers, as defined in the Covenant; in part by the nature of its shifting membership and the impact of non-member states; and in part by the range of administrative and political problems it was forced to confront. The main organs of the League were the Assembly, consisting of representatives of all the Member States; the Council, with the Great Powers self-appointed as permanent members and others (eleven states in the last days of the League) elected by the Assembly; and the Secretariat. The powers of the League were only loosely defined, the authors of the Covenant realising that they were launching an unprecedented institution, an epoch-making experiment that should be allowed to evolve without undue constraints. In reality the Council came to be regarded as the effective executive of the Assembly, initiating its own policies and supervising those introduced by the Assembly in more general terms.

Specific institutions were created to support the Assembly, the Council and the Secretariat. The principal legal/political bodies set up for this purpose were the International Court, two Commissions for military and disarmament affairs, the Mandates Commission, and the Minorities Committee. The main social/economic bodies were the International Labour Organisation, the Economic and Financial Organisation, the Organisation for Communications and Transit, and the Health Organisation. Bodies of a strictly humanitarian character included the Committee of the Drug Traffic, the Committee on the Traffic in Women, the Committee on the Protection of Children, and the Committee on Slavery. In addition, the Committee on Intellectual Co-operation was established, and work was begun for the benefit of refugees, originally intended as a temporary endeavour but one that turned out to be indefinitely prolonged.[4]

The membership of the League evolved over time (see Table 1.1). The original signatories to the Treaty of Versailles were necessarily included (since the League Covenant was included in the Treaty), but this gave a misleading view of what would be the subsequent membership: for exam-

Table 1.1 Membership of the League of Nations

Member	*Date of entry*	*Notice of withdrawal (effective after two years)*
Afghanistan	September 1934	
*Union of South Africa		
Albania	December 1920	(†)
*Argentine Republic		
*Australia		
Austria	December 1920	(‡)
*Belgium		
*Bolivia		
*Brazil		June 1926
*United Kingdom of Great Britain and Northern Ireland		
Bulgaria	December 1920	
*Canada		
*Chile		June 1938
*China		
*Colombia		
Costa Rica	December 1920	January 1925
*Cuba		
*Czechoslovakia		
*Denmark		
Dominican Republic	September 1924	
Ecuador	September 1934	
Egypt	May 1937	
Estonia	September 1921	
Ethiopia	September 1923	
Finland	December 1920	
*France		
Germany	September 1926	October 1933
*Greece		
*Guatemala		May 1936
*Haiti		April 1942
*Honduras		July 1936
Hungary	September 1922	April 1939
*India		
Iraq	October 1932	
Ireland	September 1923	
*Italy		December 1937
*Japan		March 1933
Latvia	September 1921	

Table 1.1 Membership of the League of Nations (cont'd)

Member	*Date of entry*	*Notice of withdrawal (effective after two years)*
*Liberia		
Lithuania	September 1921	
Luxemburg	December 1920	
Mexico	September 1931	
*Netherlands		
*New Zealand		
*Nicaragua		June 1936
*Norway		
*Panama		
*Paraguay		February 1935
*Persia		
*Peru		April 1939
*Poland		
*Portugal		
*Roumania		July 1940
*Salvador		August 1937
*Siam		
*Spain		May 1939
*Sweden		
*Switzerland		
Turkey	July 1932	
Union of Soviet Socialist Republics	September 1934	(§)
*Uruguay		
*Venezuela		July 1938
*Yugoslavia		

NOTES
* Original Members
(†) Annexed by Italy, April 1939
(‡) Annexed by Germany, March 1938
(§) Declared no longer a Member, by Council Resolution, 14 December 1939

SOURCE: F. P. Walters, *A History of the League of Nations* (London: Oxford University Press, 1960).

ple, President Woodrow Wilson was a principal architect of the Versailles peace but the US Senate later blocked American membership of the League (see below). Some states joined at a later stage or resigned, with one (the Soviet Union) expelled by Council Resolution.

The first Secretary-General of the League was Sir James Eric Drummond, who had served for two decades in the British Foreign Office.[5] The choice of Drummond was far from automatic, with various other candidates initially considered for the post (the Greek premier Eleftherios Venizelos, the Czechoslovakian president Tomas Masaryk, General Jan Smuts, Sir Robert Cecil, Sir Maurice Hankey and others). Hankey, offered the post by Sir Robert Cecil, turned it down, deciding that he 'could make a greater contribution to peace and security by continuing [his services] to the Supreme Council in Paris [as well as Secretary to the Cabinet] than in the superficially attractive post at Geneva'. Drummond too had doubts but, after delaying his decisions for a few days, accepted the post.

The signatories of the Treaty of Versailles decided, following an invitation from the Swiss government, that the headquarters of the League should be situated at Geneva. A park district, the Parc de l'Ariana, was chosen for the permanent site of the League of Nations headquarters, and plans were set in train for the design and erection of a Palace of Nations (*Palais des Nations*) as a replacement for the temporary offices of the League delegates and support staff. After three years' effort a design for the palace was agreed and on 7 September 1929 the foundation stone for the new building was laid. Enough of the building had been completed by February 1936 to allow the Secretariat to move in. The Council chamber was completed in October and the Assembly hall a year later. This was an ambitious venture. Artists and designers from many nations contributed to the furniture, decorations and works of art, with the gold and sepia murals created for the Council chamber by the Spanish artist José Maria Sert attracting particular attention. The library, containing more than 600,000 volumes, was one of the world's primary centres for books and documentation on international affairs. When President Woodrow Wilson died in 1924 the Hôtel National – the temporary League headquarters in Geneva – was renamed the *Palais Wilson*. And when, on 19 April 1946, a final Assembly session dissolved the League the Ariana Agreement, negotiated between the new UN Secretary-General and the Swiss government, stipulated that the League rights to the Ariana site would be transferred to the United Nations. The Palace of Nations had become the UN European headquarters.

THE US POSITION

President Woodrow Wilson was the principal force behind the creation of the League but he was also the main reason why the United States Senate blocked American membership. A nice historical irony. Without Wilson – despite all the impulses of Smuts, Cecil, Clemenceau and the rest – there may have been no League; with him – because he was the cause of the American absence at crucial historical junctures – the League was seriously weakened. The very personal qualities that had enabled Wilson to thrust the League on to the world agenda stimulated opposition and resentment, in both Europe and the United States: Wilson's focused commitment too easily translated into arrogance and obduracy. He always claimed to understand 'the people' better than did other national leaders. After three days in Italy he snapped at Orlando, the Italian premier, 'I know the Italian people better than you do'; just as he was able to comment, 'I am satisfied that if necessary I can reach the people of Europe over the heads of their rulers.'[6] Wilson's (second) wife, Edith, saw things differently:

> Many books have been written of this tense period, dealing with M. Clemenceau, an avowed cynic, distrustful of humanity's ability to rise to unselfish heights; with Mr Lloyd George, a political weather vane shifting with every wind that blew across the Channel lest it affect his personal fortunes; with Senor Orlando, whose ear was ever to the ground for fear Italy should not get all she hungered for . . . Amid all those complexities my husband stood practically alone . . . Seeing him grow grimmer and graver, day by day, how I longed to be a man so I could be of more help to him.[7]

None the less, it seems hard to avoid the conclusion that it was Wilson's inflexibility, his resistance to compromise, that ensured that the United States would stay outside the League.

Many of the delegates to the Peace Conference assumed that Wilson, with his primary role in the formation of the League, had the authority to deliver American membership. In fact the US President is constitutionally empowered to make treaties only 'provided two-thirds of the Senators concur'. And it soon became clear that there was powerful American opposition to the prospect of US membership of the League. It was being suggested, for example, that the League was a five-nation club rather than an all-nation League, that the Covenant threatened the US Monroe Doctrine,* that Wilson was trying to slide the Covenant through by embedding it in the Peace Treaty, that Congress powers over immigration would be reduced, and that American boys may be sent abroad to fight at the behest of the League. Wilson's political opponents in the Senate were keen to trade on such doubts and resentments: the US elections of 1918 had already produced a defeat in the Senate for Wilson's Democrat Party and Wilson himself had not been canny enough to take a major Republican with him as a member of the delegation to the Paris conference. One of the principal Republican opponents of US membership of the League was Senator Henry Cabot Lodge, chairman of the Senate Foreign Relations Committee and Wilson's long-time enemy.

Wilson did little to nurture a consensus. He had, he considered, negotiated at length in Paris, and he was not about to begin again. His depiction of his opponents as 'poor little minds' did nothing but stimulate hostility, while Lodge, refusing to adopt the extremist ploy of outright rejection of the peace terms, decided to advance a number of 'reservations' and amendments (in clear mockery of Wilson's Fourteen Points he submitted a list of precisely fourteen reservations), incorporated in the Lodge-inspired majority report of the Senate Foreign Relations Committee. The Senate was not prepared to give unqualified support to Lodge's proposals (even less was it prepared to endorse the anti-League rhetoric of extremists such as Senator William Borah), but there was unambiguous pressure for Wilson to compromise in some of the particulars of the Covenant – and, after everything, Wilson was in no mood to compromise. On 19 November 1919 the Senate refused to approve the Treaty with the Lodge amendments and then rejected also the unchanged text. The supporters of US membership of the League urged that the matter be put to the test again, and on 19 March 1920, after Wilson had struggled to campaign despite drastically failing health, the Senate voted again. The resulting vote in favour of the Lodge amendments (49 for, 35 against) did not achieve the two-thirds majority needed for ratification of the modified text. But only twelve of those voting against were Republican opponents. America's membership of the League, albeit under the terms of a modified Covenant, was blocked by 23 Democrat supporters of the League, faithfully obeying Wilson's instruction to oppose

* The 1823 statement of American foreign policy, attributed to President James Monroe, but drafted by Secretary of State John Quincy Adams, to signal US hostility to the expansion of European influence in the Western hemisphere and elsewhere.

the Lodge amendments. The Republican opponents had gambled on presidential obduracy, and America, despite the likelihood of a majority in favour of some sort of League, had been thrust on to the isolationist path. This meant that the League was increasingly perceived as a European rather than a world body. Thus Lord Grey, writing just before the final Senate vote, declared: 'Without the United States, the present League of Nations may become little better than a League of Allies for armed self-defence against a revival of Prussian militarism . . . predominantly a European and not a world organisation.'

American opposition to League membership continued in the years that followed, an attitude that would come to influence the character and effectiveness of the United Nations. Theodore Roosevelt's daughter Alice saw the Paris negotiations as 'merely a pawn in Mr Wilson's campaign for the Presidency of the Federation of the World', and Senator Borah struck a chord when he declared the League 'Britain's tool – a dodger and a cheater', as did Senator Sherman, expecting the League to 'empty upon the American people the aggregated calamities of the world and send the Angel of Death into every American home, embargo our commerce, close our exchanges, destroy our credits, leave our merchandise rotting on our piers, shut the Isthmian canal, order Congress to declare war, levy taxes, appropriate money, raise and support armies and navies, dispatch our men to any part of the globe to fight because an alien Council so willed'.[8] Even the more moderate Franklin Delano Roosevelt, dubbed by one historian a 'renegade Wilsonian',[9] saw the League of Nations as 'nothing more than a debating society and a poor one at that'.[10] In fact the American *Literary Digest* (April 1919) reported that 718 newspapers favoured the League, with 181 opposed and 478 conditional on the issue. Even Senator Lodge had been apprehensive about his chances of blocking US membership. His strategy had succeeded, in his terms, but the isolationist course could not be long sustained. Official US support was given to the League's position in September 1931 during the international crisis caused by the Japanese aggression in Manchuria (see below). In 1932 the US Secretary of State H. L. Stimson attended the League's Council meetings during the Conference on Disarmament, at the same time presenting the US view of the Far East crisis. The United States was already organising its strategic influence on the League, despite American non-membership. The US appetite to shape world affairs – despite Lodge isolationism and Wilson obduracy – could not be long denied.

THE MANDATES

Many of the League bodies were to have their counterparts in the organisation of the United Nations. However, because of the developing sensitivities over colonialism the UN Charter, in some respects more detailed than the League Covenant, contains no direct equivalent to the League mandate provisions (Article 22).*

The basic League approach in 1919 was that Germany's former colonies (in Africa and the Pacific) along with Ottoman Turkey's former Arab territories in the Middle East would be adopted by the 'advanced' nations as temporary wards until able to lead independent lives. Thus Article 22(1) of the Covenant declares:

> To those colonies and territories, which as a consequence of the late war have ceased to be under the sovereignty of the States which formerly governed them, and which are inhabited by peoples not yet able to stand by themselves under the strenuous conditions of the modern world, there should be applied the principle that the well-being and development of such peoples form a sacred trust of civilisation, and that securities for this trust should be embodied in this Covenant.

The extent to which the designated Mandatories honoured their 'sacred trust' (a phrase of Edmund Burke) can be judged. Viewed in the most pious terms, the mandate system was a selfless and enlightened route to the advancement of peoples who had long suffered under the oppression of colonialism; viewed more realistically (and perhaps more cynically), Article 22 simply transferred colonial territories from two (defeated) imperial powers to other (victorious) ones.

Today few can doubt that the assignment of mandates – in, for example, Palestine, Iraq and South West Africa (see Table 1.2) – did much to store up problems for the future. There may, however, have been little practical alternative to Article 22. 'It was impossible', observed William Rappard, the mandate system's first secretary, 'once the peace was signed to return to the *status quo ante*. Such a solution could not be adopted for practical reasons, while annexation pure and simple would have been in contradiction with the principles which secured the victory of the Allies.' Whether *de*

* The nearest UN body to the League mandate system is the Trusteeship Council (see Chapter 3). Today, as shown in particular by the UN intervention in Somalia, the United Nations may be finding its way to a fresh mandate system (see Chapter 7).

facto (as opposed to *de jure*) distinctions could be made between annexation and mandate operation became a matter for debate and an occasion for growing tension in many of the mandated territories. It is highly significant in this context that the allocation of mandates was begun by the victorious Allies before the foundation of the League: 'the Allies in reality simply doled out the mandates among themselves. This was managed by a system commonly known as "horse trading"; not surprisingly, the lion's share went to Britain and France.'[11] In fact it is clear that British and French statesmen of the day saw no distinction between mandates and colonies, openly conceding that it was the Great Powers, and not the League, that had

*Table 1.2 Mandatories and mandated territories**

Mandatory power	*Territory*	*Area (sq. km.)*	*Population (1938)*
UK	Tanganyika	932,304	5,287,929
	Togoland	33,772	370,327
	Cameroons	88,266	857,675
	Palestine	27,009	1,435,341
	Transjordan	Declared independent, 1946	
	Iraq	Declared independent, 1932	
France	Cameroons	429,750	2,609,508
	Togoland	52,000	780,699
	Syria and Lebanon	Declared independent, 1944	
Belgium	Ruanda-Urundi	53,200	3,752,742
South Africa	South-west Africa	822,909	292,079
Australia	New Guinea	240,864	587,625
New Zealand	Western Samoa	2,934	57,759
British Empire	Nauru (administered by Australia)	2,929	3,400
Japan	Caroline, Mariana and Marshall Islands	2,149	121,128

* The table is true to the source. All the listed territories are now independent of the mandatories stipulated by the League.

Source: H. Duncan Hall, *Mandates, Dependencies and Trusteeship* (London, 1948) Annex II.

allocated the former German and Turkish colonies to the victorious Allies. Thus Lord Curzon declared to the House of Lords on 25 June 1920: 'It is quite a mistake to oppose . . . that under the Covenant of the League or any other instrument, the gift of the mandate rests with the League of Nations. It does not do so. It rests with the Powers who have conquered the territories, which it then falls to them to distribute.'

The people in the mandated territories were not consulted about the decision to allocate their lands to various 'advanced' nations. There was in consequence growing resentment at what native radicals were able to depict as a foreign occupation. The Permanent Mandates Commission, reporting to the League Council, was expected to advise on 'all questions relating to the execution of the mandates'; but in effect the mandatories were given a free hand. The Commission did not send observers to the mandated territories, and would probably have been resented by the mandatories had it done so. Moreover, petitions from the territories were in general only received by the Commission with the approval of the mandatories – which meant that in reality the territories were run with little or no control by the League. It is hardly surprising – in a period of growing nationalism and hostility to traditional colonialism – that the mandated peoples frequently showed dissatisfaction with the foreign administrations. At the same time the Commission, though in the main forced to monitor events from a distance, voiced various criticisms of the mandatories.

South Africa was criticised more than any other mandatory power. Its early reports on South West Africa, said the Commission, were shoddy and so fragmentary as to be worthless, with the South African government responding by suggesting that 'great harm was done to Natives through misguided efforts at kindness'. Racial segregation in the Reserves was providing a reservoir of cheap labour, as were the jails: the High Commissioner for South West Africa, Mr Smit, explained that since the 'Native mind' was entirely different from the European's it was better to supply convicts to white employers, rather than let the blacks degenerate in prison.[12] An uprising in South West Africa in 1922, the so-called Bondelzwarts affair, was dealt with by the Commission in July 1923, following a request from the League Assembly. The 600 native rebels, most of whom were unarmed, were harshly suppressed by the South African administration. The majority report of the three-man commission of inquiry condemned the South African administration, but no action was taken. The Mandates Commission agreed that repression had taken place 'with excessive severity' which might have been prevented by 'timely personal action by the Administrator'. Subsequent criticism that South Africa was not spending enough on the advancement of the mandated peoples led Smit to comment that 'accommodation for white pupils had necessarily to be more elaborate and expensive'.

The other mandatories were equally resented by the peoples of what were in effect neocolonial territories. The Arabs, with burgeoning nationalist feeling, felt that they had been denied the independence promised by the Allies in the First World War. The provision in Article 22(4) – 'The wishes of these communities must be a principal consideration in the selection of the Mandatory – had been largely ignored, with neither Britain nor France desired by the local population. In Iraq, Feisal, even before he was installed by Britain as the intended puppet monarch, was demanding formal independence and objecting to the League mandate. He proposed that Iraq and Britain negotiate a separate treaty, but Britain objected, saying it had no authority from the League for such a course. Feisal in turn would not accept the British proposal of a new treaty that included reference to the League. At a Cabinet meeting in late-summer 1922 Winston Churchill, then Colonial Secretary, observed that King Feisal was not 'prepared to recognise the mandatory basis as he thought that the mandatory system was a slur on Iraq'. And there were problems also with the British mandate for Palestine. Here the original mandate text commissioned Britain as trustee of Palestine with the task of creating a Jewish national state (the key provision of the 1917 Balfour Declaration), while at the same time protecting the rights of non-Jews. Churchill's policy ran counter to the mandate stipulation, and so he arranged for it to be redrafted – a nice example of Great-Power manipulation of League requirements.

The situation was clear. The major powers adopted what mandates they chose and administered them, with little control by the League, as they saw fit. There was provision for non-members of the League to be granted mandates, with the United States – before the Covenant had been presented to the US Senate – being offered the mandate for an independent Armenia. In fact, the United States agreed to accept mandates for Constantinople, the Dardanelles and Armenia – and then reneged two years later. Independent Armenia, by 1921 divided up between Turkey and the Soviet Union, was left to its fate. The Great Powers selected their own mandates (or declined mandate proposals from others) and administered them as they wished. This said much about the political impotence of small states, even when seeking to function within the nominal jurisdiction of an international body.

THE MINORITIES QUESTION

The protection of minority groups, like the mandate system, has no equivalent provision in the UN Charter. In fact the Covenant does not deal with minorities but a number of treaties since 1919 include undertakings to protect minority rights, and a procedure was designed to allow petitions from minorities to be heard by the League Council. (In 1991 the United Nations took an important step towards the protection of minorities by passing Resolution 688 in the Security Council. Here a condemnation is issued of 'the repression of the Iraqi civilian population in many parts of Iraq'; see Chapter 7.) It has been recognised that the minorities question is closely linked to the question of self-determination, though often the principle 'cannot be logically applied, especially in the hotch-potch of races in Central Europe'.[13] The Covenant itself is vague in this area, a shortcoming that reinforces the idea that the Allies were little interested in supporting the aspirations of minority groups seeking protection or independence.

Numerous petitions were submitted to the League Secretariat on behalf of various minority groups. Council members and their advisors served in rotation on the many committees (more than 150 such committees between 1921 and 1929) to which each petition was submitted. The appropriate committee would then, if impressed by the petition, make representations to the appropriate government. The committee may or may not have been satisfied by the government response; if not, then it was able to air the matter before the Council or the Permanent Court – an exposure that no government would have welcomed. An obvious weakness of such arrangements was that the specific committees and the Minorities Section of the Secretariat had no status in the specific Minorities Treaties. This meant that the committees could only exert moral, not legal, pressure on recalcitrant states, and any committee successes went unpublicised.[14]

DISARMAMENT

Throughout the 1920s and early 1930s the question of disarmament was a constant preoccupation of the League. Article 8(1), reflecting the fourth of President Wilson's Fourteen Points, stated: 'The Members of the League recognise that the maintenance of peace requires the reduction of national armaments to the lowest point consistent with national safety, and the enforcement by common action of international obligations.' It was hoped that, in order to avoid another arms race that would lead to war, the drastic disarmament forced on Germany by the Treaty of Versailles would herald a worldwide disarmament. However, the Permanent Armaments Commission, created by Article 9, made little progress: the failure to achieve significant levels of disarmament must be judged one of the crucial failures of the League.

The Temporary Mixed Commission (TMC), comprising military experts from various countries, was set up to devise disarmament plans. One of the first fruits of this body was the Esher plan, named after Lord Esher who inspired it, a scheme that was soon discarded when a number of governments proved predictably hostile. None of the European powers felt sufficiently secure to agree large cuts in armaments, and it did not help that the United States had failed to join the League. When, in September 1922, the Third League Assembly adopted Resolution XIV, declaring the necessary connection between disarmament and security, the TMC redoubled its efforts – but to no avail. New ideas were seen as unwarranted threats to national sovereignty, a hazard that no national government was prepared to risk. In 1924 the Fifth League Assembly approved the Protocol for the Pacific Settlement of International Disputes, the Geneva Protocol, but this was nullified by British opposition, and that of other states, to the idea of assuming responsibility for acting against aggression around the world. Other agreements – for example, the Locarno Pact* and the Briand–Kellogg Pact† – had encouraged optimism about the possibility of international agreements to prohibit aggression, but the League *per se* was making no progress in the area of disarmament.

The Preparatory Commission, set up by the League to organise a world disarmament conference, met for the first time in May 1926. After months of clandestine diplomacy the Commission's first draft disarmament convention was held from 21 March until 26 April 1927, followed by a second that lasted from 15 April until 6 May 1929. In meetings in late 1930 a final draft was agreed, subsequently presented to the disarmament conference organised by the League Council for 2 February 1932. Agreement was reached on limiting arms expenditure, on the need for placing a ceiling on the levels of armed forces, and on the banning of chemical and bacteriologi-

* Agreement signed on 16 October 1925 (by Germany, Britain, France, Italy, Belgium, Czechoslovakia and Poland) to guarantee the post-First World War borders of the Rhineland, Belgium, France and Germany. Hitler denounced the Pact and on 7 March 1936 remilitarised the Rhineland.

† Agreement, initiated by US Secretary of State F. Kellogg and French foreign minister A. Briand and signed on 27 August 1928 by fifteen nations (ultimately subscribed to by 62), intended to prohibit war as an instrument of national policy.

cal weapons (a prohibition already effected in the 1925 Geneva conventions). But there were important loopholes. Armament budgets could be creatively massaged, and there were no mechanisms for independent audit. The agreement did not cover trained reserves, so a state could build up armed forces much larger in reality than those nominally stipulated. And there was no restriction on investment in air forces. The document that emerged from the conference had no teeth. There was nothing here to prevent the cataclysm that would soon engulf the world.

Fresh tensions were growing in Europe. In 1933 the Nazis gained power in Germany and Mussolini was posturing in Italy. When General Balbo took up his post as the Italian representative at Geneva his first contribution was to declare the League a 'limited liability company under the control of England, France and the United States' (despite US non-membership President Herbert Hoover saw no reason why the United States should not work to influence League activities: 'We should cut through the brush and adopt some broad and definite method of reducing the overwhelming burden of armaments'). After Locarno, Germany, still regarded by many as a pariah nation, was demanding equality of status with the other European powers, with the Nazis at the same time finding ways to circumvent the armament strictures of the Treaty of Versailles. Germany had been admitted to the Disarmament Conference but on 14 October 1933 signalled its intention to withdraw. On the same day Hitler declared that Germany was withdrawing from the League. A month later he commented to the Comte de Brinon of *Le Matin* (16 November 1933): 'The League of Nations is an international Parliament in which the conflicting groups of Powers can only quarrel. The differences, instead of being settled, only grow worse. But I shall only be too glad to enter into negotiations with anyone who wants to talk to me.' Now the Rhineland demilitarisation was to be ended; the *Reichswehr* (limited by Versailles to 100,000 men) was soon to contain 300,000 conscripts; armaments denied to Germany by Versailles were to be permitted (if 'defensive'); the Nazi paramilitary groups (the SA, the SS and *Stahlhelm*), as 'non-military' groups, were to be excluded from the disarmament provisions; and the Saarland, disputed by France, was to be returned to Germany (ahead of the plebiscite planned for 1935).

Germany was out of the Disarmament Conference and the League; Italy decided only to observe the disarmament talks; the United States, despite the persistent impulse to intervene, was also increasingly sensitive to isolationist voices. Germany, against the spirit and the letter of Versailles, was rearming. On 11 June 1934 the Disarmament Conference, launched with high hopes, adjourned, never to meet again. Morale in the League was at rock bottom. It would be seen with hindsight that the German Question, with all the attendant European tensions, would be a principal factor contributing to the League demise. It was not the only one.

MILESTONES TO COLLAPSE

Manchuria

On 18 September 1931 Japan invaded Manchuria, created the puppet state Manchukuo on 9 March 1932 headed by Pu Yi, the last emperor of China, and so laid down a challenge to the League and to the world. On 15 September Japan declared that Manchukuo was independent of China, whereupon China appealed both to the League of Nations and to the United States. The Japanese occupation of Manchuria proved to be a turning point in the history of the League, a wound that, in concert with other seismic events, would prove fatal.

Manchuria had long been regarded as part of the Chinese Empire, but many observers, especially Japan, saw it as not an integral part. The Chinese government held little sway in the region, governed as it was by the bandit chief Chang Tso-lin and later by Chang Hsueh-liang, his inexperienced son. At the same time there was a growing Chinese population which Japan judged would frustrate its future ambitions if action were not taken. Many disputes in the area – over finance, communications, Japanese settler rights, the role of Japanese administrators, defence and others – were combining to exacerbate local tensions. China was keen to extend its sovereignty in the North-east Provinces while Japan had an eye on the region's abundant economic resources.

It was clear that Japan, a member of the League, had violated the Covenant by resorting to force; but it was less clear what the League could do about it. Within hours of the first shots at Mukden, the League Council was discussing the Far East crisis. Japan, through representative Yoshizawa on the Council, was well prepared to argue its case, urging the importance of Manchuria to Japan and citing what it claimed were broken promises of China. The military incursion, declared Yoshizawa, was a minor matter and there would soon be direct negotiations with Nanking. Any international pressures or interventions would only make matters worse. The Council, largely impotent at a distance from the affair, was reduced to appealing to both sides to refrain from any actions that might further inflame the situation. Consultations would continue and the United States would be informed of progress. There were grounds for thinking that America might be interested in taking steps to secure a Far East peace.

Secretary of State Henry L. Stimson, eager to make moral pronouncements, was concerned to show that the United States had a strong commitment to peace-keeping. But at the same time the Manchurian crisis was geographically remote, despite America's historical focus on the Pacific region. The United States, like the League, was soon seen to be powerless: the Japanese occupation of Manchuria would not be recognised but American boys were not about to be sent across the world to fight in a distant land. There was moreover the economic crisis at home: when Franklin Roosevelt was inaugurated on 4 March 1933 he was forced to confront the virtual collapse of the capitalist system. This was no time to embark upon foreign adventures.

The Chinese delegate to the League Council, Sao-ke Sze, had urged League intervention, though it was never made clear what form this might take. Yoshizawa predictably argued against intervention and disputed also the right of the Council to send a copy of its minutes to the American President. The Council considered itself reassured by Chinese and Japanese promises that no actions would be taken that might make the situation worse; and issued a resolution that noted Japanese claims that Japan had 'no territorial designs on Manchuria' and that it would withdraw its troops 'as rapidly as possible . . . in proportion as the safety of the lives and property of Japanese nationals is effectively assured'. A week later, on 8 October 1931, the Japanese bombed Chinchow, confirming fears that Japan had further aggressive designs. Stimson said in response that the United States 'would endeavour to reinforce what the League does'; while moves to invite a US representative to attend Council deliberations were denounced by the Japanese as unconstitutional (since the United States was not a League Member).

The protracted discussions did nothing to prevent Japan's annexation of Manchuria. The League Council issued resolutions; the League-inspired Lytton Report supported the Chinese case; the Soviet Union, not yet a member, was asked to help; and Japan, as a prelude to a wider war, consolidated its hold on the newly conquered territories. In March 1933 Japan formally withdrew from the League, followed by Germany's withdrawal in October. The Manchurian episode had irreparably damaged the authority and credibility of the League. Soon it would have to face another devastating blow.

Abyssinia

The League had proved impotent to prevent or reverse the Japanese annexation of Manchuria. There were, however, still optimists prepared to argue that this was an exceptional crisis, geographically far removed from the

League's main focus of interest. This conveniently ignored the fact that the League was intended to be a world authority, an institution designed to guarantee a 'peace of the peoples'. But even if Manchuria was a distant and exceptional case could the League be relied upon to cope with crises nearer to home? Italy – with its invasion of Abyssinia (the Italo-Ethiopian War) – was soon to give an answer, and in a way that would kill the League.

Italy, poor in raw materials, had derived no benefits from the League's mandate system. Instead, it was forced to observe Britain and France, already rich, being granted mandates that they would be able to administer in their own national interests. Italy already controlled Libya, Eritrea and Italian Somaliland, and now it was beginning to contemplate the benefits that might derive from an Abyssinian adventure. The Italian General Emilio de Bono has confirmed that Mussolini began in 1933 to plan for his attack on Abyssinia.[15] The clear aim was to expand the colonial possessions of Italy. Efforts were made to generate disaffection and disorder within Abyssinia; funds were provided to enlist dissident groups and to aid road-making in Eritrea; and at the same time, while the military plans were being laid, Mussolini gave speeches to stimulate the imperial ambitions of the Italian people. On 29 September 1924 the Duce assured the Abyssinian chargé d'affaires in Rome that Italy had no aggressive intentions.

On 5 December 1934 the armed forces of Italian Somaliland and the Ogaden province of Abyssinia clashed at Wal-Wal, in a disputed area. After some days the two governments learned of the scale of the encounter: around 100 Abyssinians and some 30 Italian native troops had been killed. Predictably, each side blamed the other for the outbreak of hostilities. Emperor Haile Selassie insisted that Wal-Wal was part of Abyssinia, while the Italians claimed that it belonged to Italian Somaliland. Soon there were reports that Italian troops were massing before Gerlogubi, an Abyssinian border post; that Italian aircraft were constantly flying over the area; and that Abyssinian soldiers had been killed in fresh encounters. Haile Selassie then requested that the League Council take action to safeguard the peace. On 3 May 1935 Count Grandi, the Italian ambassador to London, was speaking of the situation in Abyssinia as 'a cancer which had to be cut out', conveying to Sir John Simon, the British Foreign Secretary, 'in veiled though unmistakable terms that Senor Mussolini was contemplating a forward policy of the most serious dimensions'. On 21 May Mussolini told Sir Eric Drummond, British ambassador to Rome, that if it was necessary to clarify the situation and to obtain security he was prepared to go to war. In the same spirit the Duce informed Sir Anthony Eden that if he had to resort to war, 'his aim would be to wipe the name of Abyssinia from the map'.[16]

The League Council, as with the Manchurian crisis, then urged both sides to negotiate to settle their differences. Nothing came of such advice, Haile Selassie having no power to push for a settlement of the dispute and Mussolini having altogether different intentions. The Italians made absurd demands for reparations for the Wal-Wal incident and, when these could clearly not be met, launched an invasion of Abyssinia on 3 October 1935. Four days later fourteen members of the League Council (all except Italy) determined that Italy had violated Article 12 of the Covenant by resorting to war to settle an international dispute. Now, in accordance with Article 16, League members were obliged to impose sanctions on Italy. On 10 October Baron Aloisi, speaking for Italy, insisted that Abyssinia was 'a country which has no government capable of exercising its authority throughout its territory, whose frontiers were not delimited, which not merely fails to mete out equitable treatment to conquered peoples, but exploits them, subjects them to slavery and destroys them'. In any case, Aloisi argued, sanctions had not been mentioned in the recent conflict between Bolivia and Paraguay; and the 1928 Briand–Kellogg Pact did not apply since Italy was simply acting in self-defence.

There was little League opposition to sanctions on Italy. Most of the League states had agreed by 31 October to observe the sanctions proposals administered by the Co-ordination Committee. There was, however, the problem of states that were not members of the League. Would they too be willing to observe sanctions? The League sent out proposals to non-Members Saudi Arabia, Brazil, Costa Rica, Egypt, Germany, Iceland, Japan, Liechtenstein, Monaco and the United States – and received replies only from Egypt and the United States (President Roosevelt stated that he could do no more than issue moral appeals to American oil producers). In the event, action against Italy was ineffective, not least because Hitler's remilitarisation of the Rhineland had weakened League resolve. France wanted action against the growing Nazi threat, and there was a growing recognition that harsh reprisals against Italy would destroy all chance of it remaining an ally against Germany: growing tensions in Europe were pushing Abyssinia down the agenda. The French premier Pierre Laval even began proposing that Italy should be awarded a mandate over Abyssinia, as a means of defusing the crisis, a manifest reward for aggression. The British Foreign Secretary, Samuel Hoare, was sufficiently impressed with this proposal to agree with Laval the 1935 Hoare–Laval Pact, whereby large parts of Abyssinia would be ceded to Italy. This unprincipled agreement led to Hoare's resignation, an event that did nothing to strengthen sanctions against Italy or to bolster the general campaign against the annexation of Abyssinia.

The Abyssinian crisis was now increasingly regarded as an unwelcome diversion from the main drama being enacted in Europe. On 4 May 1936 Italian troops entered Addis Ababa; Eden admitted that sanctions had failed; and a month later Neville Chamberlain dubbed the continuance of sanctions the 'midsummer of madness'. On 17 June Eden, speaking at a cabinet meeting, urged that sanctions be lifted, and two weeks later 44 delegates from the sanctionist states approved the termination of the sanctions policy. Abyssinia became part of Mussolini's empire. And the impotence of the League of Nations – having been well warned of Italian intentions – was advertised for all to see. The League's first and only attempt to impose international law had been brought to dismal failure. The wound would never heal.

Spain

After the League's humiliation over Manchuria and Abyssinia there was the issue of Spain, a manifest civil war that invited (and received) foreign interventions of various sorts and which for a while engaged the attention of the League. The Nazis, with bombings and other measures, contrived to aid the Franco Fascists in their opposition to the legitimate Republican government. Britain, for its part, created the odious Non-intervention Committee, 'which was to graduate from equivocation to hypocrisy and humiliation, and which was to last out the Civil War'.[17] In the wings of the League General Assembly meeting on 24 September 1936 Eden persuaded Foreign Minister Monteiro to bring Portugal into the Committee. In his speech to the Assembly Eden pledged that Britain would co-operate with the League. Dr Lamas, the Argentinian President of the Assembly, supported by other delegates, criticised the non-intervention policy since it placed the legitimate Spanish government on the same basis as the Fascist rebels, but Eden continued to support (so-called) non-intervention. When, in the following year, the Spanish representative Juan Negrin appealed yet again against non-intervention, Eden, comparing the policy to a leaky dam, declared it 'better than no dam at all'.

Again the League was shown to be impotent. There were meetings in the Assembly and the Council duly deliberated. Regular reports to the League left members in no doubt about what was happening. Sir Denys Bray and Laurence Webster, for example, reported to the League that the entire population of the Republic were being forced to live on minimum rations, which in any case were not being distributed. In the city of Barcelona a million refugees faced appalling privation. A military revolt had begun the civil war on 18 July 1936, and within the first weeks it was clear that the rebels were receiving substantial help from Italy, Germany and Portugal.[18]

The Soviet Union supplied aid, on a much smaller scale, to the Republican government. In the first weeks of the war it was obvious that the Non-intervention Agreement was doing nothing to prevent external intervention in the civil war.

At an early stage the Spanish government requested the League Secretary-General to arrange an urgent meeting of the Council to consider the flagrant German and Italian aggression against Spain. After some delay the Council met on 12 December, though none of the principal foreign ministers were present. More than half the Council members belonged to the Non-intervention Committee, and in consequence the Spanish government still had hopes that non-intervention would be strictly enforced, not administered solely in ways that benefited the Fascist rebels. Only once, at the 1937 Assembly, was the Spanish question fully faced, though it was discussed in a more perfunctory way on many other occasions. The Committee had resolved to treat both sides as having equal legitimacy, an absurd posture that undermined any initiatives that the League might have chosen to adopt. There was abundant evidence of Italian divisions in Spain; and the German bombing of Guernica and the sinking of Spanish merchant ships by Italian submarines and destroyers were widely known facts. But the League took no action, beyond various modest humanitarian gestures. Before the Spanish government collapsed in 1939 it made further futile appeals to the League for help, but nothing was done. In Spain the fascist rebels, enjoying massive support from the armed forces of the Axis powers, overthrew the Republican government and consigned the Spanish people to a brutal dictatorship.

In the cases of Manchuria, Abyssinia and Spain – in circumstances where the rule of international law was most crucially needed – the League of Nations had been found drastically wanting. With hindsight it is easy to see how its limited membership, the narrow interests of certain key members, the purblind attitudes of certain politicians and the tumultuous collocation of a number of international crises all combined – with the added ingredient of the Second World War – to consign the League to oblivion. But the record was not all gloom. There was a residual idealism, the hope of a better world, that came to inform the organisation of the United Nations and which remains alive today, despite all the cruelties and insanities. It is useful to evaluate, albeit in brief and general terms, the character and contribution of the League.

EVALUATING THE LEAGUE

The ultimate collapse of the League should not be allowed to disguise its various accomplishments, in both practice and propaganda. With the impetus of its launch, it was more successful in its early life than later, functioning 'as an instrument of international co-operation and pacification, on the whole quite impressively, throughout the 1920s'.[19] And even later there were significant achievements. Thus in 1925 the League managed to organise a peace between Greeks and Bulgars; and it ended the 1934 Columbo-Peruvian War. At the same time it gave exposure to many important causes: debates were held in the Assembly and petitions were heard by the Council. The pejorative 'talking-shop' image was at times unfair: publicity for injustice must be judged a helpful stimulus to political action for the righting of wrongs. And the League was able to bring quiet pressure on governments that might not have welcomed the exposure of unjust practices. Above all, the ideal of the pacific settlement of disputes was institutionalised for the first time in a body that enjoyed international recognition.

The impact of the League was constrained in various ways, not least by the fact that many important states remained outside the League for all or part of its existence. Germany, Italy, Japan and the United States were absent from the League for all or part of its history, though there were many times when such states contrived ways of influencing the League's procedures and decisions. The Soviet Union did not join the League until 1934, impelled to membership by fear of Hitler, but was expelled from the League in 1939 because of its war on Finland (it is interesting to remember that the aggressions of Japan and Italy did not cause expulsions). In the 1920s the Soviet Union had denounced the League as a mere contrivance of a few capitalist powers, but we have seen also that the United States was equally antipathetic to the young international body. In 1932 Roosevelt became the first Democratic candidate to denounce the League, following William Randolph Hearst's threat to use his powerful newspaper chain against any internationalist. Said Roosevelt: 'I do not favour American participation.'

Another problem of the League, which the United Nations has still not solved, was that national sovereignties were left intact, with no practical machinery established to compel respect for the Covenant. (Today, as then, powerful states can act to compel political compliance but this is more a matter of hegemony than justice.) And it should also be said that the embedding of the Covenant in the Treaty of Versailles meant that the League was necessarily tarnished with the widespread vindictive attitudes to Germany. Whatever the merits of the Treaty, its necessarily anti-German thrust was not helpful to an international body aiming to shape a new world of peace and justice. Thus the League was inevitably rooted in recent European convulsions: its unswerving support for Versailles often made the League appear a mere alliance of some states against others, a manifest handicap in a body nominally committed to the disinterested search for justice.

The League solved a number of international problems peacefully, though it is most clearly remembered for its failures. It fulfilled many humanitarian obligations, helping with the problem of post-war refugees and prisoners of war, organising the effective repatriation of hundreds of thousands of displaced people. It exerted persistent pressure against the slave trade, human exploitation in other forms, and the international drugs trade. It worked also in the fields of health and education, and pioneered the important idea of an international civil service, a significant development on which today's United Nations crucially depends. In his last year of service to the League, Secretary-General Eric Drummond declared that if the League 'were to disappear today, nearly every treaty of a political character which has been concluded during these 13 years would vanish with it . . . A state of chaos would result . . . the first task which would confront the statesmen on the League's disappearance would be to reinvent the League.' These words, spoken in 1933, were prophetic: the League was only allowed to die when its spirit and functions could be transferred to another international body.

LONG LIVE THE UNITED NATIONS

On 8 April 1946 the League Assembly met in the *Palais des Nations*. The delegates knew what had to be done and they set about their tasks in a quiet and businesslike fashion.

A number of resolutions were passed whereby the powers and functions of the League would be transferred to the United Nations; the reserve funds were distributed among the Members who had donated them; the Palace and the associated material possessions were handed over to the United Nations, with the League library and its archives assigned to the new Secretariat. Spokesmen for the Permanent Court and the International Labour Organisation gave their own addresses, aware that their respective organisations would survive the League but regretting the dissolution of the international body with which they had worked so closely. The Assembly agreed that the League of Nations would cease to exist on 19 April 1946.

Sir Robert Cecil, who had been one of the original architects of the League, spoke at the last meeting of the General Assembly:

> Let us boldly state that aggression wherever it occurs and however it may be defended, is an international crime, that it is the duty of every peace-loving state to resent it and employ whatever force is necessary to crush it, that the machinery of the [UN] Charter, no less than the machinery of the Covenant, is sufficient for this purpose if properly used, and that every well-disposed citizen of every state should be ready to undergo any sacrifice in order to maintain peace . . .
>
> I venture to impress upon my hearers that the great work of peace is resting not only on the narrow interests of our own nations, but even more on those great principles of right and wrong on which nations, like individuals, depend.
>
> The League is dead. Long live the United Nations.

2 Genesis

The United Nations, like the League, emerged out of political turmoil. Nations had again clashed dreadfully in war, states were again thrown into confusion, and again the dead were numbered in millions. The League had failed to keep the peace, but the hunger remained for an international body able to settle disputes between states without resort to military force. The conflagration of the Second World War, far from discouraging the development of international organisations, had vitally stimulated the efforts to create a successor to the League. The survivors again sought institutions that would prevent such wanton human carnage and such massive waste of treasure. The great army of 50 million dead was the silent midwife of the United Nations.

BACKGROUND

Soon after the outbreak of the Second World War the Allied powers began their planning for the creation of a new international body that would help – in the newly chastened post-war world – to keep the peace. One option would have been to sustain and develop the League, but it was tainted with failure and its shortcomings were obvious. Over Manchuria and Abyssinia it had proved impotent, and it had done nothing to counter what was in effect a Nazi invasion of Spain. The League had appealed for negotiations and calm, and even – in the case of Abyssinia – initiated partial sanctions (hastily abandoned). There were, above all, pious discussions and resolutions, but all the hand-wringing had done nothing to coerce aggressive states into acquiescence. Moreover, the League had only limited membership: lacking full American participation, but none the less subject to US pressure, the League was viewed with suspicion in the United States. The embedding of the League Covenant in the Treaty of Versailles inevitably gave the League a European focus. The new post-war organisation would need a global orientation.

In June 1941 representatives of Great Britain and the British Dominions (including Canada, New Zealand, Australia and South Africa) met in London with representatives of France, Belgium, Greece, the Netherlands, Luxembourg, Norway, Poland, Yugoslavia and Czechoslovakia. On 12 June a declaration was adopted, the so-called Inter-Allied Declaration, pledging the signatories to work for a free world, in which all people could live in peace and security. The Declaration was one of the first practical steps towards the creation of the United Nations. Two months later the US President Franklin D. Roosevelt and the British premier Winston Churchill met secretly off Newfoundland and reached agreement on the principles that should govern post-war settlements. This agreement, the Atlantic Charter, paralleled Woodrow Wilson's Fourteen Points and was later endorsed by the Soviet Union and fourteen other states at war with the Axis powers. At this time, though the United States was still officially neutral, it pledged with Britain to forgo territorial gains, to restore sovereignty to countries conquered by force, to make basic raw materials available to all nations, to promote the worldwide improvement of economic and social conditions, to ensure freedom from fear and want, to maintain freedom of the seas, and to work towards the elimination of war and a means of settling disputes between states. (It is of interest that even during the war the United States put national interest before adherence to such principles. For instance, it made significant territorial gains at the expense of Britain as a condition for supporting the British war effort.[1]) The principles came to influence the drafting of the Charter of the United Nations, but had little impact on the shaping of the post-war world.

On 1 January 1942, at Washington, D.C., representatives of 26 nations signed the United Nations Declaration ('United Nations' was the term devised by Roosevelt). A principal purpose of the Declaration, later signed by 21 other nations, was to approve the aims of the Atlantic Charter. For the first time, the creation of the organisation of the United Nations was on the serious political agenda. On 30 October 1943 representatives of Britain, the United States, the Soviet Union and China signed the Moscow Declaration on General Security, approving the concept of a new international body for the preservation of world peace. A month later, Roosevelt, Churchill and Soviet premier Joseph Stalin met at Tehran for the first inter-allied conference of the Second World War. The subjects discussed included the Soviet entry into the war against Japan, the co-ordination of Allied landings in France with the Soviet offensive against Germany, the future of Poland (disagreement here heralded the start of the Cold War), and the creation of a post-war international organisation to preserve the peace. The three leaders declared that they recognised their supreme responsibility, and what would be the responsibility of the United Nations, to work for a world without war.

The plans were already being laid. Detailed official consideration – particularly in Britain and the United States – was being given to the shape of a post-war international organisation. The US Secretary of State Cordell

Hull had begun to develop plans soon after the start of the European war, and in due course was responsible for a highly detailed study of international organisation.[2] A number of important international organisations, geared to the perceived needs of the post-war world, were already being developed. In May 1943 the United Nations Conference on Food and Agriculture was convened at Hot Springs, Virginia; and in the same year the United Nations Relief and Rehabilitation Administration was set up to tackle various problems related to the war. In 1944, at meetings in Chicago, the constitution of the International Civil Aviation Organisation was drafted; and at the Bretton Woods Conference (see below) the International Monetary Fund (IMF) and the International Bank for Reconstruction and Development (the World Bank) were established. Already much effort was being devoted to shaping the character of the post-war world. And in such endeavours the United States was the principal player.

THE US ATTITUDE

The United States, having entered the war, had no appetite for a return to the pre-war isolationism that had kept America out of the League. Roosevelt, once antipathetic to an international organisation focused on Europe, was now keen that the United States be at the heart of the new world organisation and crucially shape its development. He imagined that there might be a rerun of the type of disputation that had killed the possibility of American membership of the League, and so he resolved not to take the issue of the United Nations to Congress or to the American people until the US commitment was irreversible. This time, Roosevelt decided, the United States would not be left behind.

The Roosevelt Administration of 1943–4 was sensitive to the extent to which key Congressmen already supported the creation of a new international organisation in which the United States would play a central role. There was also the growing awareness that US membership of the League might not have saved it, since the Treaty of Versailles, including the League, was wrongly conceived from the start. One lesson was that any new international organisation could not be securely based on vindictive settlements designed to punish the defeated nations at the end of the war. It might again be necessary to restrain the Germans, and there was also the growing Soviet problem: there had been evident tensions between the capitalist world, led by the United States, and the only socialist country in the pre-war world, and with the expansion of Soviet influence in the post-war environment the tensions would be bound to increase. In circumstances of growing American awareness of such matters there was no focused opposition when Congressman J. William Fulbright, a member of the House Foreign Affairs Committee (and later Chairman of the Senate Foreign Relations Committee), introduced the 'Fulbright Resolution', urging the 'creation of appropriate international machinery with power adequate to establish and maintain a just and lasting peace'. Such machinery, some observers perceived, might suitably be used to secure for America the fruits of victory. In the Senate, Tom Connally of Texas, Chairman of the Foreign Affairs Committee, introduced a similar resolution and it was passed without trouble. The mood was plain. It seemed unlikely that there would be concerted Congressional opposition to American involvement in a new international organisation, particularly if the United States was one of its principal architects. In fact Washington was already taking the lead. At the White House, on 9 November 1943, 44 nations signed agreements for the United Nations Relief and Rehabilitation Administration (UNRRA), and by March 1944 Roosevelt had signed Congressional acts guaranteeing UNRRA $1350 million. The Administration was keenly advertising its internationalist commitment. Roosevelt himself 'had become obsessed with the idea that a genuine new world order was being made'.[3] The notion was one that, in a somewhat different context, would tantalise some of his successors.

THE BRETTON WOODS CONFERENCE

It was well understood in the United States that if America were to have maximum influence in the post-war world it would be useful to create pivotal financial institutions that no country would be able to ignore. This task was accomplished at the conference held at Bretton Woods, New Hampshire, 1–22 July 1944. The Bretton Woods Conference, a massively far-reaching event, saw the creation of the International Monetary Fund (IMF) and the International Bank for Reconstruction and Development (the World Bank), so helping to protect American dominance of global capitalism in most post-war national economies. Here it was that the United States successfully enshrined its interests against the rival capitalist states weakened by the war, laying the basis for a new world monetary system to US advantage. At the time of Bretton Woods most Third World peoples lived under colonialism and little attempt was made to represent their interests. By the time the bulk of them had gained their independence they had no chance to recast the powerful financial institutions to which they were now in thrall.

The United States pushed its interests against competing schemes advanced by the other industrial nations. The head of the British delegation, John Maynard Keynes, submitted the 'Bancor' plan whereby all the imbalances in balances of payments would be converted into a new international unit (the 'Bancor') and balanced out via a central clearing facility, so enabling balance-of-payments deficits to be financed out of the Bancor accounts of the countries in surplus. The scheme meant that the creditor states would have to contribute when creating the Bancor facility, an idea that the United States found objectionable since it assumed – rightly for the immediate post-war years – that America would have large surpluses. The US delegation pushed through the alternative White plan, named after the delegation head, which shifted the full burden of adjustment on to the deficit countries.[4] Loans would be granted to such countries, provided that stringent conditions were met. This meant that the United States had succeeded in securing the agreement of 44 states in creating the complementary institutions of the IMF and the World Bank to impose US interests on a global economic system based on free trade and free enterprise. A quota voting system, a departure from 'one country – one vote', was adopted to ensure US dominance in both institutions.

The creation of the IMF/World Bank system meant that states would have access to the main sources of world finance only if they embraced a thoroughgoing capitalist philosophy, were in consequence granted membership of the IMF, and so allowed access to funds (as appropriate) from the IMF and the World Bank. For many years the Fund concentrated on the industrial economies, with the Bank also providing loans for the rebuilding of post-war Europe: France, the Netherlands, Denmark and Luxembourg were early loan recipients. Chile, Mexico and Brazil received Bank loans in the late 1940s; and in 1949 John J. McCloy, the second president of the World Bank, declared: 'The reconstruction phase of the Bank's activity is largely over and the development phase is under way.' The IMF and the World Bank were now looking with growing interest at possibilities in the Third World.

Thus the United States had created mechanisms to facilitate its dominant influence over the world economy (see also Chapter 3). It even arranged for the IMF and World Bank headquarters to be sited in Washington, close to the political and economic establishment of US capital, rather than in New York, where the headquarters of the United Nations were to be situated and where most of the Bretton Woods representatives would have preferred to see the IMF and World Bank facilities. The symbiotic institutions of the International Monetary Fund and the World Bank are generally depicted as 'intergovernmental agencies' related to the United Nations. Any effort to understand the dominant role of the United States in the organisation of the

United Nations should give consideration to US control of the two principal bodies of world finance, the UN-related IMF and World Bank. These were the significant US achievements of the Bretton Woods Conference, the two institutions which may be said – without much exaggeration – to have given the United States a handle on the world.*

THE DUMBARTON OAKS CONFERENCE

The United States was also working on a draft of what would become the Charter of the United Nations. In early 1943 a series of staff briefings on the UN idea were presented to Roosevelt and incorporated into a 'Staff Charter', by July 1943 revised into a 'Draft Constitution of International Organisation'. Further modifications were made in August and the final document, approved by Roosevelt on 29 December, was presented to the conference at Dumbarton Oaks, a mansion on the outskirts of Washington, D.C., on 21 August 1944. Here it was, in meetings that lasted into October, that the Big Four – the United States, Britain, the Soviet Union and China – focused on the detailed planning of the shape of the new international organisation. A principal feature of the plan was the idea of a Security Council on which the Big Four plus France would be permanently represented.

The composition of the Dumbarton Oaks Conference was highly significant. Many nations had been parties to the various international declarations and agreements sired in a world at war, but now only five major powers were to have a hand in shaping the organisation of the United Nations. The United States dominated the proceedings. The American plan, now entitled *Tentative United States Proposals for a General International Organisation*, was the only document submitted in a final form. The other conference members offered ideas and suggestions but it was the US text that was proposed as the basis for discussion. Edward R. Stettinius, the head of the US delegation, moved that the American scheme be accepted for consideration and the other powers were happy to acquiesce.

It was obvious from the start that the emerging organisation of the United Nations would be biased in favour of the victorious Allies. Article 2(1) of the UN Charter was to note 'the principle of the sovereign equality

* The IMF/World Bank system was strengthened by the General Agreement on Tariffs and Trade (GATT) which, with its various annexes and schedules, is attached to the Final Act of the United Nations Conference on Trade and Development (UNCTAD), signed at Geneva on 30 October 1947.

of all' the Members of the United Nations but in reality the major victors in the Second World War came to fashion the structure of the United Nations and to run it – as far as possible in their interests* – thereafter. The Security Council would have executive power, with the General Assembly offering membership to all states not on the Council. It is significant that the Council was intended to have authority, not only over all Members of the United Nations but also over every other state as well. Thus, according to Article 2(6) the Organisation (of the United Nations) 'shall ensure that states which are not Members of the United Nations act in accordance with these Principles so far as may be necessary for the maintenance of international peace and security'. In short, the Security Council – following US proposals that had initially involved discussion with no other states, and later with only four major powers – was framed to provide it with both executive and military power over the rest of the world. It was clear that all states would be under pressure to join the General Assembly, since only then would they have the option of participating in the major forum for influencing world opinion. But the powers of the Assembly were to be strictly limited. This was to be the real talking-shop, with only the decisions of the Security Council binding on the United Nations and the states outside it.

There was little argument at Dumbarton Oaks, a fact that has surprised some later commentators.[5] In fact, the Chinese and the Russians felt flattered at being invited to attend the framing of the world's supreme political organisation. The British were content to go along with what they perceived as a continuation of the fruitful war-time alliance, and in any case were realistic in acknowledging what would be the power structures of the post-war world. In short, the US negotiators enjoyed an easy ride. Their *Tentative . . . Proposals* had matured, without substantial modification, into 'The Proposals'. On 9 October 1944 they were released to the outside world, and at once there were protests from many of the smaller nations. They had been impressed by the terms of the Atlantic Charter and what they had imagined was the flavour of American idealism, but now they were presented with a Charter that did nothing to safeguard the rights of small nations. Statesmen from these countries had not been consulted, and now it was clear that the victorious Allies intended to maintain their grip on global political power. The thrust of *realpolitik* was obvious. *Time* magazine summed up a widely held perception: 'The Proposals have many serious flaws, and they all add up to this: the plain reliance on Big-Power agreement is so desperate that no peaceful alternative is envisaged.' But what was the alternative? If the

* An aim that was largely frustrated – some today may say with good cause – by the emerging constraints of the Cold War (see Chapter 4).

United States or the Soviet Union were to refuse to accept a ruling of the Security Council, how could either state – short of a disastrous new war – be coerced into acquiescence? Big-Power agreement had always been required for the peace of the world, a circumstance that clearly signalled the political primacy of certain nations. How, in this context, could the rights of small nations be protected? The League of Nations had not solved the problem, and the United Nations was not about to. *Quis custodiet ipsos custodes?** Since the United States was clearly one of the guardians – perhaps the lead guardian – Congress accepted the fruits of Dumbarton Oaks, with minor reservations. As far as could be judged, the American people were also in agreement. There was no repetition of the League fiasco.

THE YALTA CONFERENCE

From 4–11 February 1945 Roosevelt, Churchill and Stalin, during the closing stages of the Second World War, attended the conference at Yalta in the Crimea. Here the Allied intention to receive only an unconditional surrender from Germany was restated and plans were laid for the post-war reorganisation of Europe, including the occupation of Germany by the major Allies. Attention was also given to the development of the Dumbarton Oaks proposals and to the forthcoming conference in San Francisco for the establishment of the United Nations. The conference had no formal agenda. After much discussion of military and territorial matters the Big Three turned their attention to various questions that Dumbarton Oaks had left unresolved.

There was already acceptance that unanimous agreement on the planned Security Council was essential before action be taken. This principle – that of the Big-Power veto – was reaffirmed at Yalta, though there would later be debate as to whether an abstention was equivalent to concurrence. Again it was soon clear that the major Allies were not prepared to accept any limitations on their sovereignty: the Soviet Union would not be able to interfere in American matters and nor would the United States be entitled to intervene in Soviet affairs. The subsequent use of the veto was later to emasculate what would have been many useful UN initiatives.[6] And there was also the question of representation, with Molotov arguing that the Soviet Union should have six votes, in the light of Soviet power. He noted

* 'Who will guard the guardians?'

that the British Commonwealth, by virtue of its six separate sovereignties, would have six votes. When the Americans refused to accept such arguments Molotov proposed that the Soviet Union be allowed three votes in the General Assembly: one for the Soviet Union as a whole, one for the Ukraine, and one for Byelorussia. Churchill supported the Soviet claim, reminding the Americans that the Western majority in the Assembly was secure, even if the Soviet Union were granted its original demand for six votes. Already much attention was being given to how the various power blocs in the United Nations would shape up in the post-war world. Roosevelt reluctantly agreed to allow the Soviet Union three votes in the Assembly but, with an eye on American domestic opinion, now reserved the right of the United States to an equal number. On 7 February the secret voting clauses of the proposed United Nations were finalised and signed.

There were other matters still to settle: for example, the question of the trustee lands left over from the League mandate. Here the US drafters of the new trusteeship provisions had shown more sensitivity to the aspirations of colonial peoples than did the European colonial powers. Churchill was anxious that the new provisions, entitling colonial peoples to bring their grievances to the United Nations, might weaken the British Empire, still a going concern at the end of the Second World War. No one doubted that Churchill was a staunch supporter of traditional British colonialism, resolutely opposed to any attempt to question the British presence in Africa, Asia or anywhere else. Stettinius made an effort to reassure Churchill, declaring that the UN would be interested in the Japanese mandates granted by the League, not in the legitimate territories of the British Empire. The United Nations, Churchill was prepared to accept, would not set about dismantling the European colonial order. In fact, the order would collapse, for the large part in bloodier ways than had the dissolution been managed under UN auspices.

The Yalta Conference was now concluded. After much argument – Stalin being reluctant – it was finally agreed that a fresh conference would be held at San Francisco on 25 April 1945 to formally establish the United Nations. Stalin was concerned that the agreements reached at Dumbarton Oaks and Yalta would be diluted or even cancelled if other nations were allowed their say. The shape of the United Nations had been sewn up. Why risk all that had been achieved? In fact, Stalin underestimated the US capacity to push the Charter through at San Francisco. Roosevelt, for his part, 'hoped it would be possible for the earth to have peace for fifty years, if not for eternity'. Churchill toasted the British Empire. And Stalin declared: 'The difficult time will come after the war.'

THE SAN FRANCISCO CONFERENCE

After Yalta, where President Roosevelt had looked increasingly frail, he returned to the United States to begin preparations for the San Francisco Conference. On 30 March he arrived in Warm Springs, Georgia, for a period of rest, by now so exhausted at times that he could only sit in a chair with a book in his hands. On 6 April he was working on a design for the UN stamp, asking two visiting cousins, Margaret Suckley and Laura Delano: 'What do you think of this? A simple new stamp without an engraving – on the top line "3 cents 3", on the bottom line "United States Postage", and in the middle "April 25, 1945".'[7] On 11 April Roosevelt was working on his Jefferson Day speech that he planned to deliver two days later, but on the morning of 12 April he suffered a massive cerebral haemorrhage, and was pronounced dead at 3.35 p.m., Central War Time. Roosevelt had died three weeks before the final German surrender, and two weeks before the formal establishment of the United Nations. His successor, Harry S. Truman, was sworn in, as the 33rd President of the United States, less than four hours after Roosevelt's death.

Truman later recalled the circumstances of his first meeting with his Cabinet members: 'we all sat down around the Cabinet table and then Steve Early or Jonathan Daniels [another Presidential press secretary] came in and said the newspapermen were outside and they all wanted to know if there was going to be the United Nations meeting in San Francisco in April as had been planned, and I said it most certainly was'. Truman added that 'it was what Roosevelt had wanted, and it had to take place if we were going to keep the peace. And that's the first decision I made as President of the United States.'[8]

At the invitation of the United States, delegates from nearly 50 nations convened in the San Francisco Opera House on 25 April 1945. This was an epic, though sometimes confusing, conference. The flags of 48 sovereign states were floodlit against a blue backdrop; while four great columns, symbolising the Four Freedoms, rose from the floor. The delegates, accommodated in red plush seats, surrounded the stage. From Washington President Truman wished the Conference well, whereupon the delegates were divided up into four main commissions and twelve technical committees, charged with the task of considering 547 amendments to the Dumbarton Oaks proposals. The idea that the new international body be called the 'United Nations' – Roosevelt's original wish – was accepted by acclamation; and it was decided that China, the first state to suffer aggression in the Second World War, would be the first to sign the Charter of the United Nations. In the event, the Conference 'was a mixed bag of power politics, muddy thinking, official hypocrisy, high idealism, keen good sense, legalistic nonsense, compromise and false hopes. Men could take from it almost anything they wanted'.[9] The small nations resented the dominance shown by the major Allies; and already there was growing tension between the Allies themselves, the burgeoning hostilities that would develop into the Cold War (see Chapter 4).

The American numbers one and two were Arthur Vandenberg and John Foster Dulles, both dedicated to the protection of US foreign policy in the new world order (not to be confused with the newer world order of the 1990s). Dulles in particular saw the new world organisation as a promising tool for the furtherance of US policy aims, an approach that the starry-eyed idealists of UN theory would not have recognised or accepted. Stettinius played the part of the American front man, nominally subordinate to Vandenberg and Dulles but around whom the Conference seemed to revolve. Some 282 delegates attended the San Francisco Conference, aided by an International Secretariat, mostly American citizens, already numbering more than 1000. The US armed forces provided 2262 personnel, helped by 800 Women's Volunteers, 400 Red Cross workers, and 800 Boy Scouts, providing various services, including the support of 2636 newsmen.[10] The United States paid the Conference bill of $2 million.

There were broad areas of agreement among the delegates, and also issues where the views of the Conference participants strongly diverged. There was much debate about such questions as provisions for revising treaties, the granting of independence for the trustee territories, the veto power of the permanent Security Council members, possible ways of amending the Charter in the future, the role of the International Court of Justice, the development of economic and social provisions, the powers of the Secretary-General, and how states might withdraw from the organisation of the United Nations. Attention also focused on the role of regional security agreements: would the UN have legal priority over these? What, in the new framework, would be the status of, for example, the League of Arab States and the Organisation of American States? Who would adjudicate if a clash of interests developed between a regional group of nations and the United Nations itself? Here the Security Council was given a primary role: regional treaties would not allow enforcement actions in the absence of Security Council authorisation.

There was also discussion on how decisions would be reached in the various UN organs, particularly in the powerful Security Council. Many of the medium and small powers objected to the veto arrangement for the five Permanent Members (the United States, the Soviet Union, Britain, France and China). The Big Five, beset by many questions on this issue, offered an explanation. It was pointed out that the Council of the League of Nations had operated on a basis of unanimity, which implied the power of veto.

Now the UN Security Council, allowing the participation of non-permanent members on the basis of qualified majority voting, would make the decision-making process less subject to obstruction. The permanent members of the Council, it was emphasised, had special responsibilities and so were entitled to veto decisions with which they disagreed. The Big Five assured their critics that they would not use their veto power to 'wilfully obstruct the operation of the Council'. The critics were far from satisfied with such a general statement but when it became clear that without a Big Five veto arrangement there would be no United Nations their opposition to the veto subsided.

On 26 June 1945 the San Francisco Conference concluded with the signing of the Charter of the United Nations. Throughout the world there were mixed reactions to the creation of the new international body. Small states tended to assume that the United Nations would do little more than consolidate the grip of the major Powers on post-war global politics, a view that various powerful *realpolitik* practitioners were prepared quietly to endorse. In the United States there was a widespread perception that the new international body and its institutions were 'devices to make the world safe for basically peaceful, satisfied, and progressive – if not entirely democratic – nations; the UN Charter implied the American Way of Life writ large'.[11] The United States, after working hard at Dumbarton Oaks and Yalta to define the UN framework, had now secured the creation of a new international body that could be induced to work in ways that were helpful to the development of American interests. Things did not always run smoothly – it was inevitable that there would be various US miscalculations – but in the main the first five decades of the United Nations did little to disrupt, and much to aid, the cynical prosecution of American foreign policy.

SITING THE UN HEADQUARTERS

Immense political importance attached to the decision to locate the United Nations headquarters in New York. The decision concerned – in the words of Trygve Lie, the first UN Secretary-General – 'the establishment and consequent official recognition of the world's new political centre of gravity'.[12] Europe was no longer, as it had been for centuries, the focus of world politics. A new pivotal centre had been recognised by the most powerful states, and a new phase in the world history had begun.

The question of the siting of the UN headquarters was not settled easily or without rancour: there were competing claims, and in the end winners and losers. There were, some argued, obvious merits in siting the headquarters within the borders of the United States. This would represent a useful counterbalance to the strong current of isolationism present in American attitudes. The United States would be locked into its world role and responsibilities, a circumstance that some observers viewed with misgiving. There would moreover be the important advantage of the American democratic media, the sophisticated facilities that would lubricate not only the UN's own internal activities but also ensure that its deliberations were promptly and fully disseminated throughout the United States and around the world. Trygve Lie's advisors 'all agreed that the common sense of the American people could be relied upon to play its role in safeguarding the future of the world if given a chance like this'.[13] And it was also highly significant that discussions about the siting of the UN headquarters took place in London, at a time when the capital was blacked out, with all of Western Europe in the hands of the Nazis. The European-sited League of Nations had been isolated and impotent during the Great War. There was no way that yet another European conflagration could be allowed to jeopardise the effectiveness of the headquarters of the United Nations.

The Russians surprised many Europeans by supporting the idea of a site in America (see also Chapter 4), countering the widespread feeling that Geneva was the natural location for the headquarters of the new international body. Now the Swiss had strong reservations about planting the UN HQ in Geneva, though they declared their willingness to accommodate some UN facilities on Swiss territory. Geneva was irrevocably associated with the failed League, a connection that the Swiss were keen to live down; and they were also concerned that a much-strengthened international body might compromise traditional Swiss neutrality. In due course the Swiss came to insist that any Security Council decisions involving the use of force be taken well away from Geneva or any other part of Switzerland. The Scandinavian capitals were considered as possible sites for the headquarters, as were Brussels, Paris and London; but the feeling gradually emerged that the siting would have to take into account the shift in world power. Commented Trygve Lie: 'London was no longer the world cross-roads of determinative political forces. This point had moved farther west. We had to settle on new shores.'[14] Still opinion swung from one direction to another, with the Russians even proposing Oslo at one stage. The American statesman Adlai Ewing Stevenson* reiterated the US resolve to remain above the

* Adlai Stevenson (1900–65), governor of Illinois (1948–52), US ambassador to the United Nations (1960–5).

fray, but commented that the United States would be prepared to host the UN headquarters if that proved to be the favoured option. Soon skilled Americans were lobbying in London to that effect and finally the UN Preparatory Commission's Committee Eight, representing the UN membership, voted 30 to 14 in favour of the idea that 'the permanent headquarters of the United Nations be located in the United States of America'. In fact the decision was close: a few minutes before, an amendment favouring Europe over the United States had been defeated by 25 to 23, with two abstentions. Adlai Stevenson acknowledged the final vote, noting the great honour and responsibility conferred on the American government and people.

There was still much argument about the precise location. A vote (19 to 19) in the Permanent Headquarters Commission, set up by the General Assembly, meant that a proposal to defer the matter of site selection until the Assembly's autumn session had been defeated. Now the selection of a permanent site would not be long delayed. Some states – Australia, Egypt, Syria and Iraq – favoured San Francisco against New York; while the inhabitants of various possible American locations, aware of the concept that the eventual UN headquarters might occupy a 40-square-mile international enclave, began to worry that they might lose their homes and property in the process: meetings were held to denounce the business of site selection as 'un-American and unfair'.

The Permanent Headquarters Commission then ruled that New York was one of the best options, and decided to establish the Temporary Headquarters in New York City, a decision that virtually guaranteed New York as the final site for the UN headquarters. Trygve Lie comments that in the first few weeks there was no place to work except 'cramped hotel rooms', with the Secretariat membership swelling by the week. There was already a massive accommodation problem: there had always been housing difficulties in the metropolis and now veterans were returning to New York from all over the world. Lie improvised by seeking a lease for the use of buildings on the Bronx campus of Hunter College, a women's institution under the jurisdiction of the City of New York. The lease was secured, despite opposition from some newspapers, whereupon a gymnasium and swimming pool (now empty) were converted into a Council Chamber for the Security Council, the Economic and Social Council, and the Trusteeship Council. Classrooms were converted to accommodate the Secretariat, delegates and media staff. The practical work of the United Nations, the supreme political body of the world, had begun in auspicious fashion.

Further moves were necessary before the establishment of a Permanent Headquarters, with at one time UN personnel divided between space at the

Sperry plant at Lake Success on Long Island, and the former Municipal Auditorium on the World's Fair grounds in Flushing Meadow. This latter had been used as a skating rink, but it was successfully adapted to provide the UN Assembly Hall. There were still persistent problems with the housing of staff: in one 30-day period some 1612 apartments were secured in Flushing and Manhattan. President Truman charged John W. Snyder, the Secretary of the Treasury, with the task of easing the building and housing problems while the municipal authorities helped in various ways.

There was still some organised resistance to siting the Permanent Headquarters in New York. Thus on 5 November 1946 Senator Warren R. Austin, the American First Delegate in succession to Stettinius (who had favoured San Francisco), proposed that the question of siting be amended to read: 'consideration of possible alternative sites for permanent Headquarters in the New York area and in the San Francisco Bay area'. When the Soviets learned that San Francisco was back in the frame they reaffirmed their preference for New York, at the same time muddying the waters by suggesting that the agenda item be further modified to carry the idea 'of fixing the temporary or the permanent Headquarters . . . in Europe'. For a while New York's chances faded – with fresh attention being given to the options of San Francisco, Philadelphia and Boston – until the Soviet Union reduced the field by declaring that the 'USSR Delegation will not, under any circumstances, countenance the selection of the San Francisco site, and will not go there'. The Soviets repeated their preferences for New York but said they might accept Philadelphia as a compromise.

The discussions dragged on, with fresh attention being given to the possible development of the Turtle Bay area of New York, a run-down maze of slum dwellings and slaughterhouses bordering the East River. The Rockefeller family was contacted with the idea that they might like to contribute to such a prestigious development, and in due course a letter was received from John D. Rockefeller Jr, offering the United Nations a gift of $8,500,000 for the purchase of the East River property as a new Headquarters site: 'If this property can be useful to you in meeting the great responsibilities entrusted to you by the peoples of the world, it will be a source of infinite satisfaction to me and my family.'

This concentrated many minds. An Egyptian proposal to postpone consideration of the gift was defeated by 36 votes to 6, and at last the Headquarters dispute was at an end. Within two days the Headquarters Commission had approved the gift, and on 14 December the General Assembly ratified the decision by 46 to 7, with only the Arab states, Australia and El Salvador in opposition. In 1952, six years after receipt of the Rockefeller gift, Turtle Bay saw the completion of the new Permanent Headquarters. The delegates gathered for the first time in the permanent General Assembly hall of the United Nations in October 1952 for the start of the Seventh Session. Trygve Lie declared: 'the creation of the Permanent Headquarters has been one of my greatest responsibilities to you as Secretary-General. Now, here it stands, aspiring in graceful lines but solid upon the Manhattan rock.' The organisation of the United Nations had been created out of war, fear, idealism and the *realpolitik* calculations of the Big Powers. Destined in a shrinking world to survive far longer than the League of Nations, it would not be able to avoid the controversies and military crises that would shake the planet.

3 Profile

It [the United Nations] is basically a spiritual-political institution in the line of descent from the ancient shrine at Delphi and the medieval papacy. As with those institutions, the powerful have recourse to the UN in times of crisis . . .

Conor Cruise O'Brien, 1993

The image of the United Nations offered by the perceptive Conor Cruise O'Brien* suggests an institution that functions at the behest of power, a hapless pawn manipulated to serve *realpolitik* ends.[1] This is a refreshing analysis. Behind all the dispassionate portrayals in the text-books there is another United Nations, a complex organisation operating in the real world. Here some factual information about the components of the United Nations is included, with clues also to the other reality.

THE PURPOSES OF THE UNITED NATIONS

The nominal purposes of the UN are stated in Article 1 of the Charter:

1. To maintain international peace and security, and to that end: to take effective measures for the prevention and removal of threats to the peace, and for the suppression of acts of aggression or other breaches of the peace, and to bring about by peaceful means, and in conformity with the principles of justice and international law, adjustment or settlement of international disputes or situations which might lead to a breach of the peace;

2. To develop friendly relations among nations based on respect for the principle of equal rights and self-determination of peoples, and to take other appropriate measures to strengthen universal peace;

* Conor Cruise O'Brien entered the Department of External Affairs of Ireland in 1944 and was Head of the UN Section and Member of the Irish Delegation to the UN (1956–60). He then served as Representative of the UN Secretary-General in Katanga in 1961, when he resigned from the UN and the Irish service.

3. To achieve international co-operation in solving international problems of an economic, social, cultural, or humanitarian character, and in promoting and encouraging respect for human rights and for fundamental freedoms for all without distinction as to race, sex, language, or religion; and

4. To be a centre for harmonizing the actions of nations in the attainment of these common ends.

Such ambitious but broad goals meant that the United Nations had assumed the right, with the agreement of the signatories to the Charter, to involve itself in almost every aspect of the lives of people on the planet. The UN is not involved only, as is sometimes superficially thought, in matters of peace and war, in trying to ensure harmonious relations between states. It is also nominally involved with human rights and social development, interpreted in the broadest terms: aid can be disbursed to assist health and education schemes, to fund economic development, and to help the victims of war. Here, as in other areas, problems can arise because of limitations on the UN's domestic jurisdiction. Winston Churchill was concerned that the United Nations would strengthen the hand of those agitators working to erode the British Empire, which in any case was destined soon to dissolve. Today there are many governments that would resent UN intervention in what are perceived to be domestic matters. For example, though Western governments have no problem with UN Security Council Resolution 688 (condemning Iraq's treatment of its minorities; see Chapter 7), the British government would bitterly oppose any UN attempts at intervention in Northern Ireland, either to investigate manifest human rights abuses or to bring the warring factions to the conference table. There is no way that the signatories to the Charter will allow the UN writ to run untrammelled in many of the trouble spots of the world.

In fact, despite the UN's many recent domestic interventions (in, for example, such places as Cambodia, Iraq and Somalia), Article 2(7) states: 'Nothing contained in the present Charter shall authorize the United Nations to intervene in matters which are essentially within the domestic jurisdiction of any state or shall require the members to submit such matters to settlement under the present Charter . . . .' At the same time it is declared that this principle 'shall not prejudice the application of enforcement measures under Chapter VII'. What this means in practice is that the United Nations may not intervene within states unless the most powerful governments decide otherwise. So UN intervention in the United States (for example, to oppose institutionalised racism) would be unthinkable, but

Washington could contrive UN intervention in virtually any other state. One authority has noted that the interpretation of Article 2(7) 'is still as uncertain as ever'[2] – a convenient situation for powerful states committed to using the Charter as it suits.

Public declarations as to the objectives of the United Nations are predictably high-sounding and virtuous. Thus Dag Hammarskjöld, the second Secretary-General, saw the main objectives as the prevention of armed conflict through negotiation, the prohibition of the use of force 'save in the common interest', equal economic opportunity, political equality, and the rule of law or justice. It would be unwise to dismiss such pieties, even today: genuine idealism is discernible in a battered United Nations. At the same time it would perhaps be more foolish to doubt the role of a few powerful states – even a few powerful individuals – in shaping the political agenda of the United Nations.

THE CHARTER

The Charter was the effective treaty whereby the institution of the United Nations was established: if the UN or its members act outside the terms of the Charter then they are breaking the law. However, as with any treaty, there is always the difficult question of interpretation. Many of the historic disputes within the United Nations have focused on how particular Articles in the Charter are to be interpreted, a problem that lawyers take for granted with any complex legal document. In the case of the Charter the problem is compounded by the fact that the text was drafted largely by politicians, with little input from lawyers. The resulting ambiguities and gaps have not helped the frequent need for resolute action, though they have aided governments at those many times when they have an interest in procrastination. Nor is the situation helped by the existence of five official versions of the Charter – in English, French, Spanish, Russian and Chinese – all of which are intended to carry equal legal weight. There are differences in emphasis from one text to another, and it should be remembered that many of the delegates at San Francisco were not fluent in any of the languages of the five official texts. In such circumstances, ambiguities and inconsistencies, even from one text to another,[3] were inevitable. In fact, with the major powers having the dominant influence, such problems can be reduced. A textual disagreement between Togo and the United States is likely to be soon resolved.

There are various ways in which the difficulties in textual interpretation can be tackled. Literal interpretation would be the best option, if the original drafting had been clear and unambiguous, rather than the results of several different committees at San Francisco, some of which scarcely communicated with each other. Or an effort can be made to discern the intentions of the parties to a treaty by looking, not only at the treaty itself but also at the historical context of the negotiations. Here the extant records, *travaux préparatoires* (preparatory work), may be deemed relevant, but records created prior to and during the San Francisco Conference are unlikely to be relevant to the deliberations of the many countries that joined the United Nations years after its 1945 launch. There may also be reliance on established practice, which can be helpful where there is a precedent; or on what the treaty may be reckoned to intend, which is likely to be synonymous with what the most powerful states declare. In any event it is obvious that signatories to the Charter cannot assume that membership of the United Nations confers clear and unambiguous rights and duties.

MAIN ORGANS

The Charter established six principle organs of the United Nations, which together define its broad structure and via which its purposes are to be realised:

- the General Assembly;
- the Security Council;
- the Secretariat, headed by the Secretary-General;
- the International Court of Justice;
- the Economic and Social Council;
- the Trusteeship Council.

In addition there are many crucial Specialised Agencies, some of which are inter-governmental, focusing on particular tasks of crucial interest to the United Nations. These bodies vary in the extent to which they are under the nominal control or influence of the UN: some, against original intention, have developed independent lives. There is no obligation on states, by virtue of their UN membership, to support or belong to the Specialised Agencies. This is a matter of government policy and attitudes can vary from one administration to another within the same state. At the same time it should be emphasised that some of the Agencies – such as the World Health Organisation or the International Monetary Fund – are vitally important to many countries of the world, though in a number of areas it is possible to debate whether Agency influence is baleful or beneficent.

MEMBERSHIP

At the San Francisco Conference in 1945 some four dozen states signed the Charter of the United Nations. By the mid-1960s there were some 120 Members. In April 1993 Macedonia became the 181st UN Member, an event which Macedonians – in view of the general turmoil in the area – greeted with some confusion. The state-run Macedonian television covered the General Assembly session live, and fireworks lit up the sky over the capital Skopje. An observer in the central square was quoted: 'All this struggle, all this never-ending agony, was it worth it?' Greece had opposed the republic's admission to the United Nations, causing the General Assembly to recognise the new Member under a temporary name, 'the former Yugoslav Republic of Macedonia', proposed by Britain, France and Spain. Greece also objected that the sixteen-ray 'Sun of Vergina' on the Macedonian flag – which the General Assembly decided not to hoist – was a 2300-year-old Greek emblem dating back to King Philip of Macedon and his son Alexander the Great. Becoming a Member of the United Nations is often far from a trouble-free affair.

States cannot decide to become Members of the United Nations. They can only decide to apply for membership, and then – as in any club – they have to be approved. The admission of an applicant is governed by Article 4 of the Charter which declares that membership is open to all 'peace-loving states which accept the obligations contained in the present Charter and, in the judgement of the Organisation, are able and willing to carry out these obligations'. Here, for all practical purposes, it is the Security Council that decides: 'The admission . . . will be effected by a decision of the General Assembly upon the recommendation of the Security Council.' And once a state has been accepted for membership, it can be thrown out, if it misbehaves, at the discretion of the Security Council. Thus Article 5 allows the Security Council to suspend a Member 'from the exercise of the rights and privileges of membership'; and Article 6 states that the Security Council can recommend the expulsion of a Member 'which has persistently violated the Principles contained in the present Charter'. Decisions under Articles 5 and 6 are taken by the General Assembly upon Security Council recommendation, but it is easy to see how the Council mood could be decisive. (We have often seen – not least with the spate of Security Council resolutions on

Iraq – how the United States, as the dominant Permanent Member, can induce both other Permanent Members and Third World states to vote in a particular way.)

In fact there have been no expulsions, since it is unclear what such a course would achieve: an expelled state, still recalcitrant, would be removed from the eye of the Security Council. Nor have there been any sustained withdrawals on a voluntary basis. (The Covenant of the League of Nations included a withdrawal provision, and so seemingly encouraged a number of states to depart, thereby weakening the League. The UN Charter contains no such invitation.) In 1965 Indonesia withdrew from the United Nations in protest at the election of Malaysia as a non-permanent member of the Security Council; but then in 1966, as if nothing had happened, simply resumed its seat.

There have been occasional protracted disputes about membership. The recent Greek opposition to Macedonian membership was a relatively minor matter, whereas the question of Chinese membership – after the Communist takeover of China in 1949 – was a controversy of major proportions (see Chapter 5). There is no doubt that the United Nations, whatever the criticisms levelled against it, retains a unique prestige. All states seem keen to protect their membership, confined as it is for most states and for most of the time to the General Assembly, and subject as it is for most states and for most of the time to the whims and machinations of the Permanent Members of the Security Council.

On 26 May 1993 the Security Council recommended to the General Assembly that Eritrea and Monaco be granted UN membership. On 28 May the Assembly approved the Council recommendation, bringing to 183 the total number of United Nations Members. Two months later on 28 July, Andorra became the 184th UN Member.

THE GENERAL ASSEMBLY

The General Assembly is the only UN body that contains all UN Members – which, from a democratic perspective, makes it the most important institution within the United Nations. Sadly, the Assembly has few powers. It may discuss any matters within the scope of the Charter, with annual sessions held from mid-September through December and rarely lasting longer than January or February; and with special sessions called by a majority in the Assembly or at the request of the Security Council.[4] All Member States are represented in each of the seven principal committees (six of which are numbered) that correspond to the Assembly's main areas of interest: I – the Political and Security Committee; II – the Economic and Financial Committee; III – the Social, Humanitarian and Cultural Committee; IV – the Trusteeship Committee; V – the Administrative and Budgetary Committee; VI – the Legal Committee; and the Special Political Committee.

A rite of ceremonial initiation begins each Assembly session. The head of the delegation from which the President was selected the previous year now acts as temporary President. He gavels the Assembly to order and then requests a minute of prayer or silent meditation, after which the members of the Credentials Committee are selected and the new President elected by secret ballot (the results are usually predetermined by consultations with regional groups). Chairmen are then elected for the seven Main Committees (again following consultation among groups). The Committee chairmen, like the Assembly Vice-Presidents (21 in all), are usually elected by acclamation. In addition to the Main Committees there are Procedural Committees, Standing Committees and Ad Hoc Committees. As may be imagined, there is much talk and little scope for practical action.

The General Assembly may, according to Article 10 of the Charter, 'discuss any questions or any matters' within the scope of the Charter and 'may make recommendations to the members of the United Nations or to the Security Council'. Similarly, Article 11 entitles the Assembly to 'consider', 'discuss', 'make recommendations' and 'call the attention of the Security Council to situations that are likely to endanger international peace and security'. It may initiate studies and make recommendations in the areas of law, culture, health, human rights, and so on (Article 13), and may 'recommend measures' to bring a 'peaceful adjustment' in any situation deemed 'likely to impair the general welfare or friendly relations among nations' (Article 14). The Assembly also has the power to approve the UN budget, state contributions being roughly related to the size of gross national products. Article 19 states that a member in arrears shall have no vote in the General Assembly, a provision that is generally ignored: the United States, along with various other members, is usually in heavy arrears.* The Assembly has few powers beyond the nominal budgetary authority, though its deliberations and votes may have a moral impact on recalcitrant states (unless powerful enough to ignore Assembly opinion).

* In September 1992, at a time when the United States was celebrating the post-Gulf War authority of the United Nations, the outstanding US debt to the UN was $757 million.

There is no sense in which the General Assembly is a world parliament. The various Ministries and Specialised Agencies do not come directly under the Assembly: they have their own assemblies and determine their own policies, and the Assembly has minimal influence. Member States, moral pressure apart, are quite at liberty to ignore the Assembly's deliberations. It is also useful to note that the Assembly is not representative of peoples but of governments: individual states may be totally undemocratic but (as regulated by Article 18) all Members have specific voting rights. The Assembly has been compared to the conferences and congresses of the nineteenth century, whereby the Concert of Europe – often enjoying more practical power than the Assembly – discussed the important issues of the day.[5]

In the early days of the United Nations the Western powers enjoyed a majority in the General Assembly, and so were keen to advertise its powers as a means of escaping the Soviet veto in the Security Council. But with the later growth of the Afro-Asian bloc the US-led West became increasingly hostile to a body that was likely to oppose Western imperialist policies, and so majority wishes in the General Assembly were increasingly ignored by the Western powers. With the dissolution of the Soviet Union in the early 1990s, the United States – no longer faced with the problem of a predictable Soviet veto on the Security Council – concentrated with renewed commitment to developing its dominance within the Council. The General Assembly, more than ever, was confined to empty talk.

THE SECURITY COUNCIL

The Security Council, the most powerful UN body, consists of fifteen Member States: five Permanent Members (the United States, Britain, France, Russia and China) and ten non-permanent members elected for two years by the General Assembly. According to current practice, five non-permanent places are filled by Afro-Asian states, two by Latin American states, one by an Eastern European state and two by Western European and other states (these latter being mainly the white members of the Commonwealth).

It is significant that the US-dominated Security Council has considerable powers defined by the Charter (and facilitated by the *realpolitik* circumstances of its current situation). Article 24(1) notes that UN Members 'confer on the Security Council primary responsibility for the maintenance of international peace and security, and agree that in carrying out its duties under this responsibility the Security Council acts on their behalf'. Or, in effect, the 180-plus Members of the United Nations give the Security Council – in reality the Permanent Members chaperoned by Washington – a blank cheque to act as it wishes, with extensive powers. In fact Article 24(2) notes that 'specific powers' granted to the Security Council 'are laid down in Chapters VI, VII, VIII and XII' of the Charter. It is further noted (in Article 24(3)) that the Security Council shall submit annual special reports for the consideration of the General Assembly, but only 'when necessary', and who will decide? It is emphasised (Article 25) that: 'The Members of the United Nations agree to accept and carry out the decisions of the Security Council in accordance with the present Charter.' Thus the Security Council – in effect the US-led Permanent Members – has the power to take binding decisions, with no need to consult the broad membership of the General Assembly.

The voting procedure of the Security Council is defined in Article 27: each member shall have one vote and decisions on procedural matters 'shall be made by an affirmative vote of nine* members'. Furthermore, 'Decisions . . . on all other matters shall be made by an affirmative vote of nine members including the concurring votes of the permanent members; provided that, in decisions under Chapter VI . . . a party to a dispute shall abstain from voting.' This means that each Permanent Member of the Security Council can veto non-procedural questions, a provision that recognises the realities of power politics in the world: if, under a different constitution, a majority vote were carried in the Security Council against the United States how could such a decision ever be enforced? And there is also the question, already mentioned, as to whether an abstention constitutes 'concurrence'. In fact, the practice of not treating abstentions as vetoes was recognised as lawful by the International Court of Justice in the *Namibia* case.[6] An associated matter, whether absence is equivalent to a veto, has not been settled with any certainty. In June 1950 the Security Council, with the Soviet Union absent, passed a resolution for Member States to intervene in Korea to oppose what the West was branding as Communist aggression (see Chapter 5). At the same time it has been pointed out (Akehurst, 1991, p. 213) that the Soviet absence was a violation of Article 28(1): 'The Security Council shall be so organised as to be able to function continuously. Each member . . . shall for this purpose be represented at all times . . . .'

Whether – as is stated in Article 27(3) – a party to a dispute shall abstain from voting in decisions under the peace-keeping Chapter VI is similarly open to dispute. It is not always possible to establish who is party to a

* Originally seven.

dispute – for the simple fact that there is often much clandestine involvement. Even when a state's involvement is clear there has been little opposition to such a state voting in the Security Council, a circumstance that again suggests a recognition of power politics in the real world: who will gainsay a US decision to vote?

In the early 1950s, partly because of the veto, the Security Council was often unable to act decisively to resolve international crises. Often problems were tackled outside the United Nations: consider, for example, the Berlin talks on Germany (1954), the Vienna discussions on Trieste (1954–5), the Geneva discussions on Korea and Indo-China (1954), the negotiation of the Austrian State Treaty (1955), and the Geneva Summit Conference (1955). Many questions (Kashmir, Algeria, Tunisia, Guatemala and problems of the Middle East) were brought to the United Nations, which then proved itself powerless to act. In the 1960s, with the United States becoming increasingly disenchanted with the General Assembly, there was a fresh focus on the power of the Security Council. In 1965 the membership of the Council was increased from eleven to fifteen, with the number of affirmative votes required to carry a resolution raised from seven to nine (so reducing the required proportion). This change in effect gave the Permanent Members a greater pool of smaller states from which the votes could be trawled to guarantee the majorities required. The most powerful states, the veto apart, would agree a course and then organise the necessary votes in the Council. Today – with the pliant Russia replacing the recalcitrant Soviet Union – it is even easier for the US-led Western states to achieve the desired majorities.

The procedures and deliberations of the Security Council are nominally defined by the relevant Articles in the Charter and by the Provisional Rules of Procedure.[7] At the same time the powerful states have scope for 'softening' (ignoring) some of the more stringent requirements when they choose. There is always the problematic question of textual interpretation, and even when there is a consensus there are no practical means of ensuring the compliance of powerful states.[8] It is hard to avoid the conclusion that the Security Council is defined and run for the benefit of a small number of powerful countries. Against this circumstances, rooted in the origins of the United Nations and the current shape of power politics, there is little scope for appeal.

THE SECRETARIAT

Sir Eric Drummond, the first Secretary-General of the League of Nations, had worked to establish an international civil service in Geneva. This body

– drawn from some 30 countries but in practice largely European – was to provide the basis for the Secretariat of the United Nations. A vastly enlarged staff had to be created but many of the practices and some of the officials of the now defunct League were carried over. Today the international civil service consists of tens of thousands of individuals, working for the United Nations itself and deployed over the many Specialised Agencies. The supreme administrative section of the Secretariat is the office of the Secretary-General. He may be regarded as the world's loftiest and most influential civil servant.

Chapter XV of the UN Charter defines the character of the Secretariat. It comprises (according to Article 97) a Secretary-General and such staff as the organisation may require, with the Secretary-General 'appointed by the General Assembly upon the recommendation of the Security Council'. Again the power of the Council is manifest. The Secretary-General is required to serve as the chief administrative officer of the organisation, acting in that capacity 'in all meetings of the General Assembly, of the Security Council, of the Economic and Social Council, and of the Trusteeship Council' (Article 98). He is required to 'bring to the attention of the Security Council any matter which in his opinion may threaten the maintenance of international peace and security' (Article 99). The Secretary-General and his staff shall not be instructed by any government, and UN Members shall respect 'the exclusively international character of the responsibilities of the Secretary-General and his staff' (Article 100). The staffing of the Secretariat shall be the responsibility of the Secretary-General (Article 101).

There has been much debate about the role of the Secretary-General. Should he be, as some proposed, 'more the general than the secretary – but where were his divisions?'[9] Or should he be a mere administrator, keen only to monitor the contributions of the members? Trygve Lie, the first Secretary-General and therefore crucially important in the early shaping of the post, resolved to adopt a middle way: 'I would listen to all my advisors and be directed by none. I had no calculated plan for developing the political powers of the office of Secretary-General, but I was determined that the Secretary-General should be a force for peace. How that force would be applied I would find out – in the light of developments.'[10] It was inevitable that Lie, like each of his successors (Table 3.1), would bring his own unique personality and experience to the post of Secretary-General.

Dag Hammarskjöld in turn noted that the establishment of 'a truly international civil service, free from all national pressures and influences . . . not only in words but in deeds' was one of the 'fundamental principles' upon which the Organisation's influence and growth depended.[11] This was an important observation at a time when small but influential groups in the

Table 3.1 Secretaries-General of UN

Name	*Nationality*	*Term of office*
Trygve Lie	Norwegian	1946–53
Dag Hammarskjöld	Swedish	1953–61
U Thant	Burmese	1962–71
Kurt Waldheim	Austrian	1971–81
Javier Perez de Cuellar	Peruvian	1982–92
Boutros Boutros-Ghali	Egyptian	1992–

United States were denouncing the Secretariat, declaring that it was populated by Communists and thus opposed to US interests (see Chapter 4). The Soviet Union also had denounced Trygve Lie for his support offered to the Americans over the Korean crisis. According to Ernest Gross, legal counsel to the United Nations (1953–6), Hammarskjöld was particularly keen to obtain from certain nations, particularly the United States, greater respect for the impartiality and international status of the Secretariat.[12] The problem of pressure from powerful states and influential regional groups was one that the Secretaries-General would have to contend with throughout the life of the United Nations.

The required international status of the United Nations influences the recruitment policy in the Secretariat. Apart from clerical and manual posts, recruitment is subject to rules about national quotas, which to an extent are designed to favour the nationals of smaller countries. The Secretary-General issues Staff Rules under powers delegated to him by Staff Regulations enacted by the General Assembly. An administrative Tribunal, set up by the Assembly, hears grievances from staff and strives to safeguard the conditions of employment. Today the Secretariat comprises an international staff of more than 16,000 men and women from some 150 countries, with an increasing involvement in the framing and holding of multilateral treaties between states. By 1990 the Secretary-General was providing a depository service for more than 300 multilateral treaties, at the same time becoming increasingly involved in the adjustment of international relations between states. The office of the Secretary-General, despite various setbacks and vicissitudes, has continued to develop. On 18 September 1961 Dag Hammarskjöld suffered a mysterious and fatal air crash over Africa, a tragedy that remains controversial. And on 4 April 1986 the UN Secretariat made available to Austria, Israel and the United States a confidential UN War Crimes Commission file on Kurt Waldheim, leading to a US Justice

Department recommendation on 24 April 1986 that he be banned from entering the United States as a private citizen. Such events have damaged the office of Secretary-General but today it is an increasingly important element in international negotiations. The Secretary-General, unlike the Security Council, has few powers, but there is growing evidence that his efforts can make a difference.

THE INTERNATIONAL COURT OF JUSTICE

The International Court of Justice at The Hague, created at the 1945 San Francisco Conference, was the culmination of decades of development. The Hague Conference of 1899 had seen the establishment of the Permanent Court of Arbitration, a device for the pacific settlement of international disputes. The League of Nations involved the creation of the Permanent International Court of Justice, also at The Hague; though in the event this court was excluded from hearing the disputes that were most likely to lead to war. In April 1945 the US government invited a Committee of Jurists to meet in Washington to study how a new international court could be integrated in the United Nations system. The Statute of the New International Court of Justice (with the optimistic 'Permanent' dropped) was added to (in some interpretations, embedded in) the Charter of the United Nations. All members of the UN are *eo ipso* parties to the Statute of the Court. In addition, Article 93(2) of the Charter allows states that are non-members to become party to the Statute 'on conditions to be determined in each case by the General Assembly upon the recommendation of the Security Council'. However, efforts to date to develop the International Court as a body whose 'compulsory' jurisdiction members are obliged to acknowledge have not been successful. Powerful states have ignored the Court when they felt that their interests could be best achieved in other ways, and 'inconvenient' Court rulings – as when the United States was condemned for violating international law in waging aggressive acts against Nicaragua – have been similarly ignored. In short, the Court is massively limited in its rulings because there is no method of enforcement. This is a problem that afflicts many UN agencies when the interests of powerful states are an issue.

The Court consists of some fifteen judges, with five elected every three years to hold office for a period of nine years. Both the Security Council and the General Assembly must secure a majority for a vote to be passed. If a state appearing before the Court does not have one of its own nationals on the Bench it is allowed to appoint a judge for the particular case, a provision that seems to tell against the Court's impartiality but which is likely to reassure litigants that their views will be seriously heard. The smaller states, often at a disadvantage when in confrontation with powerful members, suggested in 1945 that the Charter make provision for compulsory jurisdiction. The great powers predictably objected to such a facility.

The Court is not open to private individuals, only to states. It has always refused to consider the many requests and petitions addressed to it by individuals. A state may choose to represent one of its nationals in a complaint against another state but then the dispute is between states and does not involve the individual as a party. It is also significant that simply because a state has access to the Court does not mean that the state is obliged to have its disputes with other states settled by the Court. The states must consent since, because the Court has no powers of coercion, international justice is still largely an optional matter.

There are various ways in which the consent of states may be expressed. It is stated in the Statute that Court jurisdiction 'comprises all cases which the parties refer to it and all matters specially provided for in the Charter of the United Nations or in treaties and conventions in force' (Article 36(1)). Or a state may be keen to accept the jurisdiction of the Court in disputes that have not yet arisen, where a state indicates a willingness to appear before the Court when the anticipated dispute occurs: there are various treaties and conventions where the signatories bind themselves in advance to appear before the Court, should a dispute arise. Again, the matter of Court jurisdiction can itself become a complex issue in circumstances where states disagree. Where agreement on jurisdiction cannot be established the Court has no powers. Once the question of jurisdiction is resolved a state is likely to be responsive to the Court's judgment, even in the absence of coercive powers: there is moral pressure on a state to observe a ruling from a prestigious source. According to the Charter (Article 96) the Court may also be asked by either the General Assembly or the Security Council 'to give an advisory opinion on any legal question'. Such opinions are not intended to be binding, but they carry political weight and are usually influential.[13]

THE ECONOMIC AND SOCIAL COUNCIL

In the late summer of 1939, a few days before the start of the Second World War, the Bruce Commission delivered a report to the League of Nations, urging the creation of a high-powered council to organise and expand the League's economic and social activities. The war prevented the establishment of such a League council but the idea survived until the 1945 San Francisco Conference where the Economic and Social Council was created as one of the principal organs of the United Nations. Article 55 of the Charter states that the United Nations,

> With a view to the creation of conditions of stability and well-being which are necessary for peaceful and friendly relations among nations . . . shall promote: (a) higher standards of living, full employment, and conditions of economic and social progress and development; (b) solutions of international economic, social, health, and related problems; and international cultural and educational co-operation; and (c) universal respect for, and observance of, human rights and fundamental freedoms of all without distinction as to race, sex, language, or religion.

It further declared (Article 60) that the responsibility for discharging these functions 'shall be vested in the General Assembly and, under the authority of the General Assembly, in the Economic and Social Council'. Chapter X of the Charter defines the composition, functions and powers, and procedures of the Economic and Social Council.

The Council comprises some 54 members who individually serve for three years, with eighteen members elected each year to replace the eighteen members whose three-year term has expired. Council members each have one vote and proposals are passed by simple majority. The Council serves as a central forum for consideration of international economic and social issues; initiates studies and makes recommendations; promotes human rights; calls conferences and drafts conventions; negotiates agreements with the Specialised Agencies (see below) and co-ordinates their activities; and performs a wide range of associated functions. Its subsidiary bodies include various functional, regional and standing committees, and a number of expert bodies (on such subjects as crime, development planning, international tax matters, and the transport of dangerous products). More than 600 non-governmental organisations have consultative status with the Council, some making functional contributions to the Council's work.

THE TRUSTEESHIP COUNCIL

The Charter (Article 73) recognises that some peoples 'have not yet attained a full measure of self-government' and recognises that 'the interests of the inhabitants of these territories are paramount'. It is also declared that UN members 'accept as a sacred trust the obligation to promote to the utmost . . . the well-being' of these peoples. Chapter XII, framed under the residual circumstances of the League mandate and under the conditions created by the Second World War, defines the terms of an International Trusteeship System to deal with the mandated territories, territories 'which may be detached from enemy [Axis] states', and 'territories voluntarily placed under the system by states responsible for their administration'. It is further noted (Article 83) that the Security Council will exercise all the functions of the United Nations 'relating to strategic areas, including the approval of the terms of the trusteeship agreements and of their alteration or amendment'. Chapter XIII defines the composition, the functions and powers, and the procedure of the Trusteeship Council.

Once the Council had been established the General Assembly created the Trusteeship and Administration and Information about Non-Self-Governing Territories Committee, while the Secretariat established a special department run by one of the Secretary-General's deputies. In 1945 the Soviet government insisted that the trusteeship system be provisional and that a deadline be specified for the countries striving for independence. Against this suggestion the Western powers managed to secure the alternative formula of 'self-government or independence' without giving specific dates – so managing to breathe some life into traditional European colonialism. On 12 November 1961 the Soviet government demanded the total dissolution of the Trusteeship Administration created by the Western powers on 19 October 1945 (five days before the establishment of the other major UN organs). The Soviet move was vetoed by Britain and the United States, but the competence of the Trusteeship Council was considerably limited when it was subordinated to the Decolonisation Committee.

The broad aims of the Trusteeship System were fulfilled to the extent that by the 1980s only one of the original Trusteeships remained: the Trust Territory of the Pacific Islands, administered by the United States. The UN Decolonisation Committee remained resolute in demanding the independence of this residual Trusteeship. Of the 'principal organs' of the United Nations the Trusteeship Council is unique in that the bulk of its responsibilities have disappeared followed social and political change throughout the world.

THE SPECIALISED AGENCIES

In addition to the many agencies operating solely under the auspices of the 'principal organs' of the United Nations there are a number of intergovernmental Specialised Agencies that relate to the UN by special agreements but which have a separate and autonomous existence. Some of these are older than the United Nations: for example, the International Telecommunication Union (ITU) was founded in 1865; the Universal Postal Union (UPU) in 1874. The International Labour Organisation (ILO) was created in 1919, under the Treaty of Versailles, as an autonomous body associated with the League of Nations. According to an ILO/UN agreement approved on 14 December 1946 the International Labour Organisation, striving to help working people throughout the world, became the first Specialised Agency to be associated with the United Nations.

Other Specialised Agencies include:

- the Food and Agriculture Organisation (FAO), founded on 16 October 1945 at a Quebec conference, a date observed since 1979 as World Food Day;

- the International Civil Aviation Organisation (ICAO), created on 4 April 1947 after a convention drawn up at the 1944 International Civil Aviation Conference in Chicago had been ratified by 26 states;

- the World Meteorological Organisation (WMO), with its origin in the International Meteorological Organisation created in 1873, and subject to the Convention that became effective on 23 March 1950;

- the International Maritime Organisation (IMO), formerly the Inter-Governmental Maritime Consultative Organisation, established by a convention ratified by 21 states on 17 March 1958;

- the World Intellectual Property Organisation (WIPO), with origins in the 1883 Paris Convention for the Protection of Industrial Property and the 1886 Berne Convention for the Protection of Literary and Artistic Works, created in 1967 and on 17 December 1974 became a specialised UN agency;

- the International Fund for Agricultural Development (IFAD), established by an agreement adopted at a UN conference on 13 June 1976, opened for signature on 20 December 1976, and entered into force on 30 November 1977;

- the United Nations Industrial Development Organisation (UNIDO), established by the General Assembly in 1966 to promote the industrialisation of the developing countries.

There are in addition such pivotal agency bodies as the financial organisations (the IMF, the World Bank, the International Development Association and the International Finance Corporation); the United Nations Educational, Scientific and Cultural Organisation (UNESCO); the United Nations Children's Fund (UNICEF); the World Health Organisation (WHO); and the International Atomic Energy Agency (IAEA).

THE FINANCIAL ORGANISATIONS

The Articles of Agreement for the International Monetary Fund (IMF) and the International Bank for Reconstruction and Development (the World Bank) were drawn up at the 1944 Bretton Woods Conference (profiled in Chapter 2). The IMF began life on 27 December 1945 when representatives of states whose quotas amounted to 80 per cent of the Fund's resources had deposited their ratifications. The IMF Articles were subsequently amended in 1969 and 1978. The nominal purpose of the Fund is to expand world trade by developing international monetary co-operation, and to contribute thereby to increased employment and improving economic conditions in all the Member States. In reality, acting in concert with the World Bank and the other leading financial institutions, the IMF works to expand and consolidate the grip of the most powerful capitalist organisations on world resources. The IMF/World Bank axis was created as a strategic force, a fact that is rarely emphasised in mainstream descriptions of global finance.

Each of the Fund's 150-plus member countries is represented by a governor and an alternate governor on the Board of Governors, the organisation's highest authority. A member's voting power reflects the scale of its contribution to the Fund's financial resources. Twenty-one executive directors, chaired by the Managing Director, conduct daily IMF business.

For most of the Fund's history the Soviet Union showed no interest in applying for membership, perceiving that the IMF and the World Bank were created essentially to protect the world capitalist monetary system. The Russia of President Yeltsin has adopted a different policy. Other once-socialist states (such as Poland and Czechoslovakia) became members but later resigned under the pressures of the Cold War; Hungary and Romania, now with heavy credit requirements in the West, have recently joined the Fund. The vast majority of Third World states are IMF members, but despite their numbers the developing countries have virtually no say in the running of the Fund. The Bretton Woods Conference served to consolidate the international power relations among the industrial countries, and then as now the Third World nations had little leverage. The egalitarian element in the management committee voting arrangements has been progressively eroded to the disadvantage of the developing states, which today means that the five leading industrial countries are allowed the lion's share of the votes. These states (the US, Britain, Germany, France and Japan) are thus in a position to dominate the operation of the Fund, since their quotas – determined by their economic power – are used to influence their voting strengths. Thus the strongest capitalist powers have the strongest voting weight in the operation of the Fund.[14] In such circumstances we are not surprised to encounter frequent Third World comments to the effect that the IMF serves mainly to consolidate the power and privilege of the richest states while doing nothing to advance the economies of the poorest nations.

It is significant that successive debt-relief packages, nominally designed to aid Third World states, have done no more than reduce the gap between what such countries are scheduled to pay and what they are able to pay; and that actual debt-relief initiatives – for example, the much-hyped Trinidad initiative made by Prime Minister John Major in 1991 – are rarely fully implemented. In mid-1993 Africa's debt, as a glaring example, was $30 billion higher than in 1989. The World Bank itself has commented that efforts to adjust the debt burden on the poorest states has 'left much to be desired in terms of restoring growth and social welfare'. The debt predicament of Third World states sometimes pushes them into a desperate quest for financial independence. Thus in March 1993 Kenya, following a similar effort by Zambia in 1986, moved to escape from the crushing IMF burden.[15] President Moi and the Finance Minister Musalia Mudavadi declared that the Fund and the World Bank had broken pledges to Kenya, and that IMF/World Bank policies were 'dictatorial and suicidal'. Officials in London and Washington suggested that Kenya had no alternative to working with the international financial institutions, and that soon it would be compelled to return to the fold. One diplomat observed: 'I can't believe the Kenyan government can see a future without the Bank, the Fund or Western aid.' More than two dozen African countries have now made agreements with the IMF and the World Bank, and others shadow IMF/Bank policies. It was clear in 1993 that Kenya could not be allowed to establish a precedent that might tempt other struggling African states.

It is no accident that the IMF moved quickly to offer support for Russia's President Yeltsin in his efforts to establish a free-market economic system. In June 1992 he made a deal with the Fund which meant that a wide range of Russian enterprises would be allowed to collapse in the interest of the broad Fund strategy. One of the Fund's conditions for the support was that the Russian government cut back promised investments of 500 billion roubles (£3 billion) to save threatened firms.[16] In such a fashion the Fund, while nominally offering assistance, massively reduces the scope for Russian economic independence in the interests of world capitalist trade. Like the Fund, the World Bank was created as part of this broad economic strategy. In April 1990 Dr Michael Irwin, a senior British staff member, resigned from the World Bank, accusing it of profiteering at the expense of the world's poor.[17] He declared that the Bank's austerity programmes for developing countries 'result in the poor suffering the most'.

The IMF/World Bank axis is supported by other financial/commercial institutions. The International Development Association (IDA) was established in 1960 as an affiliate to the World Bank to broaden the scope of lending to poor countries. Another body, the International Finance Corporation (IFC), is a separate legal entity closely associated with the World Bank. A principal IFC role is to finance private enterprise throughout the world, bringing together investment opportunities and stimulating the flow of private capital into schemes expected to generate good returns. All IFC powers are vested in a Board of Governors which consists of the Governors and alternates of the World Bank, who represent IFC members. In addition, such bodies aim to work in sympathy with the General Agreement on Tariffs and Trade (GATT), established in Geneva on 30 October 1947. A principal GATT objective is to 'liberalise' the conditions of world trade, which in reality means exposing the most vulnerable markets to exposure to foreign capital. Of the GATT Uruguay Round of Multilateral Trade Negotiations, launched in September 1986, the one-time president of Tanzania, Julius Nyerere, observed: 'in area after area of the Uruguay Round's detailed negotiations, Economic Colonialism is attacking the independent nations of the Third World and seeking to secure control of strategic points in their economies . . . this attack is being pointed by the Transnational Corporations of the world, in whose interests the Industrialised Countries are acting, while at the very same time their governments protect other domestic industries and economic sectors even contrary to the existing GATT rules which they now wish to extend and twist!'[18]

The situation is that a group of Specialised Agencies, gaining status and credibility from their UN connections, are working to further a common global financial strategy. In essence the objective is to advance the interests of world capitalism, an objective largely indifferent to the well-being of most of the world's population. All the endeavours of the United Nations need to be understood in the context of the realities of global financial power.

THE UN EDUCATIONAL, SCIENTIFIC AND CULTURAL ORGANISATION

The United Nations, at its best, symbolises a range of cultural values intended to bring harmony and advancement to the peoples of the world. The UN Educational, Scientific and Cultural Organisation (UNESCO) – though often criticised by commentators unsympathetic to its aims and methods – has worked hard to develop such a cultural framework, striving in particular to improve the lot of Third World peoples. The UNESCO Constitution was adopted on 16 November 1945 in London by representatives of 44 states. At the same time a Preparatory Commission was created to operate until the Organisation formally came into existence on 4 November 1946. Two months later, a UN/UNESCO Agreement was approved by the UN General Assembly, recognising UNESCO as a Specialised Agency of the United Nations. The Organisation also entered into agreements with other Specialised Agencies (ILO, FAO, WHO, WIPO and so on), and with various intergovernmental agencies not belonging to the UN system (the African Development Bank, the Council of Europe, the Ibero-American Bureau of Education, the League of Arab States, the Latin American Centre for Physics and so on). The text of the UNESCO Constitution, amended in 1976, notes:

> That since wars began in the minds of men, it is in the minds of men that the defences of peace must be constructed; That ignorance of each other's ways and lives has been a common cause, throughout the history of mankind, of that suspicion and mistrust between the peoples of the world through which their differences have all too often broken into war; That the great and terrible war which has now ended was a war made possible by the denial of the democratic principles of the dignity, equality and mutual respect of men, and by the propagation, in their place, through ignorance and prejudice, of the doctrine of the inequality of men and races; That the wide diffusion of culture, and the education of humanity for justice and liberty and peace are indispensable to the dignity of man and constitute a sacred duty which all the nations must fulfil in a spirit of mutual assistance and concern . . . the peace must therefore be found, if it is not to fail, upon the intellectual and moral solidarity of mankind.

The Constitution then sets out how UNESCO should implement this principled approach to human culture. Education is to be guided and expanded; science and technology are to be developed to enable states to exploit their own resources; national cultures and identities are to be preserved; communication facilities are to be expanded to facilitate the wider dissemination of information; and the social sciences are to be promoted as a means to the advancement of justice, peace and human rights. UNESCO projects have focused on the biosphere, tensions leading to war, racism, ecology, artistic creativity, the protection of archives, and the preservation of oral traditions. Efforts have been made to develop infrastructures through the International Programme for the Development of Communication; and studies have focused on the role of the media in establishing a new economic order. The General Conference of UNESCO, composed of the representatives of some 160 member countries, meets biennially to determine policy and to approve the budget. The 50-member Executive Board is elected by the Conference and is responsible for supervising the UNESCO programme approved by the Conference.[19]

Some member states, concerned at what they perceived as UNESCO's Third World focus and its leftist slant, have criticised its policies and administration. On 2 January 1985 the United States withdrew from the Organisation, to be followed by Britain on 5 December 1985. Timothy Raison, the UK Overseas Development Minister, told the House of Commons that the £6.4 million saved would be spent on Third World aid projects which were 'thoroughly worth doing, unlike much of UNESCO's work'. The Labour opposition disagreed with the government's decision to withdraw. Bill Clinton, when President-elect, declared that a US move to rejoin UNESCO was high on his agenda, stimulating speculation that Britain would follow suit.

THE UNITED NATIONS CHILDREN'S FUND

The UN Children's Fund (UNICEF) was created (as the UN International Children's Emergency Fund) by the UN General Assembly on 11 December 1946. In 1953, when the words 'International' and 'Emergency' were dropped, the General Assembly extended UNICEF's mandate indefinitely, and the organisation began to focus on the problems of malnutrition, disease and illiteracy afflicting millions of children throughout the world. In 1965 – because 'it has fulfilled the condition of Alfred Nobel's will, the promotion of brotherhood among the nations' – UNICEF was awarded the Nobel Peace Prize.

The organisation has semi-autonomous status within the United Nations, reporting to the Economic and Social Council and the General Assembly.

Its 21-member Executive Board is selected by the Council and is responsible for the development and administration of UNICEF policies. The body is wholly dependent on voluntary financial contributions, about three-quarters of which derive from governments and the rest from the general public in countries across the world. UNICEF is currently supporting children's programmes in more than 100 countries in Africa, Asia, the Americas and the Eastern Mediterranean with a total child population of around one billion. The UNICEF-assisted countries are divided into various groups, according to their perceived levels of need. A principal task is to offer immediate assistance in case of emergency, while at the same time developing long-range programmes for children in developing countries.

THE WORLD HEALTH ORGANISATION

The World Health Organisation (WHO) was established on 22 July 1946 when 61 states adopted the WHO Constitution; ratification took place on 7 April 1948 – now known as World Health Day – when the Constitution came into force. On 1 September 1948 WHO took over the activities of *Office International d'Hygiene Publique*, the League of Nations health organisation, and the peace-time functions of the UNRRA Health Division. The main WHO organ is the World Health Assembly, convened annually and composed of delegates from all member states. The WHO headquarters are in Geneva, but the activities of the Organisation have been largely decentralised to six regional associations. Any state, UN member or not, can become a WHO member by achieving Assembly approval of their application by simple majority vote.

In 1977 the General Assembly declared the WHO objective to be the attainment by all peoples of a level of health that will allow them to lead a socially and economically productive life. A blueprint for health for all by the year 2000 was worked out, with special focus on the need for primary health care, the essential levels of care that can be established at a cost that individual communities and states can afford. It was emphasised that priority should be given to nutritional requirements, safe water supplies, the control of communicable diseases, and the dissemination of existing knowledge to tackle the health problems of developing countries.

The Organisation has worked to improve health levels as widely as possible. Thus in 1967 began a global campaign to eradicate smallpox within ten years. At that time, some 131,418 cases were reported in 43 countries, but by the mid-1980s WHO was able to announce that the smallpox plague no longer existed. During the mid-1970s a long-term programme was developed to immunise children in the developing countries against diphtheria, tetanus, whooping cough, poliomyelitis, measles and tuberculosis. At the same time WHO supported the national control of tuberculosis by means of regional and national seminars and training schemes. WHO and UNICEF together tackled the African cholera problem, while WHO was making significant progress in reducing the incidence of malaria. In 1973 the International Health Regulations were amended to reflect the increased surveillance of epidemiological disease on an international scale.

The on-going WHO research programme involves the co-ordination of research workers in member countries, with more than 500 national institutions designated by WHO as collaborating centres. In the 1980s a special programme was developed for the treatment of six widespread tropical diseases: malaria, schistosomiasis, leprosy, filariasis, trepanosomiasis and leishmaniasis. WHO also researches cancer and encourages the standardisation of terminology and cancer-control services. The International Agency for Cancer Research in Lyon, France, is an autonomous body within the WHO framework. WHO has also collaborated with the World Bank, FAO and the United Nations Development Programme (UNDP).

Throughout 1993 the World Health Organisation continued to develop its global programme to combat AIDS. On 7 June in a keynote speech to open the AIDS conference in Berlin, Dr Michael Merson, director of the global WHO campaign, charted the 'relentless advance of HIV'. At that time the total number of AIDS cases stood at around 2.5 million – a 20 per cent increase on the previous year. Dr Merson claimed that the global response to AIDS was 'inadequate and unrealistic'; and that an effective campaign for education and condom distribution could halve the total of new infections. He commented that the cost estimated by WHO would be around $2.5 billion – 'a fraction of the cost of Desert Storm [the US-led war against Iraq], and it would hardly buy one can of Coke for every person in the world'. More than 15,000 delegates from 166 countries attended the WHO-sponsored conference.

However the main publicity for WHO in 1993 focused on the fractious controversy over the re-election of WHO director-general, Hiroshi Nakajima, widely criticised but heavily backed by the Japanese government which donated $51 million to WHO in 1992. Nakajima has been accused of alienating most of his staff and leading donors, including the United States and the European Community, and of seeking votes in exchange for favours. It has also been said that Nakajima, in addition to his disruptive management style, lacks the necessary communication skills since he understands neither French nor English. Early in 1993 the United States threatened that WHO would suffer if Nakajima were to be re-elected for a further five-year term.[20] In the event, Nakajima was re-elected by an 18-to-13 vote, suggesting that WHO would face a troubled future. Soon after the re-election was announced, fraud detection experts from the UK's National Audit Office were called in to investigate WHO staff and payment records at Geneva, and there were signs that the World Health Assembly was keen to challenge the Executive Committee vote. The issues to be investigated included the awarding of substantial contracts to member delegates (from the Philippines, Sierra Leone and the Seychelles) who voted for Nakajima.[21] The audit eventually detected 'lapses, shortcomings and deficiencies', but no direct link to the controversial re-election of the Japanese director-general.

This episode has been taken as signalling a shift in influence from the Western world to Japan. In earlier times the US-led faction would have had little difficulty in securing their man to head a key UN-linked body. If a WHO director-general can be re-elected against vigorous lobbying and veiled threats from Washington, is it possible that other UN organisations will come to be headed by individuals lacking the approval of the West?

THE INTERNATIONAL ATOMIC ENERGY AGENCY

The International Atomic Energy Agency (IAEA) was established in 1957 'under the aegis of the United Nations', with the requirement that the Agency report annually to the General Assembly and, as necessary, to the Security Council and the Economic and Social Council. The Agency is nominally intended to promote research and development into the peaceful uses of nuclear energy, and to oversee a system of safeguards and controls governing the possible misuse of nuclear materials for military purposes. The Agency has an interest in the Non-Proliferation Treaty (NPT), signed in 1968 by the United States, Britain, the Soviet Union, France and more than 100 other countries. The principal Treaty objective is to prevent the spread of nuclear weapons to non-nuclear states, so confining the possession of nuclear weapons to the Permanent Members of the Security Council and one or two other states (most notably, Israel).

It is significant that the IAEA was devised by Washington as a strategic device for developing a manageable nuclear status quo among the nations of the world. Thus in May 1954 the United States began secret talks with eight uranium-producing states: Britain, Canada, South Africa, France, Belgium, Australia and Portugal. The meetings took place during the drafting of the IAEA Treaty; and also later, during the early years of the Agency. The US State Department periodically issued invitations, and the meetings were held at ambassadorial level. In this way the uranium suppliers worked to establish a measure of control over the atomic ambitions of the non-nuclear powers and states that were acquiring nuclear power for peaceful purposes. The IAEA supported nuclear schemes that won its approval and produced surveys that profiled aspects of the global nuclear scene. The controls were often breached, sometimes surreptitiously and sometimes when the smaller states used their superior voting power at IAEA to maintain aid for their domestic nuclear programmes. By the mid-1950s a number of developing countries – India, Taiwan, South Korea and Argentina – had established their own atomic energy commissions.

The Agency, with the authority of the United Nations, seeks to maintain appropriate inspections of nuclear sites, and suspected nuclear sites, in an effort to guarantee the terms of the Non-Proliferation Treaty. Some of the inspections yield practical advice: for instance, a 1978 IAEA safety mission found that a nuclear site on the Bataan Peninsula was close to several volcanoes. But other inspections seemed to be oddly remiss: Israeli Premier Menachem Begin suggested that in January 1981 Iraq had hidden its military nuclear developments from IAEA inspectors, but omitted to comment on the fact that Agency efforts had done nothing to inhibit the build-up of a substantial stockpile of Israeli atomic weapons.[22] Today the Agency continues its activities, characteristically with a manifest ideological slant.

The IAEA remains largely indifferent to the Israeli stockpile of nuclear devices, while showing much interest in states to which Washington shows predictable hostility. The Agency finger is constantly pointed at such Arab states as Libya and Iraq (this latter a ravaged society still punished by harsh sanctions), and North Korea – not newly punished for lack of respect in the New World Order – is now coming in for special attention. In February 1993 North Korea refused to allow its nuclear sites to be inspected by Agency experts, whereupon the Agency proposed a special 'challenge inspection' of two sites suspected of developing atomic weapons. Analysis of material collected during earlier inspections had yielded 'major inconsistencies' in data supplied by the North Korean authorities. On 23 February 1993 a State Department official declared in Washington: 'There's a general mood to see through a resolution [a Security Council resolution demanding IAEA inspections].' Neither Russia nor China – North Korea's neighbours – was prepared to support the refusal to allow Agency inspections.

On 12 March 1993 North Korea announced that it was withdrawing from the Non-Proliferation Treaty (NPT), declaring that the decision was a 'well-justified self-defensive measure against the nuclear war manoeuvres of the secretariat of the IAEA'. The government statement also attacked US 'nuclear threats against North Korea', and urged Washington to abandon the massive military exercises being held with the South Korean army, manoeuvres that involved 120,000 troops and caused North Korea to go on to a 'semi-war footing'. Now the United States and Britain were discussing the possibility of a Security Council resolution to impose sanctions against the Pyingyang regime. China, it seemed, as a Permanent Member with a veto and also North Korea's largest trading partner, might prove an obstacle to such a course. If a resolution *were* to be passed, it would emphasise the IAEA as an authoritative UN body entitled to carry out international nuclear inspections. In April 1993 there was further attention, at a tumultuous time, to the possibility of security a UN resolution against North Korea, and reports that Western intelligence had revealed that the regime was on the brink of building its own nuclear weapons.[23] It was said that confidential IAEA documents were revealing the growing concern about North Korea's nuclear ambitions.

On 11 June North Korea suspended its threatened withdrawal from the NPT, announcing that it had 'decided unilaterally to suspend as long as it considers necessary . . . its withdrawal' from the 1970 treaty. The announcement followed a series of meetings between North Korea's Deputy Foreign Minister, Kang Sok Ju, and the US Assistant Secretary of State for political and military affairs, Robert Gallucci, at the US mission to the United Nations in New York. The talks had ended 'inconclusively'. At the same time there were reports that the North Koreans had test fired a Rodong-1 missile, an adapted Russian Scud C missile, with a range of 1000 km. Washington continued to monitor the situation but it seemed likely that the North Korean decision to remain with the NPT had – at least for the moment – prevented a US call for mandatory UN sanctions against the country.

The IAEA, like other UN-linked bodies, is having to cope with a crowded agenda in the post-Cold War world of the 1990s. With the accelerating pace of technological development, and with the inevitable inadequacy of many IAEA controls, the demands on the US-led Agency are unlikely to diminish in the years ahead.

Part II
Controversy

4 Cold War

The United Nations was born out of the Second World War. Even while the League of Nations was in its death throes there was widespread recognition that a new international body would have to be created in its stead. The League could not be revivified: its wounds were too great. Now it was discredited by its partial membership, by its failures, and above all else by the war. The Soviet Union had been expelled from the League but if there were to be a new international organisation the USSR was determined to be centrally involved in its creation. However, the Soviet Union was not the central player. The United States, immensely strengthened by the war, had worked to prepare the ground. Bretton Woods, Dumbarton Oaks, Potsdam and Yalta – all had felt the pressure of American diplomacy and growing American power. The United Nations, above all else, was an American creation. This was a circumstance that would – in concert with other developments – help to shape the lineaments of the Cold War.

During the inter-war years the United States had been much preoccupied with its own internal problems. The capitalist War of Intervention against the embryonic Bolshevik state did not immediately establish a pattern of military aggression: the Soviet Union would continue to be regarded as a pariah nation, but the use of naked force to overthrow the young communist regime was eschewed. In 1919 the US Congress passed the eighteenth amendment to the constitution and in 1920 enacted the Volstead Act, two dramatic moves intended to prohibit the production, distribution and consumption of alcohol in the United States. The measures did no more than provide an enormous boost to organised crime, but many years would pass before the US government learnt the lesson: it was not until 1933 that Prohibition was abandoned, by which time much of American industry and finance was in criminal hands. Such matters, coupled with the 1929 Wall Street crash and the Great Depression, stimulated American isolationism. Until Roosevelt's New Deal and the Second World War had removed many of America's economic problems, the United States was reluctant to play a dominant part on the world stage. With the ending of the war the pivot of world power shifted from Europe to New York.

SHAPING THE COLD WAR

The Second World War offered the United States many strategic opportunities. In various theatre of operations – throughout Europe, North Africa and Asia – America had managed to project and sustain military forces that, in many cases, would not be dislodged at the end of the war. The Soviet Union, at the war's conclusion still lacking the atomic bomb, had done the same in Eastern Europe; but it now saw itself ringed by hostile bases, many only a few miles from its borders. The United States had managed to consolidate a global shift in strategic power, a process that had begun in the early years of the war.

Britain, in 1940 in a parlous economic state, was increasingly forced to rely on American support. While Churchill was striving to cultivate the myth of a special Anglo-American relationship the United States was coolly calculating its strategic interest, well prepared to turn the British predicament to its own advantage. The isolationist thread in American attitudes remained strong, and although President Roosevelt was sympathetic to the Allied cause he was sensitive also to American public opinion: an opinion poll in May 1941 showed 80 per cent against America going to war.[1]

Churchill was quick to appeal to the United States for help, one of his first decisions as prime minister. He requested the supply of ships, aircraft, steel and other goods as essential to the British war effort; but on 16 May 1940 President Roosevelt turned down all the concrete requests. Soon, however, America was supplying rifles, machine guns and ammunition, though at the same time Roosevelt was writing that the US had no commitment to supply military aid. On 25 May Lord Lothian, the British ambassador to the United States, raised the idea that British bases might be offered to the Americans as a way of gaining their support. Churchill at first rejected the suggestion but a month later the Foreign Office repeated the idea, proposing that bases in Jamaica, Trinidad and British Guiana be offered. Now the US Congress was warming to the idea. On 13 August Roosevelt agreed to give the British 50 destroyers in exchange for long-term US bases on Newfoundland, Bermuda and in five West Indian colonies. Moreover, part of the deal would have to be made public, in order to impress the American people. In the event 'it was the British who had to make all the significant concessions . . . The number of ships they received was half that requested, the number of bases acquired by the US was twice the initial British offer . . . .'[2]

This was not all. When Sir Frederick Phillips, a senior Treasury official, met with Roosevelt and Henry Morgenthau, secretary of the US treasury, to acquaint them with Britain's financial predicament, he was advised that

Britain could sell its South American assets, which the US could then buy at knock-down prices. Such moves were well designed to support American financial and territorial interests in the post-war world. Even the Lend-Lease operations, much hyped as examples of selfless US policy, were nicely geared to American economic needs, and were precipitately ended, to the considerable inconvenience of America's European allies. On 21 August 1945, within seven days of the Japanese surrender, a White House press release stated that all Lend-Lease operations would end immediately. This sudden termination – even involving laden ships on the high seas having to perform U-turns – surprised everyone outside America. It was clear that 'any such abrupt stoppage of so vast a flow of goods in the channels of trade was bound to cause dislocation and involve suffering'.[3] Britain, in her particularly vulnerable economic situation, was very badly affected. Prime Minister Attlee commented that the abrupt termination of Lend-Lease placed Britain in a 'very serious financial position', and Churchill called it 'very grave and disquieting news'.[4] The United States had signalled above all that its principal concern was with its own financial and strategic interests.

Now the scene was set for the development of wider tensions. Roosevelt had died on 12 April 1945, his last thoughts on the Soviet question sent to the British government an hour before his death: 'I would minimize the general Soviet problem as much as possible because these problems, in one form or another, seem to arise every day, and most of them straighten out.'[5] Such advice was soon ignored. When Soviet Foreign Minister Molotov arrived in Washington on 23 April to meet Truman for the first time the US president made 'very plain to Molotov our displeasure at the Soviet failure to carry through the agreement made at Yalta about the character of a new Polish Government'. Truman chose to use 'blunt language unadorned by the polite verbiage of diplomacy'.[6] Charles Bohlen, a senior diplomat at the meeting, remarked that 'he had never heard a top official get such a scolding'.[7] Truman, 'from the eminence of eleven days in power', had laid down the law to the Russians.[8] There has been much discussion about the US shift of emphasis, about the newly emerging anti-Soviet posture.

One reason was the declared antipathy to the Soviet interpretation of the Yalta agreement on Poland. The Soviets were insisting on a United Nations seat for the Lublin government which the US did not regard as representative of the Polish people. The question was: were the Russians trying to keep the agreements – 'highly ambiguous',[9] in one view – as they perceived them, or were they intent on tearing up agreements newly made? American efforts to establish Russian perfidy were not helped by comments by Winston Churchill, whom no one could accuse of pro-Soviet bias: 'The impression

I brought back . . . is that Marshal Stalin and the Soviet leaders wish to live in honourable friendship and equity with the Western democracies. I feel also that their word is their bond. I know of no government which stands to its obligations . . . more solidly than the Russian Soviet Government.'[10] The early US hostility to the Soviet Union, clearly ignoring the caution espoused at that time by both Churchill and the surviving Roosevelt faction, almost resulted in a Soviet withdrawal from the San Francisco Conference intended by Roosevelt to establish a comprehensive United Nations. Senator Vandenberg, a key US delegate at the conference, noted in his diary (24 April 1945), speaking of ' 'Frisco': 'Russia may withdraw. If it does the conference *will proceed without Russia*. Now we are getting somewhere!' (original emphasis). Vandenberg had found Truman's abuse of Molotov 'thrilling' and was keen to shape the conference decisions to protect what he saw as America's strategic interests.

There were various sources of tension at the San Francisco Conference. The controversy over the Lublin government had not derailed the Soviet presence, probably to Vandenberg's disappointment, but other difficulties soon arose. At Yalta, Roosevelt had twice promised Stalin that the US would not support the admission of Argentina to the United Nations since, in the words of Secretary of State Cordell Hull, Argentina had become 'the refuge and headquarters in this hemisphere of the Fascist movement' and was obviously seeking 'Argentine hegemony of South America'.[11] But despite Roosevelt's assurances the US delegation was suddenly ordered to support Argentina's admission to the United Nations. Hull, from his sickbed, telephoned Stettinius to say that the US attitude had done 'irreparable harm' and that the Soviet Union 'might decide that the United Nations organization was not going to furnish adequate security to her in the future'.[12] It was not emerging that Washington's main objective was to organise an anti-Soviet majority in the UN, a policy that the prestigious journalist Walter Lippmann reckoned would have 'the most disastrous consequences'. In fact, the United Nations in its first decade served as little more than an instrument of US foreign policy: 'In the years 1946–53 the General Assembly adopted over 800 resolutions. The United States was defeated in less than 3 per cent – and in no case where important security interests were involved. In those eight years only two resolutions supported by us failed of adoption.'[13]

The United Nations had been launched, with Soviet membership intact, despite the increasingly anti-Soviet US posture. The right-wing columnist Arthur Krock reported that the Soviet Union had behaved at the conference 'as a great power and a generally cooperative one on the task in hand'.[14] The journalist James Reston noted the 'ten concessions by Russia which have contributed greatly to the liberalising of the Dumbarton Oaks proposals'.[15] But the Soviet concessions had done nothing to divert Washington from its plan to transform the United Nations into an anti-Soviet tool, a useful instrument in the developing Cold War.

At one level the United States was discouraging talk of spheres of influence, urging instead a new era of security backed by the authority of the United Nations. This posture, later abandoned, was intended to weaken the Soviet influence in Poland and elsewhere in Eastern Europe while Washington was keen to support the dictatorships of Central and South America as props for US hegemony. Some leading Americans recognised the contradiction but were prepared to live with it. Thus Secretary of War Henry L. Stimson, commenting to his assistant John J. McCloy, said: 'I think it's not asking too much to have our little region over here which never has bothered anybody.' McCloy agreed that 'we ought to have our cake and eat it too . . . we ought to be free to operate under this regional arrangement in South America, at the same time intervene promptly in Europe; we oughtn't to give away either asset.'[16] It was no accident that the UN Charter (Article 52) made provision for 'regional arrangements', which in practice imposed no constraint on Washington's developing strategic alliances around the world. At the same time the United States was forced to tolerate, at least in the short term, the Soviet control of Eastern Europe. The Polish question had not been resolved, one of the various problems that had threatened the San Francisco Conference and continued to trouble the post-war world. The abrupt ending of aid to Russia and other European countries had damaged relations between the US and other powers, with Russia and Britain, for example, having assumed that their reconstruction would be aided by a continuation of the Lend-Lease provisions. At the San Francisco Conference, Secretary of State Stettinius observed that the Truman decision was 'particularly untimely and did not help Soviet–American relations'. Truman later rescinded the order and some supplies were allowed to flow. But by now the die was cast: no one could doubt that Washington was the principal player among the states jockeying for strategic interest in the post-war world.

In late-1945 the US government 'lost' a Soviet request for financial aid but 'found' it months later. Washington agreed to discuss the loan, provided the Soviet government would pledge 'non-discrimination in international commerce', so allowing American investment in the Soviet sphere of influence. Stalin rejected the proposal and resolved to maintain 'the technical and economic independence of the Soviet Union'. The US–Soviet divide was widening. Truman claimed to have learned at Potsdam that the Soviets could not be trusted and that all they understood was force. He resolved that

US interests would be pursued, whatever the Soviet attitude and whatever the theatre of operations, including those in Asia, a pressing concern: 'As I reflected on the situation during my trip home, I made up my mind that General MacArthur would be given complete command and control after victory in Japan.'[17] Such a decision had great strategic significance: it would help to sustain the ring of military bases around the Soviet Union (and in later years would help the prosecution of the war against Vietnam). In such matters there would be no reference to the security provisions of the UN Charter: the United States was big enough to look after its own strategic interests.

Another factor was to have immense significance in the development of US relations with the Soviet Union. The successful development of the atomic bomb was a weighty consideration to throw into the scales. For example, the US possession of such a weapon would, according to Secretary of State James Byrnes, 'make Russia more manageable in Europe'; more generally, it would make it unwise for the Soviet Union to threaten American interests, wherever they were. But the start of the era of nuclear terror did not always have the intended deterrent effect. The Soviets managed to secure the Communist takeover of Czechoslovakia in 1948, and no one in Washington seriously proposed dropping atomic bombs on Moscow. Russia had not proved 'more manageable' after all: the Soviet Union would not be browbeaten, though it was clearly at a strategic and military disadvantage. The Soviet state had been ravaged by the war, making any destabilising aggressions against Western Europe extremely unlikely.[18] At the same time it was equally improbable that any country, even the United States, would be prepared to confront the military power of the Soviet Union. The rigid constraints of the Cold War were becoming consolidated, with neither of the two great power blocs having a decisive strategic advantage, at least in the short term. There were frequent tensions in Germany between the Soviets on the one hand and the Western powers on the other; there were signs of growing tensions in Asia as the Soviet Union gave increasing support to indigenous nationalist movements; and in the Middle East there were mounting US–Soviet tensions over Iran and Turkey. To obtain oil concessions from the Iranian government, the Soviets supported a revolt in the north of the country. On 6 March 1946 Secretary Byrnes sent a note demanding Soviet withdrawal. Two months later the Russians withdrew, having failed to guarantee the formation of a joint Iranian–Soviet oil company.

On 5 March 1946 Winston Churchill offered an interpretation of such events for the benefit of the American people and the wider world community. In a speech at Fulton, Missouri, as a fitting end to the Churchill premiership, he outlined his perception of the emerging Cold War. In President Truman's home state, with Truman beside him on the platform of Westminster College, Churchill addressed a capacity audience: more than 40,000 people had journeyed to Fulton, which at that time had a population of around 7000. In his speech, Churchill observed that the United States 'stands at this time at the pinnacle of world power . . . a solemn moment for the American democracy'. There was a role, he conceded, for the United Nations, but it was vital that Britain and the United States did not disarm before the new international body was made secure. He then extolled the sharing by Britain and the United States of atomic secrets, happy that 'some Communist or neo-Fascist state' had not monopolised 'these dread agencies . . . God has willed that this shall not be.' Then Churchill moved on to the most quoted part of his Fulton speech, advertising – though not with complete originality – a new term that would come to denote the central feature of the Cold War:

> From Stettin in the Baltic to Trieste in the Adriatic, an iron curtain has descended across the Continent. Behind that line lie all the capitals of the ancient states of central and eastern Europe. Warsaw, Berlin, Prague, Vienna, Budapest, Belgrade, Bucharest, and Sofia; all these famous cities and the populations around them lie in what I must call the Soviet sphere, and all are subject, in one form or another, not only to Soviet influence but to a very high and, in many cases, increasing measure of control from Moscow.

He noted that in the British Commonwealth and the United States 'Communist parties, or fifth columns, constitute a growing challenge and peril to Christian civilisation'. So Winston Churchill helped to fuel not only the Cold War as a general system of confrontation but also the Joseph McCarthy witch-hunts in particular. He concluded by urging the 'English-speaking' peoples to unite to defend their freedom and their way of life, so that 'there will be no quivering, precarious balance of power to offer its temptation to ambition or adventure'. This idea, sanctified by history, was not well received on either side of the Atlantic. Eleanor Roosevelt in her syndicated column voiced the fear that an Anglo-American alliance might provoke the creation of counter-alliances in other parts of the world. Three Democrat Senators (Pepper, Kilgore and Glen Taylor) denounced the speech as shocking, and Secretary of Commerce Henry Wallace commented that 'Mr Churchill is not speaking for the American people and their government'. In Britain, Prime Minister Attlee declined to venture an opinion, while a hundred MPs signed a motion of protest. In Russia, Stalin described the

Fulton speech as a 'dangerous act, calculated to sow the seeds of discord among Allied governments and hamper their co-operation'.

The United States did not need lectures from other quarters. Washington would pursue its own interests in its own way. The Fulton speech was followed by the Marshall Plan (see below) and the setting up of the North Atlantic Treaty Organisation (NATO), both designed to protect America's dominant economic and military position. In practice there would be no needless attention to such matters as freedom and democracy, though rhetoric about such things could usefully disguise the real economic and political objectives. On 24 February 1948 the US Policy Planning Staff in Washington emphasised the essential task facing the United States:

> We have about 60% of the world's wealth but only 6.3% of its population. Our world task in this position is to devise a pattern of relationships which will permit us to maintain this position of disparity. We should cease to talk about such vague and unreal objectives as human rights, the raising of living standards and democratisation.

Washington became increasingly committed to a defence of American interests around the world. Earlier thoughts about the US atomic supremacy might be voluntarily relinquished in favour of international control of nuclear weapons were abandoned. As long as the formidable Red Army remained intact the United States would retain its nuclear monopoly. There were many uncertainties. Soviet expansion into Iran and Turkey had been met and stopped, but Soviet hegemony in Eastern Europe could not be usefully challenged. In pursuing its interests around the globe Washington would be forced to consider an unsympathetic Soviet Union, a considerable military power that would itself soon have access to nuclear weapons.

This was the context in which the United Nations was forced to develop. It was essentially an American creation, largely American financed (until, in later years, US governments deliberately delayed their payments), and with the United States as its dominant member. The State Department career man Robert Murphy summed up a widespread political attitude in the US when he commented that he saw the United Nations as an organisation that could be used to serve American foreign policy. When the UN could not be used in such a fashion it could be ignored.[19] Such an interpretation inevitably portrayed the United Nations as a passive entity, to be exploited when convenient and to be deliberately disregarded at other times. There was also another view: to the effect that the UN was a subversive organisation, a front for 'communists' (see 'The "Communist" UN', below). Between those American factions intent on exploiting the United Nations as a route to advancing US foreign policy and those who would have been content to see the organisation collapse, there were few prepared to view the UN in idealistic terms, to support the international body as a realistic cornerstone of world security.

One of the earliest clues to the prevailing ideology of the United Nations was its response to the Greek civil war. In December 1946 the Greek government appealed to the UN for assistance, claiming that the Communist states of Albania, Bulgaria and Yugoslavia were interfering in its affairs. A UN commission was set up and the charges were completely substantiated. It was found that men and arms were entering Greece to aid the Communists, while ethnic Greeks north of the border were being recruited to support the Communist cause. Less attention was given to US aid designed to build up the Greek Royal Army or to the British forces that entered the country to prevent the emergence of a popular regime. Thus: 'The decisive factor in the ensuing struggle for power was the British Army, which entered the country as the Germans left.'[20] The British administrators were content to support the Greek police force that had served the Nazis. British troops moved through the country to crush nationalist opposition, while the pro-Nazi National Guard followed them to 'pacify' the regions. The United Nations expressed little interest in such matters.

Trygve Lie, the first Secretary-General of the United Nations, detected 'many ominous signs of the developing cleavage between the Western powers and the USSR during 1946'.[21] The disputes about the character of the governments of Eastern Europe, the problems of the Paris Peace Conference, tensions within the UN over Iran and Greece – such issues were not well designed to give the new body a harmonious launch on to the world scene. On 14 June 1946 the UN Atomic Energy Commission assembled at Hunter College to investigate the possibilities for eliminating 'atomic weapons and . . . all other major weapons adaptable to mass destruction', for limiting nuclear power to peaceful applications, and for developing safeguards 'by way of inspection and other means to protect complying States against the hazards of violations and evasions'. The US representative, the 75-year-old Bernard M. Baruch, introduced a proposal (the 'Baruch Plan') for the creation of an International Atomic Development Authority to control the development of atomic energy throughout the world, at the same time emphasising to the delegates that the choice was between 'world peace' and 'world destruction'.

In the end the Baruch Plan foundered: not least because, after protracted discussions, the Soviet Union rejected the ownership and operation of nuclear facilities by an international body (they would instead remain in national hands and be subject to inspection), and insisted that serious violations calling for the UN-imposed punishment would be referred to the Security Council, where the Soviet Union would be able to use the veto. The Plan failed to prevent the onset of the nuclear arms race, just as today it seems unlikely that the UN-linked International Atomic Energy Agency (IAEA) will be unable to block the spread of nuclear weapons throughout the world. The collapse of the Baruch Plan in 1947 set the seal on the dimensions of the Cold War. Throughout 1946 military representatives of the Permanent Members of the Security Council met in private sessions of the Military Staff Committee (see Article 47 of the UN Charter) with a view to developing protocols for the organisation of UN military forces. Such discussions, like the Baruch Plan, came to nought. The Military Staff Committee came to be seen as 'a symbol of disappointed hopes . . . put aside for a better day'.[22]

Other disputes within the United Nations focused on the admission of new members ('a dreary succession of deadlocks' – Lie), with 21 applications for membership still pending as late as 1953; and on the increasingly ambitious US interventions in various parts of the world. On 12 March 1947 President Truman asserted the American right to provide military and economic assistance to regimes threatened by Communism. The first fruit of the Truman Doctrine was a $400 million package of aid for Greece and Turkey, intended to shore up right-wing authoritarian governments. It was difficult to square such developments with the declared US principle that the United Nations was the 'cornerstone of its foreign policy'. Trygve Lie records that 'the Truman Doctrine burst like a bombshell upon the world with no advance notice whatever'. The US government did not bother to notify its own UN representative, Ambassador Austin, in advance; and many friendly UN members and the Secretary-General were similarly kept in the dark. Senator Vandenberg, himself not always sensitive to the global role of the United Nations, was driven to protest that the US State Department had blundered in ignoring the UN in so cavalier a fashion. Again Washington had advertised the central principle of its foreign policy: it would pursue its strategic objectives in its own way in its own time. The United Nations would be exploited where possible; where not, it would be ignored.

The basic document in which the United States government articulated its Cold War assumptions is National Security Council (NSC) memorandum 68 (April 1950); 'the cold war is in fact a real war in which the survival of the free world is at stake.'[23] The dichotomy is childishly simple, an advertiser's dream. On the one hand is the fiendish Kremlin ('The implacable purpose of the slave state [is] to eliminate the challenge of freedom'); on the other is the sublime United States (a 'free society' marked by 'marvelous diversity', 'deep tolerance', 'lawfulness' and other benign qualities, deriving 'its strength from its hospitality even to antipathetic ideas'). The United States, it was emphasised, had an 'essential tolerance . . . generous and constructive impulses . . . absence of covetousness'. The struggle between Good and Evil would be 'momentous, involving the fulfillment or destruction not only of this Republic but of civilization itself'. It almost went without saying that the United States had 'the responsibility of world leadership' in these dire circumstances. Since the Kremlin wanted to dominate the world, all nations must be enlisted on the side of righteousness: 'the idea that Germany or Japan or other important areas can exist as islands of neutrality in a divided world is unreal'.

The memorandum demanded a massive increase in armaments, while conceding that the US military budget was already twice that of the Soviet Union and its economic strength four times as great. The US armed forces were 'dangerously inadequate' because the United States now had the daunting responsibility of running the world. The US must 'foster the seeds of destruction within the Soviet system' to 'hasten [its] decay', at the same time avoiding all negotiations because any agreements 'would reflect present realities and would therefore be unacceptable, if not disastrous, to the United States and the rest of the free world'. And having, in the earlier rhetoric, praised American 'deep tolerance', the US must now overcome such weaknesses as 'the excesses of a permanently open mind' and 'the excess of tolerance'. The 'labor unions, civic enterprises, schools, churches, and all media for influencing opinion' must be insulated from 'evil' influences. There would, in such a context, be a 'necessity for just suppression'. The memorandum, as a prestigious NSC product, was one of the highest-level government planning documents. It helped to shape US attitudes and policies for the duration of the Cold War.[24]

THE 'COMMUNIST' UNITED NATIONS

Roots

Another strand in American opinion was that the United Nations existed essentially as a subversive force on the US mainland. Was it not the case that avowed Communists had supported the creation of the UN organisation? Thus Earl Browder, one-time leader of the United States Communist Party, declared in his book *Victory and After*: 'The American Communists worked energetically and tirelessly to lay the foundations for the United

Nations, which we were sure would come into existence.' Similarly, the Communist periodical *Political Affairs* (April 1945) emphasised the importance of ensuring that the capitalist countries became committed to the new international body. The Soviet Union would be a powerful voice in the Security Council, able to prevent independent action against Communist states:

> Victory means more than the military defeat of Nazi Germany. It means the collapse of anti-Soviet policies and programs as dominant tendencies within the capitalist sector of the world. It means that the policy predominant during the interwar years of attempting to solve the world crisis at the expense of the Soviet Union is replaced by the policy of attempting to solve the crisis through cooperation with the Soviet Union.[25]

A few months later a pamphlet entitled *The United Nations* gave details of how some Communists viewed the new body. The San Francisco Conference had met to bring an end to war, but 'everyone knows that war cannot be abolished until imperialism is abolished'. In such circumstances there were four reasons why Communists should support the United Nations: the Soviet Union would be protected by the veto; capitalist foreign policy would be frustrated; colonial territories would be broken up; and the new international body would eventually create a worldwide Soviet system.[26] In 1953 the House Committee on Un-American Activities heard testimony from Colonel Jan Bukar, a former Czechoslovakian army intelligence officer, that a General Bondarenko had declared at the Frunze Military Academy in Moscow: 'From the rostrum of the United Nations, we shall convince the colonial and semi-colonial people to liberate themselves and to spread the Communist theory over all the world. We recognise the UN as no authority over the Soviet Union, but the United Nations serves to deflect the capitalists and warmongers in the Western World.'[27]

In 1953 Dr Marek Stanislaw Korowicz, a UN delegate from Poland, defected to the United States and appeared before the House Committee on Un-American Activities. He testified that 'the UN is considered as one of the most important platforms for Soviet propaganda in the world . . . The UN organisation offers a parliamentary platform to the Soviet politicians, and from this platform, they may preach to the populations of the entire world and do their subversive propaganda.'[28] Even the siting of the UN headquarters in New York has been instanced as a triumph for Soviet subversion. The New York location made it easy for the 'Communists in the United Nations' to reach directly to the American people, and for 'their spies and espionage agents posing as delegates and staff' to gain entry to the United States under full diplomatic immunity.[29]

To some American observers there was an evident Communist master plan for world domination, a subversive scheme in which the United Nations had a central role to play. One observer, G. Edward Griffin, summarised what he and others saw as 'the Communist blueprint for world conquest via the United Nations':

1. Consolidate total working control of the United Nations into Communist hands as rapidly as possible.

2. Use the United Nations to break up the colonial territories of non-Communist countries.

3. Use the United Nations as a vehicle for subversion, espionage and propaganda within the non-Communist member nations.

4. Induce the non-Communist member nations to abandon any strong independent foreign policy of their own by turning this function over to the United Nations.

5. Maneuver the non-Communist member nations into establishing socialism at home as the necessary transition stage to Communism and to become dependent economically on the overall international socialist control and direction of the UN.

6. Induce the stronger non-Communist member nations to transfer full control of their military forces to the United Nations. After this, no resistance will be possible. The world will be Communist.[30]

In its early years the United States functioned as little more than a tool of US foreign policy, despite the supposed 'Communist blueprint'; but by the mid-1950s, with colonial territories beginning to achieve independence and UN membership, the United States found it harder to guarantee its majorities in the General Assembly. In consequence, there began a period of general US antipathy to much of what the bulk of the United Nations membership wanted to achieve. Early right-wing critics of the new organisation were content to denounce the new world body as an agent of international subversion. They redoubled their efforts when they claimed to have discovered Communist influence at the heart of the UN, in the staffing of the Secretariat.

The Secretariat

In the early 1950s a number of influential Americans – Roy Cohn (Chief Counsel to Senator Joe McCarthy), Senator Pat McCarran (co-author of the McCarran–Walter Act, 'the most severe anti-red law on the books') and others began a systematic attack on the American employees of the UN Secretariat.[31] To activists such as McCarthy, Cohn and McCarran it seemed that merely to co-operate with the UN's international functions was a sign of subversive intent. The attack on UN staff was only part of the wider McCarthy crusade.

Trygve Lie recorded that nothing in the UN Charter or in the Staff Regulations 'bars a Communist from being a member of the United Nations Secretariat; nor could there be in an organization that embraces both Communist and non-Communist members'.[32] At the same time Lie declared that he would not want American Communists in the Secretariat, since they would not be representative American citizens. But he had no fear 'of espionage or sabotage or other threat' – for the simple reason that there was nothing to spy on in the United Nations: 'the United Nations was about as barren a field for spies as could be imagined'. Trygve Lie noted the 'unreasoning fear and intolerance' of Communists in the United States and mentioned also European friends who wondered if Fascism was beginning in the US. At one stage an unidentified witness before a Senate Judicial Subcommittee declared that the Secretariat was under Communist domination and that Trygve Lie was himself a Communist tool – a manifest absurdity. Soon, as the Cold War began to roll, there were hysterical statements that the United Nations harboured 'a nest of Communist spies', and there were calls for a 'clean-up' of the UN Secretariat. 'The public outcry in the United States . . . grew to appalling proportions, while the morale of the Secretariat slumped badly.'[33] When in October 1952 a number of UN staff members were forced to appear before a Senate Judicial Subcommittee and pleaded the Fifth Amendment, there was a rising clamour for stern action against alleged Communists working in the United Nations.

It was at this time that Senator McCarran, chairman of the Internal Security Subcommittee, introduced a bill 'to prevent citizens of the United States of questionable loyalty to the United States Government from accepting any office or employment in or under the United States'. Any US citizen wanting to accept a post with the UN would first have to obtain security clearance from the Attorney General, and a similar clearance would also have to be obtained by any US citizens already in UN employ. The bill had ample provision for non-compliance: 'Whoever, being a citizen of the United States . . . shall willfully fail to comply . . . shall be fined not more than $10,000, or imprisoned for not more than five years.' Trygve Lie noted that the only precedent he could discover for such a law was the edict enacted in 1927 by Fascist Italy to prevent Italian opponents of Mussolini from becoming members of the Secretariat of the League of Nations. There, however, the penalties for non-compliance were less severe than in the McCarran legislation (a fine of not more than 5000 lire and a prison term of one year).

At the same time President Truman moved to facilitate FBI investigations of US citizens employed by, or considering employment by, the UN Secretariat. Some US members of the Secretariat welcomed such moves as a means of clearing themselves, though there were protests – by American and European staff – at Lie's decision to allow the US authorities to carry out fingerprinting and to run investigations in the UN headquarters building, nominally international territory. This was the rather dismal end to Trygve Lie's immensely difficult period at the United Nations, a term of office which both laid the basis for the new international body and saw the discouraging consolidation of the Cold War framework. Recalling the end of his term as Secretary-General, Lie chose to remark that the world struggle for freedom 'still has its home front' in America: 'Although the Secretariat of the United Nations cannot fight the battle which is properly to be left to the American liberal tradition, it must stand guard against the assaults which continue to be made against its international integrity and ideal.'[34] Some observers may feel that such words have a singular resonance in the 1990s when Washington has worked to suborn the United Nations in various ways.

The Case of Alger Hiss

The attack on Secretariat staff in particular and the wider McCarthy purges in general had many victims. A few, by dint of special circumstances, stood out and are still remembered today. Of these, Alger Hiss is perhaps the best known example. To the rightist witch-hunters in the United States, Hiss was the supreme example of the well-placed individual who used his position and privileges to subvert his country. Alger Hiss, in contrast, has always maintained his innocence of the charges made against him and the injustice of his subsequent punishment.

Alger Hiss achieved an impressive record at the Harvard Law School, attracted the attention of Professor (later Justice) Felix Frankfurter, and served a year as secretary to Justice Oliver Wendell Holmes. After spending time with a New York law firm he became involved in Roosevelt's New Deal activities in 1933, joined the State Department in 1936, and accompanied Roosevelt to Yalta. Critics of Hiss, trying to establish his circumstantial guilt, noted that it was at Yalta that the Soviet Union was promised three votes in the United Nations General Assembly against the one vote allowed to the United States. Thus, 'even if Roosevelt had been inclined to protest this absurd agreement, he was up against the demands of Joe Stalin and the advice of Alger Hiss'.[35] The critics also noted that Hiss was the executive secretary of the Dumbarton Oaks Conference in 1944, held to determine the future shape of the United Nations. He was also the chief planner and executive of the 1945 San Francisco Conference at which the UN organisation was launched. Here he was the acting secretary-general and responsible for organising the American delegation; he signed the passes granted to visitors. A report in *Time* magazine noted:

> At San Francisco, he [Alger Hiss] and his Secretariat of 300 (mostly Americans) will have the drudging, thankless clerk's job of copying, translating and publishing, running the thousands of paper-clip and pencil chores of an international meeting. But Alger Hiss will be an important figure there. As secretary-general, managing the agenda, he will have a lot to say behind the scenes about who gets the breaks.[36]

Alger Hiss also worked on the steering and executive committees responsible for drafting the Charter of the United Nations. He did not perform the task on his own but was obviously in a position to influence the eventual shape of the document. It was the responsibility of Hiss to carry the freshly written document – contained in a watertight box with a parachute – back to Washington by plane for final ratification by the Senate. Throughout this entire period, it was later revealed, Alger Hiss was under surveillance by the FBI as a suspected Communist agent.

It is now claimed that the FBI had evidence of Hiss's subversive activities as early as 1939 and frequently issued security reports to present the facts to the Justice Department.[37] Various former Communists have been paraded to testify that they knew and worked with Alger Hiss as a member of the American Communist Party. On 3 August 1948 Whittaker Chambers, accused of involvement in a Communist spy ring, testified before the House Un-American Activities Committee that Hiss had been active in underground Communist espionage. On 5 August Hiss refuted the charges in such a 'convincing and effective'[38] a manner that one member of the Committee was driven to declare: 'We've been had! We're ruined!'[39]

The FBI head, J. Edgar Hoover, today much discredited, threw all his resources into the effort to secure a perjury conviction against Hiss; in this endeavour he was assisted greatly by the energetic work of the ambitious investigator, Richard Nixon. Before the start of the first trial of Alger Hiss on 31 May 1949, Hoover had assigned some 300 FBI agents to work on the case. When the government prosecutor Thomas Murphy made the mild observation that the Bureau agents had not managed to find Hiss's typewriter, Hoover instructed his aides to search Murphy's files to see whether the prosecutor might be 'unfriendly towards the Bureau'. The first Hiss trial ended on 7 July 1949 in a hung jury (8–4 for conviction), whereupon Richard Nixon demanded an examination of Judge Samuel H. Kaufman's fitness for the bench. This initiative succeeded in discrediting the trial and in launching a fresh trial on 17 November with a new judge, Henry W. Goddard, and a new prosecution strategy. This time, Hoover, Nixon and the army of Bureau agents were rewarded. On 21 January 1950 Alger Hiss was found guilty of perjury and sentenced to five years' imprisonment, 'a disaster for American liberalism'.[40]

The verdict served the witch-hunters well, boosting Hoover's repressive efforts and adding a bogus credibility to the McCarthyite campaigners. The Hiss case now made it easy for the McCarthyites 'to exaggerate the dimensions of the internal Communist menace and to whip up a storm which did not last long but left ruin in its wake'.[41] The verdict on Hiss was also advertised as a vindication of those claiming that the United Nations organisation was no more than a refuge for subversive elements, an alien presence on American soil.

On 29 October 1992 Alger Hiss, then aged 87, claimed that his name had finally been cleared by a senior advisor to the Russian president, Boris Yeltsin. For 40 years Hiss had proclaimed his innocence. Three times the Supreme Court had turned down applications to examine the Hiss case. Now General Dmitri Volkogonov, the chairman of the archives of the old Soviet Union, was prepared to declare: 'Not a single document – and a great amount of materials have been studied – substantiates the allegation that Mr A. Hiss collaborated with the intelligence services of the Soviet Union.' A frail Alger Hiss commented: 'Inside, I had the confidence . . . it's just an instinctive feeling, that there would be an eventual happy conclusion that I would witness.'[42]

UNESCO

The American agitation against the alleged Communist infiltration of the United Nations organisation did not stop at the Secretariat. In July 1948 Robert C. Alexander, second-in-command of the State Department Visa Division, testified in Congress that 'Communist agents' were entering the United States under the cover of various UN agencies, with the United

Nations Relief and Rehabilitation Administration (UNRRA) 'the greatest offender'. At the time such testimony disturbed mainstream US government opinion since it provided ammunition to those conservatives who wanted to derail US support for the United Nations. Alexander proposed also that the United States take military action against Communist governments producing too many refugees: accepting exiles from socialist countries 'even for humanitarian reasons' served only to drain off 'the properly discordant and recalcitrant elements' in those states, so propping up Soviet rule.

The UNRRA may have been judged by Alexander to have been the worst offender in tolerating Communist infiltration into the United States, but other UN bodies came in for equal (or greater) criticism from other quarters. UNESCO (the United Nations Educational, Scientific and Cultural Organisation) was destined to attract particular vilification.

In April 1955 Congressman Lawrence H. Smith of Wisconsin described the United Nations in general and UNESCO in particular as 'a permanent international snake pit where Godless Communism is given a daily forum for hate, recrimination, psychological warfare against freedom, and unrelenting moral aggression against peace'.[43] The same year the American Legion, at its annual national convention, formally passed the following resolution:

> *Resolved*, that the American Legion urges Congress to repeal the law creating the United States Commission for UNESCO and its Secretariat; and that Congress deliver mandates to all administrative departments of the United States Government to desist from further dissemination of UNESCO and US Commission for UNESCO materials, reports and programs within the territorial jurisdiction of the United States.

In the face of a rising clamour against UNESCO, increasingly depicted as a Communist-dominated body, the US State Department was forced to issue a statement noting that some people had been 'making misstatements about UNESCO, some of them attaining the proportions of deliberate misrepresentation'. In fact, the US government came to believe much of the criticism levelled against UNESCO, a capitulation that eventually led to US withdrawal of 1985.

Again it was an easy matter to find Communists prepared to exploit UNESCO for their own purposes; and *former* Communists were particularly eager to provide useful testimony. Thus the former Communist Josepf Z. Kornfeder noted that 'UNESCO corresponds to the agitation and propaganda department in the Communist party. The department handles the strategy and method of getting at the public mind, young and old.'[44] It was also noted that Alger Hiss and the similarly denounced Harry Dexter White had helped to create UNESCO, just as the English communist Elen Wilkenson, who later preferred to call herself a socialist, became president of the UNESCO preparatory commission.

The anti-UN writer G. Edward Griffin offers many examples of what he considers to be the pro-Communist propaganda disseminated by UNESCO.[45] His examples include the depiction of pro-UN figures as wholesome and intelligent, criticism of race discrimination in the United States, and support for such subversive doctrines as 'human adjustment', 'group consciousness' and 'social cooperation'. He comments (p. 150):

> If we would but open our eyes and look, we would be shocked at the extent to which this UNESCO virus has spread. On Flag Day in a school in White Plains, New York, American children were presented with a flag at an impressive ceremony in which even the city government participated. It was not Old Glory [the Stars and Stripes]; it was the flag of the United Nations.

In the same way UNESCO is denounced for proposing a convention against discrimination in education, a proposal denounced in 1961 by five Congressmen (Ashbrook, Ayres, Bruce, Hiestand and Martin) as intended to deliver 'the entire American educational system into UNESCO international control'.[46]

Such arguments and agitation have always represented a substantial body of American opinion. As the United States found it increasingly difficult to guarantee a majority in the UN General Assembly, Washington developed an increasingly antipathy towards most of Assembly opinion. There were ways in which the United Nations could still be used by Washington, not least as a convenient forum for expressing support for sympathetic dictatorships and for consolidating regional alliances; but for the most part Washington found it best to preserve a strategic distance from much of the UN membership. For the US policy-makers the United Nations had a role to play, but they were mostly preoccupied with the strategies of *containment* and *rollback* that in large part came to define the character of the Cold War.

FROM CONTAINMENT TO ROLLBACK

The Policy of Containment

The United States was quite prepared to make routine declarations about its commitment to the UN organisation, but equally keen to emphasise that the United Nations would not be allowed to limit US freedom of action. In a 1946 speech that foreshadowed the announcement of the Truman Doctrine a year later, Secretary of State James Byrnes stated: 'We have joined with our allies in the United Nations to put an end to war. We have covenanted not to use force except in the defense of law.' And then came the caveat. 'But as a great power and as a permanent member of the Security Council, we have a responsibility to see that other powers live up to their covenant. And that responsibility we also intend to meet.'[47] There would be no 'unilateral gnawing away at the status quo': the United States would act to protect its perceived strategic interests and those of its capitalist allies. The Byrnes speech, following Churchill's 'Iron Curtain' speech at Fulton a few days earlier, clearly showed the tone of the times. The United States, 'as a great power', would insist that other nations behave themselves; for which purpose, Byrnes declared a few days later, 'our military strength will be used'.

This was the doctrine of 'containment', whereby forces perceived as hostile to the interests of the United States (whether such forces were Communist or independent nationalist factions) would be opposed by military, economic and other means. The doctrine, developed in particular by the 'Riga School' of the US diplomatic service, represented mainstream political thinking in the immediate post-war years and was set to be the dominant influence on American foreign policy in future decades. One of its most forceful advocates was the diplomatic advisor George F. Kennan who, on 22 February 1946, produced his now famous 'long telegram'. Here, in terms that prefigured the tone of the notorious 'Cold War' National Security Council memorandum 68 (April 1950), Kennan articulated the characteristic American hostility to the Soviet leadership:

> Thus Soviet leaders are driven by necessities of their own past and present position to put forward a dogma . . . This thesis provides justification for that increase of military and police power in Russia state, for that isolation of Russian population from the outside world, and for that fluid and constant pressure to extend limits of Russian police power which are together the natural and instinctive urges of Russian rulers.

There was no hope in such circumstances for a 'permanent *modus vivendi*' with the United States 'if Soviet power is to be secure'. Instead the Soviet leadership would do anything to undermine the Western powers, to 'work towards the destruction of all forms of personal independence, economic, political, or moral'. Kennan concluded that there were 'many foreign peoples' who 'are less interested in abstract freedom than in security . . . We should be better able than the Russians to give them this.'[48]

The Kennan telegram was well received. Byrnes reckoned it was a 'splendid analysis'; the Secretary of State for the Navy, James Forrestal, enthusiastically despatched copies to all Navy offices; and the State Department sent copies to all the diplomatic missions abroad. Kennan was asked to lecture on the 'elements of Soviet behaviour' for the benefit of academics and policy planners. The 'containment' concept was now being given wide publicity. Still, on occasions, it was deemed useful to make reference to the United Nations. Thus on 28 February 1946 Secretary of State James Byrnes declared: 'We will not and we cannot stand aloof if force or the threat of force is used contrary to the purposes and principles of the [UN] Charter.' A month later, *Time* magazine informed its readers that Iran, Turkey and Manchuria were 'infected with Communist contagion' and that Saudi Arabia, Egypt, Afghanistan and India were 'exposed'.[49] Those who recommended *rapprochement* in preference to containment were side-lined or – as in the case of Secretary of Commerce Henry Wallace – discharged from office. The policy of containment was not the only option for the United States at the end of the war. However, it did accord well with the 'direct historical experience and structural exigencies of American politics',[50] and it was the doctrine that prevailed.

The new containment policy was first practised early in 1946 to block the use of troops by the Soviet Union to further its interests in Iran. The issue was referred to the UN Security Council and the Russians were forced to recognise Western superiority in the Near East and in the United Nations. The UN had fulfilled the role it was to play many times in future years: it had provided a forum for the issuing of American threats. There were many ways in which the UN Charter could be cited to support the unilateral policy of containment.

At the second session of the Paris Peace Conference, which began on 25 April 1946, the United States made no effort to meet Soviet demands. Thus the US negotiators rejected the demand for high reparation payments (arguably justified in view of Soviet losses[18]), the demand for Four-Power control of the Ruhr region, the Yugoslav claim to Trieste, and the demand for a mandate on Libya (a former Italian colony). Vandenberg, happy with progress, noted that 'Byrnes has "stood up" 100%'. The Soviet delegation was forced to relinquish virtually all its claims. The mandate issue was referred to the United Nations, thus exposing Soviet claims to the American veto; and Trieste was established as an autonomous city under UN control. At the same time the policy of containment was showing its first military manifestations.

On 7 August 1946 the Soviet government proposed that Turkey renounce the 1936 Montreux Convention which had established Turkey's right to control the passage of warships from states with borders on the Black Sea through the Straits; and that joint Turkish–Soviet defences be established on the Straits. The Soviet suggestions were not extravagant: in October 1944 Churchill had acknowledged the Soviet justification, and the Potsdam Conference had approved the Soviet proposal for a revision of the Montreux Convention. Now, however, the policy of containment meant that the Soviet proposals had to be rejected by the United States. Washington protested to the Soviet government, urged Turkey to defend itself, and sent warships to the Eastern Mediterranean. A month later the US government announced that American warships would be permanently stationed in the area.

Such events – coupled with the disputes over Greece, Eastern Europe, the post-war status of Germany, the control of nuclear weapons, and other matters – all combined to consolidate an escalating Cold War in which the US-inspired policy of containment was a central feature. By the time the Truman Doctrine came to be articulated it did no more than give expression to the received American wisdom. On 12 March 1947 President Truman, in an address to Congress, declared:

> At the present moment in world history nearly every nation must choose between alternative ways of life . . . One way of life is based upon the will of the majority, and is distinguished by free institutions, representative government, free elections, guarantees of individual liberty, freedom of speech and religion, and freedom from political oppression. The second way of life is based upon the will of a minority forcibly imposed upon the will of the majority. It relies upon terror and oppression, a controlled press and radio, fixed elections, and the suppression of personal freedoms. I believe that it must be the policy of the United States to support free peoples who are resisting attempted subjugation by armed minorities or by outside pressures.

This unilateral resolve 'to support free peoples' – with no reference whatever to the security provisions of the UN Charter – led to the North Atlantic Alliance of 1949 and the Pacific Security Pact of 1951. It also yielded such pivotal events as the development of the Marshall Plan and the creation of the Central Intelligence Agency (CIA).

The Marshall Plan and the CIA

The US scheme for the rebuilding of Western Europe, the European Recovery Programme, was designed to defeat Communism in Europe and to restore the shattered economies of Europe, so giving scope for the development of US trade and the raising of American living standards. The philosophy behind the Programme was first expressed, at least in part, by Secretary of State George C. Marshall in a speech at Harvard on 5 June 1947. Here he recognised that Europe 'must have substantial additional help, or face economic, social and political deterioration of a very grave character . . . the consequences to the economy of the United States should be apparent to all. It is logical that the United States should do whatever it is able to do to assist in the return of normal economic health in the world.' From these initial thoughts sprang the highly significant overt and covert elements of the Marshall Plan. In particular, the Marshall Plan became 'the keystone to containment'.[51]

It was clear, surveying the rubble of the Second World War, that something had to be done about Europe. The view that prevailed in the United States, following the clear thrust of the Truman Doctrine and the policy of containment, was that American policy-makers should aim to 'restructure the war-damaged world in such a way that rebuilt nations would have a predilection toward the United States'.[52] This would be a central purpose of the Marshall Plan, to be accomplished not only by the munificent disbursement of aid and investment in the ravaged industries of Western Europe. There was to be another element, covert and politically important, which by its nature has received little public scrutiny. There were European countries, such as France and Italy, with large Communist constituencies. In the shared interests of defeating European Nazism and Japanese fascism, the Allies had been keen to tolerate pro-Soviet propaganda that necessarily stimulated leftist European parties. Now, by whatever means to hand, it was required to throw socialism into reverse to make the world safe for (largely) American investment. To this end, the US policy-makers discovered that covert methods could be useful in implementing aspects of the Marshall Plan. The Office of Policy Coordination (OPC) was created to help with the practical application of details of the Plan: 'the complementary efforts of the Marshall Plan and the OPC afford a first view of fully integrated interventionism in the Cold War; that is, the first attempt to fully integrate economic aid and covert political activism'.[53]

In 1947, under the terms of the National Security Act, the CIA was created out of the Central Intelligence Group.* At first the Agency was not a powerful body but when it decided to focus on national economic estimates its activities increased and it was soon attracting extra funding. On 14 December 1947 President Truman authorised a National Security document (NSC 4/A), specifying covert psychological activities for Eastern and Central Europe. The Special Procedures Group (SPG) was established under the auspices of the Office of Special Operations, a clandestine element of the CIA. Covert CIA operations in Europe began in 1947, and were greatly expanded in scope and number thereafter. It is of interest that covert action was not specifically mandated under the National Security Act, though NSC 68 had called for a clear Cold War offensive that invited covert operations. The ambitious staff of the CIA, many of them officers from the war-time Office of Strategic Services (OSS), soon saw the advantages of using the Marshall Plan as a vehicle for covert operations. It was not one-way traffic. The managers of the Marshall Plan realised that they stood to benefit by having access to a covert capability.

This meant that the Marshall Plan, advertised as selfless American aid to Europe, was a principal vehicle in the Cold War, in part using CIA covert methods to attack and destabilise popular political parties in Europe.[54] This was but the start of the clandestine operations that the CIA would wage for decades around the world, a sustained US policy of global disinformation, destabilisation, torture, murder and genocide that won the approval of successive American Presidents. This was the real politics behind the public propaganda. It did not have much to do with the Charter of the United Nations.

Rollback

The policy of containment had a more ambitious component – rollback.[55] The more extreme advocates of containment reckoned that it was not enough to tolerate a status quo in which the Soviet Union had considerable influence, not only in Europe but elsewhere around the world. Containment policy could be 'liberally sprinkled with rollback goals'[56] – it might be possible to defeat Communism everywhere.

Many of the elements of rollback have been amply described in the public domain by such researchers as Bodenheimer and Gould (1989),

* A principal architect of the CIA was the former Nazi general Reinhard Gehlen, who worked closely with the Chief of US Army intelligence in Europe, General Edwin Sibert (see Simpson, 1988).

Pisani (1991), Christopher Simpson[57] and others; though the full tale has still to be told. Rollback has involved such elements as the NSC 10/2 memorandum of 18 June 1948 (authorising 'subversion against hostile states, including assistance to underground resistance movements, guerrillas and refugee liberation groups'), NSC 58 of 14 September 1949 (aiming at the 'gradual reduction and eventual elimination of preponderant Soviet power from Eastern Europe'), NSC 68 (finally signed by Truman on 30 September 1950, and thereafter used to justify a rollback policy in Eastern Europe), specific economic policies and specific military initiatives. As just one example, Frank Wisner, a former CIA chief of clandestine operations, estimated in 1951 that some 35,000 Soviet police officers and Communist Party cadres had been killed by US-backed Nazi guerrillas in the Ukraine since the end of the Second World War, and similar campaigns of assassination in other parts of the Soviet Union were being supported by the United States and Britain.[58] One of the main features of the rollback campaign was the US protection offered to Nazis, including war criminals, deemed useful in the global anti-Communist crusade. Thus Simpson, award-winning American investigative journalist, notes: 'By 1953 *the CIA was willing to finance and protect not simply former Nazis and Gestapo men but even senior officers of Adolf Eichmann's SS section Amt IVB4, the central administrative apparatus of the Holocaust*'[59] (my italics). No one who knew about such things could doubt that Washington would be well prepared to manipulate the newly hatched United Nations in the interests of American foreign policy.

The US policy of containment, with its many rollback elements, was one of the principal shaping forces of the post-war world. The preamble of the UN Charter notes the determination of the 'peoples of the United Nations' to 'save succeeding generations from the scourge of war'; and Article 2(1) declares that the 'Organisation [of the United Nations] is based on the principle of the sovereign equality of all its members'. But behind such sentiments was the brutal world of *realpolitik*, where (mainly US-sponsored) interventions could be launched into scores of countries around the globe – involving, quite literally, millions more human casualties. The issues with which the United Nations was forced to contend for the first 45 years of its life were shaped by the cruel inevitabilities of the Cold War.

5 Issues – I

The founders of the United Nations had envisaged a truly international body. The problems of membership that had afflicted the League of Nations would be solved. The sovereignty of individual states would be respected, as would regional agreements and the burgeoning corpus of international law. At the same time regional treaties would be subservient to the Charter and the UN-linked International Court would have authority to adjudicate disputes between states. Such was the ideal. In fact it was not long before the UN encountered fresh membership problems and before powerful states again pursued strategic objectives against both the spirit and the letter of the Charter.

However, such realities of international politics did not prevent UN involvement in the affairs of dozens of countries across the world. During the first 45 years of its existence the United Nations was a party, major or minor, to virtually all the significant disputes of the period. Many of the problems were inherited from the League, while others sprang up unheralded in the post-war world: all were viewed through the distorting prism of the Cold War.

THE PALESTINE QUESTION

The historic Jewish struggle for land and human rights predated by centuries both the League and the United Nations. The long agony of a dispossessed and persecuted people would reach its climax in the twentieth century with the Holocaust, in which a Christian nation would commit unspeakable outrages against humanity.[1] It is one of the supreme ironies of history that the obsessively anti-Semitic Adolf Hitler was one of the main forces behind the creation of the modern state of Israel.

With the defeat of the Ottomans in the First World War, Britain assumed the Palestine mandate on behalf of the League. At the end of the Second World War an economically tottering United Kingdom had little stomach for its mandated responsibilities in such a troublesome area. On 2 April 1947 the British government requested 'the Secretary-General of the United Nations to place the question of Palestine on the agenda of the General Assembly at its next regular session'. The government pledged that it would present to the Assembly 'an account of their administration on the League of Nations mandate and . . . ask the Assembly to make recommendations, under Article 10 of the Charter, concerning the future government of Palestine'; and Britain further asked the Secretary-General to summon a special session of the General Assembly at which a special committee could be created to consider the matter. On 28 April the representatives of 55 UN Members met, appointed the United Nations Special Committee on Palestine (UNSCOP), and then adjourned. Four months later, on 1 September, the Committee – comprising representatives from Australia, Canada, Czechoslovakia, Guatemala, India, Iran, the Netherlands, Peru, Sweden, Uruguay and Yugoslavia – submitted its report. The key recommendations of the majority report were that the British mandate should be terminated, that by September 1949 Palestine should be partitioned into sovereign Jewish and Arab states, and that Jerusalem should be internationalised. On 26 September 1947 the British Colonial Secretary, Arthur Creech-Jones, announced to the United Nations that Britain had decided to leave Palestine, and a Foreign Office spokesman ominously predicted that chaos would follow. On 8 October the High Commissioner for Palestine declared:

> I think it is essential that the people of this country [Palestine] should realise that withdrawal is really meant. It is essential that they should see what the effect of it will mean . . . [it is] physically possible for Britain to go, leaving nothing to replace her in Palestine [but only] misery, distress and chaos.[2]

The international community had delivered 'a *clear victory for the principle of partition*'[3] (original italics). The Arabs in Palestine and elsewhere watched with dismay as on 29 November 1947, by a vote of 33 to 13 (with 10 abstaining), the UN General Assembly voted at its Second Session to authorise the creation of a Jewish state on Arab land. Efforts were made, before the vote, to bring the Jews and Arabs together. The Jews signalled their willingness to accept partition even though their new territory would be much less than that promised to them in the 1917 Balfour Declaration. The Arabs, seeing no justice in an imposed sacrifice of Arab land, pledged that they would reject partition. The scene was set for all the turmoil of future decades.

The British government, having declared its intention to surrender the mandate, seemed keen to create as much disorder as possible: 'the British had managed to convince everyone that their departure would lead to chaos, and they proceeded to do their best to make it so'.[4] Now the British government was committed to divesting itself of power as quickly as possible, content to hand over the administrative responsibilities 'to whatever community was locally in the ascendant'.[5] This was a recipe for chaos. Fighting soon broke out between Jews and Arabs, and quickly developed into a full-scale civil war.

The United States, a principal player in this situation, had vacillated throughout the period in which the Jews were gaining their nation state. On 30 March 1948, perceiving the escalating Palestinian chaos, Washington expressed its opposition to forcible partition and urged that the problem be reconsidered by the UN General Assembly. For the United States, there were practical concerns: General Eisenhower, the Army Chief of Staff, was worried that if Washington were forced to send troops to Palestine to police the peace it might be necessary to reintroduce the draft, an option that the American people would not tolerate. And might a forcible partition encourage increased Soviet influence in the area? Confronted with such considerations, 'Truman attempted a political somersault: indefinite postponement of partition and the transfer of Palestine to the aegis of the UN Trusteeship Council.'[6] There were, however, practical considerations of a different kind to throw into the melting pot, and it was these that were to prove decisive.

President Truman was facing re-election in 1948 and he desperately needed the Jewish vote in New York, California and elsewhere. Moreover, there was the matter of campaign funds. The ardent Zionist, Abe Feinberg, organised a fund-raising drive for Truman that netted $100,000 (big money in 1948) within two days of a presidential appeal for cash. Other well-placed Jews, such as the jewellery store magnate Ed Kaufman, made their own financial contributions, and such matters worked well to concentrate the presidential mind. Stephen Smith, brother-in-law of John F. Kennedy, has been quoted: 'two million dollars went aboard the Truman train in a paper bag, and that's what paid for the state of Israel'.[7] Soon after his second inauguration, President Truman offered formal recognition to Israel.

The state of Israel had been born, following the support of the international community and the crucial American backing, but the Jewish celebrations were short-lived. Within days of the chaotic ending of the British mandate, the Arab states launched an invasion of Palestine in defiance of the United Nations. When the Security Council met on 15 May 1948 to consider the deteriorating situation it was confronted with a cable from the Egyptian Minister of Foreign Affairs: 'Egyptian armed forces have started to enter Palestine to establish security and order . . . .' The Permanent Members of the Security Council unanimously appointed Count Folke Bernadotte, a member of the Swedish royal family and the president of the Swedish Red Cross, as UN Mediator, who would endeavour to negotiate a secure truce. On 17 September the Zionists assassinated Count Bernadotte and the UN observer Colonel Serot.

The UN Secretary-General Trygve Lie – later to execrate the 'enormity, the barbarism, the primeval stupidity' of the assassinations – appointed Dr Ralph Bunche as Acting Mediator (later awarded the Nobel Prize for Peace), and after difficult and protracted negotiations an uncertain armistice was eventually achieved. On 11 May 1949 Israel was admitted to the United Nations, and Lie subsequently wrote in the introduction to the fourth annual report to the General Assembly that the establishment of the state of Israel was 'one of the epic events of history, coming at the end not merely of thirty years, but of two thousand years of accumulated sorrows, bitterness and conflict', and it symbolised 'historical forces beside which the present ideological conflict appears to be a transitory phenomenon'. In April 1951 Trygve Lie visited four of the states whose forces had been on the battlefields in 1948; and he noted 'hatred – bitter hatred'. It was not difficult to discern the seeds of future conflict. The nominal 1949 Armistice Agreement remained in force, but it would prove insufficient to prevent new wars in the years to come.

THE KOREAN WAR

In 1945, under the the terms of the agreements made at Cairo, Yalta and Potsdam, Korea was occupied by the Soviet Union and the United States. After a 40-year occupation, the Japanese had been expelled, and now the Koreans were keen to govern their own land. However, the US position was plain: the Koreans were reckoned 'incapable of assuming governmental control over their own country'[8] – and so different arrangements would have to be made. Washington succeeded in establishing a demarcation line at the 38th Parallel. On 10 October 1945 the United States Military Government in Korea (USAMIGIK) declared itself the only legitimate government in South Korea, and demanded an end to the pronouncements of 'irresponsible political groups', many of which comprised nationalist Koreans struggling to achieve independence. The behaviour of the US authorities 'crystalized a large part of Korean thinking into an anti-American mold' and caused the people to feel that 'the liberators had become the oppressors'.[9] On 14 February 1946 the United States sponsored a Representative Democratic Council, an undemocratic body headed by the authoritarian Syngman Rhee, who had the support of the capitalists and large landlords. While the US authorities in the South were cramming the jails with the opponents of the Rhee regime, the nationalist Kim Il-Sung in the North was dividing one-half of the land between 725,000 landless peasants, so achieving popular support.[10] In 1947 the US Assistant Secretary of State conceded that 'many Koreans feel they are worse off than they were under the Japanese', and a public opinion poll conducted by the American authorities showed that a majority of South Koreans preferred Japanese occupation to American.[11]

In September 1947 Washington proposed that the Korean question be handled by the United Nations, while John Foster Dulles contrived an Interim Committee (or 'Little Assembly') in the UN to sidestep the Soviet veto. On 14 November the General Assembly created a United Nations Temporary Commission on Korea to work towards Korean independence. After the Soviet authorities had refused to allow the Commission access to the North, it reported that elections held in the South 'were a valid expression of the free will of the electorate of that part of Korea'. The United Nations, prompted by Washington, had given its stamp of approval to the dictatorial Rhee regime, dominated by 'landlords and members of the old aristocracy', responsible for the 'near-extinction of civil liberties' and apt to favour such methods as the razing of villages on 'a vast scale'.[12]

In these circumstances of growing tension between the two halves of Korea, the government of (Nationalist) China, under prompting from Washington, submitted a resolution at the 423rd Security Council meeting held on 8 April 1949. The aim of the resolution was to secure the admission of South Korea (the Republic of Korea, a 'peace-loving State') to the United Nations. The Soviet Union vetoed the resolution on the ground that the General Assembly had given no mandate whatsoever for the establishment of a puppet government in South Korea. It was further alleged that the US had created the Interim Committee in order to circumvent and violate the UN Charter. A second Soviet veto on this question was cast at the 704th meeting of the Security Council held on 13 December 1955, and a third Soviet veto cast at the 790th Security Council meeting on 9 September 1957 (after the Soviet Union had failed to carry resolution amendments to admit *both* Koreas to the United Nations). A further resolution, submitted on 9 December 1958 by France, Japan, Britain and the United States, was similarly vetoed by the Soviet Union. All but the first of these resolutions followed the Korean war, a cataclysmic event that did no more than achieve massive human slaughter and solidify the national divide. It was the first major conflict in which the United Nations, under US prompting, was to become embroiled.

There is controversy about the origins of the Korean war, a circumstance that is not immediately apparent from the bulk of the Western literature in this area.[13] In particular, there is dispute about who began the war. The actual onset of military conflict was not witnessed by the UN Military Observer Group in the field or by the Seoul-based UN Commission on

Korea. The Observer Group subsequently made statements based on information supplied by either the US military or the South Korean government. However, on 27 June 1950, the day after the start of hostilities between North and South, the UN Commission issued a cable proposing that '[the Security] Council give consideration either invitation both parties agree on neutral mediator either to negotiate peace or requesting member governments undertake immediate mediation'. The Commission had not been able, in the short time available, to establish responsibility for the onset of hostilities; so it urged mediation, rather than sanctions or force, as the proper UN response. On the same day *The Manchester Guardian* commented that the objectives should be 'the cessation of hostilities, withdrawal of troops, and, above all, the exclusion of the Great Powers from the conflict'. The United States, seemingly eager for conflict, ignored the recommendation of the UN Commission and immediately authorised armed US intervention. President Truman instructed American air and sea forces to give 'cover and support' to the Korean government troops, and ordered the Seventh Fleet into the zone between China and Formosa (so intervening in the Chinese civil war). At the same time Washington called upon the Security Council to impose sanctions against North Korea. Various observers noted how this speedy use of the Security Council contrasted with Washington's indifference to the possible role of the UN in other disputes. Thus the UN 'was brushed aside in Greece . . . no troops and planes were sent to fight the Dutch when they defied a UN cease-fire order [in Indonesia] . . . Nor did the United States mobilise the UN to save the infant Israeli Republic . . . .'[14]

The Security Council resolution had gone far beyond the imposition of sanctions on North Korea. Faced with the *fait accompli* of US military intervention (at a time when the Soviet Union was absent from the Security Council), the Council responded by authorising 'such assistance to the Republic of Korea as may be necessary to repel the armed attack and to restore peace and security in the area'. The Security Council had moved hastily, on the basis of only slender information and against the advice of its own authorised Commission, to underwrite the pre-existing US intervention and to give a green light to further escalation of the conflict. Nor, it has to be said, was Trygve Lie the most balanced judge of the affair. In the words of one commentator, Lie's language describing the circumstances of the Korean war (*In the Cause of Peace*, 1954 chs 18 and 19) is 'so heavily biased, emotive and loaded, his charges against Communist countries so unsubstantiated, as to be more appropriate for a US State Department spokesperson than for a Secretary-General of the United Nations'.[15]

The United States made no pretence of observing the UN Charter requirement (Article 47) that a 'Military Staff Committee' be established 'to advise and assist the Security Council on all questions relating to the Security Council's military requirements for the maintenance of international peace and security'. Instead the so-called United Nations forces (no blue berets here) were made subject to General Douglas MacArthur, without any UN constraint on MacArthur's freedom of action. As with the 1991 Gulf war against Iraq, the UN was used in Korea as a flag of convenience for a United States already resolved on military intervention. The authority of General MacArthur was established via the mechanism of UN Resolution 84 introduced on 7 July 1950 by Britain and France, the usefully pliant US allies. The resolution demanded that 'all members providing military forces and other assistance . . . make such forces and other assistance available to a unified command under the United States'; and that 'the United States . . . designate the commander of such forces'. Britain, France and the United States were completely untroubled that this resolution – assigning all power to Washington – was in direct violation of Article 47(3) of the UN Charter.

The ensuing war, appallingly destructive, resulted in further violations of the UN Charter, not least of the specific resolutions that had authorised so-called United Nations involvement in the first place. The Security Council, under US prodding, had authorised the re-establishment of the *status quo ante*, but soon MacArthur demonstrated much greater ambitions; namely, the 'liberation' of North Korea. It has been pointed out that four-fifths of all US casualties occurred after the authorised UN aim of expelling the North Koreans from the South had been accomplished. One estimate suggests 2,415,601 total casualties, exclusive of North Korean civilians;[16] another suggests four million.[17]

General MacArthur's unauthorised invasion of North Korea resulted in mainland China (now Communist) entering the war, and in serious American thought being applied to the possible use of the atomic bomb against the Chinese. General Emmet O'Donnell was keen to use the A-bomb as soon as possible (the Chinese will 'understand the lash when it is put to them'), and President Truman himself seemed responsive at times to such advice. On 30 November 1950 Truman declared at a press conference that nuclear bombs might be used against the enemy and seemed to imply that MacArthur would take the decision.[18] This spurred Prime Minister Clement Attlee to hurry over from London to dissuade the US President from any precipitate action. In the event the US forces did not get to use atomic bombs: they had to be content with experimentation on a massive scale with a new weapon called napalm. The United Nations, dominated by the US, had authorised military action in Korea. Now Washington felt free to decide how it would prosecute the war, and which specific UN provisions it would violate in furtherance of its strategic objectives.

CHINA'S ADMISSION

The West had 'lost' China to Mao Tse-tung and his Communists, despite strenuous efforts by Washington to prevent this happening. Massive resources had been sent to Generalissimo Chiang Kai-shek, Washington's client in the Chinese civil war and in the Second World War. After the defeat of the Japanese, Peking was surrounded by Communist forces, whereupon US Marines were ordered to prevent the fall (or the 'liberation') of the city. At the same time US transport planes were ferrying in Chiang's troops to prevent the collapse of Shanghai to Mao's forces, just as they transported some 500,000 Nationalist troops all over China and Manchuria to prevent a Communist victory. American troops were involved in attacks on Chinese villages, in battles with Communist forces, and in the massive disbursement of aid to the Nationalist groups. In 1946 there were about 100,000 US military personnel in China, and by 1949 the US military aid to the Nationalist forces amounted to around $3 billion.

All Washington's efforts came to nought. All the aid had not succeeded in creating military forces that could defeat the Communists; or in propping up the massively corrupt civilian administration. Raids continued to be launched into 'Red' China: as late as April 1951 a few thousand troops with CIA advisors invaded China's Yunan province, but were soon expelled; just as CIA advisors guided Nationalist invasions of China in 1952. Diminishing levels of harassment were maintained until the early 1960s, but all such military endeavours were seeming increasingly futile. Only one realistic option remained to Washington: 'Red' China could be prevented from taking its legitimate place in the United Nations.

On 29 December 1949 the Soviet Deputy Foreign Minister, speaking in the Security Council, disputed the right of the delegate of Nationalist China (now confined to the offshore island of Formosa) to continue to represent China in the Council. The Kuomintang delegation, declared Yakov A. Malik, represented no one at all and it should immediately vacate its seat. The statement was unprecedented. No member had been challenged in such a fashion before. Malik advanced no formal motion but the campaign for the seating of Mao's China had begun. On 10 January 1950 Malik announced his instructions from the Soviet government to the effect that the 'representative of the Kuomintang group', Dr T. F. Tsiang, be expelled from the Security Council at once. Since Tsiang did not represent China he was not entitled to participate in the Council's business. Moreover, until Tsiang was expelled the Soviet delegation would not participate in the work of the Security Council, a decision that was supported by a draft resolution. When the Soviet motion was defeated, Malik demonstratively stood up and left the chamber, the second Soviet walkout from the UN (the first was over the Iranian dispute) and the one that allowed the Security Council to 'legitimise' the US intervention in Korea. It was made clear that the Soviet Union would not recognise as legal any Security Council decision made while China's UN seat was wrongfully occupied. In fact, the Soviet delegate was absent for some six and a half months, while China was forced to wait more than two decades for its rightful place on the Security Council.

Secretary-General Trygve Lie, uncertain how to proceed in these circumstances, decided to consult with Secretary of State Dean G. Acheson in Washington. He cannot have been surprised at the outcome. The United States would *not* recognise Peking when US properties were being seized, when American consular offices were being closed, and when US citizens were being kidnapped; and Washington would *not* tolerate the seating of the new Communist regime in the United Nations. Nor would it be useful for the General Assembly to discuss the question. It is obvious that Lie was not unsympathetic to such observations. He himself declared in 1954 that the Peking government 'had become the enemy of the United Nations'. Peking's soldiers 'were used deliberately to kill the defenders of the United Nations Charter, and those who were carrying out the resolutions of that body in the Korean conflict . . . No nation can shoot its way into the Organisation.'[19] Mao's China, decided Lie, 'faces a difficult trial before it in faith and in truth can be accorded representation'.[20]

Each year from 1951 to 1960 efforts to raise the China question in the General Assembly were routinely blocked by US-orchestrated majority decisions; in 1961 the question was accepted for discussion for the first time. But in the early 1960s the anti-Peking majority was reinforced as the Soviet Union abandoned its support for the Chinese case, and as the Chinese invasion of India in 1962 stimulated opposition to Chinese membership (see Table 5.1). In 1965 – following a fruitless argument between Britain and the United States on one side and France and the Soviet Union on the other over voting rights and peace-keeping costs – there was a swing in Peking's favour. Then, with the Cultural Revolution and the Red Guards, the pendulum swung again. Peking floated the idea of a rival United Nations, while the Russians became even more hostile as the Sino-Soviet

Table 5.1 General Assembly votes on China's admission

Year	*Total UN Membership*	*For Peking*	*Against Peking*	*Majority Against*
1961	104	36	48	12
1962	110	42	56	14
1963	111	41	57	16
(There was no voting at the 19th Assembly that began in December 1964.)				
1965	117	47	47	0
1966	121	46	57	11
1967	122	45	58	13
1968	126	44	58	14
1969	126	48	56	8

SOURCE: Andrew Boyd, *Fifteen Men on a Powder Keg* (London: Methuen, 1971).

conflict escalated into actual border skirmishes. In 1969 there was again a marked improvement in China's position: a relatively small majority against Peking's admission meant that only a few states would need to shift to secure a Communist China on the Security Council. Increasingly it seemed that Washington's two decades of politicking against Peking's membership had not succeeded in securing a permanent exclusion of the most populous nation on earth. It was also becoming obvious that Peking should be admitted, if only to subject it to the beneficial influences of states that deemed themselves more civilised; problem states may be best dealt with by admission rather than by exclusion. Thus, if membership was to be considered 'in terms of the functional requirements of the organization, it should be regarded as particularly important to encompass trouble-spots and trouble-makers, to give the United Nations the best possible basis for dealing with the ills that plague the world'.[21]

It was now obvious that the admission of Peking would not long be delayed. In 1970 the drift of opinion was clear, though it was not until the end of 1971, at the end of U Thant's term as third UN Secretary-General, that Peking finally took its proper seat as a Permanent Member of the Security Council. Kurt Waldheim, fourth Secretary-General, recorded that 'the most signal event of my first year in office had been the admission of the People's Republic of China'.[22] He noted what had become obvious to everyone: that 'it strained all credulity for a government exercising authority over a population of 16 million on an island off the Chinese mainland to claim to speak for one billion Chinese, one quarter of the human race'.

According to Waldheim the Chinese were 'very open about their problems', not used to having to take up a position 'on each and every problem in the world'. And Peking soon demonstrated its commitment to the United Nations: premier Chou En-lai offered to increase Peking's stipulated cash contribution to the organisation.

THE VIETNAM MORASS

The decades-long Vietnam conflict had much in common with the Korean turmoil (see above): an arbitrarily divided country, a massive US military incursion, sporadic American efforts to cloak illegality in UN authorisation, and millions of Asian dead and wounded, victims of Western technology and Western genocide. In one particular the Korean and Vietnamese conflicts were very different: whereas Vietnam succeeded in expelling the foreign invader (and then confront a ravaged land, a mutilated people and merciless trade sanctions), Korea remains divided, a constant symbol of Cold War *realpolitik*.

For centuries the Vietnamese fought against colonial incursions: Chinese, French, Japanese, British, American. At the start of the Second World War, Vietnam – a single country – was part of French Indochina; the French were pushed out and the Japanese became the new colonial masters. When Japan was defeated in 1945 and forced to withdraw from Indochina, the communist Ho Chi Minh, a revolutionary hero who had fought against first French and then Japanese colonialism, declared Vietnam an independent republic. The Declaration of Independence, issued in Hanoi in late 1945, began with familiar words: 'All men are created equal. They are endowed by their Creator with certain inalienable rights; among these are Life, Liberty, and the pursuit of Happiness.' For a few short weeks, and for the first time in its modern history, Vietnam was an independent national state, free of foreign occupation. The Western powers were determined to ensure that this unusual situation did not persist.

The British, under General Douglas D. Gracey, invaded Vietnam in 1945. Of the nationalist Vietnamese forces, celebrating their new independence, Gracey himself remarked: 'I was welcomed on arrival [in Saigon] by Viet Minh . . . I promptly kicked them out.'[23] At the same time the French were working to re-establish their former colonial position. However, the Vietnamese had found a new confidence and a new determination, inducing *The Times* in London to warn the French of the 'new spirit of nationalism' in Indochina and to recommend that the new wave of colonialists try 'guidance rather than repression'.[24] The Vietnamese, the West was surprised to learn, had no wish to be guided or repressed by foreigners on their land; and so, their new republic already aborted by Western invaders, the Vietnamese again took up arms against foreign colonialists, again faced decades of agony until Vietnam could again assert its national independence.

Over the next eight years the United States funded about 80 per cent of the French war effort, contributing financial assistance of around $1 billion. By 1954 the French were losing the war against the Viet Minh, and as a last-ditch stand some 20,000 French troops were parachuted into a valley in enemy territory known as Dien Bien Phu; it was here that the French suffered their final and most crushing defeat. The Americans contemplated the situation with growing alarm and considered their options. Admiral Radford, Chairman of the Joint Chiefs of Staff, supported by John Foster Dulles, urged that atomic bombs be dropped from 500 aircraft to prevent a French defeat, but Eisenhower decided against this recommendation. The French were defeated and the United States stepped into the military vacuum. In 1954 the Geneva Conference stipulated a demarcation line to facilitate the disengagement of the Viet Minh and French forces. Article 6 of the Final Declaration of the Conference (21 July 1954) stipulated that the military demarcation line was 'provisional and should not in any way be interpreted as constituting a political or territorial boundary'. While the Americans were not signatories to the Geneva Accords they declared that they would not disturb them. At the same time the US began its systematic sabotage of the elections scheduled in the Geneva Accords (Article 7), for a reason made clear by Eisenhower: 'I have never talked or corresponded with a person knowledgeable in Indo-Chinese affairs who did not agree that had elections been held at the time of the fighting possibly 80 per cent of the population would have voted for the Communist Ho Chi Minh as their leader . . . .'[25] An unremitting military onslaught on the Vietnamese people was much to be preferred to democratic elections.

Any US recourse to the United Nations was necessarily less than had been possible during the Korean conflict: the Soviet Union was now firmly seated in the Security Council and would have quickly vetoed any American attempt to gain UN authorisation for a fresh war in Asia. The French had made its own appeal to the United Nations, while Vietnam was still a French colony, that Vietnam be admitted as a new Member to the international body. This draft resolution, submitted on 13 September 1952, was vetoed by the Soviet Union, already keen to support the Democratic Republic of Vietnam in the north. In explanation of its veto the Soviet Union cited the earlier claim of Vietnam after the defeat of the Japanese:

> Vietnam has been an independent sovereign State since 2 September 1945 following upon the Allied victory over Japan, to which it contributed heavily in bloodshed and resources. It was recognised by France by the Agreement of 6 March 1945. The Government of the Democratic Republic of Vietnam was regularly appointed by the Vietnam National Assembly after the general elections of 6 January 1946, which were based on the principle of universal, secret and direct suffrage.[26]

Throughout the Vietnam conflict the West had been ambivalent about increasing the UN involvement in the issue: it would have been useful to gain a UN authorisation – however bogus – for the military onslaught on the Vietnamese people, but a growing UN interest might constrain Western policies. In April 1953 Secretary of State Dulles found that the British and the French were strongly opposed to any moves to secure a UN solution to the Vietnamese conflict, simply because a UN debate on Vietnam might expand to cover the increasingly restless French colonies elsewhere, particularly in North Africa.[27] Subsequent US 'support' for UN supervision of the elections specified in the Geneva Accords was disingenuous since Washington knew that it could rely on opposition by Britain and France to any such UN involvement – again because of the precedent that this would establish for the situations 'in North Africa and elsewhere'.[28] At the same time Washington, confident of its dominant position at the United Nations, was prepared to exploit the international body where it could be turned to advantage.

On 4 August 1964 the United States launched an attack on North Vietnam from the sea, while UN ambassador Adlai Stevenson asked for an urgent Security Council meeting to consider the situation created by 'deliberate attacks of the Hanoi regime on United States naval vessels in international waters'. According to Washington, North Vietnamese torpedo boats had made two unprovoked attacks on American destroyers in the Tonkin Gulf off the coast of North Vietnam. The Security Council met on 5 and 7 August to discuss the crisis. Nothing was achieved. Because of the prospect of a Soviet veto the US had no chance of securing an anti-Hanoi resolution, and in any case the facts of the dispute were unclear: Hanoi claimed that the US ships had been in North Vietnamese territorial waters and had fired first, and that one specific incident, the alleged second engagement on 4 August, was pure American invention. In fact, a subsequent investigation by the US Senate Foreign Relations Committee found that the Americans had not even seen any hostile craft on 4 August, much less been attacked by them.[29] However, Washington's lies had now laid the basis for the escalation of the Vietnam war.

Now the US judged it prudent to minimise any possible involvement of the United Nations. In February 1965 the first American combat units arrived in South Vietnam, the start of a massive escalation; and UN Secretary-General U Thant realised the futility of calling for a meeting of the Security Council, a move that would not have been welcomed by any of the Permanent Members. Soon there were reports that U Thant was attempting secret diplomacy[30] – if true, an initiative that did nothing to arrest the gradual slide into a vast new war on the Asian mainland. The relatively pacific Adlai Stevenson had been working to discuss options with U Thant: progress was not furthered when, on July 14, Stevenson collapsed and died in a London street near the American embassy.

Secretary-General U Thant himself made frequent efforts to bring the conflict to an end, though without success.[31] On 24 May 1966, in an address delivered in Atlantic City, U Thant noted that the world had been watching 'the inexorable escalation of the war in Vietnam with increasing anxiety . . . the temptation to win a military success may still prove stronger than the more prudent call to reason'. And so it proved. On 25 July 1965 special adviser to President Lyndon Johnson, Clark Clifford, had set the course that was to be followed over the coming years: 'I do not think it advisable to go to UN . . . A resolution in the UN with all the dramatic debate it would produce is bad for us.'[32]

During 1965 more than 200,000 US troops were sent to Vietnam; and in 1966 200,000 more. In 1968 the US troops in Vietnam numbered more than half a million, and they were no nearer to victory. Bombs were being dropped at a rate unprecedented in human history: Vietnam received a bomb tonnage greater than everything dropped in the Second World War, including the two atomic bombs. And the war escalated to Cambodia and Laos: in 1971 alone, more than 800,000 tons of bombs were dropped on Laos, Cambodia and Vietnam, with some 3600 B-52 raids over Cambodia in one fourteen-month period. As with Korea, the Asian dead and wounded were numbered in the millions.

In 1975 the Americans were finally forced to leave Vietnam, to leave a desolate land and a ravaged people. In revenge, Washington put pressure on the world community to put Vietnam in quarantine, to block all humanitarian and development aid. On 15 November 1976 eleven UN members submitted a draft resolution to the Security Council, recommending that Vietnam be admitted as a member of the United Nations. The United States blocked the resolution, declaring its doubts about Vietnam's willingness to carry out the obligations of the UN Charter, obligations 'that embraced not only the maintenance of international peace and security, but also the observance of human rights'.[33]

APARTHEID AND RACE

Throughout its history the United Nations has been sensitive to the question of apartheid and the associated issues that it raises. In 1954 Trygve Lie commented: 'The South African problems of the status and treatment of the Indian minority, and of the fate of Southwest Africa, the former German colony and League of Nations Mandate, have consistently beset the United Nations; and the South African government's policy of *apartheid*, of separation of the races, threatens to become a third.'[34]

Apartheid was introduced in South Africa as an official policy in 1948: under its provisions the overwhelming majority of the population were denied basic human rights. Today, at the time of writing in 1994, many of the apartheid provisions have been dismantled, from 'petty apartheid' to discriminatory legislation of the most fundamental kind. There has also been a repeal of the laws that defined the constitution in racial terms: de facto white power is still enshrined in the character of the South African state though multi-racial elections have been proposed for April 1994.

The United Nations first discussed the racial policies of South Africa in 1946, when India complained that the government had enacted laws against South Africans of Indian descent. The UN General Assembly introduced the issue of apartheid into its agenda in 1952, and during the 1950s made repeated appeals to the South African government to revise its legislation in the light of the UN Charter. Such appeals gained no positive response, the South African government repeatedly claiming that the UN had no right to interfere in the internal affairs of the country.

On 21 March 1960 the South African police fired on peaceful demonstrators at Sharpeville, protesting against the requirements that all Africans carry 'reference books': 69 people were killed, 180 wounded. The Security Council met, at the request of 29 African and Asian members, to discuss 'the situation arising out of the large-scale killings of unarmed and peaceful demonstrators against racial discrimination and segregation' in South Africa. The Council issued a statement declaring that the South African situation might, if continued, endanger international peace and security; and it called upon South Africa to abandon the policy of apartheid. In 1962 the General Assembly urged Member States to break off diplomatic relations with South Africa and to cease trading with that country. An 18-Member Special Committee against Apartheid was established to monitor South Africa's racial policies and to report to the General Assembly and the Security Council.

In 1963 the Security Council called on all states to voluntarily stop the shipment of arms to South Africa, and both the Council and the Assembly asked South Africa to release people imprisoned for opposing the country's racial policies. In 1966 the General Assembly proclaimed 21 March as the International Day for the Elimination of Racial Discrimination, in memory of Sharpeville; and the following year the United Nations Educational and Training Programme for Southern Africa was launched by the Assembly to grant scholarships to students from South Africa and Namibia for study abroad. In 1970 and 1972 the Security Council again exhorted Member States to observe the voluntary arms embargo.

Such declarations continued through the 1970s and 1980s, with results that can be debated. In 1977 the Security Council made the arms embargo mandatory, the first time that such an action had been taken against a Member State under Chapter VII of the Charter, a move that allowed for military enforcement of the ban. In December the Assembly adopted the International Declaration against Apartheid in Sports, urging the exclusion or expulsion of any country practising apartheid from international and regional sports bodies. In 1985 Kurt Waldheim, one-time UN Secretary-General, noted that in South Africa, 'the situation remains wholly intractable'.[35] The international protests continued, and by the 1980s it was clear that events were moving in South Africa. Detentions without trial continued, leading to further Council and Assembly condemnation: in 1987, for example, the Security Council expressed concern about a South African decree (10 April) prohibiting all forms of protest against detentions without trial, and demanded that South Africa repeal this further repressive law.

On 11 February 1990 the African National Congress (ANC) leader Nelson Mandela was released from Victor Verster prison in South Africa after 26 years of incarceration. Britain and the United States had prepared the ground for apartheid,[36] and had for decades been unwilling to take decisive action against it, despite all the declarations and proclamations from the international community (it has even been suggested that the CIA supplied the South African government with the information that led to the arrest and imprisonment of Mandela). Now the freeing of Mandela, following protracted and worldwide agitation, was applauded by the international community (though some of the adulation was dripping with hypocrisy). A victory had been won for African emancipation, though the real fruits are not yet evident in the creation of a stable and democratic South African state. To the extent that real change is already manifest, the UN General Assembly deserves much credit for its persistent efforts over many years to defeat apartheid.

FROM SUEZ TO LEBANON

On 26 July 1956 the Egyptian leader, President Gamal Abdel Nasser, nationalised the Suez Canal, so beginning a chain of events that was to have many consequences over the coming years. His speech, delivered before a huge crowd in Alexandria, aroused enormous enthusiasm throughout the Arab world and forced the Western powers to consider what actions they could take. In August the British premier, Anthony Eden, declared that Britain might 'be faced with the choice of slow strangulation of her economy' if no satisfactory settlement could be found; and he noted the determination of the French to achieve a satisfactory outcome. There was also the matter of the United Nations. Was this a situation in which the UN could be activated, or would British and French interests be best served by extra-UN actions?

Prime Minister Eden was aware that the United States was discouraging any approach to the United Nations, but was prepared to argue that action could be taken by Britain and France without a violation of UN membership obligations: it would be legitimate to 'use force within the Charter'. Lord Salisbury, at the heart of Tory thinking, hoped that the British government would make an approach to the United Nations before launching a military operation; and, striking a different note, Lord Kilmuir declared that 'while it would be wrong to disregard the UN, it would be equally wrong to allow the real issue to be eroded by ineffective international debate'. The real issue, of course, was that a substantial part of Western opinion was prepared to regard Nasser as a 'second Hitler', a title that is always held in reserve for opponents of Western strategic interests. At a Cabinet meeting on 11 September Kilmuir and Salisbury argued that if Nasser was not prepared to accept the terms of the Suez Canal Users' Association (SCUA) plan, whereby users would employ their own pilots and pay dues to Egypt as they saw fit, then 'force' would not be 'inconsistent' with the UN Charter. Eden had his mandate for a military attack on Egypt. There would be no attempt to work through the authority of the UN Security Council.

The sidelining of the United Nations was soon obvious. US Secretary of State John Foster Dulles still opposed any approach to the international body, claiming that Eden had told him that Britain 'was in no hurry to go to the UN' (though Eden denied this). Eden was prepared to have the crisis discussed in the Security Council, but only as a prelude to independent British action. There were important developments to take into account. The Soviet Union was continuing to equip Nasser; and the French, struggling to suppress the Algerian rebellion, seemed increasingly eager to attack Egypt, possibly in alliance with the Israelis. Now the UK, against the wishes of Dulles, had gone to the Security Council, but essentially only in order 'to clear the decks for action' (according to Selwyn Lloyd).[37] The UN Secretary-General Dag Hammarskjöld did his best to ensure the success of the talks, but there was a substantial British interest in their failure, and fail they did. The negotiations were largely desultory; by mid-October 1956 Prime Minister Eden had decided that early military action was the best course.

On 29 October Israeli forces attacked Egypt through Sinai, as agreed with the British and French, and French aircraft began dropping supplies to the Israeli troops. The next day, Eden informed the House of Commons that if Egypt did not accept an ultimatum for Egyptian compliance Anglo-French forces would intervene 'in whatever strength was necessary'. A Commons vote resulted in a government majority of 52, with 218 votes against, somewhat less than a consensus in favour of war. The United States, increasingly alarmed at developments, introduced a resolution in the Security Council demanding an Israeli withdrawal and the consequent removal of the Anglo-French ultimatum. The French and the British vetoed this resolution and a similar one proposed by the Russians, with Eden protesting that any demand for Israel to withdraw to her own frontiers was 'a harsh demand'. The ensuing conflict led to an allied victory, to no one's surprise, and to moral defeat.

On 7 November the UN General Assembly passed a resolution demanding that the British, French and Israeli troops immediately withdraw from Egyptian territory; but Eden refused to comply. By now a UN force was being despatched to take over the allied 'police action' but the British were keen to maintain a presence in the area, if only to clear the obstructions from the Canal and to retain a bargaining chip against Nasser's presumptions. Dag Hammarskjöld departed for Cairo and Selwyn Lloyd flew to Washington, where President Eisenhower refused to meet him. Hammarskjöld reported that Nasser would not negotiate until the British and French had left the area. On 23 November the General Assembly debated a resolution censuring Britain and France, passing the resolution the next day by 63 to 5, with 10 abstentions. Selwyn Lloyd then informed Dag Hammarskjöld that the British would relinquish power to the UN force in about four weeks, whereupon Hammarskjöld replied that this was too long a delay.

The British, French and Israeli humiliation was complete: condemned by the international community, they had no choice but to admit – albeit not always publicly – that their military initiatives had been ill-judged, counter-productive and in violation of international law. Inadvertently the allied aggressors gave the United Nations some experience in peace-keeping: the United Nations Emergency Force (UNEF) was the first of its kind. UNEF was used to supervise the troop withdrawals and was deployed on Egyptian territory, with Egypt's permission, to act as a buffer between the Egyptian and Israeli forces. It patrolled the demarcation line and the international frontier to the south of the Gaza Strip. In May 1967 UNEF was finally withdrawn at Egypt's request.

On 5 June 1967 fighting again broke out between Israel, on the one hand, and Egypt, Jordan and Syria, on the other. The UN Security Council called for an immediate ceasefire, but there were further days of conflict before hostilities ended. At that time Israel had occupied Sinai, the Gaza Strip, Jordan's West Bank, and part of Syria's Golan Heights. The UN Secretary-General, now U Thant, stationed observers of the United Nations Truce Supervision Organisation (UNTSO) in the Golan and Suez Canal areas to oversee the ceasefire, while on 4 July the General Assembly called on Israel not to alter the status of Jerusalem, now largely under the control of Israeli forces. A few months later, on 22 November 1967, the Security Council unanimously adopted Resolution 242 – still not implemented nearly thirty years later – which proposed: the withdrawal of Israeli armed forces from the occupied territories; the termination of all claims or states of belligerency; respect for and acknowledgement of the sovereignty, territorial integrity and political independence of every State in the area; and their right to live in peace within secure and recognised boundaries, free from threats or acts of force. In short, Israel must withdraw from the Arab lands occupied in 1967; and the state of Israel must be recognised by its Arab neighbours.

The Council asked Secretary-General U Thant to appoint a special Middle East representative to encourage negotiations with a view to implementation of Resolution 242. The Swedish Gunnar V. Jarring was appointed for this task, though no progress was made. Negotiations continued intermittently until 1973 but then collapsed. The Security Council showed no stomach for the imposition of sanctions, or even the use of force, to ensure Israeli compliance. Other subsequent resolutions on Israel (for example, 465, 476, 478, 673 and 681) – referring to such matters as the illegal building of settlements on Arab land, the observance of human rights, the failure to observe 242, and illegal alterations to the status of Jerusalem – have been routinely ignored by successive Israeli governments.

In 1968 the UN General Assembly established a Special Committee to Investigate Israeli Practices Affecting the Human Rights of the Population of the Occupied Territories; and in 1974 reaffirmed 'the inalienable rights of the Palestinian people in Palestine' to self-determination, national independence and sovereignty. The Palestinian people were recognised as a principal party in the negotiation of a Middle East peace, and the Palestine Liberation Organisation (PLO) was invited as an observer in the work of the

Assembly and at UN international conferences. In 1977 the Assembly called for an annual observance of 29 November as the International Day of Solidarity with the Palestinian People. On 26 March 1979 a peace treaty, known as the Camp David Accord, was signed between Israel and Egypt. Many Arab states regarded this fresh development with dismay: the anti-Israel Arab alliance had at last been breached, and the Egyptian threat to Israeli security had been removed. The Council of the League of Arab States, convened in Baghdad in November 1978, demanded non-recognition of the treaty. At the same time the UN General Assembly moved to condemn 'all partial and separate treaties' that violated Palestinian rights, and declared that the Camp David Accord had no validity in so far as they claimed to determine the future of the Palestinian lands occupied by Israel. Fresh efforts were made to arrange a Middle East peace conference at which the PLO would be represented.

In the early 1970s, with growing tension on the Israel–Lebanon border, there was an increasing threat of fresh military conflict. In 1972 Israel attacked Palestinian camps in Lebanon, in reprisal for Palestinian raids on Israeli territory. Following a Security Council decision, UNTSO set up a cease-fire observation operation in the Israel–Lebanon sector. In 1978, after a further Israeli incursion into Lebanon, the Security Council established the United Nations Interim Force in Lebanon (UNIFIL) to confirm the withdrawal of Israeli forces, to restore peace, and to help the Lebanese government to restore its legitimate authority in the area.

The Israeli forces withdrew from Lebanon on 13 June 1978 but handed over their positions to effective proxies: Lebanese forces supported and supplied by the Israelis. The area, a part of Lebanese territory, has remained an Israeli 'security zone', still outside the effective control of the Lebanese government. In July 1981 a cease-fire came into effect, until the massive Israeli invasion that began on 6 June 1982. UNIFIL positions were overrun or bypassed, some 20,000 Lebanese fatalities resulted, and the Israeli forces swept through the country as far as Beirut. The Security Council demanded a cease-fire and a total withdrawal of all Israeli forces, a decision that the Israeli government completely ignored.

On 1 August the Security Council asked the Secretary-General to send UN military observers to monitor the situation in and around Beirut. A cease-fire went into effect on 12 August and the UN observers, now assigned to the Israel–Lebanon Mixed Armistice Commission, were established as the Observer Group Beirut (OGB). Soon the Israelis were launching armed incursions into Beirut, acts that again earned the condemnation of the Security Council as violations of cease-fire agreements and UN resolutions. On the evening of the 16 September Phalange units protected by the

Israelis entered the Sabra and Shatila Palestinian refugee camps and massacred several hundred men, women and children. The General Assembly and the Security Council condemned the massacre, and there were calls for the application of the Geneva Convention pertaining to the protection of civilians in war-time.

The situation remained tense. The US Secretary-General, now Javier Perez de Cuellar, convened various meetings between Israeli and Lebanese representatives at UNIFIL headquarters, but no lasting solution was achieved. Israel continued to maintain its unilaterally declared security zone in southern Lebanon, and there are still frequent armed clashes between Arab guerrilla groups on the one hand and the Israeli forces and their proxies on the other. The expulsion of Palestinians from the occupied territories in 1992 – part of an on-going policy of external exile – did nothing to ease tensions on the Israeli–Lebanese border, in the occupied territories, or in Israel itself. However, the scene was set for dramatic developments (see 'The Israel Exception', Chapter 7).

UNDERMINING THE CONGO

A principal task of the United Nations in the 1950s – and one that Winston Churchill had anticipated with dread – was to aid the dissolution of the European colonial order. This task was to have particular significance in Africa. The crisis in the Congo was the main problem that faced the second UN Secretary-General, Dag Hammarskjöld; it was the one that led to his death.[38]

The Republic of the Congo (later the Republic of Zaire) secured its independence from Belgium on 30 June 1960. Within weeks disorder had broken out, and the United Nations was soon drawn into the morass: in one view, to bite off 'more than the world organisation could chew'.[39] The Congo comprised more than 120 tribes, with no dominant grouping. Its borders, as in much of the rest of Africa, had been drawn in the imagined interests of European colonialism, with no thought given to ethnic or other pragmatic boundaries, so storing up massive problems for the future. The Belgians had allowed no African to rise above sergeant in the army, and no effort had been made to educate the indigenous population. In the Congo of 1960 there were some sixteen college graduates among the Africans, and not a single black doctor, lawyer or engineer.

As the disorder escalated Belgium sent in troops, with the declared aim of protecting and evacuating Europeans. On 12 July 1960 the Congolese government, headed by the charismatic Patrice Lumumba, asked the United Nations for military assistance to resist Belgian aggression. On 14 July the Security Council demanded that Belgium withdraw its troops and authorised the Secretary-General to provide military support to the Congolese government until such time as the national forces were able to achieve the required levels of security throughout the country. Within two days the first troops of the United Nations Operation in the Congo began arriving to assist the Congolese government maintain the independence and territorial integrity of the new nation; at its peak the UN force reached a total of some 20,000 military personnel. The intervention of the international body was not one of the UN's most glorious achievements.

With Lumumba as premier, Joseph Kasavubu had become Chief of State, a position that he would soon exploit by dismissing the popular Prime Minister. On 11 July Moise Tshombe – with his supporters pro-Belgium in spirit – declared Katanga Province independent of the Congo, so adding fresh fuel to the fire. It has been argued that the Belgians may have planned the Tshombe revolt: he was highly sympathetic to Western interests; keen to protect, for example, the huge Union Minière mining company that controlled most of Katanga's mining interests. Lumumba flew to Elizabethville, the Katanga capital, in a hopeless attempt to prevent the Katanga secession. Tshombe's troops refused to let Lumumba leave the airport; Tshombe would not see him, and he was forced to return to Leopoldville. By now the forces of the United Nations Operation in the Congo – or *Force de l'Organisation des Nations Unis en Congo* (ONUC) – were beginning their rapid build-up. The first four days saw the arrival of 770 Ghanaians, 460 Ethiopians, 1250 Moroccans and 1020 Tunisians. Soon afterwards 700 Guinean troops arrived, and troops were sent also from three European, one Asian and one Hispanic-American nation. Sweden transferred 635 men from their UNEF duties in Palestine.[40] A principal difficulty was the collapse of civil order. ONUC, intended originally as a peace-making and peace-keeping force, found itself responsible for civil administration, a role for which it was ill-equipped.

Lumumba flew to the United States in a vain effort to generate opposition to the Tshombe breakaway: Tshombe was now a darling of the West, offering a clear route to the perpetuation of economic colonialism at the heart of the Congo. On 5 September, to the delight of Western leaders (and probably under their prompting), the Congolese Chief of Staff Kasavubu dismissed Lumumba from office, an act that at once plunged Leopoldville into chaos. Hammarskjöld's ONUC struggled to maintain order but now the main Congolese factions – Lumumba (backed by the Soviet Union), on the one hand, and Kasavubu and Tshombe (backed by the United States, Belgium and other Western powers) – were now in direct confrontation. The dismissal of Lumumba had prepared the way for a military coup, an illegal (but Western-supported) act that was to be performed by Colonel Joseph Mobutu, a US protégé set to begin a reign of terror. Lumumba – the only leader in the Congo with a reasonable claim to democratic support – was captured by Mobutu's soldiers, beaten and abused in front of him, and then handed over to Tshombe, his arch-enemy, for 'safe-keeping'. On 13 February 1961 Patrice Lumumba was murdered.

The United Nations had proved largely powerless. ONUC had achieved a measure of control, but in the event only to aid the Mobutu coup. The most credible Congolese leader, Lumumba, had been arrested, severely beaten, marched away by troops under Belgian command, and killed soon afterwards. The UN recognised President Kasavubu, a Mobutu ally, as Congolese head of state – and the Soviet Union and much of black Africa was horrified. In their eyes Dag Hammarskjöld had been totally discredited by his seeming toleration of the pro-West factions in the Congo, a posture that had led to the collapse of democracy and the establishment of a military regime highly sympathetic to Western economic imperialism. At the Fifteenth Session of the UN in September 1960 the Soviet leader Nikita Khrushchev stated: 'Conditions have reached the point where the post of Secretary-General, who alone directs the staff and alone interprets and executes the decisions of the Security Council and the sessions of the General Assembly, should be abolished.' Khrushchev then proposed what came to be known as the Troika Concept, whereby the office of the Secretary-General would be expanded to three members.[41]

The Congo episode had provided material for all those – of whatever political view – who wanted to discredit the United Nations. The propagandists of the Right advertised the 'tragedy' of the UN being driven to support the Communist-inspired doctrine of anti-colonialism (as though only Communists believe in national independence).[42] And for those who cared to look, there was abundant evidence of Western 'dirty tricks'.[43] The United States had provided a fund of $100,000 to support the coup against Patrice Lumumba; a CIA scientist, Joseph Scheider, was sent to the Congo with a 'lethal biological material' for Lumumba's assassination, and Mobutu was seen as having been 'discovered' by the CIA. There was little chance for Dag Hammarskjöld to evaluate such matters. On 17 September 1961, in mysterious circumstances, his plane crashed in the Congolese jungle on a flight from Leopoldville to Ndola, Rhodesia. This fatal accident – if accident it was (some suspected sabotage)[44] – left the UN in general and ONUC in particular in some disarray. It was left to Hammarskjöld's successor, U Thant, to pick up the pieces.

The UN involvement in the Congo was the most significant of its kind on the African continent, and it did not end with the death of Hammarskjöld. U Thant managed to gain the acceptance of a plan for the joining of Katanga and the Congo Republic, a federal scheme that would ensure Katanga's virtual independence; but there were still problems. In late 1962 Tshombe's troops began firing on ONUC positions, and a UN helicopter was shot down. This in due course led to Tshombe's defeat, whereupon he flew to exile in Spain, stopping first at a Swiss bank in Geneva.

On 30 September 1966 the Security Council met to consider Congolese complaints that Portugal was allowing its African territories to be used by mercenaries organising incursions into the Congo. Subsequent complaints of this kind led to a Security Council resolution on 10 July 1967 condemning any state that tolerated the recruitment of mercenaries and the provision of facilities for them. Portugal denied involvement, but on 18 July 1969 Zambia made fresh charges that Portugal had violated Zambian territory with bombing raids and military incursions. In December both Senegal and Guinea charged that Portugal had allowed its military forces to commit acts of aggression against their territories.

The long agony of Africa was set to continue. Subject to adverse trade conditions imposed by the IMF/World Bank stranglehold on the continent, and still subject to the baleful legacy of colonialism and Cold War *realpolitik*, African tribulations would continue – and, in many respects, intensity – in the period up to the 1990s. Civil war, famine, Great-Power interest, UN involvement – all were destined to combine over the wretched misery of Somalia (see Chapter 7).

THE CUBA CRISIS

Since the Cuban revolutionary leader Fidel Castro took power in the name of the people in January 1959, overthrowing the US-backed dictator Fulgencio Batista, the popular regime and the Cuban people have been subjected to a merciless catalogue of economic blockade, terrorism and military aggression. Successive American presidents have supported assassination attempts against Castro, armed invasions of Cuba, countless air and sea raids by Cuban exiles, sabotage of oil refineries, destruction of railway bridges and chemical plants, the poisoning of cane fields, the burning of sugar mills and warehouses, the rigging of international markets against Cuba, attacks on Cuban fishing boats and merchant vessels, the shelling of hotels from offshore, and much else besides.

The survival of Fidel Castro's massively popular regime, through more than 30 years of terrorist onslaught, military aggression and economic blockade, is one of the most remarkable achievements of modern political endeavour. It is also the context against which the Cuban (Missile) Crisis of 1962, with UN involvement as a largely passive bystander, should be considered. Cuba was expecting a fresh US invasion at any time. In such circumstance, the willingness of the Cuban government to welcome Soviet weapons, even nuclear devices, on its territory was an unremarkable policy. The United States had practised an identical policy against the territory of the Soviet Union for many years.

On 14 October 1962 American U-2 aircraft flying over Cuba detected a site near San Cristobal which gave every appearance of a location being prepared for Soviet missiles. Two days later, President John F. Kennedy discussed the matter with his closest advisors, and US ambassador to the United Nations, Adlai Stevenson, was briefed on the possible threat to American security. On 18 October Washington had decided that the first of the Soviet missiles imported into Cuba could be made ready for launching against the United States within 24 hours. Two days on, ignoring the assertions of Soviet foreign minister Andrei Gromyko that the installations were no more than anti-aircraft defences, Kennedy imposed a naval blockade around Cuba. This was in itself technically an act of war, a flagrant interference with traffic on the high seas, with no UN authorisation.

At the same time the US called an emergency meeting of the UN Security Council, ready to present the other permanent members with the *fait accompli* of the American blockade. Kennedy had already rejected Stevenson's advice that consideration should be given to an abandonment of the illegal US base at Guantanamo on Cuba, or a dismantling of the Jupiter nuclear missiles close to the Soviet borders. Many observers were quick to note that Washington assigned to itself military and territorial privileges that it was keen to deny to others. Now Kennedy announced to the world that the US navy would intercept any ships bound for Cuba that were carrying 'offensive weapons'; and that premier Khrushchev should 'move the world back from the abyss of destruction' by removing the missiles. Stevenson presented a draft resolution to the Security Council demanding the immediate removal of Soviet missiles and bombers from Cuban, authorising U Thant to send UN observers to Cuba, and proposing both an end to the American 'quarantine' when the weapons had gone, and subsequent US–Soviet talks about 'measures to remove the existing threat'. The Organisation of American States (OAS), following prompting by Secretary of State Dean Rusk, backed the US position by a vote of 19–0, with

Uruguay abstaining. Stevenson cited this evident support in his speech to the Security Council on 23 October, condemning the Soviet action.

The Cuban representative, Mario García-Inchaustegui, invited to join the debate, urged the Council to condemn America's 'act of war' in imposing the naval blockade. He declared that Cuba would never permit UN observers to enter Cuban territory, and was in this only partly supported by the Soviet representative Valerian Zorin, who proposed that UN observers should verify the removal of 'all foreign bases on foreign territory' – a suggestion that Washington would obviously reject. On the next day of debate, Zorin submitted a Soviet draft resolution condemning the United States for 'violating the United Nations Charter and increasing the threat of war', and demanding that the blockade be abandoned. In the event, the Soviet government was not prepared to risk a military confrontation with the United States: Soviet vessels approaching Cuba changed course, and subsequent negotiations achieved a deal that could be agreed by the US and the Soviet Union, with little attention paid to Cuba's role in the affair.

The final meeting of the Security Council on this issue took place on 25 October 1962. Here Zorin recklessly challenged Stevenson to produce evidence of the Soviet military build-up on Cuba – which Stevenson was well prepared to do. He proceeded to unveil to the Council enlarged air photographs of the Soviet missiles sites, forcing Zorin to attempt a denial, which proved totally unconvincing. Three days later, Vasily Kuznetsov replaced Zorin on the Cuba issue, while Nikolai Fedorenko became the new Soviet ambassador at the United Nations. U Thant became involved in two months of detailed negotiations until the crisis was finally concluded in January 1963. He had managed to remain on speaking terms with Fidel Castro, furious at how he had been sidelined by the major powers; and to function as a crucial bridge between Kennedy and Khrushchev. On 7 January 1963 U Thant received a joint letter from the Americans and the Soviets thanking him for his efforts and declaring that the matter would no longer require the attention of the Security Council.

The Cuba Crisis was at an end. Some sort of accommodation – much of it secret – was reached between the American and Soviet governments, though Washington continued to declare its unremitting hostility to the Cuban regime. The economic blockade remained in place – later to be declared by the United Nations a violation of international law – and was even strengthened by later US Presidents (a last act of President Bush, 30 years after the Cuban Missile Crisis, was to impose further restrictions on the vestigial trade with the Cuban people).

CYPRUS INVADED

Turkey had ruled Cyprus for three centuries until Britain took it over in 1878 to strengthen the imperial route through the Mediterranean and the Suez Canal to India. After the Second World War the Greek Cypriots began their campaign for *enosis* (union with Greece), a movement that was at first vigorously resisted by the British administration of the island. In 1954 the Greek government brought the case to the UN General Assembly, which at first shelved the question and later supported the idea of negotiations to achieve a solution. By this time the Greek Cypriots lost their patience and launched EOKA (the National Organisation of Cypriot Struggle) to fight against the British and any Cypriot elements prepared to support the traditional colonial regime. The campaign was led by George Grivas (who used the pseudonym of 'Dighenis', a legendary hero whose feats included leaping across the straits between Cyprus and Turkey), a Cyprus-born ex-officer of the Greek army who had been involved in right-wing political activity in post-war Greece. The Greek Cypriots, also enjoying the support of their Ethnarch, Archbishop Makarios, began a war of terrorist subversion against the British colonial power. By 1958 the British resolve had been almost totally eroded. There were increasingly violent clashes between Greek Cypriots and Turkish Cypriots. In 1959 a nominal agreement was reached between the prime ministers of Greece and Turkey, Karamanlis and Menderes, and the British on a plan for Cypriot independence. Pressure was exerted to induce Makarios and Fazil Kuchuk, the Turkish Cypriot leader, to countersign the agreement.

Cyprus became independent in 1960, with provision for British sovereignty over two coastal base areas. Greek Cypriot ambitions for *enosis* would be abandoned, while partition (what the Turks dubbed 'double *enosis*') would be equally prohibited. The Turkish Cypriots would be guaranteed 30 per cent of parliamentary seats and of police and civil service posts. Makarios became President and Kuchuk Vice-President, both with veto power over parliamentary and ministerial decisions. It proved to be no more than a dog's breakfast. By 1963 there was government deadlock, increasingly violent denunciations from every political quarter, and the growing threat of fighting between the various communities.

On 21 December 1963 there were violent clashes in the streets, with hundreds of casualties on both sides and thousands of families driven from their homes. Four days later, Turkish warships sailed towards the island and Turkish aircraft flew over Nicosia. The pro-Greece Cyprus government complained to the UN Security Council of Turkish aggression, and on 4 March 1964 the Council unanimously recommended the establishment of the United Nations Peace-keeping Force in Cyprus (UNFICYP) to restore peace, maintain law and order, and promote a return to normal conditions. Now U Thant began the onerous task of trying to recruit a suitable UN force for the purpose. Canada, Sweden, Finland, Ireland, Brazil and Austria were all approached; all except Sweden refused, though Canada and Ireland later changed their minds. The United States and Britain offered cash, and the Indian General Thimayya was appointed UN commander of the 6100-strong force, 'never enough to force the UN will . . .'.[45]

The precise scope for UN action was unclear. There were frequent clashes between the Greek and Turkish forces on the island, and the local UN commanders had no authority for independent initiatives. It was impossible to disarm the two sides, even if Cypriot 'sovereignty' had been ignored. The British had originally objected to the sending of a UN force, declaring that it would simply meddle in an area of importance to British strategic interests. So not all the governments prepared to support UNFICYP were enthusiastic about its role. U Thant struggled to address the difficulties, declaring to the Security Council in September 1964: 'I intend to proceed on certain assumptions and to instruct the Commander of the Force accordingly.' At the same time he was obliged to resist demands from the Cyprus government that the Turkish Cypriots be suppressed and the equivalent demands of the Turkish Cypriots that action should be taken to restore the now-defunct constitutional structure.

On 15 July 1974 a *coup d'état* by the Greek-Cypriot National Guard against President Makarios was quickly followed by a Turkish invasion of the island. The Turkish troops soon established Turkish-Cypriot control over the northern part of Cyprus. UNFICYP struggled to separate the warring factions, arranging local cease-fires, patrolling the battle zones, and working to protect foreign nationals. When the *de facto* division of the island became apparent, UNFICYP adopted the role of maintaining a buffer zone between the two sides, at the same time carrying out a range of tasks for the World Food Programme and the UN High Commissioner for Refugees.

Talks held between the two sides in December 1974 and January 1975 made little progress, and on 13 February 1975 all contacts were broken off when the Turkish-Cypriot leadership announced the creation of the 'Turkish Federated State of Cyprus'. The Security Council expressed regret at this unilateral initiative and called for fresh talks, asking the Secretary-General (now Kurt Waldheim) to convene the representatives of both sides under his auspices. Talks began on 28 April 1975 in Vienna and further negotiations were held later that year. Minor matters were settled but no heed was paid to repeated demands that all foreign troops leave the island.

More talks were held every year thereafter, but no progress was made. In December 1982 UN Secretary-General Javier Perez de Cuellar noted in a report to the Security Council that time was eroding the 'window of opportunity' for the solution of the Cyprus problem. In May 1983 the Turks rejected a General Assembly resolution, declaring that it undermined the basis for further negotiations. Six months later, on 15 November, the Turkish-Cypriot authorities proclaimed the 'Turkish Republic of Northern Cyprus', an initiative that was unambiguously denounced three days later by the Security Council as illegal and invalid. Further talks, sponsored by the UN Secretary-General and designed in part to reverse the Turkish initiative, achieved nothing. Today UNFICYP remains in place, carrying out its worthwhile tasks but serving as a further reminder that once the United Nations has put troops into a trouble spot they may be there for decades (see Chapter 7).

THE BETRAYAL OF RHODESIA

For many months before the 1964 General Election in Britain, negotiations had been going on between Ian Smith, the Rhodesian premier, and the British government. The aim had been to find a formula whereby independence could be granted to Rhodesia on the basis of a constitution that would satisfy the small white minority and the four million black Africans in the country. Smith and his colleagues were demanding a constitution that would guarantee white minority rule for an indefinite period; the black Africans wanted 'one person, one vote'.

It seemed for some time that the situation could be reconciled, despite the extreme positions of the two factions. But when the Labour Party, under Harold Wilson, returned to power in October, there was still no agreement, and Smith repeatedly intimated that he was contemplating an illegal seizure of independence. Despite subsequent talks and dire threats from the British government (which at the same time ruled out the use of force), Ian Smith made his unilateral declaration of independence (UDI) on 11 November. The illegal Proclamation of Independence, couched in convoluted words reminiscent of the eighteenth-century American Declaration of Independence was quickly denounced by the world community.

The immediate British reaction was to ban certain imports and to take various other economic measures to put pressure on the Smith regime. The UN Security Council met to discuss the crisis, expressed its opposition to the 'continuance in time' of the new situation, and called upon all states to 'do their utmost' to sever economic relations with Rhodesia; the resolution was not given mandatory status. On 9 April 1966 the Council expressed support for a tightening of sanctions on Rhodesia; and on 16 December, firming up its stand, determined 'that the present situation . . . constitutes a threat to international peace and security'. The British Labour government, seemingly tolerant of the illegal act against the British Crown, gave various signs that it would block any proposals for stern action by the Security Council.

In December the British Foreign Secretary George Brown declared that the British government would oppose any efforts by the UN to take action against Portugal or South Africa if they refused to comply with any mandatory Council resolutions against Rhodesia, arguing that the situation 'must not be allowed to develop into a confrontation – economic or military – involving the whole of southern Africa'. In March 1968 the illegal Smith regime hanged five Africans, whereupon 36 African governments demanded UN action to bring the situation to an end. It also emerged at this time that South Africa had sent troops into Rhodesia to support the racist regime, a highly significant development that pushed the British government into no more than demanding firmer economic sanctions.

In the event the sanctions were comprehensively violated by Portugal, South Africa and other states, neglecting their obligations under the UN Charter; and many British companies, continuing their illegal trading, helped the Smith regime to survive. When Wilson went to the United Nations to explain the British position he faced a walk-out of the bulk of the African delegates. The UN had not been prepared to take the resolute action that would have ended the illegal Smith regime. The situation dragged on through the 1970s until the black Africans, through armed struggle, managed to overthrow the white racist government. In 1980 – despite all the sanctions-busting, the illegal support provided to Smith by other racist regimes, and all the procrastination at the United Nations – Robert Gabriel Mugabe became the first black Prime Minister of an independent Zimbabwe.

THE CAMBODIAN AGONY

The US onslaught on Cambodia grew out of various historical circumstances, most of them mediated by the pressures of the Cold War. In particular – much against its collective will – Cambodia was to become a player in the Vietnam war, earning it the Third World right to be comprehensively bombed, to the point that Cambodian casualties came to be numbered in millions. The 'killing fields' of Cambodia were not launched by the Khmer Rouge Leader Pol Pot but by the bombers of the United States.

In 1955 US Secretary of State John Foster Dulles visited the Cambodian leader, Prince Norodom Sihanouk, to secure Cambodian membership of the South East Asia Treaty Organisation (SEATO) to broaden the American military posture in the region. On this occasion the pressure exerted by Washington did not work. Sihanouk later commented: 'I considered SEATO an aggressive military alliance directed against neighbors whose ideology I did not share but with whom Cambodia had no quarrel.' When it was clear that John Foster Dulles, 'an acidy, arrogant man', was making no progress, his brother, CIA Chief Allen Dulles, soon arrived with documents 'proving' that Cambodia was about to fall victim to Communist aggression. Sihanouk remained unconvinced: 'There was nothing for the secret service chief to do but pack up his dubious documents and leave.'[46] With this decision, Sihanouk sealed the fate of Cambodia, consigning that relatively peaceful land to the ministrations of the CIA, B-52s and Pol Pot.

Washington was forced to acknowledge that Sihanouk could not be bullied into joining the American military alliance. In May 1957 an influential National Security Council (NSC) paper commented that 'the United States has been unable to influence Cambodia in the direction of a stable government and non-involvement in the communist bloc'. The following year Vietnamese troops supported by the United States invaded Cambodia, while Carl Strom, the US ambassador to Cambodia, declared that American aid was provided only on the understanding that it was used to resist 'Communist' aggression; in no circumstances could it be used against an American ally. In 1963 Sihanouk refused to accept further US aid, claiming that the United States had supported attempts to overthrow the Cambodian government.[47] The investigative journalist William Shawcross has noted that 'NSC papers of the period . . . confirm that Washington saw Thai and Vietnamese pressure across the borders as one of the principal weapons to be used in an effort to move Sihanouk toward a more pro-American position'.[48] The CIA was also helping to organise Cambodian groups (for example, the Khmer Serei and the Khmer Krom) opposed to Sihanouk's rule. The French, jealous of their own colonial past, were not happy to see the escalating American involvement in what had been a sphere of French influence. But the die was cast: in 1964 American aircraft began bombing Cambodian villages as part of the escalating Vietnam war. When, in May 1965, American bombers killed or wounded dozens of Cambodian villagers the Cambodian government severed diplomatic relations with the United States.

In March 1969 there was a massive escalation of the US aggression against Cambodia. American policy, now under the direction of President Richard Nixon and National Security Affairs Advisor Henry Kissinger, became focused on the possibility of a crushing military victory in the Asian war. One consequence of this developing policy was massive B-52 'carpet bombing' of Cambodian villages, an appallingly brutal business that was kept secret from the American people.[49] On 18 March 1970 Sihanouk, while visiting the Soviet Union, was deposed by Lieutenant-General Lon Nol and Prince Sisowath Sirik Matak, two of his leading ministers. There is abundant evidence that Washington helped to organise the coup.[50] Sihanouk took refuge in China, where he formed a government in exile. Lon Nol abolished the monarchy, dissolved the legislature of Cambodia (now more widely known as Kampuchea) in 1971, and, the following year, made himself President.

In April 1970 US and South Vietnamese troops invaded Kampuchea, forcing the pro-Sihanouk and Communist groups to withdraw deeper into the country. By the end of 1971, Washington had succeeded in bringing the war to the whole of Kampuchea. The B-52 bombing raids continued until August 1973, with sporadic ground fighting maintained thereafter. Washington provided massive aid to Lon Nol, amounting through the period 1970–5 to $1.18 billion in military supplies and $503 million in other forms of assistance. Then there was a shift in US policy. The forces of the Royal Government of National Union of Kampuchea (the Khmer Rouge) launched a major offensive, the reduced aid to Lon Nol failed to prevent a government collapse, and a new administration was established under Khieu Samphan. On 5 January 1976 the government named the country Democratic Kampuchea, and on 20 March a general election was held for the 250-member People's Assembly. Khieu Samphan now replaced Prince Sihanouk, who had returned to the country in September 1975, as Head of State; and Pol Pot became Prime Minister.

Hostilities broke out in December 1978 between Democratic Kampuchea and Vietnam, now reunited after the final expulsion of the Americans. The UN Security Council, following a request from Democratic Kampuchea, met in January 1979 to consider a draft resolution demanding strict adherence to the principle of non-interference in the internal affairs of states, a cease-fire, and the withdrawal of all foreign troops from Kampuchea. Now Vietnam, following an invasion of Kampuchea involving some 100,000 troops, had succeeded in establishing a pro-Vietnamese government in what was now dubbed the People's Republic of Kampuchea (PRK), headed by Heng Samrin, a former division commander in the Khmer Rouge. The PRK had met substantial resistance from the beginning, and from the jungles in the west and south Khmer Rouge rebels continued to harass the government.

In late 1979 the UN General Assembly discussed the issue at the request of five Asian states (Indonesia, Malaysia, the Philippines, Singapore and Thailand). The Assembly adopted a resolution calling for the withdrawal of all foreign forces from Kampuchea, appealing to all states to refrain from interference in Kampuchea's internal affairs, and declaring that the Kampuchean people should be free to choose their own government. An appeal was made to all states and relevant national and international bodies to send relief aid to the civilian population. A 1980 decision of the General Assembly resulted in the convening of an International Conference on Kampuchea in July 1981 in New York. The Conference – in the absence of the Soviet Union, Vietnam, Laos and several non-aligned nations – adopted the Declaration on Kampuchea, reaffirming the basic principles for a political settlement but failing to achieve much else.

The Khmer Rouge now seemed keen to improve its international image. In the early 1980s it adopted a united-front strategy; while at the same time Pol Pot, branded with massive atrocities against the Kampuchean people through the 1975–9 period, withdrew into the background. With Khieu Samphan as chief spokesman, the Khmer Rouge then formed the Coalition Government of Democratic Kampuchea (CGDK), including the two non-Communist factions of Prince Sihanouk and Son Sann. By the late 1980s the PRK, with Vietnamese support, had consolidated its position, though fighting continued. The PRK was supported by Vietnam, the Soviet Union and its allies; the CGDK in which the Khmer Rouge was the dominant faction – was supported by the United States, China and many other nations. The United Nations – through both the General Assembly and the Security Council – continued to urge a negotiated settlement of the dispute between the various contending Kampuchean factions. The scene was set for a deeper UN involvement (see Chapter 7).

THE IRAN–IRAQ WAR

The war between Iran and Iraq, that began in September 1980 and continued for most of the decade, represented yet one more confrontation between the regions that in history were broadly known as Persia and Mesopotamia.[51] Again the causes of the conflict through the 1980s were complex but focused on border disputes, particularly on disagreements about the Shatt al-Arab waterway. The UN response to the outbreak of hostilities was speedy but in the short term largely ineffectual.

On 28 September 1980 the Security Council passed Resolution 479 calling for a cessation of hostilities and mediation. Saddam Hussein expressed his government's willingness to observe a cease-fire, provided that Iran accepted Iraq's terms regarding the Shatt al-Arab and 'other usurped Iraqi territory' and agreed to 'abandon its evil attempts to interfere in the domestic affairs of the region's countries', at the same time ending its occupation of three islands in the Gulf. Iran rejected the UN call for a cease-fire and gave no sign that it would accede to Saddam's specific demands. The fighting continued and there were renewed efforts to secure UN mediation for a negotiated settlement. A Security Council statement in late September urged both sides 'to refrain immediately from any further use of force and to settle their dispute by peaceful means and in conformity with principles of justice and international law'. The Council continued to support the efforts of Secretary-General Kurt Waldheim to arrange negotiations, with Olof Palme of Sweden appointed the UN Special Representative from 1980 to 1982, making various trips to the region in the effort to secure a negotiated peace.

The UN offered to provide observers to monitor a cessation of hostilities in the region of the Shatt al-Arab waterway, but the proposal was rejected. Both sides proved intractable: Saddam gave the impression of talking from a position of strength, while the revolutionary regime in Tehran had no doubt that the conflict was between Good and Evil. Waldheim himself noted 'the most important' lesson taught by this Gulf conflict was: 'that, despite the daily growth in the armaments of the two super-powers, they are themselves unable or unwilling to prevent the occurrence of a shooting war or of stopping one that has broken out'.[52] This held lessons too for politicians contemplating the escalating conflicts on the 1990s.

On 12 July 1982 the Security Council passed a further resolution calling for a ceasefire and a withdrawal of the various contending forces to the international border. Tehran rejected the proposal and the next day, at the start of the holy month of Ramadan, launched a fresh offensive. Later in the year there were further military initiatives from both sides and further UN calls for a cease-fire. In October, with an Iranian push for Baghdad involving between 50,000 and 70,000 troops, yet again the Security Council demanded an end to the hostilities. Iraq, now on the defensive, agreed to the cease-fire but Iran rejected it outright. On 1 June 1984 the Security Council condemned (by 13 votes to 0) attacks on vessels passing through the Gulf to trade with Kuwait and Saudi Arabia. A demand was made for all states to recognise free navigation in the Gulf, and the Secretary-General, now Javier Perez de Cuellar, made fresh efforts to bring to an end a conflict that was again engulfing the population centres of both sides.

In January 1985 the Secretary-General, with the agreement of both Iran and Iraq, sent a fact-finding mission to the area to investigate an incident in a prisoner-of-war camp in Iran and to report on other matters. It was found that prisoners were being mistreated on both sides, evidence of a clear failure to observe the 1949 Geneva Convention relative to the Treatment of Prisoners of War. Further Security Council statements in 1985 expressed deep concern over renewed hostilities, with Secretary-General Perez de Cuellar declaring on 26 March that he was 'deeply disturbed by the continuing conflict between Iran and Iraq'. He reiterated his belief that 'the earliest possible cessation of hostilities, followed by progress towards a negotiated settlement, is essential to end the unconscionable carnage caused by this conflict'; and in April 1985 Perez de Cuellar travelled to Tehran and Baghdad in a vain effort to end the war. Iran signified that it doubted the impartiality of the United Nations, saying that it would cease hostilities if Iraq was condemned as the aggressor and if reparations were paid. Iraq laid down its own demands, insisting that a comprehensive cease-fire within a specific timetable must be agreed.

On 20 July 1987 the Security Council unanimously passed Resolution 598, no more remarkable than the earlier Council decisions but one that was destined to be more influential. Resolution 598 stipulated a number of provisions:

- a cease-fire and withdrawal to internationally agreed borders;
- despatch of a UN team to supervise the cease-fire;
- release of prisoners of war;
- Iran and Iraq to co-operate with UN mediators to achieve an acceptable settlement of disputed issues;
- restraint on the part of other states with a view to preventing escalation of the conflict;
- exploration of the idea of an impartial body to determine responsibility for the conflict;
- UN experts to assist in reconstruction and stabilisation.

The war was not yet over. Iran presented a seven-point plan for the implementation of 598, and on 15 October Perez de Cuellar submitted a four-paragraph document to the Security Council, linking a truce with other peace moves. The Council commended the Secretary-General's proposals and urged him to set up machinery for the implementation of Resolution 598. Increasingly, it seemed that the United States had developed a 'tilt' in favour of Iraq, and that this was evident in the deliberations of the Security Council. Already there were hints of the 'Iraqgate' (or 'Saddamgate') scandal that before long would rock the American political Establishment. There were still evident differences between the permanent members of the Security Council about how Resolution 598 should be implemented, and when the Secretary-General introduced a plan on 15 October for its implementation it was rejected by Baghdad, observing that the new document required the simultaneous implementation of various 598 provisions, whereas Baghdad wanted implementation in the order specified in the resolution itself.

In the event, the broad terms of the resolution came to be accepted, even by Khomeini. Iran felt it had no option but to accept the new UN resolution, though Khomeini's feelings were plain: 'God knows that were it not that all our honour and prestige should be sacrificed for Islam, I would never have consented . . . I repeat that accepting this [resolution] was more deadly to me than taking poison'; Khomeini had submitted himself 'to God's will and drank this drink for His satisfaction . . . Accepting the UN resolution does not mean that the question of war has been solved. We should be prepared for *jihad* . . .'[53] Baghdad too found it possible to accept Resolution 598, and without any reference to God or *jihad*.

The important Security Council resolution had now been accepted by both parties to the dispute, a year after it was unanimously approved by the Council. On 8 August 1988 the Council approved the implementation details of 598, and the Secretary-General specified 20 August as the time for a truce. The war had accomplished nothing – except huge loss of life and prodigious waste of resources. Saddam Hussein proclaimed a three-day holiday beginning on 9 August to celebrate Iraq's 'great victory'. Already the ground was being prepared for another devastating Gulf war.

CENTRAL AMERICA

All the states of Central America have proved powerless against US imperialism, and for the most part the United Nations has done little to curtail American abuse of some of the poorest countries in the world. The pattern has been constant for more than a century: frequent US invasions, support for murderous proxies, economic pressures – used separately or in concert to protect US company interests in the region. Nicaragua was first invaded in 1854 when the United States sought to avenge an alleged insult to the millionaire Cornelius Vanderbilt. The US Marines again invaded in 1909, as they frequently did in the surrounding countries; and during the period 1912 to 1933 (apart from one year) Nicaragua was under constant US military occupation. This led to the murder in 1934 of Augusto Sandino, the rebel hero, and to the installing of the Somoza dictatorship, sure to protect US interests. The ensuing events, grimly oppressive, were characteristic of the region. Men, women and children were tortured and executed, the bulk of the population reduced to destitution.

A sporadic and widely supported rebellion, a protest at repression and the grossest forms of exploitation, gained momentum through the 1970s; and in 1979 the brutal US-supported regime of General Anastasio Somoza was overthrown by the Nicaraguan people. The cost of the struggle was 50,000 lives and a devastated country. The United States set about reversing this unacceptable blow to its fortunes. In March 1981 CIA Director William Casey presented detailed proposals for covert actions against Nicaragua – as well as against Afghanistan, Laos, Cambodia, Grenada, Iran, Libya and Cuba. On 9 March 1981, a few weeks after taking office, President Ronald Reagan authorised terrorist action against Nicaragua, still a ravaged land and one of the poorest countries in the world. On 1 December he agreed a covert-action plan calling for the creation of a terrorist force funded to the tune of $19 million.

In March 1982 the popular Nicaraguan government asked the UN Security Council to meet, in view of the 'worsening of tension in Central America, with the ever-increasing danger of a large-scale military intervention by the armed forces of the United States'. Washington denied the allegations as without foundation, at the same time charging the Nicaraguan government with aggressive conduct designed to destabilise neighbouring countries – most of them, though Washington did not remark the fact, US-supported dictatorships. In December the CIA reported to Congress that it had succeeded in creating a 4000-strong anti-Nicaraguan commando (that is, terrorist) force. Now the counter-revolutionaries ('contras'), many of them ex-members of Somoza's National Guard, were ready to enter Nicaragua, from the US-protected bases in Honduras, to destroy Nicaraguan farms and clinics, to murder teachers, nurses and engineers – anything to re-establish the American grip on the small country.

A draft resolution was presented to the Security Council appealing to all Member States to refrain from the direct, indirect, overt or covert use of force against any country of Central America and the Caribbean: the resolution was blocked by the United States.

On 4 November 1984 Nicaragua held a general election while struggling to cope with US-inspired terrorist invasions deep into its territory. Washington had constantly charged the Sandinista regime with lacking a democratic mandate, but when the election came the US did all it could to sabotage it. Thus John Oakes, a former senior editor of *The New York Times*, commented that 'the most fraudulent thing about the Nicaraguan election was the part the Reagan administration played in it . . . United States embassy officials in Managua pressured opposition politicians to withdraw from the ballot in order to isolate the Sandinistas and to discredit the regime . . . it tried to torpedo the election.' The election – declared by international authorities to be secret, free and fair – delivered a resounding victory to the Sandinista regime, 61 National Assembly seats going to the government, 35 to the opposition. The only recourse for Washington was to call the election a sham and to step up its terrorist attacks on the peasant nation.

A group of nations – Columbia, Mexico, Panama and Venezuela (the so-called Contadora Group) – initiated a series of consultations with five Central American governments (Costa Rica, El Salvador, Guatemala, Honduras and Nicaragua) in an effort to find a negotiated settlement to the problems facing the region. Their 1984 scheme, the 'Contadora Act on Peace and Co-operation in Central America', found support from various Latin American states and was delivered to the UN Secretary-General in July 1986.

In May 1983 the Security Council had again met at the request of Nicaragua to discuss a terrorist invasion 'by counter-revolutionary Somozist forces operating out of Honduras and financed, trained and supported' by the United States. It was now widely known that the CIA had trained the contras in their terrorist methods. The CIA manual, *Psychological Operations in Guerrilla War*, made available to the contras, includes sections on 'implicit and explicit terror' and gives details of how Sandinista officials could be 'neutralised'. Countless examples of atrocities by the contras, all acting under the aegis of the United States, were documented. On 13 October 1983 the contras massacred 47 people in the town of Pantasma; in November 1984 the contras attacked the coffee farm La Sorpresa, killing seventeen men, women and children; on 9 November 1986, at El Nispero, the contras murdered two old women, a young mother, two children and two Sandinista soldiers. Through this period the contras managed to killed some 30,000 people, in circumstances of horror: eyes gouged out, castrations, breasts cut off, lips sliced, tongues removed, throats slashed, disembowellings . . . Today the accomplishments of President Reagan's 'freedom fighters' are widely acknowledged.

The UN Security Council met on several occasions in 1984, 1985 and 1986 to consider Nicaragua's complaints of US-backed military incursions and terrorist atrocities. In April 1985 a Nicaraguan draft resolution condemning the illegal mining of Nicaraguan ports by US forces was vetoed by the United States. A month later the Council unanimously reaffirmed Nicaragua's right to decide freely its own political, economic and social systems without outside interference; it called upon Nicaragua and the United States to resume talks. The United States, despite the Security Council resolution, subsequently refused to re-enter negotiations.

In July and October 1986 the Council met at Nicaragua's request to consider the dispute that on 27 June had yielded a Judgment of the International Court of Justice. On 9 April 1984 Nicaragua had filed an application to begin proceedings against the United States on the grounds that Washington was using military force against Nicaragua and intervening in its internal affairs, so violating the country's sovereignty. On 10 May the Court rejected a US request that the case be removed from its agenda, and called upon Washington to stop laying mines in Nicaraguan ports. A Judgment on 26 November 1984 found that the Court had jurisdiction to entertain the case and that Nicaragua's application was admissible. On 27 June 1986 the International Court of Justice, the supreme legal body of the United Nations, ruled that the United States was in violation of international law, that it should desist from its illegal actions, and that reparations should be paid to Nicaragua.

Washington responded to the Court's ruling by refusing to recognise the jurisdiction of the Court, a decision that should be set against Article 93(1) of the UN Charter: 'All Members of the United Nations are *ipso facto* parties to the Statute of the International Court of Justice', and Article 94(1): 'Each Member of the United Nations undertakes to comply with the decision of the International Court of Justice in any case to which it is a party.'

The General Assembly considered the political situation in Central America during its 1983, 1984 and 1986 regular sessions. In 1983 the Assembly condemned acts of aggression against the states of the region, recording the particular gravity of attacks launched against Nicaragua, the mounting human carnage in El Salvador and Honduras, and the massive increase in the number of refugees in the region – circumstances signifying the appalling suffering of the people of Central America, and all the result of US policies. The General Assembly expressed continuing support for the purposes and principles of the draft Contadora Act and urged the Contadora Group to persevere with its efforts to secure a peaceful settlement to the region's problems. In 1993 an authoritative UN report implicated the US-backed authorities in El Salvador in torture, assassinations and other atrocities through the period of the 1980s' civil war, a conflict in which the vast bulk of the Salvadorean people struggled to overthrow their US-supported oppressors.

OTHER MATTERS

Most of the issues profiled in this chapter have been concerned with such matters as war, external aggression, civil strife and national sovereignty. In all these cases the United Nations has been involved to the extent that it was able to fulfil its various roles in peace-making, peace-keeping, truce monitoring, aiding refugees, disengaging combatants, providing a forum for discussion, adjudicating issues, and related activities. This chapter makes no attempt to provide an exhaustive listing of all the issues – between the founding of the United Nations and the ending of the Cold War – in which the United Nations has been engaged in such tasks. For example, no mention has been made of the UN role in securing the withdrawal of Soviet forces from Afghanistan, in launching the massive aid programme in Bangladesh in 1971, in addressing the India–Pakistan dispute over Kashmir, or in helping Namibia (formerly South West Africa) to achieve independence after a South African-fuelled conflict (with US acquiescence) that cost around one million lives.

It is also useful to note such UN activities as the efforts to secure disarmament, the on-going support for human rights (following the establishment of the Commission on Human Rights in 1946),[54] the collection and dissemination of information, the development of international law, efforts to secure economic and social development, and work to protect the environment. Much of the UN endeavour to achieve investment and national economic development focuses on support for private companies, so reflecting the free-enterprise orientation of IMF/World Bank strategies. At the same time there is some discussion of the possibility that global corporations, with their global responsibilities, should be chartered by some world organisation, such as the United Nations. This would mean that private economic and commercial power, like all forms of authority, would have to be sanctified by a system of law that took due account of the larger global interest. Such a provision would go far beyond, for instance, current GATT regulations, though it is hard to imagine how enforcement could be guaranteed.

The attractiveness of legal constraints over large companies – in the interest of ecological or other human-rights considerations – is obvious, but it is difficult to see how multinational corporate power could ever be tamed by a United Nations committee with few staff and a limited budget. However, it is vital to realise that many UN efforts will continue to be made in a global environment where organisations of immense power are working to an entirely different agenda. The central problem facing the United Nations in the future will be how to develop on a worldwide basis the crucial concept that the proper principle of politics is morality rather than exploitation for private profit.

THE COLD WAR PRISM

Most national and international political affairs from the birth of the United Nations to the collapse of the Soviet bloc were influenced more by the exigencies of the Cold War than by the efforts of the United Nations. Throughout this whole period the UN had a significant impact, more on some issues than others, but its work was necessarily constrained by what powerful states would allow. In these circumstances Washington was inevitably the principal player. Much of the machinery of the United Nations and the UN-linked bodies had been designed by Americans with an eye on American interests; and where, for whatever reason, the machinery did not serve US strategy it could be ignored.[55] Moreover, Washington was always prepared to buy votes in the United Nations. Thus J. William Fulbright, the distinguished Arkansas Senator from 1945 to 1974 and long-serving chairman of the Senate Foreign Relations Committee, declared: 'Because we had lots of money . . . we could send aid all around the world to gain the support and allegiance of various countries . . . That is, in part, how we got so many votes on our side in the United Nations. We could usually win on any question . . . .'[56]

Hence the two-track US policy on the United Nations throughout the period of the Cold War: the exploitation of UN mechanisms wherever possible, including massive levels of 'jury tampering' through the buying of votes; and ignoring the United Nations, wherever necessary, either by unilateral military aggression or covert programmes of terrorism and subversion, using the CIA and other agencies. We can debate the extent to which this two-track policy has been affected by the ending of the Cold War, by the fresh opportunities presented to Washington in the environment of the 'New World Order'.

6 Towards the New World Order

For more than 40 years the United Nations had been shaped and constrained by the Cold War. The UN scope for action had been defined by the circumstances of political power in the real world, and while the United Nations was striving to develop its various roles the Cold War itself was undergoing its own evolution. The pressures exerted by the US-sustained policies of *containment* and *rollback* (see Chapter 4) – allied to the inevitable inflexibility of the command economy – succeeded in eroding the cohesion of the Eastern bloc. By the early 1980s there was growing pressure for reform in the Soviet Union, a development that had its counterparts in all the satellite states.

The tumultuous events that were to shake Eastern Europe and bring the end of the Soviet Union have been variously depicted as a 'revolution', a 'new reformation', a 'disintegration' and a 'collapse'. Within a few short years an authoritarian Old Order – ossified in rigidity and repression – had been overthrown. There were to be dramatic consequences for all states, for all alliances, and for the United Nations. Would this seismic shock to the global scene facilitate new opportunities for peace, a new route to international harmony? Or would the new shape of global power relationships bring fresh constraints, new problems to frustrate the efforts of the peacemakers? In particular, what would be the impact on the United Nations?

THE DISINTEGRATION OF EASTERN EUROPE

By the mid-1980s massive pressures for change had built up in the Soviet Union. At the same time there were parallel developments in the satellite states. None of the events happened in isolation: as their various consequences fed across national boundaries, they combined to feed the growing sense of crisis. Under Leonid Brezhnev the Soviet Union had seen important developments. Between 1960 and 1970 gross social product had doubled and more than trebled by 1980. There had been a significant improvement in living standards and a dramatic expansion of education and health facilities. But such developments could not disguise the tensions at the heart of the system: the bottlenecks in industrial production, the economic distortions caused by the excessive military budget, the growing aspiration for a consumer-orientated society. The creaking economic and social order came to be nicely symbolised by the failing health of the Soviet leader: in January 1976 Brezhnev had been briefly declared dead following a stroke, and thereafter his health continued to deteriorate.

Brezhnev died on 10 November 1982, having performed a two-hour stint in the reviewing box at the anniversary Red Square parade two days earlier. On 12 November it was announced that Yuri Andropov had been elected the new General Secretary of the Communist Party. But Andropov too was in poor health, his effective power destined to last only a few months. His last public appearance was in August 1983 and it became known that he was being treated for kidney disease at the Central Committee Hospital near Moscow. On 11 February 1984 it was announced that Andropov had died after a long illness. Two days later Konstantin Chernenko, a frail 72-year-old, was elected General Secretary. In bad health, Chernenko was known to have a history of lung disease. His last public appearance was at the end of December 1984, and he died of heart failure on 10 March 1985 following problems with his lungs and liver. The long-serving Andrei Gromyko proposed Mikhail Gorbachev as the new General Secretary of the Communist Party, the third in as many years. Gorbachev was 54 years old, the youngest member of the Politburo, and in good health. The scene was set for a new political agenda that would lead to the disintegration of Eastern Europe and the collapse of the Soviet Union.[1]

No one knew better than Gorbachev the need for economic and political reform in the Soviet Union and throughout the satellite states. With much talk of *perestroika* ('reconstruction' or 'restructuring') and *glasnost* ('openness') he set about the business of reform. However, despite his clear awareness of the shortcomings of the Soviet system, Gorbachev was still – in important respects – a leader in the traditional Soviet mould. He remained an essentially Party man, keen to promote economic and managerial reform, but resolutely opposed to any form of political pluralism that would undermine the unique status of the Communist Party in the Soviet Union. Gorbachev helped to set in train a host of reforms that would gather pace until they engulfed him. At the Party Congress in July 1990 Gorbachev acknowledged that the simple replacement of leading officials was 'not a panacea', that more was needed; in October he acknowledged that the 'inertia of the old thinking' had been responsible for the failure to meet the challenge of the times. It was this failure that had led to the collapse of the old power relationships, the rapid disintegration of the old Soviet/Eastern European order (see Table 6.1).

In August 1991 an attempted 'old-guard' coup against Mikhail Gorbachev led to his resignation and the emergence of Boris Yeltsin, darling of the

Table 6.1 Chronology of East European disintegration, 1985–94

1985	
11 March	Mikhail Gorbachev elected General Secretary of Soviet Communist Party
December	Boris Yeltsin becomes leader of Moscow Communist Party
1986	
6 January	Gorbachev sacks 77-year-old Mayor of Moscow in continuing purge
5 March	27th CP Congress approves radical 15-year programme of reform
1987	
January	Charter 77 demands greater democracy in Czechoslovakia
27 January	Gorbachev delivers key speech to Moscow plenum on reform
August	Anti-Soviet protests in Baltic capitals
28 November	Gorbachev withdraws four Soviet divisions from Eastern Europe
29 November	Polish referendum to sanction radical reforms
1988	
January	Nationalist unrest over Ngorny-Karabakh
March	Hungary grants asylum to thousands of Romanian refugees
May	Hungary's Kadar and entire Party old guard ousted; violence at unofficial May Day rallies in Poland; solidarity leaders arrested after strikes in Gdansk
June	Debt crisis in Poland strengthens Western leverage; Ngorny-Karabakh parliament makes appeal to Supreme Soviet; thousands protest against Yugoslav austerity measures
July	Serbian leader invokes idea of restoring Serbia to independence; Ngorny-Karabakh Party leadership votes to secede from Azerbaijan
August	Lenin shipyard in Gdansk sealed off
October	Protests in Hungary on anniversary of 1956 uprising; newly legalised flags of Latvia and Lithuania fly over mass meetings
November	Estonia declares its sovereignty
1989	
January	Yugloslav Prime Minister resigns; Albanians try to turn Kosovo into independent republic

Table 6.1 Chronology of East European disintegration, 1985–94 (cont'd)

February	Hungary decides to adopt multi-party system; Vaclav Havel convicted of inciting protests in Czechoslovakia
March	Six senior CP leaders in Romania publish open criticism of government
April	Lech Walesa publishes his 'Letter to the Polish Electorate'
August	Solidarity government established in Poland
September	Radio Free Europe opens a Budapest office
October	Hungarian Communist Party votes for its own dissolution; East Germany's Erich Honecker ousted; Hungarian Republic formally established
November	Bulgaria's Zhivkov ousted; supreme Soviet approves large degree of autonomy for Baltic states
9 November	East German government opens Berlin Wall
22 November	Demonstrations in Czechoslovakia against Communist government
24 November	Most of Czechoslovakian praesidium resigns
27 November	General strike in Czechoslovakia
December	Czechoslovakia's Husak ousted: Havel elected president; Bulgarian Communist Party paves way for multi-party system; opening of Brandenburg Gate between East and West Berlin; IMF pushes for economic restructuring in Poland
8 December	East German Communist Party Congress in emergency session
22 December	Arrest of Nicolae and Elena Ceausescu in Romania
25 December	Ceausescus executed by firing squad
26 December	Iliescu named provisional president of Romania
1990	
January	Romanian government repeals repressive laws, charges Ceausescu with genocide; Albanian leader announces democratic and economic reforms; Polish Communist Party suspends its activities
2 January	Entire Ceausescu politburo arrested
March	Lithuania declares independence from Soviet Union; Soviet troops begin to leave Hungary

Table 6.1 Chronology of East European disintegration, 1985–94 (cont'd)

April	Right-wing election victory in Croatia
May	Travkin leaves Communist Party and founds Democratic Party of Russia; Yeltsin elected president of Russian Federation
June	Elections in Bulgaria give Socialist Party majority over Communists and Monarchists; Civic Forum in Czechoslovakia wins overall majority with Communists in second place
July	World Bank opens Warsaw office; IMF chief visits Russia to discuss economy
2 July	Gorbachev advocates 'parliamentary' role for Soviet Communist Party
August	Gorbachev declares state ownership 'chief cause of the present chaos'; Hungary joins Council of Europe; Serbs threaten to seek extended frontier; Muslim demonstrations in Croatia
October	German state elections
December	Walesa wins landslide victory in Polish presidential elections; Gorbachev says: 'Actually, I'm going round in circles.'
1991	
January	Russian 'conservatives' in rich region make sovereignty claims; 50- and 100-rouble notes no longer legal tender in Russia
March	Rallies and protest demonstrations banned in Moscow; Albanian Communist Party wins election, President loses seat, unrest blamed on Serbs
April	G7 nations discuss 'New World Order' and how to handle emerging Soviet free market
May	Soviet–Romanian security pact signed
6 May	Supreme Soviet creates constitutional court
June	Albanian Communist Party resigns following general strike; Czechoslovakia launches privatisation programme
July	Gorbachev attends G7 summit
August	Attempted coup in Moscow; Soviet Communist Party suspended; Azerbaijan declares independence; Lithuania outlaws Communist Party; Gorbachev resigns from Soviet Communist Party, proposes that CP dissolve itself

Table 6.1 Chronology of East European disintegration, 1985–94 (cont'd)

October	Russian officials suggest taking over most Soviet functions, especially the control of nuclear weapons; Russian government takes over responsibility for past Soviet debts
November	Movement to develop the CIS after collapse of the Soviet Union; extensive money laundering in Hungary becomes apparent; non-Communist leader elected in Bulgaria; G7 nations take steps to ease Russian debt problems
December	Disintegration of the Soviet Union and announcement of the CIS by the 'big three' former Soviet republics; Norway recognises independent Russia; Supreme Soviet votes itself out of existence; United States recognises independence of republics
1992	
June	G7 nations agree to aid package only if Yeltsin accepts IMF terms
1 October	Russian government launches massive privatisation campaign
2 November	Yeltsin declares state of emergency in parts of Russia hit by violence
9 November	Yeltsin and premier John Major sign security treaty
9 December	Bolshevik sweet factory sold to private interests
1993	
January	Troops deployed on Moscow streets to combat huge rise in crime; Central Bank designs 50,000- and 100,000-rouble banknotes
2 April	West reschedules $80 billion Russian debt
3–4 April	United States promises at Vancouver summit to lift trade restrictions on Russia; G7 nations to office in Moscow; $1.6 billion aid programme for Russia agreed
14 April	G7 nations meet in Tokyo to plan $30 billion aid package
25 April	Four-part referendum held in Russia; both Yeltsin and parliament claim victory
30 April	Polish government passes privatisation bill allowing millions of Poles to become shareholders in 600 state-owned enterprises
1 May	Riots in Moscow after police stop protesters from marching into Red Square

Table 6.1 Chronology of East European disintegration, 1985–94 (cont'd)

12 May	Yeltsin continues administration purges, announces intention to bypass the Congress of People's Deputies; he and parliamentary opposition both work to produce alternative constitutional drafts
13 May	Signs in Moscow as rouble crashed that Yeltsin was considering reintroducing state control over key industries; constitutional court to examine Yeltsin's decision to bypass parliament
14 May	Tensions develop in the Russian 'war of the constitutions'
18 May	Soviet coup trial dismissed, as book *Kremlin Plot* is judged to violate the principles of a fair trial
20 May	Ukraine premier resigns following battle with President Kravchuk
24 May	Russian government and central bank promises IMF to limit credits to state enterprises to reduce monthly inflation rate to 10 per cent – setback to Russian industrial lobbies
26 May	Leaders of Russian republics urge Yeltsin to accept a truce in the 'war of the constitutions' and to combine Yeltsin and parliament versions
28 May	Yeltsin prevents Vice-President Rutskoi from meeting journalists in the Kremlin; Poland's premier Hanna Suchocka loses no-confidence motion by one vote; President Walesa considers calling new elections
29 May	Walesa calls new elections
30 May	Solidarity trade union threatens to call a general strike in Poland
1 June	Russia's parliamentary speaker, Ruslan Khasbulatov, suggests national referendum to resolve the 'war of the constitutions'
2 June	Yeltsin advisers urge him to state-manage constitutional conference
4 June	World Bank's International Finance Corporation (IFC) considers partial pull-out from Ukraine if country's government does not pay for membership; Yeltsin imposes draft constitution
7 June	Anatoly Gorbunov and his 'moderate nationalists' win Latvian poll; Russian parliamentary delegates help to draft Yeltsin's post-Soviet constitution; Russia stalls over pact with European Community
8 June	Russian delegates, including Yeltsin supporters, propose compromise constitution

Table 6.1 Chronology of East European disintegration, 1985–94 (cont'd)

9 June	Khasbulatov accuses Yeltsin of seeking to impose an 'anti-Communist dictatorship'
10 June	Yeltsin apologises for saying that all Russia's councils (*soviets*) were incompatible with democracy
13 June	Nearly one-third of Russia's parliamentary delegates threaten resignation if the parliament continues to block a new constitution; industrial strikers in Ukraine demand resignation of President Kravchuk
27 June	Deadlock in drafting of new Russian constitution; Walesa refuses invitation to attend Solidarity trade union convention; Estonia suspends law forcing ethnic Russians to take Estonian nationality
29 June	Black Sea fleet officers threaten mutiny against presidents of Russia and the Ukraine
2 July	Ukrainian parliament claims ownership rights over former Soviet nuclear weapons on its territory, but says Ukraine intends to become non-nuclear
7 July	Trial of Russian coup plotters postponed until 7 September amid doubts that trial will ever take place; Yeltsin supporters urge early meeting of parliament to push through Yeltsin constitution
8 July	G7 states agree $3 billion package to help large-scale privatisation of Russian industry; Kuchma calls for state of emergency in Ukraine
10 July	Russian parliament claims Sevastopol as property of post-Soviet Russia
12 July	Yeltsin applauds parliamentary acceptance of draft constitution enshrining private property and new system of governance ('We are on the right path. We have found a consensus.')
18 July	Czech and Slovak republics agree to introduce proper border controls
24 July	Confusion in Moscow as government announces that all pre-1993 banknotes will go out of circulation tomorrow; Yeltsin seemingly taken by surprise by this decision
25 July	Yeltsin rushes back from Washington to Moscow after condemning his own government's decision on banknotes
26 July	Yeltsin softens the money reforms; Georgia and rebel Abkhazia agree ceasefire

Table 6.1 Chronology of East European disintegration, 1985–94 (cont'd)

27 July	Yeltsin dismisses Security Minister Barannikov; Gerashchenko, head of central bank, defends his money reforms
29 July	Russian parliamentary delegates summoned to Moscow for crisis session
3 August	Violence breaks out in Chechenia; Russian troops maintain high state of alert in nearby North Ossetia
7 August	Yeltsin's lawyers find no evidence to implicate Gorbachev in 1991 coup attempt; UN Secretary-General calls for UN military observer mission to be sent to Georgia
12 August	Yeltsin threatens dissolution of Russian parliament; demands early elections
13 August	Yeltsin vows to prevent Russia from fragmenting like the Soviet Union; Kostikov, a Yeltsin spokesman, denounces separatist feeling in the Russian republics as 'geopolitical nonsense'
19 August	Yeltsin denounces the parliament and the Russian White House that two years before he had defended against the coup plotters
22 August	Russian trade minister, Sergei Glazyev, 'hounded out' of office; Yeltsin demands early elections
30 August	Yeltsin agrees to withdraw remaining Russian troops from Lithuania; Ukraine procrastinates over vote of confidence
1 September	Yeltsin suspends Rutskoi; Rutskoi comments: 'How can I comment on a decree issued in violation of the law?'
10 September	Ukrainian premier Kuchma resigns saying that political opposition has made it impossible for him to introduce market reforms; Rutskoi banned by Yeltsin from using official country house
16 September	Yeltsin returns Gaidar to Russian cabinet
19 September	Former Communists and their allies, the Democratic Left Alliance (SLD) win Polish elections; Walesa says he will accept the voters' verdict and accept an ex-Communist prime minister
21 September	Yeltsin dissolves Russian parliament; Rutskoi denounces 'overt coup' and declares himself acting head of state; Khasbulatov confirms Rutskoi as President; Major and Clinton applaud Yeltsin's dismissal of elected parliament

Table 6.1 Chronology of East European disintegration, 1985–94 (cont'd)

22 September	Russian parliamentary delegates continue to meet; Defence Minister Grachev expresses support for Yeltsin; former Soviet republics rally to Yeltsin's support; armed forces say they will keep out of the dispute; Gorbachev rushes back from Italy to Moscow
23 September	Armed clashes at Moscow military facility; IMF calls for G7 nations to aid Yeltsin; Khasbulatov states that Yeltsin had made a *coup d'état*
24 September	Grachev orders troops of the Ministry of Internal Affairs (MVD) into Moscow; troops seal off Russian parliament; rebel delegates vow to fight on
26 September	Rutskoi, on the balcony of the parliament, states: 'We will fight to the last cartridge. There will be blood.'
27 September	Pro-parliament protests take place in Moscow; predictions made of military onslaught on White House; Abkhazian rebels seize Black Sea port of Sukhumi; Kravchuk takes over direct control of Ukraine government to speed up market reforms
28 September	Council of Europe takes first step to admit Romania; Yeltsin cuts electricity, water and other supplies to White House; trucks in Moscow carry slogans: 'Yeltsin is an American agent'
29 September	Yeltsin sets deadline for delegates to leave White House; Georgian rebels complete their capture of Abkhazia; the White House delegates refuse to hand over their arms, violating an agreement reached in talks between Rutskoi and Yeltsin officials
1 October	Yeltsin restores electricity supply to White House
2 October	Street battles erupt in Moscow; Rutskoi reads appeal to Russian people: 'Rise up and join the fight against dictatorship'
3 October	Anti-Yeltsin protestors lift siege of White House, sack the mayor's office, and attack the main television station; after the street battles leave hundreds of dead and injured, Yeltsin regains control; calls in paratroops
4 October	Tanks bombard White House; troops storm the building; 300 people, including delegates, leave building with hands over their heads; hundreds of people dead and injured
5 October	Yeltsin moves to ban opposition parties; to close down anti-Yeltsin newspapers; and to set in train the trials of Rutskoi, Khasbulatov and others; Yeltsin establishes night-time curfew; official figure of 127 dead with 600 injured thought to be a low estimate

Table 6.1 Chronology of East European disintegration, 1985–94 (cont'd)

6 October	Yeltsin consolidates power; begins purge of political enemies; maintains state of emergency
8 October	Parliament now crushed; constitutional court abolished; opposition parties banned; anti-Yeltsin newspapers closed down; show trials projected for elected parliamentarians; West applauds Yeltsin's democratic initiatives
11 October	Shevardnadze decides to take Georgia into Commonwealth of Independent States (CIS); Yeltsin declares that elections for both houses of Russian parliament will be held on 12 December
12 October	Yeltsin aide states that Yeltsin may delay the parliamentary elections scheduled for December and hold them next year
13 October	General Makashov, involved in the attack on the television centre, is charged with organising mass disturbances; Yeltsin announces that he will not hold presidential elections in December, but says they will take place on 12 June 1994; Poland's ex-Communists agree coalition with Polish Peasant Party
14 October	Walesa accepts premier Waldemar Pawlak, the candidate put forward by the left wing coalition; Russia's Security Minister Golushko urges the need for the 'constant monitoring' of political parties
16 October	Yeltsin aides urge speedy action to remove the body of Lenin and the remains of other Soviet heroes from the Kremlin
17 October	Pro-Yeltsin party meets, despite supposed ban on all political gatherings
18 October	Yeltsin continues to issue a spate of decrees, including making state awards to soldiers who showed loyalty to him in battle for the White House, and transferring powers away from the elected parliament
19 October	Moscow mayor announces intention to remove Lenin's body from the Red Square mausoleum; the Socialist Party of Working People (SWP) resolves to fight December election but to exclude members of the banned Communist Party of the Russian Federation (CPRF) from joining its ranks
20 October	Yeltsin aide, Sergei Filatov, states that June (1994) presidential election may not take place

Table 6.1 Chronology of East European disintegration, 1985–94 (cont'd)

22 October	Yeltsin begins to withdraw political power from the provinces; Ukraine states that its missiles are still pointed at the West and will be used as bargaining chips
23 October	Speculation that Moscow rebels may be hiding in underground city
25 October	Parliamentarians in Ukraine state that the government will ratify the Start 1 (Strategic Arms Reduction Talks) treaty by the end of the year
26 October	Georgian government, with Russian support, regains control of the Black Sea port of Poti; Russian troops make a 'show of strength'; Poland's former Communists assume power, but Walesa warns them not to reverse reforms; Russian 'centrists' predict that new parliament will have similar composition to that crushed by Yeltsin
29 October	Russian trade union federation drops plan for national strikes in the wake of heavy pressure from Yeltsin; Rutskoi in hospital with high blood pressure
2 November	Reports of disillusionment with the 'revolution that never was' in Bulgaria (95 per cent of economy still in state hands); Russian economy continues to slump; Yeltsin berates his cabinet for ineptitude
6 November	Romania racked by corruption; IMF 'holds whip hand' over Romania's suspended loans; Yeltsin reneges on pledge to face electors in June 1994; Shevardnadze regains control in Georgia
7 November	Police prevent Moscow celebration of 76th anniversary of Bolshevik revolution; new Yeltsin constitution finalised (vast new presidential powers)
10 November	Yeltsin's Electoral Commission bans 8 political groups (a third of the total from forthcoming election); Russia sends troops to Georgia
15 November	Anxiety in West about possibility of Russian colonialism
21 November	Reports that 40 per cent of Russia's new entrepreneurs are gangsters
25 November	Yeltsin orders political parties not to criticise him; Moscow threatens military measures if NATO absorbs former Warsaw Pact members; Yeltsin threatens to ban critical television broadcasts
28 November	Megaoil (US) accused of training Azeri soldiers; fresh Moscow–Kazakhstan tensions; Gorbachev criticises Yeltsin

Table 6.1 Chronology of East European disintegration, 1985–94 (cont'd)

30 November	New Yeltsin move to ban political opponents
2 December	Ukraine urged to give up nuclear arms; former Warsaw Pact states woo NATO
5 December	Growth of Russian mafia; Hungarian premier Antall ill
13 December	Ultra nationalist Zhirinovsky wins substantial support in new parliament
29 December	Germany bans 'ranting' Zhirinovsky
1994	
1 January	Signs of Yeltsin backtracking; Zhirinovsky talks of Third World War
5 January	Georgia's former president Gamsakhurdia 'has committed suicide'
7 January	Signs of anti-Yeltsin parliamentary pact; NATO offers loose links with former Warsaw Pact states
11 January	Yeltsin opens new parliament; Clinton, in Moscow, tries to reassure Yeltsin about evolving NATO influence in Europe

West, as the new Russian president. Now the Soviet Union was rapidly falling into chaos and collapse, with the republics proclaiming their independence, territorial disputes erupting into violence, and the internal Soviet social and industrial structures falling into disorder. After a series of national initiatives in the states of the old Soviet Union, a new structure – loose, ill-defined and uncertain – the Commonwealth of Independent States (CIS) emerged, in the hope that some of the traditional economic and strategic relationships could be preserved.

The West, keen to support the free-market reforms of the authoritarian Yeltsin, proposed various aid packages which scarcely seemed to address the magnitude of the problems in what was now a chaotic Russian Federation. Yeltsin himself, after various confrontations with the residual Soviet parliament, held a four-question referendum in April 1993 which gave him qualified support. It still seemed unclear how the collapse of Eastern Europe, the dismemberment of the Soviet Union, the emergence of a Yeltsin-dominated CIS – and all the attendent civil strife, nationalist rivalries and increasingly Mafia-run enterprises – could be brought by Western policy-makers within the orbit of the so-called New World Order. It was unclear also what the implications were for the United Nations.

ANOTHER WORLD ORDER

The disintegration of the Soviet/Eastern European bloc necessarily had a host of military and economic consequences. The world had been accustomed to a bipolar power structure, with the possibility of Mutually Assured Destruction (MAD) affording some nightmarish form of security. The United States, though temporarily constrained in some of its more ambitious plans – in particular, the desire to bring the Soviet bloc within the grasp of world capitalism – was able to shape the political course in most of the countries of the world. In this framework there was no doubt that the Soviet Union would have been able to co-operate – had the occasion arisen – in the slaughter of tens of millions of human beings. Its status as a military superpower meant that it had clearly established its reputation as a potential mass murderer on a horrendous scale. But to the extent that the Soviet Union was forced to compete with the United States, the great people's state was at an obvious – and ultimately decisive – disadvantage. Throughout its history the Soviet Union had been compelled to function in a reactive mode: it worked desperately to catch up with the United States in the possession of nuclear weapons; the Warsaw Pact was formed as a response to NATO; the Soviet Union, not the United States, came to be ringed by hostile military bases. While post-Second World War Western Europe, Japan and other states were being reconstructed in the American mode, the Soviet Union – in a state of virtual siege – struggled for survival in apparent isolation. The isolation was in part imposed by prescient Western policy-makers, in part self-selected by the political idealogues in the Kremlin. It was none the less real, a debilitating condition that would feed Russian paranoia and prohibit consideration of new ideas that might have tempered the rigidities and repression associated with the command economy. Thus the Soviet Union and its authoritarian East European acolytes, trapped in an unequal struggle, slid – at first slowly and then with dramatic momentum – into apocalyptic collapse. The result was not quite what the Western policy-makers might have imagined.

At first the situation seemed clear. The Soviet Union – traditionally hyped as a demonic giant that a virtuous and reluctant America was forced to confront – had obligingly disappeared: the American Way had prevailed and the world was safe for all the Christian virtues that the CIA, death squads and napalm had exemplified so elegantly in their protection of world capitalism for more than four decades. It now seemed that Washington would be able to tighten still further the global grip it had managed to establish during the period of its confrontation with the Evil Empire. But there were problems. The United States, once a massive creditor nation, was now in deep debt: the arms race had contributed to huge trade and budgetary deficits that would inevitably force a change in political direction. The signs were clear through the terminal years of the Soviet Union, and once it had passed into history the doubts about the imagined omnipotence of the United States were voiced on every side. Perhaps even Washington would have great difficulties in coming to terms with the post-Soviet world, an unfamiliar environment in which spies and arms manufacturers, policy-makers and Washington war-mongers were no longer quite sure what they were about.

The 1991 Gulf War (see Chapter 7) raised many new questions. In particular, how would the United States aim to tackle the aftermath to a vast new Western onslaught on a Muslim state? Would the US be able to fill the post-war power vacuum?[2] Was the United States really set to 'police the universe'?[3] It now seemed too simplistic a model for the shrinking world, still beset by racial tensions, a massive economic imbalance between the poor nations and the rich, and many of the traditional ambitions of nation states. It was left to J. K. Galbraith, Emeritus Professor of Economics at Harvard, to suggest that poverty should be addressed as the 'prime source of world disorder';[4] though others were also emphasising that a 'new world order' based on a successful conclusion to the Gulf War was a totally unrealistic expectation.[5] It was still possible to assert that the US President was 'set to police the planet',[6] but a new perception was starting to shape the slogans. To many observers the New World Order had collapsed weeks after the end of the Gulf War, when Washington cynically refused to help the desperate Kurds who had struggled to rise up against Saddam; and other unresolved disputes were soon contributing to the sense of disillusion. Thus the journalist Peter Jenkins commented on the shape of 'a new world disorder',[7] and Martin Woollacott reported on 'The New World what?'[8] It was soon apparent that the complexities of the post-Cold War world were combining to throw the Clinton administration into confusion and equivocation.[9]

The ending of the Cold War had thrown many traditional policies into question. The old Soviet Union had, for example, supported Cuba over decades, but now all aid was stopped and the Cuban people, suffering under the illegal US blockade, were powerless to halt their gradual slide into destitution. The corollary was that Washington was no longer forced to save the world from Communism, a circumstance that was to have economic and political consequences around the globe. The structure of the world finance system is largely a Cold War product:

> . . . to an extent Gatt, the development of multinationals, the global capital market and the asymmetric use of world trade on which the Japanese and eastern Asian economies based their growth are all in part cold war phenomena . . . Now that it is over, the world economy will change its contours dramatically.[10]

This suggests the likelihood of fresh tensions in a global capitalist environment no longer able to rely on the stabilising cement of enduring anti-Communist policies. The troubles in the Uruguay GATT round, focusing above all on the growing tensions between Washington and Europe, have been much advertised; but there is a more radical interpretation of the current difficulties in the economic relationships between the erstwhile allies against Communism. In one view, the world trading arrangements are defunct, no longer able to cope with the pressures of the post-Cold War world. Thus the economist Lester Thurow, Dean of the Massachusetts Institute of Technology's Sloan School of Management, declares:

> The GATT–Bretton Woods trading system is dead. It died not in failure but at the normal end of a very successful life. Logically a new Bretton Woods conference should now be under way. But politically, it cannot be called. Such a conference can only occur if there is a dominant political power that can force everyone to agree. In 1944 the United States was such a power . . .[11]

It is highly significant that the United States is no longer a 'dominant political power' in the sense considered. The US *military* dominance is not in question, though America's parlous economic situation is forcing military cut-backs. What is clear is that the United States is being forced to address the implications of a tripolar economic world – based on the production capabilities of Europe, America and Japan – in which Japan is in the economic ascendant. And there is also the persistent Russian problem. Boris Yeltsin has initiated the most ambitious privatisation programme of any former Communist country; and has managed to produce unprecedented levels of crime, a collapse in industrial production, a massive erosion of social services, and hyperinflation (prices rising 30 per cent a month in mid-1993). The old Soviet Union's foreign debt of £47 billion is due to be repaid by 1995, and fresh help from the G7 nations has only added to the debt burden. What is to be done?

It is against these circumstances that the United Nations will evolve, its role and powers shaped as ever by what powerful states will allow. The growing economic constraints on Washington will increasingly restrict its scope for manoeuvre in both the General Assembly and the Security Council. The IMF/World Bank/GATT axis still has enormous clout in the global economic framework, giving the Western political Establishment a handle on the economic management of most countries in the world; but it is marginally less easy for Washington to buy UN votes than it was in the good old days. Russia and other states are still obliged to keep an eye on their economic interests when performing in the various chambers (and corridors) of the United Nations, but today the global political scene is fluid and uncertain. Power is more diffuse than it was at the height of the Cold War: there are pros and cons in this.

AND THE UNITED NATIONS

The ending of the Cold War and the growing economic power of Germany and Japan on the world stage inevitably focused attention on how the United Nations should function in the new world environment. Many observers saw a clear case for a reform of the UN structures, an improvement in its decision-making apparatus, a revision of Security Council membership (see Chapter 8). There seemed to be a general consensus on the pivotal role of the United Nations in the imagined New World Order, though less agreement on how this role would be translated into policies and actions in the real world. In what disputes was the UN equipped to intervenc? Was there scope for an impartial application of principle, now that the old US–Soviet rivalry was at an end? Or would powerful states continue to manipulate or ignore UN organs, as had happened too often in the past? In fact, the disintegration of the Soviet Union gave Washington – at least in the short term – fresh scope for manipulation of the Security Council to further perceived US interests. The most glaring example of this was the 1991 Gulf War; it was not the only one.

The end of the Communist threat quickly induced American policy-makers to speculate on how the United Nations could be further exploited to US advantage. The collapse of the Soviet Union meant that there was no longer a focus for a coalition of nations against US interests. It was fortuitous that George Bush – one-time CIA chief and one-time US ambassador to the United Nations – was American President during the final death throes of the Soviet Union. No one was better placed to see the fresh opportunities. Suddenly the United Nations – after decades of ambivalence and hostility to any UN voices that queried American global hegemony – was a friend of the international body. When Kuwait was liberated President Bush declared: 'This is a victory for the United Nations, for all mankind, for the rule of law and for what is right.' Again it was easy to ask whether the United Nations was a 'world voice or US puppet?'[12]

One initial complication was the question of what was to happen to the Soviet seat on the Security Council when the Soviet Union was no more. There was even a hint that Moscow might lose its seat at the 'UN top table'.[13] In the event Moscow did not need to worry. Now that the free-marketeer Boris Yeltsin was suitably ensconced in the Kremlin it well suited Washington to have another right-wing Permanent Member in the Council. Little discussion was needed, no public negotiations: in no time at all Boris Yeltsin was planted in the Security Council seat formerly occupied by the Soviet representative, and Washington's grip on power seemed secure.* Again after a while the position seemed less clear. Russia's ethnic links to the Serbs added confusion to at least one escalating crisis, and Yeltsin's uncertain grip on domestic power meant that on occasions he was forced to look uncomfortably over his shoulder. Washington sometimes wondered whether the solid Yeltsin, free-marketeer and authoritarian democrat, was all he was supposed to be.

The pundits continued to speculate about what could be expected from the United Nations in the New World (dis)Order. Would a post-Cold War UN at last be able to work in the way that its founders intended? (And what way was that?) Or would the international body remain relatively impotent, inevitably sidelined by the growing power of the multinational corporations, recalcitrant nation states, and the obvious military hegemony of the world's one surviving superpower? Much of the speculation was soon overtaken by events. There was soon an accumulation of disputatious issues in which the United Nations was involved; this gave a clear indication of the UN scope for action in the new political environment. It is useful to glance at some of these issues.

* The transfer of the permanent seat from the erstwhile Soviet Union to Russia, without a vote in the UN General Assembly, was in blatant violation of Article 108 of the UN Charter. The current Russian permanent seat on the Security Council is therefore illegal.

7 Issues – II

There is historical continuity in all events in the real world; that is, a full understanding of any circumstance or epoch can be approached only by seeking out prior causes. The problem here is that this implies the need for an infinite regress, an agenda beyond the capacities of even the most diligent historian. All the issues profiled in the present chapter have their roots in events that preceded the start of the Cold War and the origin of the United Nations. Thus the UN, itself a historical product, came to its involvement in the various disputes in circumstances that were shaped *in toto* by prior causes. In seeking to understand the developing role of the United Nations it is important that such considerations be borne in mind. In what was clearly a new phase of UN operations it was still easy to detect the residual detritus of Cold War mind-sets and the persistent burden of *realpolitik*. It is important to note also that the disintegration of the Soviet Union did not mean that the United Nations would cease to be manipulated in the interest of powerful states. The anti-Communist containment/rollback crusade was no longer needed, but there were still vital interests to be protected.

THE IRAQ QUESTION

On 2 August 1990, in the context of an escalating crisis, Iraqi forces invaded the small Emirate of Kuwait. The circumstances of this aggression, as with all sociopolitical events, were created and conditioned by complex historical factors.[1] It is enough to mention here the traditional Iraqi claims to the territory of Kuwait, the unambiguous American advice to Saddam Hussein that he adopt aggressive oil pricing policies,[2] and the manifest 'green light' that Washington gave to Saddam's invasion.[3] Such matters are crucial to an understanding of the Iraqi aggression and will continue to be discussed. Here, the principal concern is the shape and extent of the involvement of the United Nations in the crucial context of a rapidly deteriorating Soviet Union.

On the day of the invasion the UN Security Council adopted Resolution 660 (14 votes to 0, with Yemen abstaining), citing Articles 39 and 40 of the Charter, condemning the invasion, and demanding an immediate and unconditional withdrawal of all Iraqi forces. There was also a demand that

Iraq and Kuwait begin 'intensive negotiations' to settle their differences. It was Resolution 660 that, in the absence of Iraqi compliance, was to serve as the springboard for more than a dozen further Council resolutions that were to be approved over the coming months. Throughout this entire period the United States was the principal architect of the resolutions: they were designed essentially to bolster US policy and, significantly enough, where a resolution could not be secured – as with the post-war imposition of 'no-fly' zones – Washington showed its willingness to act in defiance of international law. Many of the resolutions, once approved, were selectively interpreted according to the whims and interests of powerful Member States. Many examples could be given but here we need only consider the application of Resolutions 661 and 678.

Resolution 661 (6 August 1990) was passed (13 votes to 0, with Cuba and Yemen abstaining) to impose comprehensive sanctions on Iraq, following its failure to comply with the withdrawal demand set out in Resolution 660. This was a highly punitive resolution since, allied to the freezing of overseas Iraqi assets and a ban on Iraqi oil sales, it denied the Iraqi people adequate supplies of food and medicine. The governments of the United States and Britain, when pressed, cited clause 3c in the resolution ('but not including supplies intended strictly for medical purposes, and, in humanitarian circumstances, foodstuffs') to demonstrate that no attempt was being made to deny the Iraqi people the essentials of life. But since there was a *de facto* ban (through asset-freezing and the oil sales ban) on the importation of medical supplies and foodstuffs, the operation of 661 was a violation of international law which prohibits the deliberate starving of civilian populations in time of war. *In early 1994, three years after the ending of the Gulf War, the sanctions on Iraq remain in place.*

The American decision to use force in the Gulf was taken long before the sympathetic (but not overwhelming) vote in Congress and long before the 'enabling' Security Council vote enshrined in Resolution 678. This resolution authorised Member States 'to use all necessary means to uphold and implement 660' (demanding an Iraqi withdrawal from Kuwait). This crucial resolution, even as it stands, was not unanimously supported by the members of the Security Council: China, as a permanent member, decided to abstain, and Yemen and Cuba – non-permanent members without a veto – voted against. Today the conventional wisdom assumes that Resolution 678 entitled the 'Coalition' powers to use force: this is frequently asserted and rarely discussed. However, it is arguable that 678 did *not* authorise the use of force, in the absence of further specified protocols; and that moreover its subsequent application was a violation of the UN Charter.

It is clear that Secretary of State James Baker did not regard 'all necessary means' (the wording of 678) as synonymous with 'the use of force'. The Soviet Foreign Minister Eduard Shevardnadze, alarmed at any reference to *force* in a possible Security Council resolution, signified acceptance of 'all necessary means' as a compromise – which at one stage Baker rejected as too indefinite: 'the Bush administration did not want a domestic debate on the meaning of a UN resolution'.[4] But the compromise wording did not solve the problem. Force could only be used in the Gulf if it could be shown to be *necessary*, and who was to decide? Resolution 678, as drafted, gave no guidance. There was no reference to the role of the UN Sanctions Committee, which might have been able to report on the effects of the measures already taken under Resolution 661; and no requirement that the Security Council meet again on 15 January (1991), the stipulated deadline, to decide what further action was necessary.

This meant that the Member States were free to interpret 'necessary' as they chose – a clear intention of Washington. The United States could take a unilateral decision on war, without any further reference to the United Nations, any time after the deadline date for Iraqi withdrawal. There was no longer any role for the Security Council; Secretary-General Perez de Cuellar, already greatly disturbed by the course of events, no longer had any part to play. Some observers protested in vain that the so-called 'use of force' resolution did not entitle Washington to act without reference to the United Nations. Thus on 14 January 1991 Lord Gifford and other lawyers in Britain emphasised that Resolution 678 'is not a blank cheque for the United States to pursue its own ends by its own means'. When, on 13 January, Perez de Cuellar met Saddam Hussein in Baghdad he urged the Iraqi president to 'deny the warmongers their opportunity'. When Saddam commented that: 'These are American resolutions . . . What the United States want at present is the thing that is passed [678] and not what the Security Council wants', the UN Secretary-General replied: 'I agree with you as much as the matter involves me.'[5] The position was plain. The United Nations had been deliberately excluded from the picture: the 1991 Gulf war was contrived, initiated and run by the United States, exploiting the UN as a 'flag of convenience'. Already the evidence was beginning to accumulate about how Washington intended to use the United Nations in the post-Cold War world.

The United States had learned much from the Vietnam fiasco. Washington's willingness to run a campaign of genocide in Vietnam – *without* a nominal UN sanction – had run into all sorts of problems, not least with the increasingly agitated American people. If there were to be fresh genocide, this time in the Middle East, it would clearly be useful to first obtain what could be passed off as United Nations backing. Washington obviously believed that there was much to be said for such a flag of convenience, as shown by the strenuous US efforts to contrive the support of as many UN members as possible.

After unremitting pressure on King Fahd had secured a Saudi 'invitation' that the United States send forces to the Gulf,[6] Washington turned its attention to other states that could be usefully cajoled, bribed and threatened. One early step was to donate $8 billion-worth of military equipment to Turkey, strategically situated with a shared border with Iraq. Washington declared also that the IMF/World Bank would facilitate $1.5 billion-worth of low-cost loans to Turkey. Syria was offered arms, and when Iran agreed to aid the blockade of Iraq, substantial loans from the World Bank were suddenly forthcoming. A $15 billion Egyptian debt was waived, while non-permanent members of the Security Council were given particular attention: Ethiopia was offered an investment deal and Zaire was promised military aid and debt forgiveness. There were even attempts to win over Cuba, against whom Washington had waged a merciless economic war and organised thousands of terrorist acts for more than 30 years: Fidel Castro was one of the few jury members who refused to be bought. Minutes after Yemen had registered its negative vote against Resolution 678 a senior American diplomat told the Yemeni ambassador: 'That was the most expensive "no" vote you ever cast.' Within days the US had stopped its $70 million aid programme to Yemen, one of the poorest countries in the world. The World Bank and the IMF moved to block Yemeni loans, and some 800,000 Yemeni workers were abruptly expelled from Saudi Arabia. The Yemeni 'no' vote – an entirely legitimate sovereign decision under the UN Charter – cost the impoverished Yemen about $1 billion, adding greatly to the suffering of the Yemeni people. Zimbabwe, initially hostile to Resolution 678, eventually voted in favour after threats that an IMF loan would be withdrawn, while Ecuador was warned by the US ambassador of the 'devastating economic consequences' that would follow a 'no' vote. The famine-stricken Sudan, rash enough to voice support for Iraq, was denied a shipment of food.

The permanent members of the Security Council could be relied upon. A supine United Kingdom, in this matter little more than a subdivision of the US State Department, would cause no problems; and France, often more independent, had no wish to rock the boat. The Soviet Union, on its last legs, was desperate for Washington's favour; and China – like so many other states – was prepared to be bought off. China was keen to win US approval after the Tiananmen Square massacre and a new loan would not come amiss. Once it was clear that China would do no more than abstain on the crucial Resolution 678, the World Bank quickly deposited a further $114 million in Peking. The Chinese scholar Liu Binyan commented:

'Since August [1990] . . . Beijing has skilfully manipulated the Iraqi crisis to its advantage and rescued itself from being the pariah of the world.'

The old Washington tactics of bribery and threat had worked again, although now there was an important difference. The debt-burdened United States was forced to parade a begging bowl: the Saudis were pressured to offer funds, and soon Germany and Japan were being invited to make contributions to the war chest. Here were the clues to a new US strategy: states around the globe would be pressured to serve as paymasters to American mercenaries fighting to protect US interests.

The ending of the Gulf War did not bring peace and security in the area. Washington contemplated with seeming indifference the desperate plight of the Iraqi minorities, while the harsh sanctions continued to add to the suffering of the Iraqi people. In March 1991 a UN mission led by Martti Ahtisaari, Under-Secretary-General for Administration and Management, visited Iraq to assess the humanitarian needs of the people. The resulting report was widely publicised because of its depiction of conditions in post-war Iraq as 'near-apocalyptic'. For the Iraqi people the war was not over: now, through massive destruction of the country's infrastructure and the punitive continuation of sanctions, they were forced to suffer increasing levels of disease, malnutrition and starvation.[7] Nor could the prospect of a further military onslaught on Iraq be ruled out. President Bush, frustrated at the survival of Saddam Hussein, was clearly seeking an excuse for a fresh confrontation. The general pretext was that the Iraqi president had failed to observe the terms of the many UN resolutions, a charge that became increasingly unsustainable as the months wore on.[8] In mid-July 1990 a UN inspection team reported that most of Iraq's nuclear equipment had been destroyed during the war, and what remained could not be used to manufacture nuclear weapons. Over the following months UN teams destroyed much of the residue of Saddam's 'weapons of mass destruction' capability and, despite frequent Iraqi confrontations with UN inspectors, it became increasingly difficult to argue that Saddam still posed a threat to the region.

The war had been an American initiative, despite the unending hype about the 'Coalition' and the 'UN forces'. There was no reference made to the Security Council to authorise the launching of the air offensive after the deadline had expired neither the UN Sanctions Committee nor the Secretary-General were given any part to play as the human slaughter continued; no effort was made to revive the Military Staff Committee specified in Article 47 of the UN Charter; and in the theatre of war there was no UN command, not a blue beret or a blue helmet to be seen. After the war the character of the UN inspections became clear. In September 1991 the UN Secretary-General, Perez de Cuellar, rebuked the head of the team of

UN inspectors and the deputy head of the UN special disarmament commission for feeding seized Iraqi documents directly to Washington rather than to UN officials.[9] Again the United States had contrived to use the UN as cover for its own strategic activities.

On 11 May 1993 the chief UN official in Baghdad warned that the United Nations was withdrawing its guards from northern Iraq as a first step to ending the aid programme through lack of funds.[10] The UN's Department of Humanitarian Affairs (DHA) had appealed earlier in the year for $489 million to cover its Iraq operations for the next twelve-month period but less than $2 million had been pledged. It had proved possible to tap the treasuries of the world to sustain a vast military onslaught on one relatively small country, but the need to support the hundreds of thousands of civilians thrust into privation by the war was a less pressing concern. A UN official commented: 'It's not just the guards who are affected, it's our whole programme. With the guards gone, however, there'll no longer be a visible UN presence in the country.'

The main task had been achieved. A brutal and recalcitrant nationalist leader, a darling of the West only a short time before, had been tamed; and the Western grip on strategic energy reserves had been tightened. Western aircraft, without UN authorisation and outside UN control, continued to patrol substantial tracts of Iraq; and frequent missile attacks were launched against Iraqi sites, on thin pretext or through (later admitted) error. On 27 June – without UN authorisation and to the horror of most of the international community – President Clinton ordered a Tomahawk cruise missile attack on Baghdad in retaliation for an alleged Iraqi assassination attempt on George Bush when he visited Kuwait some months before.* The 24 cruise missiles landed on Baghdad at 2 a.m., destroying much property, some of it in residential areas, and killing and maiming some dozens of Iraqis: one of the dead was Leila al-Attar, the director of the Saddam Arts Centre and an internationally respected painter. Later that morning, President Clinton, on his way to church, commented: 'I feel quite good about what transpired and I think the American people should feel good about it.'

Over the following weeks there were more US threats of military action against Iraq, with the pretext now the growing UN–Iraq tension over weapons inspectors. But now President Clinton, possibly chastened by the international condemnation of the Baghdad raid, was insisting that any military

* At the time of the raid none of the accused had been found guilty by a Kuwaiti court. It was also widely reported that the Kuwaiti-appointed defence lawyers had refused to visit their clients in jail, and that some of the defendants were beaten and tortured by the security police while in custody.

initiative would have to be multilateral. On 9 July it was announced that UN inspectors would 'seal' two Iraqi missile test sites to prevent their use until Baghdad allowed the installation of monitoring cameras. All the same time there was speculation that Iraq might be allowed to sell $1.6 billion-worth of oil over six months, but with the United Nations marketing the oil, banking the proceeds and monitoring the distribution of food and medicine that Iraq would be allowed to buy. Such restrictions implied that Iraq would never be allowed to regain control of its oil resource. It seemed likely that the harsh UN–imposed sanctions on Iraq would remain in force.

It was now clear, to anyone who cared to look, what the sanctions were achieving. In July 1993 a 'Special Alert' (no. 237), issued under the joint auspices of the UN Food and Agriculture Organisation and the World Food Programme, declared:

> . . . given normal circumstances, Iraq would not be a 'food insecure' country . . . it is a country whose economy has been devastated by the recent war and subsequent civil strife, but *above all by the continued sanctions* since August 1990, which have virtually paralyzed the whole economy and generated persistent deprivation, chronic hunger, endemic undernutrition, massive unemployment and widespread human suffering . . . a vast majority of the Iraqi population is living under the most deplorable conditions and is simply engaged in a struggle for survival; but with increasing numbers losing out in this struggle every day a grave humanitarian tragedy is unfolding. (My italics)

Thus while the United States was insisting, through the mechanism of the UN Security Council, that punitive sanctions be maintained, various UN bodies were deploring the appalling consequences of the sanctions. The FAO/WFP 'Special Alert', noting the findings of the Crop and Food Supply Assessment Mission to Iraq, highlighted

> . . . with deep concern the prevalence of the commonly recognized pre-famine indicators such as exorbitant prices, collapse of private incomes, soaring unemployment, drastically reduced food intakes, large scale depletion of personal assets, high morbidity levels, escalating crime rates and rapidly increasing numbers of destitute people . . . large numbers of Iraqis have now food intakes lower than those of the populations in the disaster stricken African countries.

In September 1993 the US-dominated UN Special Commission insisted that existing sanctions on Iraq, including the ban on oil sales, would be maintained until a 'long-term' monitoring programme had been completed. By now it was clear that Washington was insisting on banning Iraqi oil sales in order to protect the price of oil on the international markets. An increasingly cash-strapped Saudi Arabia, for example, needed to maximise its revenues to pay for a massive influx of US-supplied arms. In late 1993 Washington was consigning millions of Iraqis to destitution, disease and premature death, at least in part to protect the profits of American arms manufacturers.

The United States, exploiting the post-Cold War compliance of Russia, had succeeded in manipulating the United Nations to American strategic advantage – first in waging war on an entire people and then in determining the conditions of a merciless peace. It seemed clear that Washington would now be tempted to exploit its new-found control of the Security Council to address other matters of strategic concern. It was not long before the United Nations was again induced to underwrite US foreign policy.

THE LIBYA QUESTION

Colonel Muammar Gaddafi of Libya, long a thorn in the side of the West, was destined soon to receive fresh attention from Washington.[11] In September 1991 it emerged that the West was keen to label Libya as the sole perpetrator of the Lockerbie and UTA DC-10 bombing outrages.* To many observers this move immediately suggested a hidden agenda. There had been many earlier claims of Iranian, Syria and Palestinian involvement, and it now seemed odd that such likely culprits should be written out of the story. On 14 November Washington declared that two Libyan nationals were to be charged with complicity in the bombing of Pan Am 103 over Lockerbie, an announcement that followed a statement by CIA chief William Webster that Syria had not been involved. The UN Foreign Secretary Douglas Hurd then called for Libya to yield up the two suspects, Abdelbaset Ali Mohmed al-Megrahi and Amin Khalifa Fhimah, for trial in Britain or the United States for mass murder, commenting that 'this fiendish act of wickedness cannot be passed over or ignored'. On 16 November it was revealed that Britain and the United States were prepared to call for a worldwide trade embargo on Libya if Colonel Gaddafi did not hand over the

* A terrorist bomb destroyed Pan Am flight 103 over Lockerbie, killing all the crew and 243 passengers on 21 December 1988. A bomb destroyed UTA 772 over the Sahara, killing all the passengers and crew on 19 September 1989.

suspects. There was also talk of an approach to the United Nations. What had worked with the recalcitrant regime of Saddam Hussein might work with difficult regime of Colonel Gaddafi.

On 27 November Britain and the United States demanded that the Libyan President accept full criminal and financial liability for the Lockerbie bombing. Libya had no extradition treaty with Britain or America, the suspects had not been tried, no appeal had yet been made to the United Nations – but already Colonel Gaddafi was being told to declare himself the culprit for 'mass murder'. If he failed to comply – and what head of state could ever succumb to such threats – he would face economic sanctions within a very short time and the possibility of military action. On many occasions over the coming weeks spokesmen in both Washington and London were to declare that military strikes could not be ruled out, so violating Articles 2(4) of the UN Charter: 'All Members shall refrain in their international relations from the threat or use of force against the territorial integrity or political independence of any state . . .' In early December 1991 reports appeared that US aircraft were already carrying out practice bombing exercises ready for an attack on Libya.[12] It was now time to involve the United Nations.

A series of documents were then submitted to the UN by Britain, France and the United States, making charges against and demands on Libya with regard to the surrender of the two hostages. On 20 January 1992 the UN Security Council unanimously adopted Resolution 731 urging the Libyan Government to respond to the 'requests' that is 'cooperate fully in establishing responsibility for the terrorist acts' against Pan Am Flight 103 and UTA Flight 772. All states were urged 'individually and collectively to encourage the Libyan Government to respond fully and effectively' to the 'requests'. It was reported that the US, Britain and France were considering how much of a role the UN Secretary-General, now Dr Boutros Boutros-Ghali, should be permitted in this escalating crisis. Little mention was made of the important fact that Libya, as a signatory with the Western powers and other states to the 1971 Montreal Convention on terrorist attacks against civilian aircraft, was scrupulously observing the requirements of international law. The Western powers were less interested in this than in escalating the pressure on Libya. Would this perhaps be a new opportunity to depose Colonel Gaddafi? The US assassination attempt on Gaddafi on 15 April 1986 had failed (the bombing raids killed Gaddafi's adopted daughter and resulted in several hundred civilian dead and injured), but perhaps the United Nations could again be used to good effect.

Secretary-General Boutros-Ghali then produced two reports on the Libyan crisis, nothing that there had been a 'certain evolution' in the Libyan position. His suggestion that this should be acknowledged before punitive measures were adopted against Gaddafi 'irritated London and Washington'.[13] On 31 March 1992 – after various conciliatory offers from Gaddafi, attempts by the Arab League to secure a settlement to the dispute, and further US arm-twisting in the Security Council (China was threatened with loss of 'favoured nation' status if it did not behave) – the Council approved Resolution 748 (by 10 to 0, with five abstentions), imposing various sanctions on Libya. On 14 April the International Court of Justice, presented by Washington with the *fait accompli* of Resolution 748, ruled (11 to 5) that it could not grant Libya a temporary restraining order to prevent the imposition of sanctions.

Again the United States had demonstrated its new approach to the manipulation of the United Nations. Libya – unlike Britain, the US and France – had discharged its obligation under international law (as specified in the 1971 Montreal Convention). There was no legal obligation on Libya to surrender its two nationals (since Libya was party to no relevant extradition treaty). Not only had the Western powers, under US prompting, violated the Montreal Convention, but they had also violated Articles 2(3) and 33(1) of the UN Charter, demanding a pacific solution to an international dispute. In a detailed analysis of the dispute, Marc Weller, Research Fellow in International Law at St Catharine's College, Cambridge, concluded that Libya has responded 'in accordance with international legal requirements', noting that to secure the UN resolutions the claimant states 'had to expend considerable political capital and goodwill in the Security Council, *bullying fellow members to obtain the necessary votes, and enraging many non-members of the Council who keenly observed this spectacle*'[14] (my italics). Weller adds that the US and UK governments 'may well have contributed to, or brought about, an abuse of rights by the Security Council', and judges that it may now be necessary for the International Court to seek a judicial review of decisions of the Security Council 'if the constitutional system of the UN Charter is to recover from the blow it has suffered in this episode'.

In early 1994 the illegal sanctions on Libya, tightened by a further Council resolution (883), remained in place. On 18 August 1993 the Jamahiriya News Agency (JANA), the Libyan agency, reported that the Security Council had prohibited Libya from using air ambulances to fly critically ill patients abroad for medical treatment. The request for the permit to fly out the patients was consistent with the terms of the illicit Resolution 748 which makes provision for urgent humanitarian cases to be exempted from the air ban. JANA (18/8) reports:

> The application for a permit was presented over a month ago. The condition of the patients worsened and some of them had to be trans-

ported overland to Tunisia and by sea to Malta, despite their serious illnesses. Six year old Safaa Abdel Rasoul died as she could not be treated locally. A list of the names of those urgent cases who require treatment abroad, which has been rejected by the Security Council, has been published. It includes nationals from Libya, Egypt and Palestine.

On 20 August 1993 Fawzi Hamed al-Sultan, the President of the UN-linked International Fund for Agricultural Development (IFAD), visited Tripoli to present Colonel Gaddafi with an engraved metal plate as a token of the Fund's appreciation for his support and in appreciation of Libya's active role in combating screw-worm disease in North Africa, in co-operation with the Fund and other UN-linked organisations. As with Iraq, while the Security Council was resolute in punishing an Arab people, various UN-linked bodies were keen to emphasise other priorities.

In September there were fresh signs that the two Libyan suspects might 'volunteer' to be tried in Scotland, provided assurances be given that they would not be handed over to the United States. Alasdair Duff, an Edinburgh solicitor, confirmed that he was acting for the two men; and the Foreign Office acknowledged that it had given Libya a detailed list of assurances covering the treatment that the two suspects could expect while being held in Barlinnie prison, Glasgow. Colonel Gaddafi continued to insist that he would not bow to Western threats. On 11 November 1993 the Security Council passed Resolution 883 to attack the Libyan oil industry, the backbone of the Libyan economy.

By now Libya was enjoying considerable international sympathy and some surreptitious material support. What the United States frequently advertised as the will of the 'international community' was little more than Washington policy, meekly shadowed by France and Britain. A clear consensus on the Lockerbie issue could not be found in the Security Council, much less in the General Assembly. Washington clearly intended to push for whatever sanctions on Libya it could achieve, but few observers thought that this policy had much to do with a disinterested attack on international terrorism.

ANGOLA, NAMIBIA AND MOZAMBIQUE

The problems of Africa in the twentieth century are rooted largely in colonialism; from the times of naked military occupation, through the granting of power to white minority proxies, to the exploitative commercial arrangements whereby most of Africa is a net contributor to the wealth of the developed countries in the West. The unending African predicament runs through the whole continent, but some areas are more afflicted than others. The United Nations itself has developed a particular involvement in such states as Angola, Mozambique, Namibia (formerly South West Africa) and Somalia.

Angola, like Mozambique, went directly from fifteen years of bitter revolutionary war against European colonialism to civil and tribal conflict that, beginning in 1975, has lasted ever since. In Angola the MPLA (*Movimento Popular de Libertação de Angola*), based on the Kimbundu tribe, managed to form a government in the early days of independence. Washington had supported the Portuguese in their efforts to crush the indigenous uprisings. Thus John Marcum, an American scholar who visited the FNLA (*Frente Nacional de Libertação de Angola*) in the 1960s, commented: 'By January 1962 outside observers could watch Portuguese planes bomb and strafe African villages, visit the charred remains of towns like Mbanza M'Pangu and M'Pangala, and copy the data from 750-point napalm bomb casings from which the Portuguese had not removed the labels marked "Property U.S. Air Force".'[15] When, despite such characteristic US aid, the Portuguese colonial forces were defeated, a civil conflict soon broke out between the MPLA on the one hand and the FNLA and UNITA (*União Nacional para a Independencia Total de Angola*) on the other.

Washington moved quickly to support its chosen clients: the FNLA and UNITA – a move that stimulated Soviet and Cuban aid to the MPLA, and set the course for years of civil strife. In the US a House investigating committee admitted Washington's pivotal role in stimulating the conflict: 'this infusion of US aid, unprecedented and massive in the underdeveloped colony, may have panicked the Soviets into arming their MPLA clients'.[16] When the popular MPLA routed the US-backed factions, Henry Kissinger promised UNITA's Jonas Savimbi continued support if he maintained his military struggle against the government. The result was a bloody civil war with massive foreign intervention: by the CIA and US military personnel, be South African forces, by Soviet military advisers, and by thousands of Cuban troops. In September 1981, for instance, the Lisbon daily newspaper *Portugal Hoje* reported that South African forces were occupying parts of Angola.[17]

After President Reagan took office in January 1981 there was a dramatic increase in US aid to UNITA. In 1978 South Africa had agreed to give Namibia its independence but now, with support from the Reagan Administration, decided to renege on the agreement, so forcing both Namibia and Angola to suffer further years of war. In January 1986 Savimbi visited Reagan in the White House and was received as a hero; at that meeting

UNITA was promised US Stinger anti-aircraft and TOW anti-tank missiles, part of an annual $15 million military aid package. In June 1988 Savimbi was attacked by US Democrat Jesse Jackson as a tool of the South African regime. For years the United Nations tried to mediate in the various conflicts in the area, striving to accomplish the independence of Namibia and a settlement to the Angolan strife that would involve a withdrawal of all foreign troops, including the South Africans and the Cubans; but if settlements were to be agreed they would have to follow talks between Washington and Moscow. Also in June, while Jesse Jackson was attacking the residual colonialism in the region, Reagan was meeting Gorbachev in Moscow: the upshot was a statement that included a declaration of intent on the Angolan question. The aim was to resolve the situation by 29 September, the tenth anniversary of UN Security Council Resolution 435 which demanded a South African withdrawal from Namibia.

Now the negotiations began in earnest. Representatives of Angola, Cuba, South Africa and the United States held talks in London, then in New York, and finally in Geneva. The agreement signed on 5 August 1988 in Geneva and ratified three days later laid down a timetable for ending the wars in Angola and Namibia. In summary, it included the following important provisions:

- a ceasefire and withdrawal of the remaining six hundred South African troops;
- negotiations to establish a timetable for Cuban withdrawal and to address such matters as US and South African aid to UNITA, Soviet and Cuban aid to the MPLA, Angolan aid to the ANC, and how to fund the proposed UN peace-keeping force;
- the UN plan for Namibian independence to be put into operation on 1 November 1988, with elections to establish a Namibian constituent assembly by 1 June 1989;
- withdrawal of South Africa's 50,000 troops from Namibia, except for a 1500-man force in two southern bases;
- a UN force of 7500 to be sent to Namibia as a peace-keeping guarantee.

Many of the ingredients for continued conflict were left in place. Many observers doubted that South Africa would leave Namibia, a valuable colony; and aid would continue to be disbursed to the various client factions. The United Nations had assumed direct responsibility for Namibia (then South West Africa) in 1966, recognising SWAPO (the South West Africa People's Organisation) as representative of the Namibian people, but more than two decades were to pass before the significant achievement of the 5 August agreement. In fact, despite all the doubts, Namibia achieved its nominal independence in 1990. The Angolan situation remained largely unresolved.

In September 1992, after an uncertain sixteen-month ceasefire, it was announced that the MPLA and UNITA would form a coalition after nationwide elections.* As the date for the UN-sponsored elections approached there were many outbreaks of violence throughout the country, and growing doubts that the United Nations would be able to achieve an orderly transition to democracy. Already Jonas Savimbi was indicating that if he lost the elections he might be unwilling to accept the results: 'If UNITA does not win the elections, it [*sic*] has to be rigged. If they are rigged, I don't think we will accept them.' And there was also the problem of ensuring a fair ballot. The UN had placed some 800 observers around the country, using helicopters and planes to transport election materials and personnel to remote areas, but it was easy to see the UN effort as inadequate; for example, in the Mavinga municipality there were just two UN observers to monitor 84 polling stations. On 27 September 1992, two days before the first day of the two-day elections, a UN helicopter carrying observers crashed in Uige province, killing the four Russian crewmen and the eleven Angolan passengers.[18]

The MPLA, led by President Jose Eduardo dos Santos, won a majority, though smaller than the early results had suggested. Against expectations the elections had been well conducted, UN and independent observers praising the orderly conduct of the voting.[19] Soon Savimbi, bitterly resentful of the poll results (MPLA 49.5 per cent, UNITA 40.6 per cent), was giving a strident broadcast on the UNITA *Voice of the Black Cockerel* radio station: 'The MPLA wants to cling to power illegally, tooth and nail'; if, he added, the government refused to address the alleged vote-rigging then UNITA would be forced 'to take a position which might deeply disturb the situation in this country'.[20] Savimbi praised the UN assistance with the cease-fire and the elections but declared that he might not accept the judgement of the international community that the vote had been fair. On 5 October the UNITA generals withdrew from the newly unified Angolan armed forces.

* Both factions were soon discounting the possibility of a coalition between the MPLA and UNITA, though each side agreed to give posts to leading members of the defeated opposition.

The UN Security Council then sent a crisis mission of four senior representatives (from the United States, Russia, Morocco and Cape Verde) to Angola in an attempt to persuade Savimbi not to plunge the country into a fresh civil war. Margaret Anstee, a special representative of the UN Secretary-General, later commented that the meeting had gone well ('I think that we're making some progress'). A few days later the South African Foreign Minister Pik Botha declared his support for Savimbi's charges of electoral fraud. The UNITA leader had succeeded in delaying the MPLA announcement of final victory, and by now the situation was rapidly deteriorating. The United States had long backed Savimbi. Now that he had so clearly demonstrated his hostility to democracy, how would Washington respond? On 20 October 1992 the US State Department acknowledged that UN observers had found 'no major evidence of systematic or widespread fraud'; and then called for a fresh presidential election.

Within days the civil war had started again: UNITA forces surrounded Luanda, the Angolan capital; British workers in Angola were seized; and the UNITA movement took control of the provincial capital of Huambo, at the same time attacking other cities. The UN Security Council demanded an immediate end to the violence and approved a resolution threatening action against any party that violated the UN-orchestrated peace accords. By the beginning of November the death toll in Luanda alone was put at around 1000, though by that time a shaky cease-fire had been established. On 6 November the United Nations chief peace-keeper Marrack Goulding arrived in the Angolan capital in an attempt to prevent a return to full-scale civil war. Already thousands of tonnes of food and medical supplies had been stolen from UN warehouses by UNITA, and the UNICEF leader in Luanda, Nicholas Alipui, commented that if 'under duress our items are used for military purposes, there is nothing we can do'.

UNITA now controlled various regions, compounding health and food-supply problems. Angolan officials were refusing to allow UN distribution of food to such regions until the rebels agreed to accept the UN-sponsored elections and their results. Already UN officials were warning that the endemic tuberculosis in the north-east was being exacerbated by lack of medicines. Margaret Anstee, after further talks with Savimbi on 24 November, said that the meeting 'was very constructive, we are making progress'. Days later, a further cease-fire was agreed, only to be broken with heavy fighting around Uige and a further slide into civil war. UN officials, desperate to keep negotiations alive, spoke of skirmishes and manoeuvres but were reluctant to mention war. By now there were widespread criticisms of the UN posture. Why had the United Nations treated UNITA with kid gloves? Why had there been such a lukewarm response to Savimbi's violation of the peace accords? Why were there no blue helmets on the ground to guarantee the peace?[21] There were also ample signs of US equivocation. On 8 October Herman Cohen, the Assistant Secretary of State for African Affairs, told Congress that Washington would establish diplomatic relations with Angola once the UN had certified the elections. UN Resolution 785 (30 October 1992) had endorsed the elections as free and fair, but Washington still refused to give recognition to the democratically elected government in Angola.

In early January 1993 UN Secretary-General Boutros-Ghali issued a fresh condemnation of renewed violence in Angola, and also deplored the search of a UN camp in southern Angola by MPLA police. At the same time the Security Council seemed reluctant to take further action to bring the conflict to an end, declaring that it would be reluctant to extend its monitoring mission beyond the end of the month without evidence of effective peace negotiations. Already the UN presence had been criticised as paltry: only 210 military observers and 77 police observers in a country at war (more than ten times this number had been sent to Mozambique).

With the spread of the war, there were significant MPLA gains: UNITA forces were pushed out of cities they had occupied, and by mid-January Savimbi himself had been forced to flee. Even now there were signs that the UN representative, Margaret Anstee, was struggling to maintain an even-handed approach between UNITA and the MPLA (that is, between the democratically elected government, sanctioned by UN Security Council Resolution 785, and the rebels): Savimbi had 'been absolutely consistent with me. He says he wants peace, and that he don't believe there is an answer in war. There have been many things that have happened that have thrown doubt on that, but also thrown doubt on both sides.' In late-January 1993 it was reported that UN Secretary-General Boutros-Ghali was resigned to the failure of the peace-keeping efforts in Angola, and that the United Nations personnel might be withdrawn from the country. He recommended that all UN staff should leave by 20 April unless a ceasefire had been achieved and realistic negotiations begun. Now one million Angolans were facing starvation. Soon there was growing evidence of the UN pull-out, with the United Nations Angola Verification Mission (UNAVEM), headed by Margaret Anstee, closing 41 of its 67 monitoring stations throughout the country. At the United Nations headquarters in New York the Angolan Foreign Minister, Venacio de Moura, provided evidence of South African involvement in the illegal resupply of UNITA forces.[22]

At the end of February UNITA representatives failed to arrive for projected peace talks in Addis Ababa. The meeting was postponed at a time when Huambo was suffering new devastation at the hands of UNITA forces equipped with helicopters and a wide range of sophisticated weapons. One consequence of UNITA's failure to attend the new talks was mounting pressure on President Bill Clinton to recognise the legitimate MPLA government. Within days the city of Huambo had fallen to UNITA, whereupon the rebels said they were willing to attend fresh peace talks in Geneva. Now Savimbi, long touted by Washington as a model African democrat, was rumoured to be in hiding in South Africa, and the Clinton Administration was declaring that there were no obstacles to the establishment of relations with the elected Angolan government. On 25 March the US Congress criticised Clinton's tardy response to the worsening civil war in Angola, and called for US recognition of President Jose dos Santos's elected government. At the same time a joint resolution of the Senate and the House of Representatives condemned the refusal of Savimbi to negotiate a ceasefire, noting that the Savimbi-provoked conflict had resulted in '20,000 deaths, more than 1 million persons displaced, and 3 million persons threatened by hunger, disease, and land-mines'. A few days later it emerged that *in 1987 South Africa had come close to dropping an atomic bomb on Luanda.*[23] Fresh peace talks resulted in a further stalemate as UNITA refused to give up the areas that it still controlled.

On 19 May 1993 the Clinton Administration formally recognised the MPLA government of Angola, so reversing long-standing US policy. Washington had supported the Portuguese colonial power, funded efforts to destabilise the MPLA government, and impaired the UN efforts to counter Savimbi's illegal rejection of the 1992 election. Now, with a dramatic volte-face, Washington had brought new hope to the region. There still remained the need for the UN Security Council to act decisively to bring peace to Angola.

With much of the attention of the world focused on such regions as Somalia and Bosnia, the Angolan conflict continued to claim a dreadful human toll. On 8 July representatives of Russia, Portugal and the United States convened in Moscow in an attempt to end a war that was then resulting in around 1000 deaths a day through direct military action and the consequent starvation it brought in its wake. Most of the deaths were being caused by shellfire, disease and hunger in the crowded towns under siege by Savimbi's UNITA forces, for many years trained and equipped by the United States. An agreement with UNITA had allowed the UN to fly food relief to all areas but now relief planes had been prevented from flying to Cuito, Malanje and Menongue. UNITA, in direct violation of the UN-brokered election, now controlled Huambo, a provincial capital, Soyo, a centre for on-shore oil production, and other towns.

The World Food Programme had suspended emergency aid flights after one of its aircraft had been hit by UNITA forces; a new agreement was being sought, but WFP officials were not optimistic. One UN estimate suggested that some 100,000 people had been killed in fighting over the previous six months, with two million more now in danger of starvation. It was increasingly acknowledged that an effective arms embargo on UNITA, long a US proxy and with friends in Portugal and South Africa, was a totally unrealistic option. In any case, there were still massive stockpiles of arms supplied by Washington through the 1980s. In August, with a rapidly escalating food shortage, the United States asked the World Food Programme to scale down its demands because of the cost.

In September 1993 the UNITA rebels launched a diplomatic campaign in an attempt to prevent a Security Council sanctions initiative that would tip the balance of power in the region. Such an initiative – in any event likely to be diluted by Washington – would close UNITA's offices in Europe and the United States (still at this time allowed to function despite Savimbi's violation of UN measures), jam UNITA's clandestine radio (set up by the CIA), and block Savimbi's supply lines from Zaire and South Africa. At this time it seemed unlikely that the US-dominated Security Council would have any appetite for taking decisive action against a long-term Washington proxy.

The course of events in Mozambique followed the same broad pattern. After a long guerrilla war, FRELIMO (*Frente de Libertação de Moçambique*) succeeded in expelling the Portuguese colonial power, whereupon external forces – notably from Rhodesia and South Africa – set about trying to overthrow the new nationalist government. The Rhodesian Central Intelligence Organisation set up RENAMO (the Mozambique National Resistance Organisation) to begin an armed insurrection against the FRELIMO regime. When Rhodesia became independent in April 1980, RENAMO was forced to move its bases to South Africa. The rebel forces were transported by South African ships, planes and helicopters, and were soon in a position to establish bases in Mozambique itself. When, on 19 October 1986, the Mozambique President Samora Machel was killed in a plane crash in South Africa, there was widespread suspicion of foul play; there were suggestions of South African sabotage and even that South African aircraft had shot down the plane.

After years of armed struggle the FRELIMO regime moved significantly to the right, abandoning much of its earlier socialism and taking steps to establish a free-market economy on the Western model. However, this gradual shift did not generate a secure peace. Talks in September 1992 between President Joachim Chissano and the RENAMO leader Alfonso Dhaklama were expected to yield a peace deal, but Dhaklama pulled out at the last minute. Again there was the familiar pattern of millions of people put at risk of dislocation, famine and disease. The UN involvement, as in Angola, had failed to achieve a settlement. The United Nations continued to press for peace talks, and on 4 October Chissano and Dhaklama both put their names to an agreement. But there were doubts that the peace would hold.

Within weeks fighting had again broken out, with RENAMO occupying the port of Angoche in the northern province of Nampula. The offensive continued and more towns fell to the fresh rebel onslaught. A new truce was arranged and also a new UN-brokered peace agreement. By now it was reported that the war was coming to an end, after some one million people had been killed in the sixteen-year conflict. On 16 December 1992 the UN Security Council voted to send 7500 troops and civilians to Mozambique to monitor the cease-fire and the planned elections. It was estimated that UN Operations in Mozambique (ONUMOZ) would cost more than $330 million by the time its mandate expired at the end of 1993. In the event, because of the UN's slow progress, the planned elections were delayed until May 1994; by March 1993 none of the UN-authorised 7500 personnel had arrived in Mozambique to organise the demobilisation of the contending forces. The UN representative in Mozambique, Aldo Ajello from Italy, stated that the United Nations would not make the same mistakes that were made in Angola: the election campaign would not begin until all the government and RENAMO forces were disarmed. In late 1993 the situation remained fraught but the fragile truce was still holding. It was increasingly clear that Savimbi's UNITA, if unchecked, would work to undermine both the planned Mozambique elections and South Africa's projected transition to majority rule.

THE EL SALVADOR AGONY

For more than two decades the United States sustained in El Salvador – one state among several unfortunately situated in Uncle Sam's 'backyard' – a sequence of regimes interested only in the repression of the people to the economic advantage of wealthy Salvadorean families and US corporations. Washington pursued its task in this region by massive injections of military aid, by training soldiers and interrogators, and by sanctioning the use of death squads. From 1980 to 1986 the United States supplied El Salvador with more than $2 billion in aid, 85 per cent of which yielded weapons of various types: planes, helicopters, small arms, machine guns, napalm bombs, oxygen reduction bombs, cluster ('flesh-shredding') bombs, and much else besides. The widespread use of terror affected all sections of society, while death squad leaders – in particular, Roberto d'Aubuisson – were acknowledged as such by US personnel and other observers. Thus Robert White, former US ambassador to El Salvador, testified before the House Subcommittee on Western Hemispheric Affairs:

> From the first day in office the Reagan White House knew – beyond any reasonable doubt – that Roberto d'Aubuisson planned and ordered the assassination of Archbishop Oscar Arnulfo Romero . . . The administration of President Carter classified ex-Major Roberto d'Aubuisson, accurately, as a terrorist, a murderer, and a leader of death squads.

The 1980 Annual Human Rights Report of the Council for Hemispheric Affairs labelled El Salvador and Guatemala the worst human rights violators in Latin America: neither regime would have lasted a month without prodigious US military aid. In 1981 a US Congressional delegation visited the region and produced a report that includes testimony from refugees on how the Salvadorean army bombed and burned villages, raped children before bayoneting them, shot defenceless peasants from helicopters, and massacred fleeing civilians. The journalist Edouard Bailby reported how the refugees hid in the forests in fear of 'the killer commandos who come from El Salvador'; just as David Blundy of *The Sunday Times* recounted that the Salvadorean army was engaged in the 'mass extermination of thousands of peasants'. This grim catalogue of repression and massacre, today well attested and well documented, was long of concern to human rights groups and to the United Nations. For many years no action was possible since El Salvador was one of Washington's key client states.

After persistent efforts, the United Nations managed to arrange fresh talks between the El Salvador government and the popular leaders of the left-wing guerrilla group, the FMLN (Farabundo Martí National Liberation Front). In March 1990 UN Secretary-General Perez de Cuellar presided over a ceremony in Geneva at which the two sides agreed to negotiate a speedy cease-fire to be supervised by the United Nations, a framework for building democracy, the improvement of human rights, and the reintegration of FMLN members into civilian life. Shafik Handal, a senior FMLN commander, noted that the involvement of the United Nations had provided 'a degree of seriousness and weight lacking in the past'. The breakdown of negotiations the previous October in San José, the Costa Rican capital, had been followed by the bombing of trade union headquarters in which ten people had died, and the launch of a new FMLN offensive; in November came news of the notorious murder of six Jesuit priests by Salvadorean army personnel. Now it was being recognised that neither the FMLN nor the government could win a military victory and that a peaceful solution might be the best option for the war-weary factions. On 26 July 1990 the two sides signed a human rights agreement under UN auspices, at a time when government-backed death-squad killings were on the increase, according to a report by Amnesty International. At least 45 people were murdered between January and August, exceeding the previous year's total: 'The extent and nature of the abuses and the fact that human rights violations have been committed with almost total impunity under this and previous governments has left little doubt of official complicity.' In November, while the FMLN was launching fresh attacks on military installations, the UN General Assembly adopted by acclamation a resolution calling on the guerrillas and the government to continue their peace talks. At the same time Perez de Cuellar appealed to the rebels for restraint.

In February 1991 it became increasingly clear that a principal obstacle to the success of the fragile peace talks was President Cristiani's unwillingness to reform his US-backed army. The UN mediator, Alvaro de Soto, produced a working paper to fix a timetable for army reform but it seemed unclear how government compliance could be achieved. On 10 March elections were held to choose a new parliament and municipal authorities, under UN-framed rules agreed by all parties; but the OAS (Organisation of American States), monitoring the procedures, had estimated that some half million Salvadoreans might be prevented from voting in view of persistent government violations of human rights. Four days before the election, the UN Economic and Social Council expressed 'its serious concerns at the persistence of politically motivated violations of human rights, such as summary executions, abductions and enforced disappearances'.

An unprecedented 121-strong UN human rights mission (ONUSAL) began work in El Salvador in July 1991 to monitor the government/FMLN agreement reached the previous year. The mission was intended to monitor the cease-fire, once achieved, and to pressure both sides into observing their human rights obligations. This was the first UN initiative of its kind, designed in part to discourage violence against the civilian population (a UN official commented: 'The mere fact of being here is a dissuasive element'). Washington, now providing an extra $21 million military aid to the government, was unenthusiastic about the ONUSAL initiative: 'The US is not impartial in this whole thing', observed a source close to the negotiations. 'They support the talks but they are an ally of the government. They only speak to one side, which affects their view of the process.'

At the end of 1991, during the final hours of Perez de Cuellar's ten-year period as UN Secretary-General, the parties signed an agreement to end the civil war that had claimed some 70,000 lives. The ceasefire would begin on 1 February, the FMLN guerrilla forces would be broken up and the Salvadorean armed forces would be reduced by 50 per cent. The agreement, achieved on New Year's Eve, signalled a fresh optimism in the country, with the rebels even prepared to give Washington the benefit of the doubt. Thus Jorge Melendez, a top FMLN commander, declared: 'The North Americans are now clearly interested all over Latin America to reform military dictatorships and police forces that are barrels of rotten apples hiding criminals and drug traffickers.'[24] But there were still immense difficulties to overcome. In a report released in September 1992 the Washington-based human rights group Americas Watch criticised the ONUSAL mission for being 'timid in openly criticising the government on human rights matters, even when its own investigations have pointed to state involvement in abuses'. In particular, 'With its public silence, ONUSAL – far from doing anything to break the cycle of impunity – runs the risk of contributing to it.'*

After various delays in the peace process, the government agreed on 10 October to purge its forces by 15 December, and the FMLN leaders agreed to dismantle their forces by that date. Tension was increased for a time when a right-wing death squad issued a threat that it would kill FMLN leaders; but soon, it accordance with the negotiated settlement, the guerrillas were destroying their weapons under the careful scrutiny of UN officials. FMLN leaders submitted an inventory of their arsenal (5200 pieces of equipment, plus dozens of anti-aircraft missiles) before – to cries of 'Long live the FMLN' – publicly destroying machine guns and other items. In December a final 2000 guerrillas handed their rifles to UN peace-keepers.

In February 1993 the UN Economic and Social Council issued the report of Pedro Nikken, the 'Independent Expert on El Salvador' appointed by the Secretary-General to investigate the human rights situation.[25] In addition to reporting on continuing extrajudicial executions, attacks, death threats and other matters, the report notes the earlier agreement to establish a Commission on the Truth to investigate, amongst other things, the responsibility for human rights abuses during the period of the civil war. In March the UN Secretary-General Boutros-Ghali issued a four-page statement (SC/5570,

* There were interesting similarities between UN derelictions in Angola and El Salvador: both UNAVEM and ONUSAL displayed a manifest tilt in favouring the erstwhile US proxies, in refraining from robust criticisms of the manifest illegalities of UNITA and the Salvadorean government.

18 March 1993) welcoming the report of the Commission on the Truth. President Cristiani urged postponement of elements of the report, fearing the impact of its contents. Here it was: a 600-page document finally establishing the guilt of the US-backed Salvadorean army in a horrendous catalogue of human rights abuses.[26] The El Salvador Deputy President, Francisco Merino, described the UN report as 'absolutely insulting'.

The UN Truth Commission had established the factions, and in many cases the individuals, responsible for the bulk of the atrocities through the period of the twelve-year civil war; but there were few signs that any action would be taken against the rapists, torturers and murderers. President Cristiani had offered an amnesty to all the guilty parties, eager above all to praise the historic role of the Salvadorean army: 'The soil of this country has been bathed by the blood of the best soldiers, fertilising in this way the wish of the Salvadorean people to live in peace and freedom.' There would be no action against the named individuals[27] now known to be responsible for a catalogue of atrocities. Nor would any attempt be made to arraign a principal culprit – the United States – before any judicial body or before the court of world opinion. The Truth Commission was too timid by far to charge Ronald Reagan, George Bush and other leading politicians and policy-makers with complicity in a whole range of atrocities in El Salvador. Thus Harold Pinter, writer and political activist, notes: 'there is another and quite substantial body of people which also walks free, indeed has not been charged. This body includes the American "military advisors", the CIA, Elliot Abrams, former head of the US Latin American Desk, Jeane Kirkpatrick, former US ambassador to the United Nations, former Secretary of State Al Haig, and ex-Presidents Reagan and Bush.'[28] The evidence of US complicity is substantial and cannot be gainsaid.[29]

THE ISRAEL EXCEPTION

It is now widely perceived that Israel enjoys a unique relationship with the United Nations. Despite its failure to comply with a host of UN resolutions no action is ever taken – beyond private talks and public appeals – to force compliance: there is never the real possibility of UN sanctions against Israel, much less the prospect of a Security Council-sanctioned use of force. The most glaring example of Israeli non-compliance is its rejection of Resolution 242 (22 November 1967), but there are many other examples. Israel is currently in violation, to a greater or lesser extent, of Resolutions 338, 465, 476, 478, 672, 673 and 681. One of these, Resolution 681, is of particular relevance to a violation that was to be perpetrated in the evolving circumstances of the so-called New World Order. Resolution 681(3), approved on 20 December 1990, 'Deplores the decision by the Government of Israel . . . to resume the deportation of Palestinian civilians . . . .' It would not be long before a further act of deportation would offend the conscience of the world and lead to a further act of Israeli non-compliance with a Security Council resolution.

After further alleged actions by Hamas, the extremist Palestinian organisation acting in the occupied territories, the Israeli authorities sealed off the West Bank and the Gaza strip on 14 December 1992 in the search for Muslim terrorists. Three days later, the Israeli government went ahead with the mass deportation of 383 Palestinians thought to be Hamas supporters; 34 more Palestinians from the Ketziot prison in southern Israel were deported a few hours later. The Israeli army escorted the deportees to Israel's northern border and deposited them, with a little food and water, in Israel's self-styled security zone in southern Lebanon. Even Washington felt obliged to condemn this action of one of its most favoured client states. The US Secretary of State Laurence Eagleburger sent a message to the Israeli government expressing 'strong objections' to the act, which was seen as a flagrant violation of international law. The UN Security Council joined in condemning the deportation and in unanimously approving Resolution 799, a unique US-supported denunciation of Israel's further violation of international law.

This important resolution notes that Israel, 'in contravention of its obligations under the Fourth Geneva Convention of 1949, deported, on 17 December 1992, hundreds of Palestine civilians from the territories occupied by Israel since 1967, including Jerusalem'; and further:

> Strongly condemns the action . . . Reaffirms the applicability of the Fourth Geneva Convention of 12 August 1949 to all the Palestinian territories occupied by Israel . . . Reaffirms also the independence, sovereignty and territorial integrity of Lebanon . . . Demands that Israel, the occupying Power, ensure the safe and immediate return to the occupied territories of all those deported . . . .

The resolution also requested the Secretary-General to send a representative to discuss the serious situation with the Israeli government, and to report back to the Security Council. In a formal statement UN Secretary-General Boutros-Ghali commented that he had learned of the Israeli action with 'grave concern'. The UK Foreign Office, speaking for Britain as EC President, declared that the Israeli action was a violation of international law.

Few observers thought that Israel would take any notice of the widespread outrage and the unambiguous attitude of the United Nations. One diplomat was quoted: 'On past form, it is unlikely they will comply. The pattern has always been that Israel hears the UN resolution and then does what it intends to do anyway.'[30] In the early hours of the morning the deportees had been dumped in a wilderness, with no obvious means of support; but, significantly enough, neither any Western power nor the United Nations was prepared to suggest punitive action against Israel in the event of deliberate non-compliance with Resolution 799. Bill Clinton, at that time US President-elect, commented that he was 'concerned'. Soon the Lebanese government was stating its unwillingness to accept the deportees or to underwrite the Israeli action by feeding them. When sympathy actions were staged in the Gaza strip, Israeli troops fired on the protesters, killing a ten-year-old girl and five other Palestinians.

After some initial hesitation, the Israeli Supreme Court rejected an appeal from the Palestinians that the deportations be reversed, and the projected Middle East peace process seemed increasingly fragile. Still no serious effort was being made to put pressure on Israel to observe its obligations under international law and the demands of Security Council resolution. The United Nations aid agency, UNRWA, protested against the shootings in the occupied territories which had now resulted in several child deaths, though the protest had no discernible effect on the Israeli posture. On 25 December the Israeli prime minister, Yitzhak Rabin, blocked Red Cross supplies bound for the Palestinian deportees. Few observers doubted that the Israeli government's own species of 'ethnic cleansing' would be resolutely implemented. Two days later, Rabin informed the visiting UN envoy James Jonah that the Israeli government had no intention of reversing the mass deportation: 'the Israeli government has decided to fight, without mercy, the terrorism, of Islamic extremists. I will not permit a single Israeli citizen to be in contact with the expelled.' The Israeli Foreign Minister, Shimon Peres, commented to Jonah that the Security Council resolution was 'one-sided in that it did not relate to the reasons the Hamas people were deported – it did not mention the murders [of Israeli soldiers by Muslim militants]'.

By the end of December, under mounting international pressure, there were signs that the Israeli government was prepared to compromise. On 29 December the Israelis agreed to let a Red Cross medical team through the Israeli lines to treat the ailing deportees if the Lebanese government allowed through a food convoy. Lebanon rejected the offer, declaring that James Jonah would be wasting his time if he were to raise the issue on his arrival from Israel. On 3 January 1993 the Palestinian deportees appealed to sympathisers to stop smuggling food to them because such action attracted Israeli shelling. Two days later Israeli Minister of Justice David Libai unexpectedly attacked the deportation decision: 'the authorities have given themselves the possibility to put people . . . on buses or on a boat and deport them without giving them any right to be heard to prove they are the right people . . .' At the same time UN Secretary-General Boutros-Ghali warned that he might recommend Security Council action to force compliance with Resolution 799.

Israel was now being forced to admit that at least some of the Palestinians had been deported in error. On 23 January RAF helicopters picked up seventeen deportees, most of them wrongly expelled, from the makeshift Palestinian camp; four of the men were sick and wounded. On 26 January Boutros-Ghali took the unprecedented step of declaring that the Security Council should take 'whatever measures are required' to force Israel to reverse its deportation order. 'There is a growing perception', said the Secretary-General, 'that the Council, by not pressing for Israeli compliance dose not attach equal importance to the implementation of all of its decisions.'[31] No one imagined that Washington would allow such a call to be approved in the Security Council, and so it proved. As international pressure grew for a UN debate on a possible sanctions resolution on Israel, the Israeli government moved to diffuse the issue by offering a compromise: perhaps as many as 100 deportees would be allowed to return, and the rest after only a year. The horse-trading, a manifest violation of Resolution 799, was enough to enable Washington to squash any residual thoughts about the imposition of mandatory sanctions on Israel. The Israeli proposal was obviously inconsistent with Resolution 799(4): '*The Security Council . . . demands that Israel . . . ensure the safe and immediate return . . . of all those deported.*' The US Secretary of State Warren Christopher commented: 'The US believes that this process is consistent with UN resolutions . . . further action by the Security Council is unnecessary and could even undercut the process under way . . .'[32]

Again the character of the Israel exception had been well demonstrated. Washington had not been quick to allow Saddam Hussein to pick and choose which Security Council resolutions he wanted to observe; yet Israel was seemingly licensed to violate international law and to ignore consequent UN resolutions. This was not helpful to the projected course of the Middle East peace talks. What was not widely known at the time was that parallel talks between Israel and the Palestine Liberation Organisation (PLO) were in progress, talks that were set to achieve a historic measure of agreement.

On 25 July 1993 Israel began a fresh military offensive against Lebanon with the declared aim of crushing the pro-Iranian Hizbollah groups in the south of the country. The massive offensive – by land, sea and air – in a matter of days brought the estimated number of displaced people to around 250,000, with hundreds of civilians killed and wounded. A UN official in southern Lebanon said that hundreds of houses had been destroyed over a four-day period. The Secretary-General of Hizbollah, Sheikh Hassan Nasrallah, declared: 'We will not back down no matter how big the sacrifices are . . . Neither Israel, America nor France can force us to submit to their will.' The United Nations was powerless to prevent the Israeli aggression, the largest Israeli invasion of Lebanon since the ill-fated 1982 incursion; and Washington did no more than urge restraint on both sides. A month later, with the high-profile Middle East peace talks apparently stalled, the details of secret Israel–PLO negotiations began to emerge.

Israel had ignored the United Nations on the Palestinian deportees (in mid-August a phased return was agreed), Lebanon had been subjected to a new aggression (with UN observers powerless to influence events), and the US-brokered peace talks were achieving nothing. Washington's failure to break the negotiation deadlock led to the United States being marginalised when Israel and the PLO reached accord in Oslo. The plan – at odds with everything that Washington had urged over the previous months – was quickly commandeered by the US as an excuse for a new spasm of White House theatre. On 13 September 1993 the Israeli prime minister Yitzhak Rabin and PLO leader Yasser Arafat shook hands in Washington to signal the new accord. The PLO would be granted a measure of autonomy in Gaza and in the Jericho region of the occupied West Bank, with further developments projected for the years ahead. The Palestinian movement was divided, with much of the Arab world uncertain how to react.

The United Nations had played no part in securing the historic agreement, whatever its merits; and for once Washington had been kept at arms length (until the time arrived for public advertisement). The Israeli–PLO accord, reached in secret in Norway, had been negotiated by only a few interested individuals, with many parties to the dispute excluded. Now, however, Washington had reclaimed its central part on the stage, with talk of even putting US troops into Golan ('to secure the peace'); and the UN-linked World Bank was declaring that it was keen to become involved in the new Middle East situation. The scene was set for a new chapter in the endless saga: there was much speculation about the new twist in the plot but it was easy to identify the principal players.

THE SOMALIA MANDATE

In the nineteenth century Somalia, like most of the rest of Africa, was subject to the European scramble for land. The British, the French and the Italians all built up interests in the region, a typical geopolitical circumstance that piled up problems for the future. In the Second World War the British conquered the Italian territories of Abyssinia, Somaliland and Eritrea; and in 1948 contemplated uniting the British and Italian Somali lands with the Ogaden. Here Britain was opposed by Washington and Moscow, both making their own strategic calculations. Italy was told to prepare Italian Somaliland (Somalia) for independence in 1960: on 1 July of that year Somalia and British Somaliland united to form a homogenous independent nation. For a brief time a multiparty democracy was in place, soon to be overthrown by the Soviet-backed army. In 1974, Haile Selassie was deposed in Ethiopia (erstwhile Abyssinia) while fighting a war with Somalia. The new Ethiopian government swung to the left, whereupon Somalia quickly abandoned its pro-Soviet stance and looked for support from the West.

Thus Somalia, originally carved up between the European colonial powers, became a pawn in the Cold War. Its protracted confrontation with (now) Cuban-backed Ethiopia had a devastating effect on the country; in one period in the late 1970s the Somalis lost 8000 men, three-quarters of their tanks and half their planes. Somalia, now run by an increasingly authoritarian government, was set for the long slide into chaos and famine in the 1980s and beyond.

The UN presence in Somalia was never a happy one. The desultory efforts of the United Nations in the 1980s to achieve a peaceful settlement to the civil strife, to cope with the flood of refugees and to bring order to the country were always inadequate. Until the 1990s the Somali question was never a priority on the agenda of the Security Council, and even when the UN efforts were increased there was much criticism of UN 'bungling' in Somalia. It was acknowledged that Somalia represented one of the world's worst man-made disaster areas, and the UN impact continued to be desultory. By January 1992 critics of the United Nations were charging that the international body, despite its huge resources, had not acted as an effective peace-maker, had not brought adequate humanitarian relief, and had even hampered the efforts of the other aid agencies. Specifically, it was said that the visit of special UN representative James Jonah to Mogadishu on 3 January was ill-prepared, that UN staff did not consult with other aid workers, and that the UN's bureaucratic structure hampered its efforts to bring humanitarian assistance.[33] In July, eighteen months after the collapse of the central government authority in Somalia, the UN sent a small group of observers to monitor the fragile ceasefire agreed by the principal combatants, General Mohammed Farah Aideed and Ali Mahdi Mohammed. The deployment of the 47 UN observers was delayed following charges that a UN relief aircraft had been used to transport Somali banknotes printed in Britain and destined for the troops of Ali Mahdi.

Secretary-General Boutros-Ghali, now urging the Security Council to address the mounting tragedy in the country, acknowledged that the 'complexity of the situation . . . combined with almost total absence of central, regional or local government, pose enormous operational difficulties for the United Nations'. Between May and August the United Nations had shipped some 22,000 tonnes of food aid to Somalia, only a third of the total earmarked for the country. Now, with around 1.5 million Somalis close to starvation, UN aid was being suspended in Mogadishu because of the lack of security at the port. Said one head of a relief organisation: 'The UN are not in touch with the reality here. Their biggest mistake was to come late and then not do enough.' In August a 24-strong UN team, led by Peter Hansen of the Department of Humanitarian Affairs, arrived in Mogadishu to herald the projected 500-strong UN force intended to guard the convoys. At that time, weeks after their arrival, the batch of 47 observers had not yet left their compound because of security and other problems. Following a supportive resolution passed in the US Senate, Secretary-General Boutros-Ghali was said to be 'shopping for troops' to send to Somalia.

On 16 August 1992 Somali fighters attacked a UN relief ship, stripping it of fuel oil and stealing 200 tonnes of food aid. Aid workers declared – following a US promise to send 145,000 tonnes of extra food – that the priority must be to secure Mogadishu port, while at the same time the UN Brigadier-General Imtiaz Shaheen announced that he could not say when the 500 UN guards would arrive. On 28 August the first US aid flights, Hercules aircraft marked with Red Cross insignia, began arriving in the relatively secure town of Beletuen, 250 miles north of Mogadishu. At the same time an aid worker was commenting that the UN may be 'a million light years away from achieving anything'; said one source: 'The UN is still squabbling among itself about who is responsible for co-ordinating the UN operation. The United Nations Development Programme has refused to make its resources available to the Department of Humanitarian Affairs.' Mike Aaronson, overseas director of the Save the Children charity, commented that there was 'a shameful degree of in-fighting between UN agencies who pursue their own interests'. Boutros-Ghali was advised to visit Somalia himself 'to bang a few heads together'. Nicolas Hinton, the Save the Children director-general, stated on 29 August: 'The UN, in terms of its life after the Cold War, is a shambles. If you look at Somalia, what you see is an ill-equipped, ill-informed and unco-ordinated response. The UN and the international community should have acted months ago. Lack of attention and lack of planning have already cost thousands of lives.' Now it seemed clear that a lack of co-ordination between UNICEF, the UN Development Programme (UNDP), the UN High Commissioner for Refugees (UNHCR) and the World Food Programme was creating serious obstacles to progress. On 31 August the UN announced another 79,200 tonnes of food for Somalia; two weeks later, the first UN guards, 40 Pakistani soldiers, arrived in the country, with another 460 troops scheduled to be flown in by the end of September.

The US Navy now declared that it was sending 2100 Marines to Somali territorial waters to support US military planes transporting UN troops to Mogadishu. A clear escalation in the US/UN presence in the region had begun. On 29 October the UN special envoy Mohammed Sahnoun resigned, adding to the chaos in the country; he remarked that he was 'disappointed generally' with the 'lack of support' shown by the United Nations hierarchy. In November there were further criticisms that the UN peace-keepers were failing to protect the food shipments.[34] At the same time the US senators Paul Simon and Howard Metzenbaum, after a ten-day trip to Somalia, were urging the UN to accept the immediate use of American planes to transport 3000 UN troops to Somalia. By now the 500 scheduled troops had arrived in the country, with a further 3500 authorised by the Security Council. Now, for the first time, Washington was suggesting that it might send 30,000 troops to protect the aid convoys. Mark Bowden, African director of Save the Children, commented: 'It would put the whole relief operation in jeopardy, as well as the personal safety of our staff, and it would undermine or destroy the remaining local structures, such as the committees of elders, who should be supported and strengthened if there is to be any hope of Somali society being reconstituted.' The real need was for the United Nations itself to develop a coherent long-term strategy. President-elect Bill Clinton offered an opinion: 'What I think we should do is wait until the options are narrowed.'

It was now clear that Secretary-General Boutros-Ghali was moving to support a massive deployment of force in Somalia. In a letter to the Security Council he declared: 'There is now no alternative but to resort to Chapter VII of the Charter [which authorises the use of force if necessary]. The focus of the Council's immediate action should be to create conditions in which relief supplies can be delivered to those in need.' He noted that the Council could frame a resolution authorising the intervention of US troops, to be replaced later by a conventional UN peace-keeping force. The alternative would be to place the American troops under UN control, an option that Washington would never sanction. President-elect Clinton refrained from endorsing any large-scale commitment of American ground troops in Somalia.

On 3 December 1992 the UN Security Council voted to approve Resolution 794, authorising the further deployment of 3500 personnel in the United Nations Operation in Somalia (UNOSOM), authorised by Resolution 775, and authorising also action under Chapter VII of the UN Charter, allowing Member States 'to use all necessary means to establish as soon as possible a secure environment for humanitarian relief operations in Somalia'. Washington had secured its blank cheque: it was authorised to send troops, whenever it wanted, to the African mainland. President Bush announced to the US troops that they would be 'doing God's work'; and took pains to assure Somalia and other African countries that the United States had no ulterior motives: 'We do not plan to dictate political outcomes. We respect your sovereignty and independence.' Baroness Chalker, the British Minister for Overseas Development, commented that the long-term political solution in Somalia was 'not the job of the American troops, that is the job of the UN'; British troops would not join the planned intervention in Somalia. President-elect Clinton, now prepared to support 'God's work', described the planned operation as a 'historic and welcome step'.

On 6 December the United Somali Congress, the most powerful of the military factions, warned of the danger of a 'new colonisation', and called for talks on the planned intervention. It was of some passing interest that some days after the UN vote in the Security Council Washington had not informed the UN peace-keeping force in Somalia of the planned American intervention; said one senior UN officer: 'We only heard about it on the radio.' Some aid workers were quoted as having doubts about the 'shoot to feed' policy.[35]

Early on the morning of 8 December 1992 American troops came ashore to seize Mogadishu's airport and other important sites as the first stage of the UN-authorised intervention. The forces of the media were already well positioned, eager to report the arrival of the US troops. One reporter was told, 'Get your hands up!', while dozens of troops walked up through the dunes into the glare of television lights. It was a historic military intervention, the first in history where television staff had secured the beachhead before the troops. A top UN official in Mogadishu commented: 'The operation stinks of arrogance. All this bullshit about 80 per cent of food being looted and all that – it's all very well stage-managed by the United States. That's why there is no co-ordination with the UN or the relief agencies. This whole operation is a test case for future conflict resolution. It's as if the

US had a new vaccine they wanted to test. Now they have found an animal to test it on.'[36] President-elect Bill Clinton observed that the mission 'has merit, and an artificial timetable cannot be imposed upon it'.

The impact of the mission, 'Operation Restore Hope', was uncertain in the weeks that followed. Some Somalis were successfully disarmed, including ones who had been guarding UN food convoys, fresh tensions developed between Washington and the United Nations over the precise role of the American troops,[37] and there seemed little chance that the US-imposed administration would survive an American departure. Some of the food convoys were offered effective protection but whole areas of the Somalian hinterland remained unaffected by the US presence. On 31 December President George Bush arrived in Somalia, having announced 'the concern that all Americans feel . . . These are humanitarian concerns . . . it is proper that the president show this concern to the people over there.' Early in January large-scale clan fighting broke out again in Mogadishu and ordinary Somalis despaired at the failure of the troops to disarm the various warring factions. Said one Somali university lecturer, an erstwhile supporter of the intervention: 'If the Americans are not going to take those people's guns away, then they may as well pack up and go home.' Two days after President Bush's departure, UN Secretary-General Boutros-Ghali arrived in Mogadishu: as the UN headquarters were pelted with stones, he was forced to take refuge with US Marines. It was obvious that the UN-backed force had failed to establish order in the Somali capital, even in the region where the US troop concentrations were at their strongest.[38]

There were frequent eruptions of violence in Mogadishu and the surrounding areas. A number of Somali gunmen were shot dead by US Marines in the capital; and on 13 January, as peace talks foundered, an American soldier was killed in an ambush of a night patrol near Mogadishu airport. By February 1993 there were growing signs that Washington was prepared to hand over the peace-keeping task to the United Nations. According to Farouk Mawlawi, a UN spokesman in Somalia, the UNOSOM force 'will deploy in all of Somalia – the north, north-east, north-west and along Somalia's borders with Kenya and Ethiopia'. There was consensus, he declared, that the proposed deployment would go ahead. Most US troops were now scheduled to leave before the end of April. On 24 February US troops killed at least nine people trying to storm the US embassy in Mogadishu. Now Washington was seeking a way out of the Somali chaos.[39] Now, said a senior UN official, the US was down-playing everything, 'because it's the only way they are going to get out of here'. Dr Abdi Mohamed Elmi Hangun, a Somali surgeon at the Mogadishu Benaadir hospital commented: 'The US were welcomed with flowers, but they will leave with blood on their uniforms.'

At a special press conference on 2 March 1993, the American special envoy to Somalia, Robert Oakley, acknowledged that aid workers and UN forces due to take over the relief effort would face a worsening crime problem despite the American intervention.[40] Said a headline on one report, 'They came, they fed – and now they're getting the hell out.'[41] The American troops were disillusioned and Washington was no longer keen to foot the bill, some $40 million a day. On 26 March 1993 the Security Council authorised 'enforcement action by UNOSOM II to secure humanitarian relief operations throughout Somalia'.[42] Resolution 814, providing this authorisation, was unanimously adopted to allow the deployment of 20,000 UN peace-keeping troops 'to complete the restoration of peace there begun by the [US-led] Unified Task Force'.

This development represented a UN commitment of immense scope. It was a virtual mandate to rebuild the political institutions of a nation ('to provide humanitarian and other assistance to the people of Somalia in rehabilitating their political institutions and economy and promoting political settlement and national reconciliation'), a commitment that went far beyond the essential requirements of peace-keeping and the support of refugees. Resolution 794 had authorised the US intervention, an initiative that had achieved mixed results. Now Resolution 814, framed to embody a much enlarged mandate, had presented the United Nations with one of the greatest challenges of its history. It was not long before the doubts surfaced. The spokesman for one of the leading aid agencies in Somalia commented in May that judging by the track record of the United Nations 'it's going to be very worrying, because they have such bad organisation'.[43] Few observers thought that the fresh UN mandate, unprecedented in scope and ambition, had any realistic chance of success.

On 5 June fighting broke out in Mogadishu when UN soldiers inspecting an arms depot controlled by the 'warlord' General Mohamad Farah Aideed came under fire. Twenty-six Pakistani soldiers were killed and 50 wounded, with three American soldiers wounded: this was the bloodiest day in the history of UN peace-keeping. Soon there was disputation about the causes of the tragedy. Some Pakistani officials blamed the United Nations and the United States for failing to ensure that the peace-keepers were properly equipped. A Western military source in Islamabad commented: 'Pakistan was asked to send troops because it is a well-disciplined army. But the UN is incredibly amateurish. It hasn't got a proper military secretariat with competent advisers. They're a shower of bumbling amateurs.' One senior

Pakistani official stated that the Americans 'were supposed to provide us with cover and they didn't'.[44] On 6 June the UN Security Council unanimously authorised UNOSOM to use force against any factions opposing its presence in Mogadishu and elsewhere.

France, Germany and the United States now sent troop reinforcements to Somalia, partly reversing the US withdrawal, with Washington announcing that AC-130 attack aircraft were being sent to the region. The situation was now rapidly deteriorating: many aid workers were now either fleeing the country or moving into secure compounds, and there was a growing likelihood of further military conflict. On 12 June American aircraft equipped with 105 mm guns and rapid-fire cannon attacked a number of selected sites in Mogadishu; and the next day launched a fresh wave of attacks, including a missile attack on Radio Mogadishu, from which Aideed had been transmitting anti-UN propaganda. US Cobra and Black Hawk helicopters joined in the assault, repeatedly attacking arms dumps and other targets. The US forces suffered no casualties but the Somalis accused the attackers of killing civilians. In one incident an attack on an arms dump containing six rusting tanks hit a house, killing an eight-year-old Somali girl. The US-led action had been no more than a revenge attack, with no prospect of a useful outcome. Already there had been many civilian casualties, and hundreds of Somalis were taking to the streets chanting 'Down with the UN!' and 'Down with the US!'[45]

On 13 June Pakistani troops securely ensconced on rooftops in Mogadishu fired on thousands of unarmed Somalis protesting against US air strikes. Twenty people were killed, including women and a young boy whose head was blown off by a high-calibre machine gun. In Benadir hospital the dead bodies were stacked 'like rubbish'; people unavoidably stepped in the blood of the wounded; and many makeshift operations were attempted without anaesthetic.[46] The UNOSOM operation, effectively sabotaged by the brutal and ill-considered US actions, had gone disastrously wrong. Now the UN forces were in military confrontation with the Somali people. On 14 June 1993 leaflets began circulating in Mogadishu bearing the dreadful words 'UN peace-killers'.

This turn of events was being seen by some observers as a new 'Clinton Doctrine' whereby the United States would be an enforcer when UN peacekeeping operations run into trouble.[47] A short time after the killing and maiming of dozens of protesting Somalis, President Clinton declared: 'If UN peacekeepers are to be effective agents for peace and stability in Somalia and elsewhere, they must be capable of using force when necessary to defend themselves and accomplish their goals.' Moreover, the use of US air power was 'essential to send a clear message to the armed gangs . . . and to strengthen the effectiveness and the credibility of UN peacekeeping forces'. At the same time there was a growing feeling that Washington's much-hyped Operation Restore Hope had achieved little and that the West had done no more than bring a further dimension of chaos and misery to Somalia.

The Somali human rights activist Rakiya Omaar, a co-director of African Rights, has pointed out that the UN peace-keepers in Somalia have liberal rules of military engagement, making clashes with the local population inevitable. By late March around 300 Somalis had been killed, some 'in self-defence, many in suspicious circumstances and others in cold-blood'.[48] Mohamed Sahnoun, a former UN envoy to Somalia, criticised UN and US actions, nothing the 'total divorce between the UN and Somalis' and the 'perception . . . that the UN is a force of occupation and that there is a hidden agenda to make Somalia a UN trusteeship'.[49] On 17 June American AC-130 Spectre aircraft launched further attacks on selected targets in south Mogadishu. Now there were renewed US efforts to capture the 'warlord' Mohammed Farah Aideed, one of the Somali leaders responsible for the chaos in the country. The UN chief in Somalia, the retired US Admiral Jonathon Howe, urged General Aideed to give himself up peacefully 'in order to ensure his safety'. Throughout June there were frequent reports that UN forces were about to capture Aideed but his whereabouts continued to remain uncertain. Now the United Nations had taken the unprecedented step of offering a reward for Aideed's capture, and other Somali leaders were learning how to capitalise on his demonisation by the US-led forces. For instance, the self-styled interim president, Ali Mahdi Mohamed, declared: 'I am satisfied, though it has been late, that the world now realises that the only obstacle to peace is Aideed. Day by day he is losing his supporters . . . Today the peace process is on the right track. If they select me again, I am ready to serve as president.' By July there were growing signs that the US forces were preparing further military initiatives to root out the recalcitrant Aideed, though many observers thought that the only outcome would be more Somali casualties.[50]

On 2 July Italian tanks and armoured vehicles were involved in a military action that left three Italians killed and 21 others wounded. An 800-strong Italian force backed by 400 Somali police had come under sniper fire. The US Quick Reaction Force arrived 40 minutes later, bringing a company of Marines and two Cobra attack helicopters, though this was insufficient to prevent Somali fighters capturing an area formerly controlled by the Italians. At the same time a US soldier found guilty of negligently killing a Somali civilian was fined $450 and demoted.[51] A week later, six Somali UN workers were shot dead in an ambush. Now there was uncertainty about the announced *Bundeswehr* mission to Somalia and the Italians were considering a pull-out if UN objectives were not clarified. On 14 July the UN Secretary-General Boutros Boutros-Ghali effectively sacked Italy's military commander, General Bruno Loi, for insubordination, whereupon Italy's Foreign Minister, Beniamino Andreatta, declared himself 'outraged'. Such matters did little to bring harmony to the UN factions in Somalia.

In July 1993 the London-based human rights group African Rights published a catalogue of human rights abuses by the UN forces in Somalia.[52] The document describes abuses in Mogadishu, Kismayo and Belet Weyn, claiming that there is 'prima facie evidence that UNOSOM forces have committed a number of grave breaches of the Geneva Conventions'. Cases are cited of an attack on a political meeting, an attack on a hospital, the demolition of houses, the force relocation of Mogadishu residents, and the killing of unarmed civilians: 'United States, Pakistani, Tunisian, Italian and other troops have been responsible. These are not cases of undisciplined actions by individual soldiers, but stem from the highest echelons of the command structure.' It is acknowledged that General Aideed is contemptuous of basic human rights: 'This, however, cannot justify abuses of rights in response. Such abuses are not merely a crime; they are a blunder. UNOSOM has lost the moral high ground. Increasingly, Somalis regard UNOSOM as another faction and Admiral Howe as another warlord.' The African Rights report lists the constructive measures that should be taken.

There were signs also that such concerns were widely shared. The various aid agencies were now criticising the increased militarisation of the Somali situation; there were clear dissent among the various national factions in Somalia; and the UN itself was showing evidence of misgivings. In August there were reports of a confidential United Nations document questioning the legality of the UN's attacks against General Aideed. The report, written by US legal expert Ann Wright seconded to UNOSOM, states that attacks without warning should be stopped, even when they are against what are thought to be legitimate targets: 'From the legal, moral and human rights perspective, we counsel against conducting military operations that give no notice of attack to occupants of buildings.' Killing occupants without giving them a chance to surrender may be depicted by some organisations and UN Member States as 'nothing less than murder'.[53]

On 8 August four American soldiers were killed by a land-mine in south Mogadishu, whereupon President Clinton promised reprisals. Three days later, a joint statement issued by the international aid agencies stated that UN tactics had caused unnecessary civilian casualties and hindered the distribution of aid: the UN in Somalia 'must be held scrupulously to higher standards of conduct'. The International Red Cross noted that 54 Somalis had been killed in the bombardment of 12 July, when four foreign journalists were then killed by the enraged crowd. On 30 August a fresh attack was launched by US forces on what was thought to be buildings used by General Aideed. In the aftermath it was found that the raid – variously reported as 'bungled', 'botched', a 'fiasco', a 'farce' – had been made against a UN building.

Throughout September there were further US-led raids against Somali targets, including women and children. On one occasion the UN military spokesman Major David Stockwell declared that women and children were regarded by the US helicopters as being combatants whether they were 'armed or not' and as 'posing an imminent threat against our soldiers' in armoured vehicles.[55] In this attack hundreds of Somali civilians, including many unarmed women and children, were killed and wounded by US Cobra helicopters. Major Stockwell declared: 'Everyone on the ground in that vicinity was a combatant, because they meant to do us harm.' Yet again the US-led UN forces had emerged as no more than the most powerful warlord faction in the region. The international aid agencies, struggling to work to an entirely different agenda, could only observe with mounting despair the growing carnage that the Washington policy-makers had brought to a stricken land.

CAMBODIA AT THE CROSSROADS

The destabilisation of Cambodia begun by the US invasion of Vietnam (see Chapter 5) continued to exacerbate the tensions in the region throughout the 1970s and 1980s, with various contending factions struggling for power and with external states ever eager to push for strategic advantage. The United Nations seemed helpless to bring peace to Cambodia, or even to secure agreement among the Permanent Members of the Security Council on a proper course of action. By 1990 the UN had established aid channels to Khmer Rouge refugee camps along the Thai border but there seemed little scope for UN initiatives to reconcile the various warring groups.

It was now beginning to emerge that Washington had an interest in supporting the Khmer Rouge, the dominant element in the Cambodian coalition allowed to occupy a seat at the United Nations and the element widely reported as responsible for near-genocide in the late 1970s.[56] Now there was the prospect that the Khmer Rouge would be allowed to return to Phnom Penh to assume again the power it had been forced to abandon in 1979. In 1990 the United Nations drew up a peace plan under which there would be an expanded UN administration throughout the country until nationwide elections could be held. The scheme legitimised the Khmer Rouge as one of the contending parties and created grave doubts about UN concern for earlier atrocities in Cambodia. The UN plan, condoning what its own Special Rapporteur described as 'genocide . . . even under the most restricted definition', aimed to give the Khmer Rouge 'the same rights, freedoms and opportunities to take part in the electoral process' as any other party. In October 1991 the various factions – the Khmer Rouge, the Khmer People's National Liberation Front, Prince Norodom Sihanouk's forces and the government – all signed the UN-brokered plan that would bring Cambodia to democratic elections in 1993. In November Prince Sihanouk made a triumphal return to Phnom Penh after thirteen years of exile; now he was to head the Supreme National Council (SNC) for the run-up to the elections. Still it proved impossible to hold the ceasefire throughout this period. Months after the signing of the peace agreement the UN forces and officials were still only beginning to establish their authority on the ground. There was almost continuous fighting throughout 1991 and many serious outbreaks in the early months of 1992. In April the Khmer Rouge directed mortar fire at several villages, forcing some 20,000 villagers to flee to safety. Again the UN was blamed for its slow deployment of troops, while charges were also levelled against the Vietnamese forces still in the country. At the same time there were reasons for optimism: UN officials were slowly building up contacts with the Khmer Rouge and other factions, and even gaining access to guerrilla base camps to identify sites where the fighters were supposed to assemble and disarm.

In July 1992 the Supreme National Council seemed to reach an impasse, with Prince Sihanouk insisting on the dissolution of the government and demanding extra powers for the Council, and the Khmer Rouge complaining that its concerns for a 'balanced' implementation of the peace agreement were not being addressed. Hun Sen, the Cambodian Prime Minister, observed: 'we can't move forward or backward. If they continue like this, I think there will be a complete collapse.' In particular, it was increasingly recognised that Khmer Rouge obduracy would prevent the second phase of the UN operation, that demanding the regrouping of guerrilla forces in UN-supervised cantonments for the surrendering of weapons. By now the United Nations had deployed 14,000 troops in Cambodia, with 1500 police and thousands of civilians supplied to join the UN Transitional Authority in Cambodia (UNTAC). It still seemed uncertain whether UNTAC's basic task, that of creating a neutral political environment for the 1993 elections, would be accomplished.

After further disputation – and mounting pressure applied by Washington, Japan and other states – the Khmer Rouge attended a UN-sponsored joint military committee for the first time in three months. In October, despite continuing Khmer Rouge recalcitrance, UN officials began the registration of voters, beginning in Phnom Penh and then moving out into the countryside. By December more than 800 registration teams, comprising 40,000 Cambodian employees supervised by 400 UNTAC officials, were operating in every area of Cambodia. At the same time many reports suggested that Cambodia, unable to contain guerrilla intransigence, was on the verge of anarchy.[57] By December the United Nations had imposed trade sanctions on areas controlled by the Khmer Rouge and the Khmer Rouge responded by seizing six UN observers, to release them unharmed three days later. Then 21 UN peace-keepers were taken hostage in Kompong Thom province, while there were growing signs that the UN forces in Cambodia were failing to win the battle for hearts and minds.[58] Early in January Prince Sihanouk announced that he would end his co-operation with UNTAC and the Cambodian government in protest against UN impotence.

The Khmer Rouge was not the only disruptive element, with UNTAC officials forced to acknowledge the Phnom Penh government's involvement in the sharp rise of assassinations, harassment and political intimidation. On 7 January 1993, in conditions of mounting tension, UNTAC assumed extra policing powers, which invited fresh criticism from the *Cambodia Times*, the only national English-language weekly. At the same time the Phnom Penh government launched a fresh offensive against the Khmer Rouge, again threatening the UN peace operation with total collapse. The Khmer Rouge was beginning a campaign of 'ethnic cleansing' against ethnic Vietnamese; in April the Khmer Rouge killed three Bulgarian peace-keepers, and the government as continuing its murder campaign against selected political opponents.

The UN officials still doggedly carried out their allocated duties, registering voters as best they could, displaying notices to inform the voters about the candidates, and fortifying the UNTAC headquarters with high-mesh fencing, extra barriers and sophisticated security devices. Now the UN sights were lowered. The Paris peace accords had proposed 'free and fair elections in a neutral political environment'; now the UNTAC officials were prepared to accept a flawed poll, one that achieved a 'minimum standard of acceptability'.

On 10 April UN Secretary-General Boutros-Ghali, having arrived in Phnom Penh to observe progress, was forced to witness the desperate flight of Vietnamese fishermen, a mass exodus precipitated by a new wave of merciless Khmer Rouge attacks on men, women and children. On the morning of Boutros-Ghali's departure, armed men executed a volunteer Japanese electoral worker and his Cambodian interpreter as they drove through Phnom Penh. Now anti-rocket screens had been erected around the United Nations headquarters. There was a growing awareness, as time ran on, that the UN mandate in Cambodia was due to expire in August; whatever was to be accomplished had to be accomplished by then. As the time of the election approached there was mounting violence throughout the country. On 19 April the Khmer Rouge attacked a village to the west of the capital, killing one Bulgarian soldier and wounding two others; and now there was growing acknowledgement that the elections would be held in an increasingly anarchic and politically fragmented society. The UN resolve remained undimmed. Thus Georges Germanou, a senior UN official in Kompong, expressed the general view that nothing short of war should be allowed to disrupt the election: 'The deficiencies will be obvious, but it may prevent full-scale civil war.'

By May 1993 UN workers had been withdrawn from some areas as a precaution against further Khmer Rouge attacks; and, as Khmer Rouge forces occupied the provincial capital of Siem Reap, there were mounting fears throughout the country of a fresh guerrilla offensive. On 4 May a Japanese UN policeman was killed in an ambush, fuelling the debate in Japan about whether Japanese personnel should be involved in policing Cambodia. There was still no sign that the widespread violence was to be allowed to disrupt the planned elections.[59]

The first day of voting was 23 May, when more than 1.5 million Cambodians ignored guerrilla threats and monsoon rains to take part in the country's first democratic elections for more than for decades. UN troops supervised 1500 polling stations nationwide, searching voters for weapons and using metal-detectors to check bags and clothes. Many disruptive incidents were recorded. At one location a group of Khmer Rouge guerrillas fired at ballot boxes; mortar shells landed at one polling station, injuring two voters; and at another about 100 Khmer Rouge guerrillas held UN soldiers and officials hostage for an hour before releasing them. Still the election proceeded, suffering less disruption than many observers had anticipated. Yasushi Akashi, the UNTAC head, made a whistle-stop tour of the country and declared: 'I think this is a good beginning for new democracy in Cambodia.' There was some surprise that the Khmer Rouge had not managed to disrupt the elections, but it was acknowledged that peace was far from secure.[60]

As the first election results emerged it was obvious that many problems still remained. There had been disruption in some areas, various factions were making charges of voting irregularities, and – as far as could be judged – no faction had achieved a secure majority. When it became clear that the government had polled somewhat less than the royalist candidates it announced that three had been voting fraud in at least four of the country's 21 provinces. The government would not, it declared, recognise the result of the election unless the United Nations nullified the first result and held fresh elections in the disputed areas. The United Nations effort had so far cost $2 billion; and Cambodia was still at the crossroads.

In the months that followed there were sporadic outbreaks of violence, continuing political tensions and much political jockeying for position. UN officials urged the political leaders to form an interim administration based on the election results, under the head of state Prince Sihanouk. Yasushi Akashi declared himself satisfied with the fairness of the elections, while the Khmer Rouge continued to denounce the Cambodian People's Party (CPP) for failing to surrender power. A Khmer Rouge spokesman stated that Sihanouk's proposals were 'the only way to resolve the Cambodian problem'. On 10 June 1993 the CPP leader Hun Sen and other political leaders told UN officials that eastern provinces were threatening to secede unless demands for an independent examination of the election results were met (Sen: 'I can no longer control the situation'). At the same time anti-UN demonstrations were staged in the eastern provinces of Kompong Cham, Svay Rieng and Prey Veng, while some ferry operators refused to provide access to UN vehicles. A self-styled secessionist zone collapsed when its leader, Prince Norodom Chakrapong, fled across the border into Vietnam.

On 16 June, after two days of talks at Phnom Penh's royal palace, a communiqué from Prince Sihanouk announced the formation of a 'provisional national government' in which power would be shared equally by the royalist party (Funcinpec), which had won the election, and the CPP. Sihanouk declared as co-chairmen Hun Sen and one of Sihanouk's sons, Prince Renariddh. The announcement came as some relief to UNTAC officials, increasingly alarmed by secessionist efforts and sabre-rattling on all sides. It was not long, however, before fresh problems emerged. In early July a band of Khmer Rouge rebels seized the twelfth-century Preah Vihear temple on the Thai border, provoking threats by the interim government of a military counterattack (Sen: 'We are ready to retake the Preah Vihear temple if the Khmer Rouge will not withdraw'). Further conflict in the province led to UN officials fleeing into Thailand to escape a mortar barrage, whereupon they were captured by Khmer Rouge guerrillas and released a few days later.

The uncertainties remained. The $2 billion spent by the United Nations had seemingly made likely the restoration of Prince Sihanouk as an unelected head of state; the power of the Khmer Rouge was largely unaffected; the CPP, defeated at the polls, was set to maintain effective power; and the country was forced to cope with 120,000 displaced people and some 10 million unexploded mines. In one view the internationally recognised election, largely fruitless as it seemed, was the UN's ticket out of Cambodia. Few observers were optimistic about the future.

THE YUGOSLAV QUAGMIRE

The turmoil in what used to be Yugoslavia has its roots – like all political disputes – in history: in such matters as nineteenth-century Balkanisation, the rivalries of external powers, the Second World War, and the collapse of Eastern Europe. A central feature of the Yugoslavia quagmire is the historical circumstance of many mutually hostile ethnic groups living in close proximity or intermeshed in the same communities. It is significant that the doctrine of 'ethnic cleansing' was not invented in recent years. In one important account the celebrated journalist Robert Fisk tells how he was able to read some of the German and Croatian Ustasha files abandoned by the retreating *Wehrmacht* in 1945. Here were the

> hundreds of Croatian military orders appropriating the homes and property of Serbs . . . Ustasha officers recorded with Teutonic thoroughness the gift to their loyal followers of farms and smallholdings from which the original Serbian or Muslim owners had been driven. 'Cleansing' was the word used in the files, for these documents were written by the men who invented that dreadful expression.[61]

More recently, war broke out in Yugoslavia in August 1990, just six months after multiparty elections had brought to an end the Communist rule in Croatia and Slovenia. Already the scene was set for the slide into chaos (see Table 7.1). The new Croatian government of Franjo Tudjman, still dominated by erstwhile Communists, was soon denounced as the direct successor to the Ustashe, the pro-Nazi Fascists who had murdered thousands of Serbs in concentration camps throughout Croatia during the Second World War. At the same time Slobodan Milosevic was pressing for the maintenance of a centralised Yugoslav state under Serbian control. The Serbian leadership in Belgrade decided that Croatia had to be held at all costs, even if Slovenia was to be lost. Already the European Community

Table 7.1 Chronology of conflict in former Yugoslavia, 1990–4

1990	
February	Multiparty elections bring an end to Communist rule in Croatia and Slovenia
August	Fighting erupts in Yugoslavia
1991	
25 September	UN Security Council Resolution 713 calls for arms embargo on Yugoslavia
8 October	UN Secretary-General Perez de Cuellar appoints Cyrus Vance, a former US Secretary of State, as his Personal Envoy for Yugoslavia
15 October	Bosnia-Herzegovina declares itself a sovereign state
23 October	Serb leader Slobodan Milosevic presents plan for a Serb-controlled 'mini Yugoslavia' to include parts of Bosnia and Croatia
1992	
2 January	Cyrus Vance convenes a meeting in Sarajevo between military representatives of the Republic of Croatia and the Yugoslav People's Army. This leads to new UN Secretary-General Boutros-Ghali sending a group of military liaison officers to observe the ceasefire
15 January	EC recognises Croatia; UN peace plan implemented in Croatia; UN Secretary-General urges creation of UNPROFOR
21 February	Security Council passes Resolution 743 to approve creation of 14,000-strong UNPROFOR for initial twelve months
29 February	Bosnia-Herzegovina again declares national independence
2 March	Mass anti-war protests in Sarajevo as Serbian gunmen begin blockage of Bosnian capital
6 April	EC and United States recognise an independent Bosnia
7 April	Security Council passes Resolution 749 to authorise full deployment of UNPROFOR
12 April	Ceasefire agreed in Bosnia
21 April	Serbs begin artillery bombardment of Sarejevo
27 April	Milosevic declares that Serbia and Montenegro now constitute new Yugoslav state
5 May	Bosnian president and Yugoslav army sign truce

Table 7.1 Chronology of conflict in former Yugoslavia, 1990–4 (cont'd)

18 May	UN pulls out of Sarejevo because of fighting between Serb irregulars and Bosnian-Muslim forces
2 June	Milosevic temporarily halts the siege of Sarajevo; Serb forces attack UN relief convoy trying to reach Sarajevo
11 June	UN convoy reaches Sarajevo
17 July	Two-week ceasefire signed in Bosnia
19 July	Ceasefire breaks down
22 July	Bosnia and Croatia agree military co-operation
27 July	Boutros-Ghali urges enlargement of UNPROFOR mandate
7 August	Security Council passes Resolution 769 to authorise enlargement of UNPROFOR mandate
26 August	Start of London peace conference; sets up Geneva peace talks to be mediated by David Owen and Cyrus Vance
6 October	Security Council passes Resolution 779 authorising UNPROFOR to monitor the agreed arrangements
9 October	Security Council orders no-fly zone over Bosnia
14 October	Boutros-Ghali announces decision to appoint a commission of experts
28 October	Owen and Vance publish peace plan and new Bosnia map; Croats and Muslims accept new proposals, but not the Serbs
16 November	Security Council authorises naval blockade of Serbia and Montenegro to enforce fuel sanctions
1993	
8 January	Serbian troops kill Bosnian Deputy Prime Minister in UN convoy
12 January	Bosnian Serbs agree provisional end to war
20 January	Bosnian Serbs agree to Vance–Owen peace plan but fighting continues
28 February	US begins relief airdrops to Bosnian towns, including Cerska
2 March	Serbs take Cerska
5 March	UN commander General Philippe Morillon struggles to save besieged Srebrenica in eastern Bosnia as Serbs take surrounding villages

Table 7.1 Chronology of conflict in former Yugoslavia, 1990–4 (cont'd)

22 March	Bosnia charges Serbia and Montenegro with war crimes
25 March	Vance–Owen peace plan signed by Bosnia's Muslim President, Alija Izetbegovic
3 April	Vance–Owen peace plan rejected by Serbs
16 April	Srebrenica taken by Serbs
18 April	UN enter Srebrenica; peace agreement signed between Bosnian Serb commander, Bosnian army chief and the UN commander
25 April	Vance–Owen peace plan rejected by Bosnian Serb parliament
1 May	Peace talks open in Athens
2 May	Vance–Owen peace plan accepted by Bosnian Serbs, pending final approval by Bosnian Serb parliament; Britain declares intention to veto plan to arm Bosnian Muslims
4 May	NATO agrees plan to deploy 75,000 troops from US, UK, Russia and France to keep peace if Bosnian Serb parliament approves Vance–Owen plan
5 May	Bosnian Serbs rewrite Vance–Owen peace plan
6 May	Bosnian Serb parliament rejects Vance–Owen peace plan
7 May	UN troops banned from Zepa by Bosnian Serbs
10 May	UN troops find Zepa a deserted ghost town
11 May	UN commander General Philippe Morillon demands more UN troops to protect UN-specified Muslim safe havens
13 May	UN helicopter shot down in Central Bosnia
22 May	200,000 refugees face famine in Tuzla
23 May	New plans agreed by US, UK, Russia, France and Spain for Bosnia peace. Plan widely denounced as shameful betrayal
25 May	UN announces plans for war crimes tribunal
30 May	UN-specified 'safe areas' repeatedly violated
10 June	Bosnian Croats attack aid convoy bound for Tuzla; kill eight Muslims
11 June	British UN forces kill two Croats attacking aid convoy near Vitez
16 June	Vance–Owen plan scrapped; new plan suggests demise of Bosnia

Table 7.1 Chronology of conflict in former Yugoslavia, 1990–4 (cont'd)

18 June	Canadian UN soldier killed; Dario Kordic, Bosnian Croat commander, accuses Muslims of killing 2000 Croats; Owen urges that Bosnia must be allowed to survive as 'viable entity'
21 June	President Izetbegovic pleads Bosnian case at EC summit; West threatens Croatia with sanctions; France opposes US case for arming Muslims
22 June	Bosnian plot to oust Izetbegovic
23 June	Islamic states at UN human rights conference clash with West over Bosnia; new peace plan discussed at Geneva
24 June	Bosnian Serbs and Croats agree three-way partition of Bosnia
27 June	Artillery battles and ground fighting between Bosnian Croats and Muslims in many Bosnian towns
29 June	Collapse of UN aid mission to 700,000 Bosnian civilians; US presses for end of arms embargo against Bosnian Muslims
30 June	Croats and Muslims battle for Mostar
2 July	Serbs and Croats isolate Muslims in Maglaj
6 July	Muslim–Croat exchange of fire kills female interpreter working for British UN forces at Vitez
7 July	Pressure on Izetbegovic to accept partition plan he describes as 'genocide'
8 July	Hurd suggests deteriorating situation could lead to UN withdrawal; Serbs and Croats together attack Muslims
9 July	Izetbegovic rejects three-way partition plan
10 July	Fighting in central Bosnia stops aid convoys; 2 million Bosnian Muslims on brink of starvation
12 July	Mortar shell kills twelve Sarajevo civilians in queue for water
14 July	Croats begin fresh wave of ethnic cleansing of Muslims; Mostar under siege
15 July	Britain urges sanctions against Croatia; pressure for extra EC funding for aid effort
16 July	Sadako Ogata (UNHCR) urges rescue of 150,000 besieged Muslims; UNHCR officials report blocking of aid convoys by Bosnian Croats

Table 7.1 Chronology of conflict in former Yugoslavia, 1990–4 (cont'd)

17 July	UN operation in crisis as France threatens withdrawal; Sarajevo authorities collect war crimes evidence
18 July	Croat government plans deportation of Muslims; UNHCR estimates 10,000 Muslims held near Mostar; Croats begin fresh ethnic purge; attack on Mostar intensifies
21 July	Serbs celebrate victory in Croatia; Izetbegovic agrees to attend fresh Geneva talks
22 July	Muslims strike back around Sarajevo; Bosnia tries to delay Geneva talks; fighting continues on Mount Igman overlooking Sarajevo; 4000 shells land on Sarajevo
24 July	Britain, France and US discuss launching air strikes against Serbs
25 July	Serbs bombard UN base at Zetra in Sarajevo
26 July	Izetbegovic arrives in Geneva for peace talks; criticises UN failure to protect 'safe areas'
27 July	Serbs fire on French UN soldiers; France urges UN and NATO to provide effective air cover
28 July	President Clinton threatens to bomb Serbs if attacks on UN peace keepers and 'safe areas' do not cease immediately; UN admits 'safe areas' do not exist
29 July	Izetbegovic pressed to accept three-way partition deal
30 July	NATO develops plan to bomb Serbs
2 August	France and Britain reject US bombing plans
3 August	NATO allies agree to air strikes; jets stand ready to 'hit hard'; Boutros-Ghali warns of UN cash crisis
4 August	US and UN vie for control of projected air strikes; Bosnian Serbs overrun Mount Igman; fighting between Muslims and Croats interrupts aid supplies
5 August	US administration split over Bosnia policy; UN launches Operation Life-line to save Sarajevo civilians
6 August	Clinton said to be serious about air strikes; new Bosnia partition plan unveiled
7 August	US threatens air strikes; UN discourages air strikes; noose continues to tighten around Sarajevo

Table 7.1 Chronology of conflict in former Yugoslavia, 1990–4 (cont'd)

8 August	Bosnian Serbs agree to withdraw from hills around Sarajevo
9 August	Wounded five-year-old Irma Hadzimuratovic arrives in England; UN troops join Serbs on Mount Igman; NATO air strike plans now uncertain
10 August	Publicity given to suffering in Sarajevo; new moves to create UN life-line to Sarajevo; Geneva talks on brink of failure; Serbs return to mountain strongholds; Owen urged to resign
11 August	Geneva co-chairmen urge Bosnian-Serb withdrawal from Mount Igman; Bosnians call for lifting of arms embargo; UN threatens air strikes
12 August	RAF spearheads rescue flights to Sarajevo; UN attacks British emphasis on child victims; UN reports early success with Operation Life-line
13 August	Serbs claim Bosnian genocide against ethnic Serbs; some Bosnian Serbs withdraw from Mount Igman
14 August	UN–UK dispute about peace missions; Dr Patrick Peillod (UNHCR) criticises 'supermarket attitude' in selecting which casualties to save
15 August	Operation Irma brings wounded Bosnians, including a minority of seven children, to Britain; at least 55 people killed in fighting between Croats and Muslims
16 August	UNHCR welcomes new offers of aid to Bosnians; British medics dismiss rescue mission as 'cynical piece of political theatre'
17 August	Ejup Ganic, Bosnian vice-president, denounces UN protectorate plan for Sarajevo as a 'stonewalling trick'
19 August	Owen presses Major to send more troops to Sarajevo; some Serbs still on Mount Igman; Owen and Thorvald Stoltenberg urge Bosnians to agree settlement
21 August	UN aid convoy reaches 55,000 starving Muslims in Mostar; UN mediators at Geneva suggest UN administration of Sarajevo
22 August	Izetbegovic, after 25 days negotiation in Geneva, says he will urge his people to reject 'final offer'; UN exposes horrors of Mostar
23 August	Croats seek trade-off for allowing UN aid to Mostar; European Community expresses doubts about proposed EC administration of Mostar

Table 7.1 Chronology of conflict in former Yugoslavia, 1990–4 (cont'd)

25 August	UN troops in corruption enquiry in Sarajevo; soldiers 'out of control'; UN aid convoy breaks Mostar siege
27 August	Izetbegovic demands better deal for Bosnia; NATO agrees to police final Bosnia settlement; UN leaves hostages in Mostar as aid convoy departs
30 August	Fighting between Croats and Muslims continues in Mostar; US and UN plan for policing of Bosnia after settlement
31 August	Bosnians urged to agree Geneva peace deal
1 September	Geneva peace talks collapse; Izetbegovic wants to safeguard return of hostages and refugees, and to reverse gains of aggression and ethnic cleansing
2 September	Clinton blames Serbs and Croats for collapse of talks; sanctions on Serbia have growing effect; Bosnia braces itself for a winter war
5 September	Sarajevo fuel supplies again cut off by fighting; thousands flee homes as Croat–Muslim fighting intensifies
8 September	Izetbegovic demands at UN Security Council: 'Defend us, or let us defend ourselves' – Council members react with 'deafening silence'
10 September	The war continues as fresh evidence emerges of a Serb–Croat alliance for the final carve-up of Bosnia
15 September	Bosnian Serbs demand the resignation of their government; Lord Owen says stalled peace plan is best offer available; Serbs claim to have shot down MiG 21
16 September	30 Bosnian Croats, including women and children, massacred in central Bosnian village
17 September	Croats raze villages before surrendering them to UN peace-keepers; Izetbegovic and Momicilo Krajisnik, senior Bosnian Serb official, reach peace deal in Geneva
18 September	Croat mines halt 100 UN vehicles
20 September	About 1000 Bosnian Serb troops rebel in Banja Luka
21 September	New peace plan collapses; the signing ceremony between Serb, Croat and Muslim leaders in Sarajevo is abandoned
25 September	Croatian troops ordered to stay in their barracks in run-up to vote in Bosnian parliament on three-way partition of Bosnia

Table 7.1 Chronology of conflict in former Yugoslavia, 1990–4 (cont'd)

26 September	UN commander complains to Croatian authorities about wounding of four French peace-keepers
27 September	Muslim leaders meet in Sarajevo to bury the idea of a multinational Bosnia
28 September	Bosnian Muslims reject latest Geneva peace proposals; demand new talks on ethnic partition of Bosnia
30 September	UNHCR says that Muslim rejection of peace plan might threaten aid operations
4 October	Nine killed as rival Muslim forces clash in Bihac; Bosnian army troops defect to Bihac rebels
7 October	UN's special war-crimes investigator accuses Croatian army of committing atrocities; Izetbegovic tells UN General Assembly that Bosnia rejects 'political vivisection' and 'ethnic cleansing'
10 October	Muslims launch fresh attack on Croat Vitez; UN resumes its evacuation of sick and wounded from Bosnia after three-day suspension of airlift
11 October	UN commander Phillipe Morillon says area might best be run as a UN protectorate
13 October	UN officials report that Serbs and Croats might be moving towards a new war in Croatia
14 October	Arrests of Albanians in Serbia's Kosovo raises new fears of ethnic cleansing
17 October	Sarajevo shaken by further bomb blasts; Bosnian Croats attack aid convoy at Prozor
21 October	Milosevic decides to dissolve Serbian parliament; new poll set for 19 December; Karadzic says he will only settle for single state incorporating all Serbs
23 October	Fikret Abdic, leader of breakaway Bihac, signs peace treaty with Karadzic
25 October	Muslims tell of massacre by Croatian soldiers in Stupni Do; one UNHCR driver killed, others wounded, in Muslim attack in Novi Travnik
26 October	UN announces indefinite suspension of aid to central Bosnia; millions – without food, clothing, shelter or warmth – face 'season of death' as winter approaches

Table 7.1 Chronology of conflict in former Yugoslavia, 1990–4 (cont'd)

31 October	Wounding of French officer forces halt to Sarajevo aid
1 November	Bosnians and Croats in Vares seek UN protection; Muslims execute Croats
2 November	Oslo talks set to fail; Croats flee Muslim assault on Vares
7 November	UN uncertain how to resume aid; Serbs urged to make land deals
9 November	Collapse of 16th-C stone bridge in Mostar; 25,000 Bosnians trapped; 40 casualties, including many children, in mortar attack on Sarajevo school
11 November	UN aid convoys attacked; Serbs pressure Muslim 'safe areas'
15 November	UN 'at loggerheads' over aid delivery as 'wicked winter' descends on Bosnia; British UN soldiers attacked at Garnji Vakuf
19 November	Douglas Hurd hints at permanent end to aid
22 November	Serbs offered sanctions deal; British forces lack adequate clothing
24 November	Reports of Serb torture and killing of Kosovo Albanians
28 November	Karadzic says Serbs will not give up conquered land
2 December	New Geneva peace talks collapse
9 December	Postponement of new peace talks scheduled for Greece
15 December	Serb protests against Milosovic but he remains confident of poll victory; wounded Bosnians to be treated in Britain
20 December	Milosovic wins absolute majority
23 December	Serbs give Bosnians new ultimatum; Christmas truce breaks down
27 December	Heavy casualties near Sarajevo
1994	
4 January	Owen objects to Croatian threats of military intervention in Bosnia; continuing shelling of Sarajevo
10 January	United States and Britain, at Brussels summit, reaffirm readiness to use air strikes to protect UN troops in Bosnia; air-strike policy endorsed by all 16 NATO members in final communiqué
20 February	NATO ultimatum, made after Sarajevo market massacre (5/2), expires after Serb withdrawals and Russian intervention

had become involved: after EC mediation the Yugoslav Serbs agreed to leave Slovenia, which meant they could now focus all their attention on Croatia.

The escalating conflict had impelled Croatia to struggle for survival as an independent state. It was cut off from Belgrade and had lost much of its land, but it introduced a new currency, new passports and an independent army. Milosevic, unable to consolidate the various Serb-controlled regions, opted for international mediation. Cyrus Vance succeeded in introducing a peace plan that brought some 14,000 UN troops into Serb-held parts of Croatia, with the task of monitoring the withdrawal of the Yugoslav army, disarming the local Serbs, facilitating the return of Croatian refugees, and establishing conditions that would lead to a final political settlement. In the event few of the conditions of the peace plan came to be met: much of the Yugoslav army withdrew but now violence was erupting in Bosnia. The Bosnian government contained Serbian, Croatian and Muslim ministers, now increasingly torn apart by the dynamics of the wider Yugoslav conflict. The descent into chaos gathered pace.

The United Nations had first become involved in the Yugoslavia quagmire when, on 25 September 1991, the Security Council unanimously adopted Resolution 713, expressing deep concern at the fighting in the country and calling on all states to implement immediately a 'general and complete embargo on all deliveries of weapons and military equipment to Yugoslavia'. The Council applauded European efforts to secure peace and invited the UN Secretary General Perez de Cuellar to offer his assistance. On 8 October the Secretary-General appointed Cyrus Vance, a former US Secretary of State, as his personal envoy for Yugoslavia. The subsequent peace plan followed Security Council Resolution 721, applauding the efforts of Cyrus Vance, and Resolution 724, approving the Secretary-General's plan for a peace-keeping operation.

On 15 February 1992, despite the remaining hostility of various Yugoslav factions, Perez de Cuellar recommended to the Security Council the establishment of a United Nations Protection Force (UNPROFOR), at the same time urging the need for prompt action. The Security Council passed Resolution 743 on 21 February, approving the report and establishing UNPROFOR for an initial period of twelve months. The clear intention was that the Force would help to establish the conditions for the negotiation of an overall settlement of the crisis within the framework of the European Community's Conference of Yugoslavia. On 7 April the Security Council authorised the full deployment of UNPROFOR, a principal aim of which was to establish the United Nations Protected Areas (UNPAs). The original mandate for UNPROFOR only referred to Croatia but it was envisaged that after the UNPAs had been demilitarised a number of UNPROFOR military observers would be redeployed in Bosnia. It was not long before UNPROFOR staff, when risks to the lives of staff had reached unacceptable levels, were forced to relocate: on 16 and 17 May 1992 about two-thirds of UNPROFOR headquarters personnel were withdrawn from Sarajevo, with about 100 remaining to arrange meetings between the warring factions and to carry out humanitarian work.

Throughout the entire crisis the impression grew that the United Nations was incapable of acting resolutely in good time. Divisions within the European Community and between the Permanent Members of the Security Council meant that UN initiatives were inevitably small-scale, tardy and inadequate. Dozens of resolutions, declarations, statements and warnings flowed from the Security Council from the time of the onset of hostilities to the eventual virtual abandonment of Bosnia in mid-1993. At every stage the United Nations had reacted to fresh events but in ways that did little or nothing to limit the escalating crisis.

In May 1992 the UN Security Council was urged by Britain, France and the United States to impose an oil embargo against Serbia, a measure that was quickly approved but which was soon judged to have little impact on the war. At the same time it was clear that deep disagreements were emerging between UN Secretary-General Boutros-Ghali and the Security Council over possible steps to protect the Bosnians from the horrors of ethnic cleansing.[62] It was also clear that Russia and China, both Permanent Members of the Security Council, were reluctant to impose comprehensive trade sanctions against Serbia, though it was unlikely that they would veto Council resolutions.[63] In any case, all the signs indicated that the limited sanctions that were envisaged would do no more than stimulate Serbian pugnacity. On 30 May the Security Council approved Resolution 757, so imposing mandatory sanctions against the Federal Republic of Yugoslavia (Serbia and Montenegro). Serbian President Milosevic responded by stating that Serbia was prepared to suffer pariah status in order to help Serbs fighting in neighbouring Bosnia and Croatia.

On 8 June the Security Council agreed in principle to send more than 100 troops to Sarajevo to take control of the airport and to protect relief supplies. It was already clear that many people were starving to death in the Bosnian capital and that both sides were fighting to gain advantage before the possible arrival of UN troops and the start of fresh negotiations. UN food convoys continued their efforts to reach Sarajevo, frequently coming under fire, and reached the city on 17 June. By the end of the month UN troops had taken control of Sarajevo airport, preparing the way for increased shipments of relief supplies. Again it was obvious that such measures, welcome in themselves as humanitarian initiatives, were doing nothing to address the wider problem of the escalating conflict. Soon there were well over 1000 troops from France, Egypt and the Ukraine at Sarajevo airport, reflecting the racial mix of the Bosnian population and advertising the humanitarian UN presence. After a meeting with Lord Carrington, Boutros-Ghali commented that 'the composition of this UN force is taking into consideration the composition of the different parts of the population in Bosnia-Herzegovina'. And in a fresh report the Secretary-General emphasised that the option of UN military action for peace-keeping purposes 'is essential to the credibility of the United Nations as a guarantor of international security'.

In July 1992 new outbreaks of fighting in Bosnia brought calls for UN involvement to protect the 70,000 inhabitants of Gorazde, a Muslim town that had been under siege for two months. Boutros-Ghali failed to respond to such pleas, preferring to emphasise instead the importance of securing the humanitarian relief effort flowing through Sarajevo airport, an operation that 'continues to hang by a slender thread'. Again the United Nations was turning down the desperate Bosnian pleas for help: there was now a sustained Serbian attack on Bosnian cities, and with the Security Council having recommended Bosnian membership of the United Nations only two months earlier, the Serbian offensive represented an attack on a sovereign UN member. Bosnia was again learning to its cost that, despite Security Council Resolution 755 urging the General Assembly to admit Bosnia as a member, the United Nations could only act to protect a country from external aggression when there was a political will to do so.[64] At the same time the European Community moved to expel the Serbian-dominated Yugoslavian rump from the United Nations.

On 4 August the Security Council demanded that prison camps in the former Yugoslavia be opened for inspection, while persistent shelling closed Sarajevo airport and brought an end to the relief operation for several days. Now the United States was pressing for a Council resolution to allow UN troops to use force to help civilians working in Bosnia, but the move was blocked by other Permanent Members. The next day, the UN High Commission for Refugees (UNHCR) announced that UN forces might be compelled to withdraw from Sarejevo because of worsening security. Within the United Nations the mood was again shifting in favour of a force option, towards approval for 'all measures necessary' to support the humanitarian programme. There were also mounting calls for the use of UN troops to stop Serbian atrocities.

By mid-September Secretary-General Boutros-Ghali was calling for a massive increase in the number of UN troops deployed in the region. On

22 September the UN General Assembly expelled the rump Yugoslavia from the General Assembly, though this further advertised divisions in the Security Council. Such measures did nothing to bring Belgrade to heel: the Serbs and their Bosnian proxies were still prosecuting the war, UN helicopters were being fired upon, and the no-fly zone was being violated with impunity.

Fresh tensions surfaced in the European Community when Macedonia applied for membership of the United Nations in January 1993; and these in turn shattered the EC's effort to present an agreed foreign policy in the Security Council. The warring factions in the former Yugoslavia, happy to contemplate the continuing UN impotence, pursued their own strategic agendas. Thus on 23 January Croatian tanks stormed across ceasefire lines, while Serb forces raided UN depots to retrieve their surrendered artillery. UN peace-keepers again came under fire, stimulating fresh appeals for an enhanced UN military role. In February the Clinton Administration, manifestly perplexed by the complexities of the crisis, hedged on the Vance–Owen peace plan, though it subsequently announced the decision to air-drop relief supplies to the beleaguered Bosnians. Now the Security Council was talking about setting up a war-crimes tribunal, though it remained unclear how anyone could ever be arraigned before it.

The conflict dragged on with no sign of an end. The Security Council voted on 31 March to give NATO aircraft the right to attack Serbian planes violating the no-fly zone, but no one imagined that this would make any difference to the course of the war. By mid-April there were reports that the UN relief operation had almost run out of funds, with food supplies for 2.3 million Bosnians almost exhausted because of international donor-fatigue and institutional squabbling.[65] On 13 April Serbian forces bombarded the centre of Srebrenica, killing perhaps as many as 80 people in a school playground. Three days later, as the killing continued, the Serbs blocked UN mercy missions and shelled the UN headquarters in the town. The Bosnian Serbs, now manifestly breaking earlier peace pledges, provoked little further UN response, except the promise of intensified sanctions. Still there was significant Western opposition to suggestions that the arms curb on the Bosnian Muslims should be lifted to allow the victims to defend themselves: Britain declared it would veto any US move to permit the arming of the Muslims.

On 5 May there were fresh tensions in the United Nations, with arguments about who should control NATO peace-keeping forces that might be sent to Bosnia. Boutros-Ghali was insisting that forces that might be deployed to implement the Vance–Owen peace plan should be under UN control, but it was obvious that Washington would not agree to any such proposal; said one Western diplomat: 'Boutros-Ghali's plan for overall political and strategic control has to be fudged if the US is to come on board.' In the event there were no concrete proposals, no plans beyond mere speculation. The so-called UN 'safe areas' in Bosnia were coming under increasing attack, and again there were calls from all sides for more UN troops with an effective military mandate. On 13 May another UN helicopter was shot down in central Bosnia after evacuating wounded Muslims from Zepa.

It was now clear that differences between the EC states and between the Permanent Members of the Security Council were quite insuperable: there was now no realistic prospect of united resolute action from any quarter to bring the Yugoslav nightmare to an end. The Clinton Administration, bereft of useful initiative, was now even talking of boycotting Security Council meetings since the US government was not yet ready for discussion. In one account, the situation at the United Nations was seen as 'a shambles';[66] in another, the Permanent Member disagreements had reached such a pitch that there was 'no possibility to determine definitely the date' for the planned meeting on the Bosnia crisis.[67]

Over the next few days an agreement was stitched together following discussions between the United States, Britain, Russia, France and Spain. On 23 May 1993 the text of the allied communiqué on Bosnia was released.[68] Few observers doubted that the bland and unoriginal text provisions were little more than a shameful sell-out, the final indication that the major powers were prepared to let the war run to its conclusion. A key provision was the UN-sponsored intention to set up six 'safe areas': in Bihac, Tuzla, Sarajevo, Srebrenica, Gorazde and Zepa. The idea was a compromise, the fruit of US opposition to the Vance–Owen plan and European opposition to Washington's impulse to arm the Bosnian Muslims.

It was soon clear that the 'safe area' provision could not be implemented: the UN forces were inadequate for the task, and the Serbs were still able to write the agenda of the war. In Srebrenica, for example, the UN peacekeepers had established a fragile peace, but only at the cost of disarming the Muslims. With the Serbs able to control any UN access to the town, they were now free to starve it into submission at their leisure. And soon there were significant violations of the other 'safe areas'. At best, they were no more than under-supplied refugee camps; at worst, destitute prisons in which tens of thousands of people could be attacked at will and systematically denied the necessities of life. A European diplomat summed up the situation: 'We've insisted on calling them "safe areas", rather than "safe havens". Maybe we should also drop the "safe" and just call them areas.'

Everyone knew the facts: naked aggression, ethnic cleansing, rape camps, the targeting of civilians, enforced exile, summary executions, torture, starvation, and the progressive dismemberment of Bosnia – recognised as an independent state by UN Security Council Resolution 755 (20 May 1992). The United Nations, unable to generate a practical consensus in the international community, remained powerless to take effective action.

THE CYPRUS SORE

We need to remember that by the early 1990s there were 48 UN resolutions calling for the withdrawal of all foreign troops from Cyprus. This dispute, like many others, had been complicated by the detritus of the colonial legacy, and by Washington's perceived strategic interest in the region.[69] On 2 August 1992 President George Bush announced that Greece and Turkey, both useful US allies in the Gulf War, had agreed to talks to resolve their differences (see also Chapter 4). Three weeks later, the United Nations published a map showing how much territory in Cyprus the Turks should give up to achieve a settlement: a UN initiative that followed three months of talks between Greece, Turkey and the United Nations in New York. Already, in late August, there were signs that the UN plan was doomed to failure. Rauf Denktash, the Turkish-Cypriot leader, had already denounced Secretary-General Boutros-Ghali for drawing a line through the island that would displace many Turkish residents. In London a spokesman for the self-styled Turkish Republic of Northern Cyprus declared: 'If we apply this map, 40,000 people will be forced to move from homes they have lived in since 1974. It is totally unacceptable to any sensible person.' In the same spirit Mustafa Gencsoy, the leader of British's Turkish Cypriot community, suggested that Washington was mainly interested in domestic electoral considerations: 'There are several million Greek voters in the US.'

Following fresh talks in November, there was a clear hardening of attitudes: in Nicosia Rauf Denktash announced that he would resign rather than sign an agreement based on the UN Security Council proposals. At the same time the United Nations made clear that it was reducing by more than half its debt-ridden activities in Cyprus. The Danish troop contingent pulled out in December, while the Canadian government announced that it would be withdrawing all its troops by September 1993. Britain said its forces would remain but expressed concern at the growing peace-keeping burden. In February the veteran right-wing Greek Cypriot leader, Glafkos Clerides, unexpectedly beat George Vassiliou in the presidential election, securing a majority of 1988 votes out of more than 350,000 cast. This was a further blow to UN plans: during the election campaign Clerides had declared that 'the UN set of ideas violates basic human rights and closes the door to EC membership'. Now the new Greek Cypriot President was calling for a delay in the UN-sponsored peace talks. Faced with this new situation, Malcolm Rifkind, the British Secretary of State for Defence, hinted at the possibility of a withdrawal of British troops (*The Independent*, 31 March 1993):

> We must find a better way of sharing the burden. We have been in Cyprus for thirty years on a UN operation. We need to replace that sort of present arrangement with a different kind of approach under which a country commits a level of forces for a finite period, and there is a clear understanding that those forces will be replaced by equivalent forces from another country.

It seemed increasingly unlikely that the UN efforts to achieve a settlement would be successful.

On 11 May 1993 Russia vetoed a British-sponsored UN resolution designed to spread the costs of the 1500-strong UN force in Cyprus among all UN members. This unexpected use of the Russia veto in the Security Council was the first since the end of the Cold War: it represented a small but significant dent in the so-called New World Order. Britain saw the Russian vote as 'disproportionate' but of greater financial than political significance. Soon London and Washington were urging Russia to change its stand.[70]

Fresh talks in May between the leaders of the Greek Cypriots and the Turkish Cypriots at the UN headquarters in New York failed to reach firm conclusions; the dimensions of the Cyprus problem seemed unchanged. In June 1993 the Canadian UN peace-keepers, whom the United Nations had failed to reimburse for the past eighteen months, began to pull out. British soldiers of the Royal Artillery took their place in the buffer zone that runs through the heart of Nicosia – to some Cypriot observers an alarming reminder of the time when EOKA guerrillas fought to rid Cyprus of the British occupation. The UNFICYP force was contracting and there seemed little hope of a permanent settlement.

WESTERN SAHARA INVADED

One consequence of the Second World War was the destabilisation of colonial territories in Asia and Africa. In North Africa the Algerian National Liberation Front (FLN) began its struggle against the French occupation in November 1954, and in Morocco an Army of Liberation launched a campaign to establish an independent republican state. Spain and France were forced to abandon their hold on the region, and when Mauritania gained its independence in 1960 both Mauritania and Morocco laid claim to the erstwhile Spanish Sahara. In 1972 Saharawi students from Moroccan schools and universities founded Polisario (*Frente Popular para la Liberation de Saguia el-Hamra y Rio de Oro*, the Saguia el-Hamra a river in the north of Spanish Sahara, Rio de Oro in the southern area).

Washington and its allies opposed Polisario on principle because of its leftist leanings but the Spanish, still under Franco, broke ranks and decided it could work with the Polisario Front. When UN representatives visited Spanish Sahara they were everywhere greeted with demonstrations in support of Polisario. On 15 October 1975 the UN mission declared that most of the people in the region were in favour of independence from Morocco; it was clear that Polisario would be the people's choice for the new administration. On 16 October the International Court of Justice, in a dramatic decision, ruled that no 'tie of sovereignty' existed between the territory of Western Sahara 'and the Kingdom of Morocco or the Mauritanian entity'. King Hassan of Morocco decided to ignore the ruling of the World Court and was supported in this by France and the United States. Soon, following Washington's blatant defiance of international law, the Moroccan army and Polisario units were fighting each other for control of the region. As many as 40,000 Saharawis were forced to flee their homes while, with US approval, Morocco and Mauritania divided up the territory between them. Polisario continued to fight a guerrilla war but Western opposition ensured that the Moroccan aggression could rely on substantial support in the United Nations. Polisario's principal ally, Colonel Gaddafi of Libya, was unreliable: he first supported the Front, then signed a unification treaty with Hassan, and two years later swung in the opposite direction.

In August 1988 UN Secretary-General Perez de Cuellar proposed a truce between the SPLA (the Saharawi People's Liberation Army, the military wing of Polisario) and Morocco, to be followed by a plebiscite in Western Sahara; and on 27 December King Hassan, reversing his thirteen-year-long stand, declared his willingness to talk to Polisario. In the early 1990s the United Nations was still struggling to establish the terms and conditions for the proposed referendum, while Polisario was accusing the Moroccan monarchy of taking steps to artificially inflate the anti-Polisario vote.

It has been further alleged that UN officials sympathetic to the Moroccan case have been involved in deliberate mismanagement and questionable practices. With elections finally scheduled for January 1992, questions were raised about the role of senior officials in the UN negotiating team and about the political competence of Johannes Manz, the UN official in charge of the operation. Alarming evidence began to accumulate that UN officials had provided confidential census lists and military information to the Moroccan government; and that officials were working to change the rules of the planned referendum to put Polisario at a disadvantage. UN documents expressed concern at the officials' attempt to aid the Moroccan government, even though Hassan was obstructing various UN efforts. Secretary-General Perez de Cuellar failed to protest when Hassan announced that he would be sending 170,000 Moroccans into Western Sahara before the vote, a clear violation of the peace plan framed by the Security Council. A diplomat familiar with the situation was quoted: 'This is potentially a serious failure in a major UN peace-keeping operation and it must cast a shadow over the reputation of the Secretary-General . . . .'[71] On 1 January 1992 Polisario called for the new UN Secretary-General, Boutros-Ghali, to demand that Morocco pull out the thousands of citizens it had sent into the territory.

In the last days of his term of office Perez de Cuellar presented the Security Council with a report proposing changes to the planned referendum. Washington and France predictably supported the new proposals, which strengthened the position of the Moroccan government, while Polisario denounced the report as 'partial, unjust and completely aligned with the position of the aggressor, the Moroccan colonists'. Faced with mounting international opposition to the new proposals, the Security Council decided to postpone adoption of the report and to ask the new Secretary-General to provide a fresh assessment by the end of February. Now it was increasingly obvious that the planned election would be indefinitely delayed.

Little progress was made through 1992 on a solution to the impasse. The Security Council, having originally framed a peace plan acceptable to Polisario, now seemed unwilling to press for an election. UN officials either resigned or were discharged after it was established that they had illicitly aided the Moroccan government; and a report from a US Senate foreign relations committee criticised both Morocco and the United Nations for procrastination. Secretary-General Boutros-Ghali failed to move the situation on, and by March 1993 there were signs that the Security Council was ready to support Morocco's annexation of Western Sahara.[72] In April a report from Amnesty International revealed that the Moroccan government had arranged the 'disappearance' of hundreds of people, most of them Saharawis. Now it was clear that the elections scheduled by the Security Council for January 1992 had been virtually abandoned, with little prospect that a new date would be set or that the conditions for a secure peace would be established. The pattern was a familiar one: as was happening in many other parts of the world – Angola, Israel, El Salvador and others – the United Nations was maintaining a manifest 'tilt' in favour of Washington's proxy factions, even where this entailed silence about known human rights abuses and obvious violations of international law.

In May 1993 a report issued by UN Secretary-General Boutros-Ghali suggested that both sides in the dispute over Western Sahara were showing 'a desire to move towards an early referendum'. In June he visited the region 'to make one more effort to seek a compromise solution', emphasising the need to achieve a settlement without further delay. Observers, aware of the region's recent history, US pressure and consequent UN vacillation, were not optimistic.

THE STRUGGLE OF KASHMIR

The long-standing dispute between India and Pakistan over the status of Kashmir represents another source of sporadic conflict which the United Nations has tried to resolve, with little success. Kashmir is predominantly Muslim, though with a large Hindu minority in Jammu. The Hindu Maharajah of Kashmir – his ancestors planted on the throne by the British – had hoped for independence in 1947 but Pakistan seized the province, whereupon the Maharajah signed a treaty of accession to India. There then followed the first Indo-Pakistan war. In 1965 fresh tension between India and Pakistan erupted in military conflict that spread to Kashmir. At Tashkent in January 1966, using Soviet good offices, the parties signed a cease-fire. With Kashmir's Muslims continuing to press for independence from New Delhi the region has remained a source of tension.

Since 1949 a small UN force has been maintained to monitor the first cease-fire agreed between India and Pakistan. Today independence demonstrations frequently take place in front of the UN offices, signalling thereby yet another well of Muslim discontent to the world community. Thus in February 1990 some 30 separate processions, involving about 500,000 men, women and children, took turns to march to the office of the UN military force in Srinagar. Many demonstrators waved Pakistani flags and those of the various militant groups organising the pro-independence movement. Within months the foreign ministers of India and Pakistan were meeting to discuss yet again the vexed question of Kashmir. The talks, held in April 1990 during a special session of the United Nations General Assembly on economic issues, were the first since an abrupt deterioration in relations had led to a troop build-up along the 500-mile border. It was now clear that fundamentalist Muslim groups wanted nothing less than for Kashmir to become an independent Islamic republic.

In 1948 a UN resolution called for a plebiscite in Kashmir, but the international body showed only desultory interest in the region thereafter. The Security Council held talks on Kashmir in January 1957, at Pakistan's request; and fresh talks, equally unproductive, were held in 1962, 1964 and on many subsequent occasions. It appeared that this was one region that failed to excite the Permanent Members of the Security Council, as though indefinite procrastination would work to resolve the tensions in the area. Thus, nearly 30 years ago, one authoritative observer remarked: 'it may yet prove that the solvent of time rather than the solutions concocted by statesmen will dispose of such issues as those which have long persisted in regard to Kashmir, Palestine, China, and Germany'.[73] The then problems of China and Germany have been settled, with new ones arising to take their place; the Palestine problem runs on; and the difficulties over Kashmir have not been resolved by 'the solvent of time'. In April and May 1993 there were reports of bomb explosions in the Kashmir city of Jammu, and of massive human rights abuses by the Indian police against Muslim Kashmiri demonstrators.[74] By August it was estimated that the Indian security forces had so far killed more than 7500 Kashmiris in the five-year revolt, with continuing persecution (*The Independent*, 16 August 1993). Appeals to the United Nations to intervene in the deteriorating situation had gone unanswered.

EAST TIMOR GENOCIDE

The emergence of President Sukarno as the first nationalist leader of independent Indonesia was not welcomed by the West. The British and the Dutch had struggled to keep Indonesia within the orbit of traditional colonialism, but had been unsuccessful. Then it was up to the CIA to remove this troublesome leader of the non-aligned and anti-imperialist movements of the Third World. President John Kennedy and British premier Harold Macmillan agreed that an attempt should be made to isolate Sukarno in Africa and Asia; a memorandum confirming the decision noted that the two Western leaders 'agreed to liquidate President Sukarno, depending upon the situation and available opportunities . . .'[75] Subsequent events, largely orchestrated by the CIA, led to the overthrow of Sukarno, the establishment of General Suharto in his place, and one of the greatest massacres of modern times, what *The New York Times* called 'one of the most savage mass slaughters of modern political history'.[76] Anyone suspected of being a supporter of Sukarno – nationalists, socialists, Communists, workers, peasants, intellectuals – was killed in a sustained massacre that spread over weeks and resulted in the deaths of at least 500,000 Indonesians (some estimates put the number of victims at well over one million). The former CIA agent Ralph McGehee has been quoted: 'I know the specific steps the agency took to create the conditions that led to the massacre of at least half a million Indonesians.'[77]

East Timor overthrew Portuguese fascism in 1974 and, under the leadership of Fretilin, a populist Catholic grouping, began to build an independent state. On 7 December 1975 Indonesia, massively equipped with US armaments, invaded East Timor and began a mass slaughter that was to claim 200,000 people – a third of the entire population – by 1980. The United States was fully involved, and continued to supply arms throughout the period, as it did thereafter. When, by 1977, the Indonesian armed forces had begun to exhaust their supply of ordnance in their onslaught on a nation of one million people President Carter took steps to increase the flow of arms.

Washington did not only supply arms to aid the extermination of the East Timorese people, but also provided reliable diplomatic support to Indonesia in the United Nations. UN Ambassador Daniel Patrick Moynihan was given the task and rejoiced in his success in blocking effective United Nations action on East Timor:

> The United States wished things to turn out as they did, and worked to bring this about. The Department of State desired that the United Nations prove utterly ineffective in whatever measures it undertook. This task was given to me, and I carried it forward with no inconsiderable success.[78]

Again Washington had successfully blocked the possibility of effective UN action, to reverse what even *The New York Times* was prepared to call 'naked aggression'.[79]

Throughout the 1980s a few advocates in the United Nations, led by Portugal, have been prepared to criticise Indonesia for its invasion of East Timor, hoping to encourage an active UN intervention. In November 1990 the United Nations expected to send a fact-finding team to East Timor to prepare the ground for a visit of Portuguese parliamentarians; but then, with little explanation, it was suddenly announced that no visit would take place until May 1991. Already there had been nearly a dozen Security Council and General Assembly resolutions calling for an Indonesian withdrawal; but with General Suharto secure as a US client, and also guaranteed British diplomatic support and military hardware, there has never been any real chance of effective UN action. On 12 November 1991 the Indonesian army fired on mourners at a funeral in Dili, the East Timor capital, killing and wounding hundreds of unarmed people. Alan Nairn, a US reporter working for the *New Yorker*, later told Reuters that he had seen 'body after body, and the soldiers kept firing at those who were still standing'. A spokeswoman for UN Secretary-General Perez de Cuellar said he deplored the loss of life.[80]

There was by now abundant evidence of Western involvement in Indonesian atrocities, both through the knowing supply of weapons and counter-insurgency equipment (and, according to some observers, personnel on the ground) and by the reliable provision of necessary diplomatic support.[81] On 29 November Perez de Cuellar announced his intention to send his own mission to conduct a 'totally independent and impartial' investigation, as if there were any doubt about what had transpired; but no other steps were proposed.

The situation remained unchanged throughout 1992 and 1993. The Indonesian army of occupation continued its policy of repression, while Washington and London provided the required levels of military and diplomatic support. On 21 May 1993 the captured East Timorese guerrilla leader Xanana Gusmao was sentenced to life imprisonment following a trial that was widely reported as violating the UN Covenant of Civil and Political Rights. It was also noted that the Secretary-General's office had 'privately expressed dismay at the ruling and may approach Indonesia on the issue'.[82] No other UN initiative was planned.

On 10 June British Aerospace (BAe) announced, with a great fanfare, that it had won a $500 million order to supply 24 Hawk military aircraft to Indonesia. It was clear that the planes could be used as strike aircraft; and that they would therefore be useful to the Indonesian authorities in their continuing genocide against the East Timorese people. Just as the British government, with others, had been happy to arm Saddam Hussein, now it rejoiced in supplying fresh arms to another murderous regime. Prime Minister John Major, celebrating the deal, commented to the House of Commons on 'the excellence of the British defence industry'.

HUMAN RIGHTS

The United Nations Charter, unlike the Covenant of the League of Nations, explicitly upholds the concept of human rights. Thus a declared purpose of the UN (Article 1(3)) is 'To achieve international co-operation . . . in promoting and encouraging respect for human rights and for fundamental freedoms for all . . . .' In February 1946 a Commission on Human Rights was established; and at its first session the UN General Assembly adopted a resolution condemning genocide as 'a crime under international law'. In December 1948 the Assembly adopted the Universal Declaration of Human Rights, which begins with a recognition 'of the inherent dignity and of the equal and inalienable rights of all members of the human family'; this recognition 'is the foundation of freedom, justice and peace in the world . . .'. There followed over subsequent years a wealth of Covenants, Conventions and Declarations – which the United Nations cannot enforce but which have great moral weight: no state would readily admit that it was in violation of any of the UN proclamations on human rights.

Today the United Nations presses for human rights within the limits of its resources and subject to the whims and self-interest of powerful Member States. Here we can do no more than glance at a few current UN activities to give a flavour of its concerns:

- In November 1990 the UN special rapporteur on torture published a survey indicating an increase in the amount of torture of children and juveniles throughout the world. Some 48 nations, four of them EC members, were investigated following the submission of well-documented claims of torture.

- In 1992 the UN stopped ranking countries according to the level of freedom enjoyed by their citizens, a year after the publication of the controversial Human Freedom Index.

- In December 1992 the UN General Assembly approved the 'Declaration on the rights of persons belonging to national or ethnic, religious and linguistic minorities'. The Declaration, lacking teeth, may represent nothing more than a statement of principle.

- In December 1992 the UN began an investigation into the anti-homosexual laws of Tasmania to determine whether they violate human rights. This followed a complaint from a gay and lesbian group to the UN Human Rights Committee.

- In March 1993 an ambitious UN-sponsored conference of 49 Asia-Pacific countries began in Bangkok to discuss human rights. A principal aim was a fundamental reassessment of the UN Declaration on Human Rights.

- In April 1993 a report by the UN Human Rights Centre said that in the first three months of the year it had received 125,000 complaints about politically motivated human rights abuses, 'only a fraction of the actual violations involving torture, mass executions, arbitrary arrests, lack of freedom of opinions, corrupt judicial systems and violence of all types including rapes'.

- In April 1993 the United States government announced that it had reversed its position and now supported the appointment of a UN High Commissioner for Human Rights.

- In May 1993 a UN report stated that the black population of the United States gains so little from the benefits of US society that, if measured as a separate country, it would rank 30 places behind the white US population on the global 'Human Development Index'.

- In May 1993 UNICEF held a press conference in Delhi to protest about the exploitation of millions of children in India. It was said that from 44 million to 100 million children from the ages of six to fourteen were working instead of attending school.

- In May 1993 a team of 150 UN and OAS human rights observers in Haiti accused the army of obstructing the monitoring of 'numerous and grave' rights violations. Proposals for the sending of a UN police force to Haiti were discussed.

- In May 1993 the Clinton Administration reaffirmed US support for the appointment of a UN High Commissioner for Human Rights. The government also expressed support for the Covenant on Civil and Political Rights.

- In May 1993 a UN report warned of the 'dangerous potential for human strife' if the worldwide growth in unemployment were not reversed. This fourth UN Human Development Report warned that new and old democracies on every continent were currently threatened by 'the issue of the 1990s'.

- In May 1993 the UN announced that it was withdrawing essential services from the remaining 40,000 Vietnamese boat people in Hong Kong camps in an effort to force them to return home.

From 14 to 25 June 1993 the United Nations staged the World Conference on Human Rights in Vienna, the first event of its kind since 1968. This momentous conference began under a shadow. Under pressure from China the United Nations refused to allow the Dalai Lama to take part as an official member. At the same time, following pressure from India, more than a dozen Sikh and Kashmiri human rights groups based in Britain, Canada and the United States have had invitations to the conference withdrawn. Protests were lodged, including one from Graham Hand, head of the UK Foreign Office human rights department. John Pace, the conference coordinator, commented in *The Independent* of 12 June 1993, that he had been forced to whittle down the number of potential participants from around 18,000 non-governmental organisations (NGOs):

> We are trying to put together an environment in which governments can decide how to implement human rights. Certain groups who want to focus on the human rights situation in one country – outfits of a denunciatory nature – are not compatible with trying to achieve a regional or international approach. This is an inter-governmental meeting. We can't focus on governments having to defend themselves.

Such a statement begs many questions: not least, *if it is the responsibility of governments to protect human rights within their regions of jurisdiction why should governments not be arraigned before the world for their manifest failures?*

Questions concerning human rights usually seem clear and unambiguous: it may not be possible to achieve improvements, but abuses are obvious. In fact, while such an uncomplicated view can generally be sustained, it is often the case that definitions of human rights rest on political assumptions – about the role of the family in society, about the balance between public and private property, about the role of the citizen and the obligations of authority. The IMF/World Bank/GATT nexus may claim commercial rights that many observers perceive as leading to naked economic exploitation. Hereditary rulers may claim rights that others see as obvious abuses of power. And Third World states may object to Western accusations of human rights abuses on the ground that rich countries have an interest in diverting attention from their own depredations of the global environment. Such ambiguities in the philosophy of human rights – a philosophy that is often politically mediated – are not adequately addressed in most current analyses.

Another key problem is the matter of enforcement. The United Nations, by almost any reckoning, is high on pious declaration (though political pressures often cause shameful silences) but low on practical implementation. The reasons are obvious: too many individuals, institutions and states throughout the world have an interest in injustice. Remove an injustice and some person, group or institution will be less rich, less privileged, less powerful; in such a context there are massive problems associated with the enforcement of human rights, even when there is broad consensus about the human rights in question. Such considerations were well illustrated by the Earth Summit that was held in Rio de Janeiro in June 1992.

THE EARTH SUMMIT

Some 180 nations participated in the Earth Summit – the United Nations Conference on Environment and Development (UNCED) – with the declared aim of protecting the global environment. It was soon clear that, despite all the pious declarations of intent, little would change: if the world were heading for environmental collapse then little would be done to change the pace or direction of the journey. The attitude of powerful self-interested organisations – usually content to pursue their economic agendas without undue advertising – was well exemplified by Lawrence Summers, chief economist of the World Bank, in a statement that formed part of a submission to the Earth Summit:

> There are no . . . limits to the carrying capacity of the earth that are likely to bind any time in the foreseeable future. There isn't a risk of an apocalypse due to global warming or anything else. The idea that the world is headed over an abyss is profoundly wrong. The idea that we should put limits on growth because of some natural limit is a profound error.[83]

If there were a world environmental crisis, it seemed that the UNCED initiative would be unable to bring it to an end.

The EC Environment Minister, Carlo Ripa di Meana, explained why he would not be going to Rio: 'The culprits are the Americans, who have won the battle of the lowest common denominator – profiting from the diplomatic complicity of all those (the Europeans amongst them, the British first and foremost) who have been content to pour out documents and declarations of "constructive ambiguity".' The reason for the US tactics of obstruction were plain: 'Whose fault is it? The winner of that prize is undoubtedly the US which was, is and will remain the great polluter of our planet . . .

There will be a party; instead of being a party to celebrate the Earth, it is in danger of revealing itself as its funeral wake.'[84] It was difficult to disguise the general pessimism. At best there was a 'Vast agenda but thin on action';[85] at worst the Rio summit was 'crumbling'.[86] Criticisms of the United States mounted when US President George Bush issued a statement that clearly violated the spirit of Rio: 'We cannot permit the extreme in the environmental movement to shut down the United States. We cannot shut down the lives of many Americans by going to the extreme of the environment.'

After two years of complex negotiations agreement had been reached on the holding of the vast Earth Summit. Well over 100 heads of state visited Rio in June 1992; when they left, the nations had agreed on:

- a treaty on climate and one on biodiversity, the latter not signed by the United States;
- a set of environmental principles – not legally binding;
- the 800-page 'Agenda 21' plan for sustainable development – not legally binding;
- the creation of a UN commission to study sustainable development;
- a small increases in Third World aid, pledged by various developed countries but not by the United States;
- a set of principles for preserving forests – not legally binding.

It was noted that the 'Earth's wretched' had won 'few favours';[87] and that 'Japan and the European Community shared the honours for greatest embarrassment at the Earth Summit. (The United States, which refused to sign the Biodiversity Treaty or pledge any increase in aid, proved unembarrassable.)'[88] At the conclusion of the Rio summit, UNCED Secretary-General Maurice Strong declared that without greater commitment from political leaders the world was heading for tragedy.

In October 1992 an unpublished United Nations study revealed that an expanse of rainforest the size of England and Wales was being bulldozed or burnt every year, a rate of destruction of more than an acre per second. A three-year study, using satellites and aerial photography, revealed that the environment had reached 'critical' levels in many of the 88 countries surveyed. At the same time, a report published by the UN Food and

Agriculture Organisation described that many plant species that could have provided new medicines had been destroyed. On 3 October 1992 it was announced that the British government was leading moves by Western nations to cut back the Rio promises of increased aid to poor countries.

On 21 April 1993 President Bill Clinton celebrated Earth Day in the Washington botanical gardens by announcing he would sign the international biodiversity treaty that had been rejected by President Bush at Rio. Clinton introduced a number of other ecological measures at this time, acknowledging that the environmental challenges had to be met: 'For too long, we have been told that we had to choose between the environment and the economy. We think you can't have a healthy economy without a healthy environment.' This shift in the White House was the most hopeful sign in a post-Rio world in which most of the world's leaders were continuing with business as usual.

Part III
Towards Reform

8 Time for Change

The United Nations is a living system; and as such it functions in highly complex characteristic ways.[1] In particular, it is subject to internal and external pressures that cause it to evolve over time. At one level the pressures are reactionary, working to shape a United Nations that will operate to protect vested interest; at another, there are pressures for genuine reform, where efforts are made to change the character of the United Nations so that it is better equipped to carry out its tasks.

The need for a reformed United Nations is widely acknowledged. UN Secretary-General Boutros Boutros-Ghali noted in recent report that 'it is in our power to bring about a renaissance – to create a new United Nations for a new international era'; and he went on to declare:

> The transition from the old to the new United Nations is neither easy nor risk-free. We are still absorbing the lessons of the end of the cold war. The bipolar competition, which carried an ever-present threat of nuclear devastation, provided strenuous framework for international relations. New and more enduring structures must not be built.[2]

In the same spirit, individual political parties in various countries have stressed their commitment to the United Nations, at the same time urging various reforms. Thus, for example, the Liberal Democrats in the United Kingdom have emphasised their belief that 'a reformed and restructured United Nations must be the cornerstone of the international institutions required for today's world'.[3] And we should also note the various campaigns for UN reform; in particular, the work of CAMDUN (Conference of A More Democratic United Nations).[4]

The reform efforts and campaigns vary widely in their ambitions. Some campaigners want to see no more than an improvement in the administrative machinery of the United Nations, a laudable aim that focuses essentially on management competence. Others look to radical reform of basic UN procedures and institutions; urging, for instance, a differently constituted Security Council or improved methods for selecting the Secretary-General. Some campaigners envisage the creation of fresh UN assemblies ('of the people'), in order to end the monopoly of the nation state. Many of the multifarious proposals for reform are mutually consistent; some are not.

THE EXPANDING ROLE

One of the consequences of the ending of the Cold War is the increased scope for United Nations activities throughout the world. This is not necessarily a beneficial development: in circumstances in which Permanent Members of the Security Council are unlikely to use their veto against Washington, there is the danger that the UN will degenerate into being little more than a US proxy, funded by the world community but mainly interested in serving American foreign policy. Secretary-General Boutros-Ghali has drawn attention to the massively expanding UN role. The work of the Security Council itself has seen 'a dramatic increase . . . In all of 1987, the Council met 49 times, whereas in the first seven months of 1992 alone there were 81 official meetings . . . 14 Security Council resolutions were adopted in all of 1987. In the first seven months of 1992, there were 46.'

The expanding UN role is particularly significant in the area of peace-keeping. In the first 40 years of its existence the United Nations established thirteen peace-keeping operations; but since 1988 thirteen new peace-keeping operations have been organised, in addition to five that are still being maintained from the earlier period. By 1993 more than 40,000 military personnel were serving under UN command around the world in operations costing more than $3 billion for a twelve-month period. The expanded responsibilities have placed increased burdens on the Secretariat.

Many proposals for UN reform or expanded responsibilities are blocked by powerful Member States. The suggestion that the United Nations should begin its own intelligence-gathering activities, in order to provide early warnings on potential conflicts, has been discovered by Washington as likely to undermine American espionage initiatives. Similarly, the US has been keen to block any suggestion that American forces operating under nominal UN mandate be brought under the control of United Nations officers.[5] At the same time increasing attention is being given to a new interventionist role of UN forces under US command. The UK Foreign Secretary Douglas Hurd has recommended that the United Nations, implicitly under Western control, adopt a fresh 'imperial' role in the post-Cold War world: 'It is putting UN blue on the map. It is an imperial role . . . It's becoming clear now that we're at a new stage in the way the world's going to have to run its affairs.'[6] On 22 September 1992 Douglas Hurd, addressing the UN General Assembly, emphasised the importance of old-fashioned diplomacy in preventing potential conflict and warned against overloading the United Nations system. There would have to be, he declared, a huge increase in the funds needed to pay for UN operations around the globe.

OILING THE MACHINE

There have been many criticisms – not always disinterested – of the administrative competence o the United Nations organisation. Many major UN operations, according to one view, have been mismanaged, leading to a waste of funds and counterproductive consequences. Thus Alex de Waal and Rakiya Omaar, then of the human rights organisation Africa Watch (now of African Rights), have referred to 'the incompetence and lack of accountability within the UN bureaucracy', suggesting at the same time the creation of independent public inquiries into such major UN operations as Somalia, Yugoslavia and Cambodia: 'Lessons for the future must be learnt and the officials responsible for needless failures must be disciplined or dismissed. This is not a matter of vindictiveness; it is a basic requirement of accountable civil service.'[7] We can recall, for example, the case of the corrupt UN officials involved in the dispute over Western Sahara (see Chapter 7).

In February 1993 an in-house UN report, delivered to Secretary-General Boutros-Ghali, spoke of 'almost surreal' budget practices and 'chronically fragmented and inadequate' internal audits. A significant charge in the report was that one UN unit responsible for internal supervision had become 'a convenient patronage dumping ground' and had recently spent some $4 million on how to manage works of art at the UN headquarters in New York. The author of the report, Dick Thornburgh, commented that the UN was 'almost totally lacking in effective means to deal with fraud, waste and abuse by staff members'. Further, there were defeats 'in nearly every aspect of personnel practice', with recruitment 'more or less haphazard' and a 'few good staff members . . . doing too much, and over-extending themselves, sometimes to the point where they have become counter-productive'. Boutros-Ghali himself had declared that one of his stated goals was fighting corruption and over-staffing in the UN bureaucracy. Not long after his appointment in 1992 he made severe cuts in the number of high-level jobs and began to trim the Secretariat's 14,000 members. In September 1992 he noted:

> A number of offices have been regrouped, related functions and activities have been consolidated and redeployment of resources have been undertaken. Unnecessary bureaucratic layers have been reduced through the elimination of several high-level posts. Lines of responsibility have been more clearly defined by concentrating the decision-making process in seven key departments at Headquarters under eight Under-Secretaries-General.[8]

Charges continued to be made about UN incompetence in Somalia, particularly after the tragic armed clashes between US-led forces and Somalis in June 1993. In January accusations of UN mismanagement were made by Major-General Lewis MacKenzie, the former head of UN forces in Sarajevo, later to be declared a UN 'safe area'. He declared that most countries were unhappy with the way that UN operations were run: 'Countries don't give their troops to the UN in trust to be killed trying to implement a really lousy ceasefire agreement arranged by a bunch of diplomats and politicians . . . That's what's happening in Yugoslavia.' He condemned the UN's headquarters as 'a nine-to-five civilian operation' and advised commanders not to get into trouble 'after 5pm New York time, or Saturday or Sunday' since there is no one 'to answer the phone'.[9]

Attention has also been given to what seemed to be the inefficient management of United Nations personnel in Mogadishu.[10] Here each day a UN helicopter ferries UN secretaries and administrators from their UN houses to the main United Nations compound a mile away. In late 1993 it was estimated to cost around $2000 to make a helicopter journey of a mile; seemingly no one had thought of bringing the UN staff to live near their work. At that time the helicopter was making the journey four times in each direction every working day. And it was also reported that personnel from UN agencies, such as UNICEF, were not allowed to share UN facilities with UNOSOM staff. Said Ian MacLeod, senior UNICEF officer in Mogadishu: 'The point is that UN agencies aren't allowed to eat with UNOSOM staff in their facilities. This is a major dispute. It's gone very high up in New York.'[11] Such matters, seemingly petty, have caused needless friction and irritation, and are scarcely what should engage the best efforts of UN representatives.

In August 1993 a series of articles produced by *The Sunday Times* (London) 'Insight' team accused the United Nations, 'funded by £7 bn of Western taxpayers' money', of being 'a bureaucracy out of control, dogged by mismanagement and financial abuse'.[12] Subsequent reports suggested that the UN was aware of the problems and was taking steps to stamp out corruption.[13] Other observers developed in detail the notion that revelations of UN corruption were unsurprising.[14] A statement from the UN Information Centre in London declared that the main Insight article (*The Sunday Times*, 15 August 1993) 'contained more than 30 factual errors' and lamented the fact that most of the UN responses to *The Sunday Times* had not been published.[15]

The debate, crucial to the future of the United Nations, is vitally important. In this context, notwithstanding the undoubted management shortcomings in the global UN organisation, it is important to remember that the United Nations has no significance and capacity beyond what is willed by its Member States. David Bryer, the Director of Oxfam, rightly commented that 'Inefficiency deserves criticism but much of the criticism commonly levelled against the UN should be more properly directed against member governments . . .'[16] Few observers doubted that there was some truth in the persistent criticisms of the United Nations but it still needed to be stressed that the international organisation could only be what the Member States – particularly the powerful countries – wanted it to be. A United Nations that was too efficient could be less easily scapegoated by those nations keen to disguise their own lack of action.

THE QUESTION OF RESOURCES

The effectiveness of the United Nations depends upon how well it is resourced. There is always the feeling that the burdens on the UN are excessive, that it is under-resourced to fulfil expectations. In June 1992 Boutros-Ghali urged member states to make armed forces available to the Security Council on a permanent rather than an *ad hoc* basis, to facilitate the rapid deployment of peace-keeping forces. Yet any such resourcing requirement would inevitably be judged within the policy frameworks of the Member States. The Western powers would probably welcome such UN 'peace-enforcement units' as helpful proxies funded by the world community, much as the way that President George Bush used his begging bowl to collect funds for the 1991 Gulf War. By contrast, smaller states would be likely to see such peace-keeping units – under the certain control of the Security Council – as a fresh tool for rich nations eager to maintain the unjust status quo in the Third World. The question of UN resourcing cannot be divorced from the policy perceptions of the different Member States.

Such considerations are well illustrated by Washington's financial debt to the United Nations. The US has long been reluctant to pay its legally binding fees or UN membership. Thus at the start of the Gulf War – at a time when President Bush was keen to praise the new UN role – Washington owed the United Nations some $451 million, $296 million for the general fund and $155 million for approved peace-keeping operations. In September 1992 Washington owed the United Nations $757 million; with the debt standing at $845.7 million – $549.5 million owed to the regular budget and $296.2 million outstanding on the peace-keeping budget – in early 1993. In February 1993 Boutros-Ghali, after his first meeting with President Bill Clinton, said that he had received 'very positive signals' over the US debt. Such tardiness in paying dues can hardly be judged helpful to the resourcing of the United Nations.

Boutros-Ghali himself has noted the problem of securing prompt payment:

> A fundamental aspect of General Assembly resolution 41/213, which called for payment in full and on time by all Member States of their assessed contributions, however, has yet to be implemented. As of September 1992 only 52 Member States had paid in full their dues . . . At the end of August 1992, I was able to pay the salaries of the regular staff . . . only through borrowing from peace-keeping funds . . . Perennial shortages, the absence of reserves and a debilitating uncertainty over the immediate future are the main characteristics of the financial situation of the United Nations.[17]

Judgements about what the UN should or should not be doing must be set against such resourcing uncertainties.

Throughout 1993 the funding problems of the United Nations became increasingly apparent. The demands on the UN continued to grow but Member States – including some Permanent Members of the Security Council – seemed reluctant to pay their nominal dues specified in the Charter. Secretary-General Boutros-Ghali made frequent appeals, at times emphasising that the United Nations was on the brink of financial collapse, but seemingly to little avail. In May he declared that money was running out for the 17,000 UN troops struggling to maintain a brief and fragile cease-fire in Croatia, with Jordan one of a number of countries threatening to pull out its UN contingent unless its costs were reimbursed. At the same time UN officials were warning that it would be hard to pay for UN guards to police the trade embargo against the Bosnian Serbs, and that the 'safe areas' policy could not be enforced without increased funding. Shortage of money was already forcing the withdrawal of the small UN contingent needed to safeguard the supply of aid to the Kurds in northern Iraq, while more than a third of the substantial bill or UN operations in Cambodia remained unpaid. The intention is that peacekeeping operations are funded according to the wealth and size of UN member states; but the United States, Japan and Russia are in massive arrears, with Britain one of the few leading countries to pay on time.[18] Part of the problem is that powerful states, with no prospect of sanctions against them, are not keen to fund operations in which they have no political interest. Thus in Cambodia, Somalia and Bosnia 'the power brokers in the Security Council, including the United States, Britain and France, who steer through the peace-keeping resolutions on which the UN secretariat must act, do not have compelling political interests in those countries'.[19] The UN debt situation for some key operations is shown in Figure 8.1.

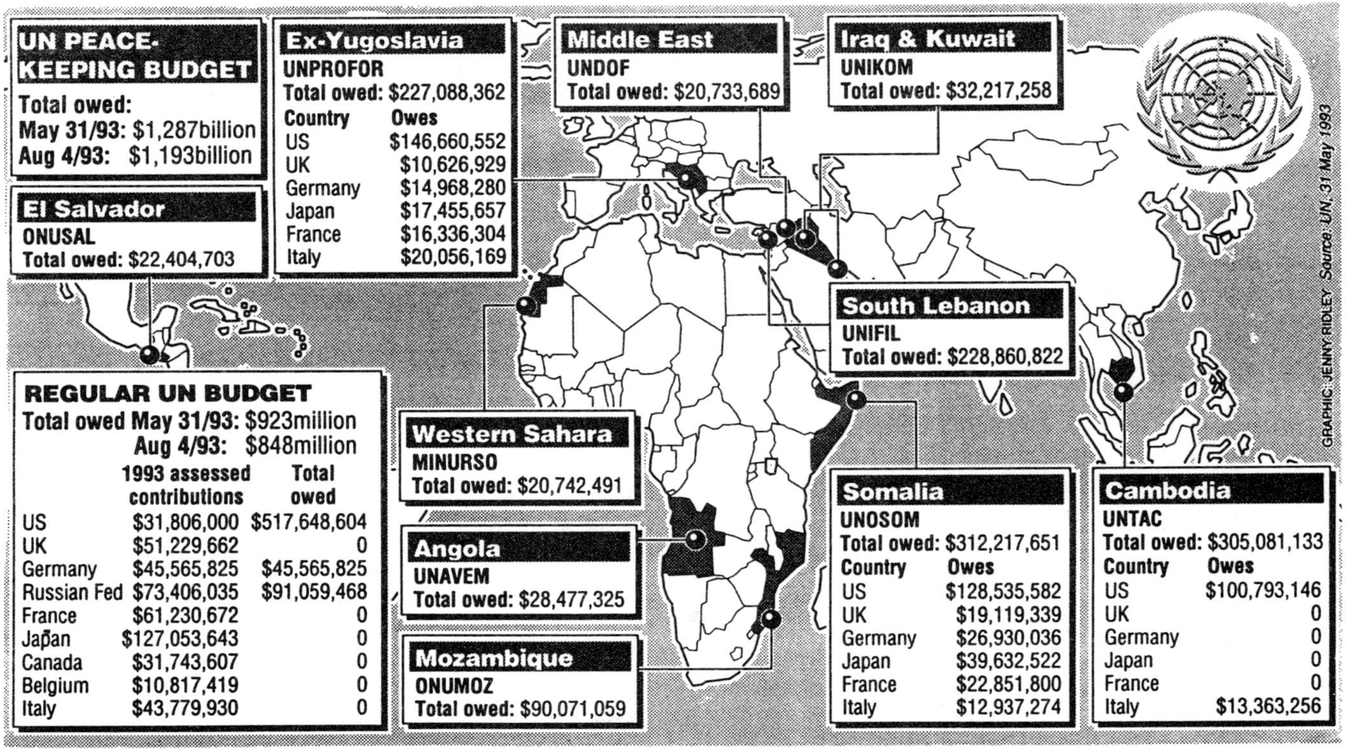

Figure 8.1 *Debt situation for some key UN operations*
SOURCE: *The Guardian* (London), 4 August 1993.

In August 1993 UN Secretary-General Boutros-Ghali appealed by letter for members in arrears to pay their dues.[20] Here he notes that the total cash reserves of the United Nations stand at $380 million, with the total monthly expense of the organisation running at $310 million; and he declares:

> Unless the United Nations receives substantial payments of outstanding assessed contributions within the next month, I will be obliged to inform the member states that the organisation is unable to enter into new financial commitments. It will not be possible to finance new missions and even existing operations will be in jeopardy . . . I should emphasise that the unprecedented demands on the United Nations, the shortfall in contributions from so many member states and the total depletion of the organisation's financial reserves render the present situation the most critical it has ever faced.

At that time the United States, the most influential UN member, owed the United Nations $836 million, by far the largest debt to the international organisation.

REPRESENTATION OF THE PEOPLE

The United Nations purports to represent the entire world community. Its sobriquets (the 'world body', the 'global forum', and so on) convey the flavour, and today, with more than 180 Members, the UN's universal character cannot be gainsaid. At the same time there is still ample scope for considering the nature of the representation. It would be difficult to argue that the institutions of the United Nations were created in a democratic spirit (see Chapter 2) or that the current UN structure is a model democratic institution. There is no sense in which the General Assembly is a world parliament with legislative powers. All UN members have a vote in the Assembly even if, in violation of Article 19 of the Charter, they persistently fail to pay their legally stipulated fees; but Assembly votes have little or no power to constrain decisions in the Security Council. It works the other way round. Most of the power in the UN resides with the five Permanent Members of the Security Council, not because they alone can command a majority in the Council but because in reality enough of the rotating members can always be bribed or threatened into supporting resolutions proposed by Washington and its allies. For people who want to see a truly democratic United Nations faithfully representing the people of the world, this is not a happy situation. There are many proposals for reform of the UN constitution.

Even if the present relationship between the Council and the Assembly were accepted there would still be the matter of how the Council should be composed in order to represent the world community. The fifteen members of the Security Council represent all continents but the powerful five Permanent Members do not: they arrived where they are because of world circumstances half a century ago. They were the victors in a war where the defeated aggressors were not to be allowed fresh powers in the newly emerging world community: it was obvious at that time that Germany and Japan could not be allowed Permanent Member status on the freshly hatched Security Council. Today the situation has changed. A reunited Germany and a reformed Japan, both now economic superpowers, may reasonably claim as much right as Britain or France to sit as Permanent Members on the Security Council. But what, if such claims were to be granted, would happen to the permanent seats of other members? Would it really be proper for Europe to have three of seven permanent seats on the Council? Perhaps Britain and France should be expelled; or perhaps there should be one permanent seat – not for Britain, France or Germany – but for the European Community. In which case, the EC would need to evolve a unified political identity: the Community would be allowed to speak with only one voice in the Security Council. And what then of other national claims across the globe? What about representation, on a Permanent Member basis, for India, Africa and Latin America? Is the Security Council to be indefinitely expanded? Or do we need expulsions? And who will decide – if not the present Permanent Members with the power of veto?

With the accelerating dissolution of the Soviet Union there was some uncertainty for a while about the Soviet seat on the Council; but in the event the matter was easily resolved. Russia, under a pro-West President Yeltsin, was given the permanent seat on the Council, but no democratic procedure was followed: the General Assembly was not allowed to determine the outcome and little heed was paid to the views of Germany or Japan. In 1991 Japan's UN ambassador, Yoshio Hatano, was already pushing for a permanent seat for Japan, the second largest contributor to the United Nations budget (he likes to quote the American Revolution slogan: 'No taxation without representation'); but Russia's accession was stitched up behind the scenes. At the time it suited the existing Permanent Members, and so that was what happened. The British government was already beginning to feel nervous about what might transpire if the structure of the Security Council were to be more widely considered: a source close to the US State Department commented that the British 'needed the question of the permanent five sewn up quickly' – and so it was. The Germans, like the Japanese, had been pushing for a permanent seat; but here earlier German statements were recycled to justify a quick elevation for Yeltsin. Was it not the case, observed a British official, that the Germans had been stressing the need to involve Russia on the international stage? In such circumstances, 'they could hardly fail to be satisfied by a proposal to bring Mr Yeltsin to New York and Russia on to the Council as quickly as possible'. US officials noted that the question of Permanent Membership of the Security Council had been conveniently shelved or another decade.[21]

It was not long, however, before the issue surfaced again, generating fresh British insecurity. On 22 January 1993 the Foreign Secretary, Douglas Hurd, responded in a speech at the Royal Institute of International Affairs to hints that the new American Administration might be interested in reforming the membership of the Security Council. A remark by the new US Secretary of State, Warren Christopher – that it might be necessary to 'bring the Security Council into keeping with modern realities' – was enough to ring the alarm bells. Said Hurd: 'If it ain't broke, don't fix it', and later denied that Britain and France would be prepared to yield their permanent seats in favour of a single European Community replacement. At the same time there were signs that the EC Commission was starting to be interested in the idea. Various EC governments, in the debate before the Maastricht agreement in December 1991, had already suggested that Britain and France should agree to give up their permanent seats on the Security Council; and on 26 January 1993 the new European Commissioner for External Affairs, Hans van der Broek, urged the need for reform of both the membership and operations of the Council. One idea was that the European Community should be represented in the Security Council by whichever EC member currently occupied the rotating presidency.

In June 1993 Madeleine Albright, the US ambassador to the United Nations, stated that Washington would work for German and Japanese permanent membership of the Security Council. London, amid fresh alarm that British power might be diluted in the Council, routinely repeated the pertinent slogan ('If it ain't broken, don't fix it') and took steps to emphasise that the existing UN Charter – specifying the five Permanent Members – remained 'a pretty good read'. At the same time it was reported that Secretary-General Boutros-Ghali would be setting up a working party in the autumn to study the question of representation on the Security Council.

There was also talk of an Anglo-French rearguard battle to oppose President Clinton's sympathy for the entry of Japan and Germany into an enlarged Security Council. Thus France's UN ambassador, Jean-Bernard Mérimée, cited the 'unwritten rules' of nuclear status in the Security Council as a means of preserving the unique status of the 'Permanent Five'. Britain has often suggested that a state must have global responsibilities to qualify for membership of the Security Council, with one official quoted as acknowledging that 'the nuclear status lurks understood in the background'.

The British and French have also tended to argue that the German and Japanese constitutional barriers against overseas military involvement would prohibit full responsibilities within the Security Council, even though there were clear signs that such barriers were being eroded. There were also reports that Washington was considering the idea that Britain and France be removed from the Security Council, replacing them with Japan and a seat for the European Community. A report by the UK Commons Select Committee on Defence warned that Britain's seat on the Security Council could be at risk unless the government protects defence spending.[22]

The UK Foreign Secretary, Douglas Hurd, frequently expressed reservations about any significant reform of the Security Council: for example, commenting to Bonn's *General Anzeiger* newspaper that 'Britain is not fundamentally against every change, but we have asked for caution'. At the same time there were signs that Britain was beginning to adjust to the inevitability of Japanese and German membership of the Security Council. On the opening day of the G7 Tokyo Summit, held in July 1993, a British diplomat was quoted as recognising that 'the debate is about widening the Security Council, including the permanent membership. There are countries who are, or who are on the way, to being able to carry out their peacekeeping responsibilities.' Soon afterwards a Japanese spokesman commented: 'Britain and France have done a lot of good on the Security Council – it's always those who feel most at risk in a hierarchy who make the greatest effort to be constructive. But Britain risks spoiling its entire image if it is perceived as digging its heels in against reform.'[23]

Few observers doubted that with the end of the Cold War the American power over the UN 'lies in its control of the Security Council'.[24] In such circumstances it seemed obvious that Washington would only permit reforms that did nothing to disturb the US hegemony over international affairs.

Debate was also focusing procedures for electing the UN Secretary-General. Here, as in many other matters, the opinions of the Permanent Members reign supreme with little attention being paid to the views of other Council Members or to the opinions of the majority of the General Assembly delegates. The campaign to find a successor to Perez de Cuellar began in late 1991, a procedure 'combining the intrigue and suspense of a papal election with the cynicism of power politics'.[25] Various candidates* were in

* The leading candidates were Prince Sadruddin Aga Khan, Boutros Boutros-Ghali, Ali Atalas, Bernard Chidzero, Gro Harlem Brundtland, Brian Mulroney, Hans van der Broek, and Thorvald Stoltenberg. The list was whittled down for the final vote in November.

the running, but it was widely acknowledged that the process was essentially obscure and haphazard. Open discussion among UN members was not encouraged and the General Assembly was expected to endorse automatically the successful individual recommended by the Security Council. Some pundits suggested that none of the favoured runners might win the place: earlier appointments – Kurt Waldheim in 1971 and Javier Perez de Cuellar in 1981 – were compromise candidates following vetoes. In the event Boutros Boutros-Ghali won the day – to Britain's great disappointment. The United States had supported the successful candidate, a not unprecedented event. Now the new Secretary-General had to prove his mettle: whatever his personal qualities, no one imagined that the selection procedure, affecting as it did the entire fortunes of the United Nations, had much to do with democracy.

Most of the proposals for UN reform assume that the broad structure of the United Nations organisation will remain unchanged. The Security Council may need to be reconstituted, the General Assembly given fresh powers, but these broad representative bodies will survive as the only first-order assemblies designed to address the social and political issues of the world community. A more radical proposal would be to abolish existing UN bodies and to replace them with others; or to graft new institutions on to a reformed UN structure. One of the most significant radical campaigns of this sort is the International Network for a UN Second Assembly (INFUSA), a movement that combined with the World Citizens Assembly (WCA), Concerned Citizens Speak and WorldCOPE to constitute the 1990s Conference on A More Democratic United Nations (CAMDUN).[26] The idea for a UN Second ('we the peoples') Assembly was first published in 1982 as a proposal that the peoples of the world should have bicameral UN representation. This meant that representation of national citizens by government delegates in the General Assembly should be complemented by a 'Second Assembly' of non-governmental delegates to provide representation of people as global inhabitants ('world citizens').[27]

All the serious proposals for UN reform are about empowerment – of abused minorities, disadvantaged social sectors, persecuted political groups, the people of the world. A principal problem – not the only one – is how power can be taken out of the hands of self-interested élites and more properly distributed in the name of justice. The central problem of the United Nations is the problem of power.

THE PROBLEM OF POWER

All states throughout history have been concerned with advancing their interests, spreading their influence and enhancing their security. This tentative political law – shaping the expansion of tribal groups, the growth of empires, the forming of military alliances – may be regarded as a natural phenomenon among multifaceted living systems with an interest in survival. But to say that something is natural says nothing about virtue. Indeed, a principal task of civilisation is to discriminate between natural processes that should be encouraged and ones that should be opposed (in defence of this doctrine we need cite only the role of medical science). In short, for our purposes, no state is *necessarily* entitled to pursue its own perceived self-interest in its own way.

The United Nations has frequently been exploited – against both the spirit and the letter of the Charter – to serve the narrow self-interest of powerful states. This clear exploitation has often taken the form of scapegoating. If leading nations want to do little in a crisis, while sounding as if they want to do much, then it is useful to be able to blame the failure on the United Nations. In this way major states can throw off their responsibilities while protecting their virtue. Thus the percipient Conor Cruise O'Brien, one-time high UN official, notes that 'falling into discredit from time to time is an important part of the UN's repertoire. One of the things the major powers value it for is its scapegoat role.'[28] And sometimes the United Nations is exploited as a cloak for action rather than inaction.

It was inevitable, given the power factors of the twentieth century, that Washington would be the lead player in the United Nations. The constitutional fabric of the UN was largely an American creation, as were most of the associated institutions – particularly the financial bodies (the IMF/World Bank/GATT nexus) – devised primarily to give Washington a handle on the world. This suggests that the United States, until recently backed by the strongest economy in the world, has always been in the best position to exploit the UN. This obvious fact has often been noted. Thus Jawaharlal Nehru, first premier of India (1947–64), observed that the United Nations 'had been a great disillusionment to him, for it was clearly an American racket'.[29] This was a circumstance that showed itself in many ways. For example, to gain a UN imprimatur for the Korean war, Washington not only launched a military initiative first, in order to present the Security Council with a *fait accompli*, but also organised disinformation (lies) in order to sway wavering delegates. Thus, when Washington did not immediately secure the necessary UN votes for its resolution, it secretly informed delegates that Russian soldiers had been captured in tanks in Korea: 'This information, which was false, seems to have swung the vote and started the UN intervention.'[30]

The United States was also in the position to influence the appointment of key UN officials, from the Secretary-General down – and to have politically 'unsuitable' officials removed from their posts. A particularly glaring example of US leverage was the discharge of UN Special Representative Rajeshwar Dayal from his post during the Congo crisis (see 'Undermining the Congo', Chapter 5). Dayal himself noted that every great power wanted to use the United Nations as an instrument of its own policy, but some powers were better placed than others to do so. During Dayal's time in Leopoldville (he had taken up his duties on 8 September 1961), 'the powers in the best position to make this use of the United Nations were the United States and, secondarily, Britain'.[31] Whereas Washington and London wanted to impose Kasavubu and Mobutu on the region – a procedure of 'highly questionable' legality – Dayal, supported by Secretary-General Dag Hammarskjöld, urged the convening of parliament and the holding of democratic elections. The Western powers, keen to secure their clients, began a propaganda campaign against Dayal, and before long his position had become untenable. Despite the unswerving support offered by the Secretary-General, Rajeshwar Dayal was forced to relinquish his post, ousted by Western pressure. Conor Cruise O'Brien later wrote:

> Mr Dayal's whole bearing . . . was extremely impressive; I found in it no trace of the 'arrogance' so persistently ascribed to him, but on the contrary an unusual degree of considerate courtesy towards his interlocutor and a dispassionate attitude, altogether worthy of a stoic, towards his own personal fate.[32]

The Dayal case was unusual in its high-profile aspect but it was not the only time when US pressure was exerted to constrain the efforts of UN officials. It is equally significant that when Secretary-General Boutros-Ghali began to disagree with Permanent Members of the Security Council a vigorous and hostile campaign was launched in the Western press.[33] Just as Dayal had been 'arrogant', so Boutros-Ghali manifested a 'harsh' style.[34] It was left to the respondent Cameron Duodu to remark that what the Boutros-Ghali affair showed was that 'the time has come for world views to prevail at the UN, rather than those of the West'. He declared: 'If the West takes the initiative and frees the Security Council from its anachronistic past, it will save the United Nations from joining the League of Nations in ignominy.'[35] Boutros-Ghali survived the campaign against him; as did Hiroshi Nakajima, the Japanese head of the World Health Organisation (WHO). Here the United States, Britain and other Western countries launched a campaign against Nakajima's re-election, with Washington on 4 May 1993 adopting the time-honoured threat that funds might be withheld. However, all the efforts failed and Nakajima was re-elected.[36]

Early in 1993 Boutros-Ghali advanced the radical proposal that the United States should relinquish the top management and budget post at the United Nations. The Clinton Administration predictably rejected the idea, insisting that if Washington were to persuade Congress to settle US debts to the United Nations then the United States would have to remain in the top management post. This incident again showed Washington's attitude to its obligations under the UN Charter. The US payment obligations could be ignored if Washington saw fit, just as rulings of the World Court could be ignored when the adjudications were against the United States.[37] Similarly, in a dramatic vote on 24 November 1992, the UN General Assembly endorsed a Cuban resolution (47/19) calling for an end to the 'economic, commercial and financial embargo imposed by the USA against Cuba'. The resolution was carried by 59 votes to 3 (the United States, Israel and Romania), with many abstentions. On 3 November 1993 the Assembly passed Resolution 48/16 by 88 votes to 4 (the United States, Israel, Albania and Paraguay), again condemning the US blockade. Washington predictably ignored these important UN votes.

The case of the 35-year US blockade of Cuba is of particular significance. The long embargo was strengthened in November 1992 when President Bush signed the so-called Cuba Democracy Act (formerly the Torricelli Bill) to prevent US subsidiaries trading with Cuba out of third countries. The impact of the US position, in circumstances where Russian aid to Cuba has ended, is that an entire nation is being denied the essentials of life: the means to sustain and develop the national infrastructure, necessary medical supplies, and adequate quantities of foodstuffs. An entire people, struggling to protect a popular revolution that is no threat to the United States, is being deliberately pushed by Washington into hunger and disease.[38]

The US policy, rigorously maintained under the Clinton Administration, represents a serious abuse of American power. To deprive an entire civilian population of food as a means of warfare is prohibited under the Geneva Convention (Protocol 1, Article 54); and, in time of nominal peace, the crime is even more odious. The historic General Assembly votes, condemning the American policy, are not legally binding, though they carry immense moral weight and must be seen as important steps in the campaign to right a great injustice. It is also important to remember that in some circumstances General Assembly recommendations have carried legal force.[39] The current US position on Cuba is a violation of international law; a clear infringement of national sovereignties (not only Cuba's); and a manifest insult to the spirit of the United Nations.

We need also to remember that the Cuban people are not the only national civilian population currently (early 1994) being condemned to destitution, disease and hunger by Washington. The Iraqi people, too, are being forced to suffer appalling privations because of the continuing punitive sanctions maintained by the US-dominated Security Council. Two of the UN's own bodies – the Food and Agriculture Organisation (FAO) and the World Food Programme (WFP) – have jointly described the effects of sanctions: 'persistent deprivation, chronic hunger, endemic undernutrition, massive unemployment and widespread human suffering . . . a grave humanitarian tragedy is unfolding'.[40]

Such issues serve to highlight the problem posed by a hegemonic United States, driven by its own strategic interests, to a United Nations organisation at least nominally concerned with international welfare. The problem focuses on Article 2(1) of the UN Charter. How are we to ensure that '*The Organization is based on the principle of the sovereign equality of all its Members'?* How are we to ensure that the 'Security Council', the 'international community' and the 'West' are more than virtual synonyms for the Washington State Department and Washington whim?

There is abundant evidence that Washington manipulated the United Nations over Iraq and Libya; that it betrayed UN resolutions on Indonesia, South Africa and Israel; that it contrived a UN 'tilt' in favour of US proxies in Angola and El Salvador; that it treats the World Court with contempt when it rules against Washington; that it uses its dominant position in the UN-linked financial institutions to further the interests of American capital; that it compounded UN problems in Somalia with its brutal military initiatives; that for years it has failed to pay its obligatory UN dues; that it exploits UN-gathered intelligence for its own purposes; that it frequently frustrates the best efforts of various UN bodies – UNICEF, WFP, FAO and others – by pushing policies designed to further a self-serving US agenda. The problem of power, particularly where the power is substantial and essentially hegemonic, is that power cannot be trusted.

Today the shortcomings of the United Nations are well publicised: cases of food aid mysteriously blocked in Sudan[41] and Liberia[42] – management incompetence, the perennial funding problems or some factions working to a hidden agenda?; US-led military abuses in Somalia; corruption among UN personnel in Bosnia and Cambodia; the subservience of the Security Council, and so the functional secretariat, to Western – primarily American – interests.[43] The weight of such criticisms, linked to the UN's manifest practical failures, has led some observers to speculate on whether the United Nations does more harm than good, to acknowledge at least that the UN 'is in trouble'.[44] However, few commentators, apart from a small fringe, call for the United Nations to be dissolved.

Much of the work of the United Nations is unsung but vital: the continuous global campaign against racism, sometimes involving criticisms of national governments;[45] UNICEF's little-publicised efforts to improve the lot of children in Brazil and elsewhere; the delivery of food aid and technological expertise to millions of suffering people around the world. And the UN keeps alive the dream of a harmonious world. With stalwart optimism Secretary-General Boutros Boutros-Ghali applauds the concept of *Multilateralism* – 'the voluntary cooperation of nations for peace and development'. Today, he declares, 'multilateralism is working more effectively than ever in history'.[46]

The credibility of the United Nations must rest on a transparent impartiality, where there are no favoured nations, no special rights conferred on wealth or military power, and no peoples – Serbs, Cubans, Iraqis, Libyans – eternally consigned to 'pariah status' to suit the strategic agenda of hegemonic powers. The UN, uniquely committed as an institution to human rights, must at all times symbolise the subversive doctrine that morality – not military dominance or economic advantage – is the proper animating principle of political endeavour. *Realpolitik*, by contrast, should be exposed as the characteristic practice of pragmatic politicians serving self-interested factions at the expense of wider communities. And there is another dimension, today too rarely discussed.

The problem of power does not focus, in the last resort, on the noise of a debating chamber, but on the control of global resources. Who owns the land? The mineral riches that it contains? And the food production that it supports? *A principal aim of powerful states in the modern world is to ensure that the United Nations and all its associated institutions are only allowed to impinge on the real world in ways that are consistent with the developing interests of the multinational corporations.* This is the fact that should be set against all the talk of UN reform, of the changing role of the United Nations in the modern world. This is the fact that should always be remembered when powerful states put pressure on the United Nations by withholding due payments, violate the spirit and the letter of the Charter, and coerce the Security Council into serving national strategic and capitalist interests rather than the good of the real 'international community'. This is the ultimate problem of power that the United Nations should be encouraged to confront.

Appendix I The Covenant of the League of Nations*

The High Contracting Parties

In order to promote international co-operation and to achieve international peace and security

by the acceptance of obligations not to resort to war,
by the prescription of open, just and honourable relations between nations,
by the firm establishment of the understandings of international law as the actual rule of conduct among Governments,
and by the maintenance of justice and a scrupulous respect for all treaty obligations in the dealings of organised peoples with one another,
Agree to this Covenant of the League of Nations.

Article 1

1. The original Members of the League of Nations shall be those of the Signatories which are named in the Annex to this Covenant and also such of those other States named in the Annex as shall accede without reservation to this Covenant. Such accession shall be effected by a Declaration deposited with the Secretariat within two months of the coming into force of the Covenant. Notice thereof shall be sent to all other Members of the League.

2. Any fully self-governing State, Dominion or Colony not named in the Annex may become a Member of the League if its admission is agreed to by two-thirds of the Assembly, provided that it shall give effective guarantees of its sincere intention to observe its international obligations, and shall accept such regulations as may be prescribed by the League in regard to its military, naval and air forces and armaments.

3. Any Member of the League may, after two years' notice of its

* The texts printed in italics indicate amendments adopted by the League.

intention so to do, withdraw from the League, provided that all its international obligations and all its obligations under this Covenant shall have been fulfilled at the time of its withdrawal.

Article 2

The action of the League under this Covenant shall be effected through the instrumentality of an Assembly and of a Council, with a permanent Secretariat.

Article 3

1. The Assembly shall consist of Representatives of the Members of the League.
2. The Assembly shall meet at stated intervals and from time to time as occasion may require at the Seat of the League or at such other place as may be decided upon.
3. The Assembly may deal at its meetings with any matter within the sphere of action of the League or affecting the peace of the world.
4. At meetings of the Assembly, each Member of the League shall have one vote, and may have not more than three Representatives.

Article 4

1. The Council shall consist of Representatives of the Principal Allied and Associated Powers, together with Representatives of four other Members of the League. These four Members of the League shall be selected by the Assembly from time to time in its discretion. Until the appointment of the Representatives of the four Members of the League first selected by the Assembly, Representatives of Belgium, Brazil, Spain and Greece shall be members of the Council.
2. With the approval of the majority of the Assembly, the Council may name additional Members of the League whose Representatives shall always be Members of the Council; the Council with like approval may increase the number of Members of the League to be selected by the Assembly for representation on the Council.

2. *bis. The Assembly shall fix by a two-thirds majority the rules dealing with the election of the non-permanent Members of the Council, and par-*

ticularly such regulations as relate to their term of office and the conditions of re-eligibility.

3. The Council shall meet from time to time as occasion may require, and at least once a year, at the Seat of the League, or at such other place as may be decided upon.

4. The Council may deal at its meetings with any matter within the sphere of action of the League or affecting the peace of the world.

5. Any Member of the League not represented on the Council shall be invited to send a Representative to sit as a member at any meeting of the Council during the consideration of matters specially affecting the interests of that Member of the League.

6. At meetings of the Council, each Member of the League represented on the Council shall have one vote, and may have not more than one Representative.

Article 5

1. Except where otherwise expressly provided in this Covenant or by the terms of the present Treaty, decisions at any meeting of the Assembly or of the Council shall require the agreement of all the Members of the League represented at the meeting.

2. All matters of procedure at meetings of the Assembly or of the Council, including the appointment of Committees to investigate particular matters, shall be regulated by the Assembly or by the Council and may be decided by a majority of the Members of the League represented at the meeting.

3. The first meeting of the Assembly and the first meeting of the Council shall be summoned by the President of the United States of America.

Article 6

1. The permanent Secretariat shall be established at the Seat of the League. The Secretariat shall comprise a Secretary-General and such secretaries and staff as may be required.

2. The first Secretary-General shall be the person named in the Annex; thereafter the Secretary-General shall be appointed by the Council with the approval of the majority of the Assembly.

3. The secretaries and staff of the Secretariat shall be appointed by the Secretary-General with the approval of the Council.

4. The Secretary-General shall act in that capacity at all meetings of the Assembly and of the Council.

5. *The expenses of the League shall be borne by the Members of the League in the proportion decided by the Assembly.*

Article 7

1. The Seat of the League is established at Geneva.

2. The Council may at any time decide that the Seat of the League shall be established elsewhere.

3. All positions under or in connection with the League, including the Secretariat, shall be open equally to men and women.

4. Representatives of the Members of the League and officials of the League when engaged on the business of the League shall enjoy diplomatic privileges and immunities.

5. The buildings and other property occupied by the League or its officials or by Representatives attending its meetings shall be inviolable.

Article 8

1. The Members of the League recognise that the maintenance of peace requires the reduction of national armaments to the lowest point consistent with national safety and the enforcement by common action of international obligations.

2. The Council, taking account of the geographical situation and circumstances of each State, shall formulate plans for such reduction for the consideration and action of the several Governments.

3. Such plans shall be subject to reconsideration and revision at least every ten years.

4. After these plans have been adopted by the several Governments, the limits of armaments therein fixed shall not be exceeded without the concurrence of the Council.

5. The Members of the League agree that the manufacture by private enterprise of munitions and implements of war is open to grave objections. The Council shall advise how the evil effects attendant upon such manufacture can be prevented, due regard being had to the necessities of those Members of the League which are not able to manufacture the munitions and implements of war necessary for their safety.

6. The Members of the League undertake to interchange full and frank

information as to the scale of their armaments, their military, naval and air programmes and the condition of such of their industries as are adaptable to warlike purposes.

Article 9

A permanent Commission shall be constituted to advise the Council on the execution of the provisions of Articles 1 and 8 and on military, naval and air questions generally.

Article 10

The Members of the League undertake to respect and preserve as against external aggression the territorial integrity and existing political independence of all Members of the League. In case of any such aggression or in case of any threat or danger of such aggression, the Council shall advise upon the means by which this obligation shall be fulfilled.

Article 11

1. Any war or threat of war, whether immediately affecting any of the Members of the League or not, is hereby declared a matter of concern to the whole League, and the League shall take any action that may be deemed wise and effectual to safeguard the peace of nations. In case any emergency should arise, the Secretary-General shall, on the request of any Member of the League, forthwith summon a meeting of the Council.

2. It is also declared to be the friendly right of each Member of the League to bring to the attention of the Assembly or of the Council any circumstance whatever affecting international relations which threatens to disturb international peace or the good understanding between nations upon which peace depends.

Article 12

1. The Members of the League agree that if there should arise between them any dispute likely to lead to a rupture they will submit the matter either to arbitration *or judicial settlement* or to enquiry by the Council, and

they agree in no case to resort to war until three months after the award by the arbitrators *or the judicial decision* or the report by the Council.

2. In any case under this article the award of the arbitrators *or the judicial decision* shall be made within a reasonable time, and the report of the Council shall be made within six months after the submission of the dispute.

Article 13

1. The Members of the League agree that whenever any dispute shall arise between them which they recognise to be suitable for submission to arbitration *or judicial settlement*, and which cannot be satisfactorily settled by diplomacy, they will submit the whole subject-matter to arbitration *or judicial settlement.*

2. Disputes as to the interpretation of a treaty, as to any question of international law, as to the existence of any fact which, if established, would constitute a breach of any international obligation, or as to the extent and nature of the reparation to be made for any such breach, are declared to be among those which are generally suitable for submission to arbitration *or judicial settlement.*

3. *For the consideration of any such dispute, the court to which the case is referred shall be the Permanent Court of International Justice, established in accordance with Article 14, or any tribunal agreed on by the parties to the dispute or stipulated in any Convention existing between them.*

4. The Members of the League agree that they will carry out in full good faith any award *or decision* that may be rendered, and that they will not resort to war against a Member of the League which complies therewith. In the event of any failure to carry out such an award *or decision*, the Council shall propose what steps should be taken to give effect thereto.

Article 14

The Council shall formulate and submit to the Members of the League for adoption plans for the establishment of a Permanent Court of International Justice. The Court shall be competent to hear and determine any dispute of an international character which the parties thereto submit to it. The Court may also give an advisory opinion upon any dispute or question referred to it by the Council or by the Assembly.

Article 15

1. If there should arise between Members of the League any dispute likely to lead to a rupture, which is not submitted to arbitration *or judicial settlement* in accordance with Article 13, the Members of the League agree that they will submit the matter to the Council. Any party to the dispute may effect such submission by giving notice of the existence of the dispute to the Secretary-General, who will make all necessary arrangements for a full investigation and consideration thereof.

2. For this purpose, the parties to the dispute will communicate to the Secretary-General, as promptly as possible, statements of their case with all the relevant facts and papers, and the Council may forthwith direct the publication thereof.

3. The Council shall endeavour to effect a settlement of the dispute, and if such efforts are successful, a statement shall be made public giving such facts and explanations regarding the dispute and the terms of settlement thereof as the Council may deem appropriate.

4. If the dispute is not thus settled, the Council either unanimously or by a majority vote shall make and publish a report containing a statement of the facts of the dispute and the recommendations which are deemed just and proper in regard thereto.

5. Any Member of the League represented on the Council may make public a statement of the facts of the dispute and of its conclusions regarding the same.

6. If a report by the Council is unanimously agreed to by the members thereof other than the Representatives of one or more of the parties to the dispute, the Members of the League agree that they will not go to war with any party to the dispute which complies with the recommendations of the report.

7. If the Council fails to reach a report which is unanimously agreed to by the members thereof, other than the Representatives of one or more of the parties to the dispute, the Members of the League reserve to themselves the right to take such action as they shall consider necessary for the maintenance of right and justice.

8. If the dispute between the parties is claimed by one of them, and is found by the Council, to arise out of a matter which by international law is solely within the domestic jurisdiction of that party, the Council shall so report, and shall make no recommendation as to its settlement.

9. The Council may in any case under this article refer the dispute to the Assembly. The dispute shall be so referred at the request of either party

to the dispute provided that such request be made within fourteen days after the submission of the dispute to the Council.

10. In any case referred to the Assembly, all the provisions of this article and of Article 12 relating to the action and powers of the Council shall apply to the action and powers of the Assembly, provided that a report made by the Assembly, if concurred in by the Representatives of those Members of the League represented on the Council and of a majority of the other Members of the League, exclusive in each case of the Representatives of the parties to the dispute, shall have the same force as a report by the Council concurred in by all the members thereof other than the Representatives of one or more of the parties to the dispute.

Article 16

1. Should any Member of the League resort to war in disregard of its covenants under Articles 12, 13 or 15, it shall, *ipso facto*, be deemed to have committed an act of war against all other Members of the League, which hereby undertake immediately to subject it to the severance of all trade or financial relations, the prohibition of all intercourse between their nationals and the nationals of the Covenant-breaking State, and the prevention of an financial, commercial or personal intercourse between the nationals of the Covenant-breaking State and the nationals of any other State, whether a Member of the League or not.

2. It shall be the duty of the Council in such case to recommend to the several Governments concerned what effective military, naval or air force the Members of the League shall severally contribute to the armed forces to be used to protect the covenants of the League.

3. The Members of the League agree, further, that they will mutually support one another in the financial and economic measures which are taken under this article, in order to minimise the loss and inconvenience resulting from the above measures, and that they will mutually support one another in resisting any special measures aimed at one of their number by the Covenant-breaking State, and that they will take the necessary steps to afford passage through their territory to the forces of any of the Members of the League which are co-operating to protect the covenants of the League.

4. Any member of the League which has violated any covenant of the League may be declared to be no longer a Member of the League by a vote of the Council concurred in by the Representatives of all the other Members of the League represented thereon.

Article 17

1. In the event of a dispute between a Member of the League and a State which is not a member of the League or between States not members of the League, the State or States not members of the League shall be invited to accept the obligations of membership in the League for the purposes of such dispute, upon such conditions as the Council may deem just. If such invitation is accepted, the provisions of Articles 12 to 16 inclusive shall be applied with such modifications as may be deemed necessary by the Council.

2. Upon such invitation being given, the Council shall immediately institute an enquiry into the circumstances of the dispute and recommend such action as may seem best and most effectual in the circumstances.

3. If a State so invited shall refuse to accept the obligations of membership in the League for the purposes of such dispute, and shall resort to war against a Member of the League, the provisions of Article 16 shall be applicable as against the State taking such action.

4. If both parties to the dispute when so invited refuse to accept the obligations of membership in the League for the purposes of such dispute, the Council may take such measures and make such recommendations as will prevent hostilities and will result in the settlement of the dispute.

Article 18

Every treaty or international engagement entered into hereafter by any Member of the League shall be forthwith registered with the Secretariat and shall, as soon as possible, be published by it. No such treaty or international engagement shall be binding until so registered.

Article 19

The Assembly may from time to time advise the reconsideration by Members of the League of treaties which have become inapplicable and the consideration of international conditions whose continuance might endanger the peace of the world.

Article 20

1. The Members of the League severally agree that this Covenant is accepted as abrogating all obligations or undertakings *inter se* which are inconsistent with the terms thereof, and solemnly undertake that they will not hereafter enter into any engagements inconsistent with the terms thereof.

2. In case any Member of the League shall, before becoming a Member of the League, have undertaken any obligations inconsistent with the terms of this Covenant, it shall be the duty of such Member to take immediate steps to procure its release from such obligations.

Article 21

Nothing in this Covenant shall be deemed to affect the validity of international engagements, such as treaties of arbitration or regional understandings like the Monroe doctrine, for securing the maintenance of peace.

Article 22

1. To those colonies and territories which as a consequence of the late war have ceased to be under the sovereignty of the States which formerly governed them and which are inhabited by peoples not yet able to stand by themselves under the strenuous conditions of the modern world, there should be applied the principle that the well-being and development of such peoples form a sacred trust of civilisation and that securities for the performance of this trust should be embodied in this Covenant.

2. The best method of giving practical effect to this principle is that the tutelage of such peoples should be entrusted to advanced nations who, by reason of their resources, their experience or their geographical position, can best undertake this responsibility, and who are willing to accept it, and that this tutelage should be exercised by them as Mandatories on behalf of the League.

3. The character of the mandate must differ according to the stage of the development of the people, the geographical situation of the territory, its economic conditions and other similar circumstances.

4. Certain communities formerly belonging to the Turkish Empire have reached a stage of development where their existence as independent nations can be provisionally recognised subject to the rendering of administra-

tive advice and assistance by a Mandatory until such time as they are able to stand alone. The wishes of these communities must be a principal consideration in the selection of the Mandatory.

5. Other peoples, especially those of Central Africa, are at such a stage that the Mandatory must be responsible for the administration of the territory under conditions which will guarantee freedom of conscience and religion, subject only to the maintenance of public order and morals, the prohibition of abuses such as the slave trade, the arms traffic and the liquor traffic, and the prevention of the establishment of fortifications or military and naval bases and of military training of the natives for other than police purposes and the defence of territory, and will also secure equal opportunities for the trade and commerce of other Members of the League.

6. There are territorities, such as South West Africa and certain of the South Pacific Islands, which, owing to the sparseness of their population, or their small size, or their remoteness from the centres of civilisation, or their geographical contiguity to the territory of the Mandatory, and other circumstances, can be best administered under the laws of the Mandatory as integral portions of its territory, subject to the safeguards above mentioned in the interests of the indigenous population.

7. In every case of mandate, the Mandatory shall render to the Council an annual report in reference to the territory committed to its charge.

8. The degree of authority, control or administration to be exercised by the Mandatory shall, if not previously agreed upon by the Members of the League, be explicitly defined in each case by the Council.

9. A permanent Commission shall be constituted to receive and examine the annual reports of the Mandatories and to advise the Council on all matters relating to the observance of the mandates.

Article 23

Subject to and in accordance with the provisions of international Conventions existing or hereafter to be agreed upon, the Members of the League:

(*a*) will endeavour to secure and maintain fair and humane conditions of labour for men, women and children, both in their own countries and in all countries to which their commercial and industrial relations extend, and for that purpose will establish and maintain the necessary international organisations;

(*b*) undertake to secure just treatment of the native inhabitants of territories under their control;

(*c*) will entrust the League with the general supervision over the execution of agreements with regard to the traffic in women and children, and the traffic in opium and other dangerous drugs;

(*d*) will entrust the League with the general supervision of the trade in arms and ammunition with the countries in which the control of this traffic is necessary in the common interest;

(*e*) will make provision to secure and maintain freedom of communications and of transit and equitable treatment for the commerce of all Members of the League. In this connection, the special necessities of the regions devastated during the war of 1914–1918 shall be borne in mind;

(*f*) will endeavour to take steps in matters of international concern for the prevention and control of disease.

Article 24

1. There shall be placed under the direction of the League all international bureaux already established by general treaties if the parties to such treaties consent. All such international bureaux and all commissions for the regulation of matters of international interest hereafter constituted shall be placed under the direction of the League.

2. In all matters of international interest which are regulated by general Conventions but which are not placed under the control of international bureaux or commissions, the Secretariat of the League shall, subject to the consent of the Council and if desired by the parties, collect and distribute all relevant information and shall render any other assistance which may be necessary or desirable.

3. The Council may include as part of the expenses of the Secretariat the expenses of any bureau or commission which is placed under the direction of the League.

Article 25

The Members of the League agree to encourage and promote the establishment and co-operation of duly authorised voluntary national Red Cross organisations having as purposes the improvement of health, the prevention of disease and the mitigation of suffering throughout the world.

Article 26

1. Amendments to this Covenant will take effect when ratified by the Members of the League whose Representatives compose the Assembly.

2. No such amendments shall bind any Member of the League which signifies its dissent therefrom, but in that case it shall cease to be a Member of the League.

Appendix II The Charter of the United Nations

NOTE: The Charter of the United Nations was signed on 26 June 1945, in San Francisco, at the conclusion of the United Nations Conference on International Organization, and came into force on 24 October 1945. The Statute of the International Court of Justice is an integral part of the Charter.

Amendments to Articles 23, 27 and 61 of the Charter were adopted by the General Assembly on 17 December 1963 and came into force on 31 August 1965. A further amendment to Article 61 was adopted by the General Assembly on 20 December 1971, and came into force on 24 September 1973. An amendment to Article 109, adopted by the General Assembly on 20 December 1965, came into force on 12 June 1968.

The amendment to Article 23 enlarges the membership of the Security Council from 11 to 15. The amended Article 27 provides that decisions of the Security Council on procedural matters shall be made by an affirmative vote of nine members (formerly seven) and on all other matters by an affirmative vote of nine members (formerly seven), including the concurring votes of the five permanent members of the Security Council.

The amendment to Article 61, which entered into force on 31 August 1965, enlarged the membership of the Economic and Social Council from 18 to 27. The subsequent amendment to that Article, which entered into force on 24 September 1973, further increased the membership of the Council from 27 to 54.

The amendment to Article 109, which relates to the first paragraph of that Article, provides that a General Conference of Member States for the purpose of reviewing the Charter may be held at a date and place to be fixed by a two-thirds vote of the members of the General Assembly and by a vote of any nine members (formerly seven) of the Security Council. Paragraph 3 of Article 109, which deals with the consideration of a possible review conference during the tenth regular session of the General Assembly, has been retained in its original form in its reference to a 'vote of any seven members of the Security Council', the paragraph having been acted upon in 1955 by the General Assembly, at its tenth regular session, and by the Security Council.

WE THE PEOPLES
OF THE UNITED NATIONS
DETERMINED

to save succeeding generations from the scourge of war, which twice in our lifetime has brought untold sorrow to mankind, and

to reaffirm faith in fundamental human rights, in the dignity and worth of the human person, in the equal rights of men and women and of nations large and small, and

to establish conditions under which justice and respect for the obligations arising from treaties and other sources of international law can be maintained, and

to promote social progress and better standards of life in larger freedom,

AND FOR THESE ENDS

to practice tolerance and live together in peace with one another as good neighbours, and

to unite our strength to maintain international peace and security, and

to ensure, by the acceptance of principles and the institution of methods, that armed force shall not be used, save in the common interest, and

to employ international machinery for the promotion of the economic and social advancement of all peoples,

HAVE RESOLVED TO
COMBINE OUR EFFORTS TO
ACCOMPLISH THESE AIMS

Accordingly, our respective Governments, through representatives assembled in the city of San Francisco, who have exhibited their full powers found to be in good and due form, have agreed to the present Charter of the United Nations and do hereby establish an international organization to be known as the United Nations.

Chapter I
PURPOSES AND PRINCIPLES

Article 1

The Purposes of the United Nations are:

1. To maintain international peace and security, and to that end: to take effective collective measures for the prevention and removal of threats to the peace, and for the suppression of acts of aggression or other breaches of the peace, and to bring about by peaceful means, and in conformity with the principles of justice and international law, adjustment or settlement of international disputes or situations which might lead to a breach of the peace;
2. To develop friendly relations among nations based on respect for the principle of equal rights and self-determination of peoples, and to take other appropriate measures to strengthen universal peace;
3. To achieve international co-operation in solving international problems of an economic, social, cultural, or humanitarian character, and in promoting and encouraging respect for human rights and for fundamental freedoms for all without distinction as to race, sex, language, or religion; and
4. To be a centre for harmonizing the actions of nations in the attainment of these common ends.

Article 2

The Organization and its Members, in pursuit of the Purposes stated in Article 1, shall act in accordance with the following Principles.

1. The Organization is based on the principle of the sovereign equality of all its Members.
2. All Members, in order to ensure to all of them the rights and benefits resulting from membership, shall fulfil in good faith the obligations assumed by them in accordance with the present Charter.
3. All Members shall settle their international disputes by peaceful means in such a manner that international peace and security, and justice, are not endangered.

4. All Members shall refrain in their international relations from the threat or use of force against the territorial integrity or political independence of any state, or in any other manner inconsistent with the Purposes of the United Nations.

5. All Members shall give the United Nations every assistance in any action it takes in accordance with the present Charter, and shall refrain from giving assistance to any state against which the United Nations is taking preventive or enforcement action.

6. The Organization shall ensure that states which are not Members of the United Nations act in accordance with these Principles so far as may be necessary for the maintenance of international peace and security.

7. Nothing contained in the present Charter shall authorize the United Nations to intervene in matters which are essentially within the domestic jurisdiction of any state or shall require the Members to submit such matters to settlement under the present Charter; but this principle shall not prejudice the application of enforcement measures under Chapter VII.

Chapter II
MEMBERSHIP

Article 3

The original Members of the United Nations shall be the states which, having participated in the United Nations Conference on International Organization at San Francisco, or having previously signed the Declaration by United Nations of 1 January 1942, sign the present Charter and ratify it in accordance with Article 110.

Article 4

1. Membership in the United Nations is open to all other peace-loving states which accept the obligations contained in the present Charter and, in the judgment of the Organization, are able and willing to carry out these obligations.

2. The admission of any such state to membership in the United Nations will be effected by a decision of the General Assembly upon the recommendation of the Security Council.

Article 5

A Member of the United Nations against which preventive or enforcement action has been taken by the Security Council may be suspended from the exercise of the rights and privileges of membership by the General Assembly upon the recommendation of the Security Council. The exercise of these rights and privileges may be restored by the Security Council.

Article 6

A Member of the United Nations which has persistently violated the Principles contained in the present Charter may be expelled from the Organization by the General Assembly upon the recommendation of the Security Council.

Chapter III
ORGANS

Article 7

1. There are established as the principle organs of the United Nations: a General Assembly, a Security Council, an Economic and Social Council, a Trusteeship Council, an International Court of Justice, and a Secretariat.
2. Such subsidiary organs as may be found necessary may be established in accordance with the present Charter.

Article 8

The United Nations shall place no restrictions on the eligibility of men and women to participate in any capacity and under conditions of equality in its principal and subsidiary organs.

Chapter IV
THE GENERAL ASSEMBLY

Composition

Article 9

1. The General Assembly shall consist of all the Members of the United Nations.

2. Each Member shall have not more than five representatives in the General Assembly.

Functions and powers

Article 10

The General Assembly may discuss any questions or any matters within the scope of the present Charter or relating to the powers and functions of any organs provided for in the present Charter and, except as provided in Article 12, may make recommendations to the Members of the United Nations or to the Security Council or to both on any such questions or matters.

Article 11

1. The General Assembly may consider the general principles of co-operation in the maintenance of international peace and security, including the principles governing disarmament and the regulation of armaments, and may make recommendations with regard to such principles to the Members or to the Security Council or to both.

2. The General Assembly may discuss any questions relating to the maintenance of international peace and security brought before it by any Member of the United Nations, or by the Security Council, or by a state which is not a Member of the United Nations in accordance with Article 35, paragraph 2, and, except as provided in Article 12, may make recommendations with regard to any such questions to the state or states concerned or to the Security Council or to both. Any such question to which action is

necessary shall be referred to the Security Council by the General Assembly either before or after discussion.

3. The General Assembly may call the attention of the Security Council to situations which are likely to endanger international peace and security.

4. The powers of the General Assembly set forth in this Article shall not limit the general scope of Article 10.

Article 12

1. While the Security Council is exercising in respect of any dispute or situation the functions assigned to it in the present Charter, the General Assembly shall not make any recommendation with regard to that dispute or situation unless the Security Council so requests.

2. The Secretary-General, with the consent of the Security Council, shall notify the General Assembly at each session of any matters relative to the maintenance of international peace and security which are being dealt with by the Security Council and shall similarly notify the General Assembly, or the Members of the United Nations if the General Assembly is not in session, immediately the Security Council ceases to deal with such matters.

Article 13

1. The General Assembly shall initiate studies and make recommendations for the purpose of:

(a) promoting international cooperation in the political field and encouraging the progressive development of international law and its codification;

(b) promoting international cooperation in the economic, social, cultural, educational, and health fields, and assisting in the realization of human rights and fundamental freedoms for all without distinction as to race, sex, language, or religion.

2. The further responsibilities, functions and powers of the General Assembly with respect to matters mentioned in paragraph 1(b) above are set forth in Chapters IX and X.

Article 14

Subject to the provisions of Article 12, the General Assembly may recommend measures for the peaceful adjustment of any situation, regardless of origin, which it deems likely to impair the general welfare or friendly relations among nations, including situations resulting from a violation of the provisions of the present Charter setting forth the Purposes and Principles of the United Nations.

Article 15

1. The General Assembly shall receive and consider annual and special reports from the Security Council; these reports shall include an account of the measures that the Security Council has decided upon or taken to maintain international peace and security.
2. The General Assembly shall receive and consider reports from the other organs of the United Nations.

Article 16

The General Assembly shall perform such functions with respect to the international trusteeship system as are assigned to it under Chapters XII and XIII, including the approval of the trusteeship agreements for areas not designated as strategic.

Article 17

1. The General Assembly shall consider and approve the budget of the Organization.
2. The expenses of the Organization shall be borne by the Members as apportioned by the General Assembly.
3. The General Assembly shall consider and approve any financial and budgetary arrangements with specialized agencies referred to in Article 57 and shall examine the administrative budgets of such specialized agencies with a view to making recommendations to the agencies concerned.

Voting

Article 18

1. Each member of the General Assembly shall have one vote.

2. Decisions of the General Assembly on important questions shall be made by a two-thirds majority of the members present and voting. These questions shall include: recommendations with respect to the maintenance of international peace and security, the election of the non-permanent members of the Security Council, the election of the members of the Economic and Social Council, the election of members of the Trusteeship Council in accordance with paragraph 1(c) of Article 86, the admission of new Members to the United Nations, the suspension of the rights and privileges of membership, the expulsion of Members, questions relating to the operation of the trusteeship system, and budgetary questions.

3. Decisions on other questions, including the determination of additional categories of questions to be decided by a two-thirds majority, shall be made by a majority of the members present and voting.

Article 19

A Member of the United Nations which is in arrears in the payment of its financial contributions to the Organization shall have no vote in the General Assembly if the amount of its arrears equals or exceeds the amount of the contributions due from it for the preceding two full years. The General Assembly may, nevertheless, permit such a Member to vote if it is satisfied that the failure to pay is due to conditions beyond the control of the Member.

Procedure

Article 20

The General Assembly shall meet in regular annual sessions and in such special sessions as occasion may require. Special sessions shall be convoked by the Secretary-General at the request of the Security Council or of a majority of the Members of the United Nations.

Article 21

The General Assembly shall adopt its own rules of procedure. It shall elect its President for each session.

Article 22

The General Assembly may establish such subsidiary organs as it deems necessary for the performance of its functions.

Chapter V
THE SECURITY COUNCIL

Composition

Article 23[1]

1. The Security Council shall consist of fifteen Members of the United Nations. The Republic of China, France, the Union of Soviet Socialist Republics, the United Kingdom of Great Britain and Northern Ireland, and the United States of America shall be permanent members of the Security Council. The General Assembly shall elect ten other Members of the United Nations to be non-permanent members of the Security Council, due regard being specially paid, in the first instance to the contribution of Members of the United Nations to the maintenance of international peace and security and to the other purposes of the Organization, and also to equitable geographical distribution.
2. The non-permanent members of the Security Council shall be elected for a term of two years. In the first election of the non-permanent members after the increase of the membership of the Security Council from eleven to fifteen, two of the four additional members shall be chosen for a term of one year. A retiring member shall not be eligible for immediate re-election.
3. Each member of the Security Council shall have one representative.

Functions and powers

Article 24

1. In order to ensure prompt and effective action by the United Nations, its Members confer on the Security Council primary responsibility for the maintenance of international peace and security, and agree that in carrying out its duties under this responsibility the Security Council acts on their behalf.

2. In discharging these duties the Security Council shall act in accordance with the Purposes and Principles of the United Nations. The specific powers granted to the Security Council for the discharge of these duties are laid down in Chapters VI, VII, VIII, and XII.

3. The Security Council shall submit annual and, when necessary, special reports to the General Assembly for its consideration.

Article 25

The Members of the United Nations agree to accept and carry out the decisions of the Security Council in accordance with the present Charter.

Article 26

In order to promote the establishment and maintenance of international peace and security with the least diversion for armaments of the world's human and economic resources, the Security Council shall be responsible for formulating, with the assistance of the Military Staff Committee referred to in Article 47, plans to be submitted to the Members of the United Nations for the establishment of a system for the regulation of armaments.

Voting

Article 27[2]

1. Each member of the Security Council shall have one vote.

2. Decisions of the Security Council on procedural matters shall be made by an affirmative vote of nine members.

3. Decisions of the Security Council on all other matters shall be made by an affirmative vote of nine members including the concurring votes of the permanent members; provided that, in decisions under Chapter VI, and under paragraph 3 of Article 52, a party to a dispute shall abstain from voting.

Procedure

Article 28

1. The Security Council shall be so organized as to be able to function continuously. Each member of the Security Council shall for this purpose be represented at all times at the seat of the Organization.

2. The Security Council shall hold periodic meetings at which each of its members may, if it so desires, be represented by a member of the government or by some other specially designated representative.

3. The Security Council may hold meetings at such places other than the seat of the Organization as in its judgment will best facilitate its work.

Article 29

The Security Council may establish such subsidiary organs as it deems necessary of the performance of its functions.

Article 30

The Security Council shall adopt its own rules of procedure, including the method of selecting its President.

Article 31

Any Member of the United Nations which is not a member of the Security Council may participate, without vote, in the discussion of any question brought before the Security Council whenever the latter considers that the interests of that Member are specially affected.

Article 32

Any Member of the United Nations which is not a member of the Security Council or any state which is not a Member of the United Nations, if it is a party to a dispute under consideration by the Security Council, shall be invited to participate, without vote, in the discussion relating to the dispute. The Security Council shall lay down such conditions as it deems just for the participation of a state which is not a Member of the United Nations.

Chapter VI
PACIFIC SETTLEMENT OF DISPUTES

Article 33

1. The parties to any dispute, the continuance of which is likely to endanger the maintenance of international peace and security, shall, first of all, seek a solution by negotiation, enquiry, mediation, conciliation, arbitration, judicial settlement, resort to regional agencies or arrangements, or other peaceful means of their own choice.
2. The Security Council shall, when it deems necessary, call upon the parties to settle their dispute by such means.

Article 34

The Security Council may investigate any dispute or any situation which might lead to international friction or give rise to a dispute, in order to determine whether the continuance of the dispute or situation is likely to endanger the maintenance of international peace and security.

Article 35

1. Any Member of the United Nations may bring any dispute, or any situation of the nature referred to in Article 34, to the attention of the Security Council or of the General Assembly.
2. A state which is not a Member of the United Nations may bring to the attention of the Security Council or of the General Assembly any dispute to

which it is a party if it accepts in advance, for the purposes of the dispute, the obligations of pacific settlement provided in the present Charter.

3. The proceedings of the General Assembly in respect of matters brought to its attention under this Article will be subject to the provisions of Articles 11 and 12.

Article 36

1. The Security Council may, at any stage of a dispute of the nature referred to Article 33 or of a situation of like nature, recommend appropriate procedures or methods of adjustment.

2. The Security Council should take into consideration any procedures for the settlement of the dispute which have already been adopted by the parties.

3. In making recommendations under this Article the Security Council should also take into consideration that legal disputes should as a general rule be referred by the parties to the International Court of Justice in accordance with the provisions of the Statute of the Court.

Article 37

1. Should the parties to a dispute of the nature referred to in Article 33 fail to settle it by the means indicated in that Article, they shall refer it to the Security Council.

2. If the Security Council deems that the continuance of the dispute is in fact likely to endanger the maintenance of international peace and security, it shall decide whether to take action under Article 36 or to recommend such terms of settlement as it may consider appropriate.

Article 38

Without prejudice to the provisions of Articles 33 to 37, the Security Council may, if all the parties to any dispute so request, make recommendations to the parties with a view to a pacific settlement of the dispute.

Chapter VII
ACTION WITH RESPECT TO THREATS TO THE PEACE, BREACHES OF THE PEACE, AND ACTS OF AGGRESSION

Article 39

The Security Council shall determine the existence of any threat to the peace, breach of the peace, or act of aggression and shall make recommendations, or decide what measures shall be taken in accordance with Articles 41 and 42, to maintain or restore international peace and security.

Article 40

In order to prevent an aggravation of the situation, the Security Council may, before making the recommendations or deciding upon the measures provided for in Article 39, call upon the parties concerned to comply with such provisional measures as it deems necessary or desirable. Such provisional measures shall be without prejudice to the rights, claims, or position of the parties concerned. The Security Council shall duly take account of failure to comply with such provisional measures.

Article 41

The Security Council may decide what measures not involving the use of armed force are to be employed to give effect to its decisions, and it may call upon the Members of the United Nations to apply such measures. These may include complete or partial interruption of economic relations and of rail, sea, air, postal, telegraphic, radio, and other means of communication, and the severance of diplomatic relations.

Article 42

Should the Security Council consider that measures provided for in Article 41 would be inadequate or have proved to be inadequate, it may take such action by air, sea, or land forces as may be necessary to maintain or restore international peace and security. Such action may include demonstrations, blockade, and other operations by air, sea, or land forces of Members of the United Nations.

Article 43

1. All Members of the United Nations, in order to contribute to the maintenance of international peace and security, undertake to make available to the Security Council, on its call and in accordance with a special agreement or agreements, armed forces, assistance, and facilities, including rights of passage, necessary for the purpose of maintaining international peace and security.

2. Such agreement or agreements shall govern the numbers and types of forces, their degree of readiness and general location, and the nature of the facilities and assistance to be provided.

3. The agreement or agreements shall be negotiated as soon as possible on the initiative of the Security Council. They shall be concluded between the Security Council and Members or between the Security Council and groups of Members and shall be subject to ratification by the signatory states in accordance with their respective constitutional processes.

Article 44

When the Security Council has decided to use force it shall, before calling upon a Member not represented on it to provide armed forces in fulfilment of the obligations assumed under Article 43, invite that Member if the Member so desires, to participate in the decisions of the Security Council concerning the employment of contingents of that Member's armed forces.

Article 45

In order to enable the United Nations to take urgent military measures, Members shall hold immediately available national air-force contingents for combined international enforcement action. The strength and degree of readiness of these contingents and plans for their combined action shall be determined, within the limits laid down in the special agreement or agreements referred to in Article 43, by the Security Council with the assistance of the Military Staff Committee.

Article 46

Plans for the application of armed forces shall be made by the Security Council with the assistance of the Military Staff Committee.

Article 47

1. There shall be established a Military Staff Committee to advise and assist the Security Council on all questions relating to the Security Council's military requirements for the maintenance of international peace and security, the employment and command of forces placed at its disposal, the regulation of armaments, and possible disarmament.

2. The Military Staff Committee shall consist of the Chiefs of Staff of the permanent members of the Security Council or their representatives. Any Member of the United Nations not permanently represented on the Committee shall be invited by the Committee to be associated with it when the efficient discharge of the Committee's responsibilities requires the participation of that Member in its work.

3. The Military Staff Committee shall be responsible under the Security Council for the strategic direction of any armed forces placed at the disposal of the Security Council. Questions relating to the command of such forces shall be worked out subsequently.

4. The Military Staff committee, with the authorization of the Security Council and after consultation with appropriate regional agencies, may establish regional subcommittees.

Article 48

1. The action required to carry out the decisions of the Security Council for the maintenance of international peace and security shall be taken by all the Members of the United Nations or by some of them, as the Security Council may determine.

2. Such decisions shall be carried out by the Members of the United Nations directly and through their action in the appropriate international agencies of which they are members.

Article 49

The Members of the United Nations shall join in affording mutual assistance in carrying out the measures decided upon by the Security Council.

Article 50

If preventive or enforcement measures against any state are taken by the Security Council, any other state, whether a Member of the United Nations or not, which finds itself confronted with special economic problems arising from the carrying out of those measures shall have the right to consult the Security Council with regard to a solution of those problems.

Article 51

Nothing in the present Charter shall impair the inherent right of individual or collective self-defence if an armed attack occurs against a Member of the United Nations, until the Security Council has taken measures necessary to maintain international peace and security. Measures taken by Members in the exercise of this right of self-defence shall be immediately reported to the Security Council and shall not in any way affect the authority and responsibility of the Security Council under the present Charter to take at any time such action as it deems necessary in order to maintain or restore international peace and security.

Chapter VIII
REGIONAL ARRANGEMENTS

Article 52

1. Nothing in the present Charter precludes the existence of regional arrangements or agencies for dealing with such matters relating to the maintenance of international peace and security as are appropriate for regional action, provided that such arrangements or agencies and their activities are consistent with the Purposes and Principles of the United Nations.

2. The Members of the United Nations entering into such arrangements or constituting such agencies shall make every effort to achieve pacific settlement of local disputes through such regional arrangements or by such regional agencies before referring them to the Security Council.

3. The Security Council shall encourage the development of pacific settlement of local disputes through such regional arrangements or by such regional agencies either on the initiative of the states concerned or by reference from the Security Council.

4. This Article in no way impairs the application of Articles 34 and 35.

Article 53

1. The Security Council shall, where appropriate, utilize such regional arrangements or agencies for enforcement action under its authority. But no enforcement action shall be taken under regional arrangements or by regional agencies without the authorization of the Security Council, with the exception of measures against any enemy state, as defined in paragraph 2 of this Article, provided for pursuant to Article 107 or in regional arrangements directed against renewal of aggressive policy on the part of any such state, until such time as the Organization may, on request of the Governments concerned, be charged with the responsibility for preventing further aggression by such a state.

2. The term enemy state as used in paragraph 1 of this Article applies to any state which during the Second World War has been an enemy of any signatory of the present Charter.

Article 54

The Security Council shall at all times be kept fully informed of activities undertaken or in contemplation under regional arrangements or by regional agencies for the maintenance of international peace and security.

Chapter IX
INTERNATIONAL ECONOMIC AND SOCIAL CO-OPERATION

Article 55

With a view to the creation of conditions of stability and well-being which are necessary for peaceful and friendly relations among nations based on respect for the principle of equal rights and self-determination of peoples, the United Nations shall promote:

(a) higher standards of living, full employment, and conditions of economic and social progress and development;
(b) solutions of international economic, social, health, and related problems; and international cultural and educational co-operation; and
(c) universal respect for, and observance of, human rights and fundamental freedoms for all without distinction as to race, sex, language, or religion.

Article 56

All Members pledge themselves to take joint and separate action in co-operation with the Organization for the achievement of the purposes set forth in Article 55.

Article 57

1. The various specialized agencies, established by intergovernmental agreement and having wide international responsibilities, as defined in their basic instruments, in economic, social, cultural, educational, health, and related fields, shall be brought into relationship with the United Nations in accordance with the provisions of Article 63.

2. Such agencies thus brought into relationship with the United Nations are hereinafter referred to as specialized agencies.

Article 58

The Organization shall make recommendations for the co-ordination of the policies and activities of the specialized agencies.

Article 59

The Organization shall, where appropriate, initiate negotiations among the states concerned for the creation of any new specialized agencies required for the accomplishment of the purposes set forth in Article 55.

Article 60

Responsibility for the discharge of the functions of the Organization set forth in this Chapter shall be vested in the General Assembly and, under the authority of the General Assembly, in the Economic and Social Council, which shall have for this purpose the powers set forth in Chapter X.

Chapter X
THE ECONOMIC AND SOCIAL COUNCIL

Composition

Article 61[3]

1. The Economic and Social Council shall consist of fifty-four Members of the United Nations elected by the General Assembly.
2. Subject to the provisions of paragraph 3, eighteen members of the Economic and Social Council shall be elected each year for a term of three years. A retiring member shall be eligible for immediate re-election.
3. At the first election after the increase in the membership of the Economic and Social Council from twenty-seven to fifty-four members, in addition to the members elected in place of the nine members whose term of office expires at the end of that year, twenty-seven additional members shall be elected. Of these twenty-seven additional members, the term of office of nine members so elected shall expire at the end of one year; and of

nine other members at the end of two years, in accordance with arrangements made by the General Assembly.

4. Each member of the Economic and Social Council shall have one representative.

Functions and powers

Article 62

1. The Economic and Social Council may make or initiate studies and reports with respect to international economic, social, cultural, educational, health, and related matters and may make recommendations with respect to any such matters to the General Assembly, to the Members of the United Nations, and to the specialized agencies concerned.

2. It may make recommendations for the purpose of promoting respect for, and observance of, human rights and fundamental freedoms for all.

3. It may prepare draft conventions for submission to the General Assembly, with respect to matters falling within its competence.

4. It may call, in accordance with the rules prescribed by the United Nations, international conferences on matters falling within its competence.

Article 63

1. The Economic and Social Council may enter into agreements with any of the agencies referred to in Article 57, defining the terms on which the agency concerned shall be brought into relationship with the United Nations. Such agreements shall be subject to approval by the General Assembly.

2. It may co-ordinate the activities of the specialized agencies through consultation with and recommendations to such agencies and through recommendations to the General Assembly and to the Members of the United Nations.

Article 64

1. The Economic and Social Council may take appropriate steps to obtain regular reports from the specialized agencies. It may make arrangements with the Members of the United Nations and with the specialized

agencies to obtain reports on the steps taken to give effect to its own recommendations and to recommendations on matters falling within its competence made by the General Assembly.

2. It may communicate its observations on these reports to the General Assembly.

Article 65

The Economic and Social Council may furnish information to the Security Council and shall assist the Security Council upon its request.

Article 66

1. The Economic and Social Council shall perform such functions as fall within its competence in connection with the carrying out of the recommendations of the General Assembly.

2. It may, with the approval of the General Assembly, perform services at the request of Members of the United Nations and at the request of specialized agencies.

3. It shall perform such other functions as are specified elsewhere in the present Charter or as may be assigned to it by the General Assembly.

Voting

Article 67

1. Each member of the Economic and Social Council shall have one vote.

2. Decisions of the Economic and Social Council shall be made by a majority of the members present and voting.

Procedure

Article 68

The Economic and Social Council shall set up commissions in economic and social fields and for the promotion of human rights, and such other commissions as may be required for the performance of its functions.

Article 69

The Economic and Social Council shall invite any Member of the United Nations to participate, without vote, in its deliberations on any matter of particular concern to that Member.

Article 70

The Economic and Social Council may make arrangements for representatives of the specialized agencies to participate, without vote, in its deliberations and in those of the commissions established by it, and for its representatives to participate in the deliberations of the specialized agencies.

Article 71

The Economic and Social Council may make suitable arrangements for consultation with non-governmental organizations which are concerned with matters within its competence. Such arrangements may be made with international organizations and, where appropriate, with national organizations after consultation with the Member of the United Nations concerned.

Article 72

1. The Economic and Social Council shall adopt its own rules of procedure, including the method of selecting its President.
2. The Economic and Social Council shall meet as required in accordance with its rules, which shall include provision for the convening of meetings on the request of a majority of its members.

Chapter XI
DECLARATION REGARDING NON-SELF-GOVERNING TERRITORIES

Article 73

Members of the United Nations which have or assume responsibilities for the administration of territories whose people have not yet attained a full measure of self-government recognize the principle that the interests of the inhabitants of these territories are paramount, and accept as a sacred trust the obligation to promote to the utmost, within the system of international peace and security established by the present Charter, the well-being of the inhabitants of these territories, and, to this end:

(a) to ensure, with due respect for the culture of the peoples concerned, their political, economic, social, and educational advancement, their just treatment, and their protection against abuses;
(b) to develop self-government, to take due account of the political aspirations of the peoples, and to assist them in the progressive development of their free political institutions according to the particular circumstances of each territory and its peoples and their varying stages of advancement;
(c) to further international peace and security;
(d) to promote constructive measures of development, to encourage research, and to co-operate with one another and, when and where appropriate, with specialized international bodies with a view to the practical achievement of the social, economic, and scientific purposes set forth in this Article; and
(e) to transmit regularly to the Secretary-General for information purposes, subject to such limitation as security and constitutional considerations may require, statistical and other information of a technical nature relating to economic, social, and educational conditions in the territories for which they are respectively responsible other than those territories to which Chapters XII and XIII apply.

Article 74

Members of the United Nations also agree that their policy in respect of the territories to which this Chapter applies, no less than in respect of their metropolitan areas, must be based on the general principle of good-neighborliness, due account being taken of the interests and well-being of the rest of the world, in social, economic, and commercial matters.

Chapter XII
INTERNATIONAL TRUSTEESHIP SYSTEM

Article 75

The United Nations shall establish under its authority an international trusteeship system for the administration and supervision of such territories as may be placed thereunder by subsequent individual agreements. These territories are hereinafter referred to as trust territories.

Article 76

The basic objectives of the trusteeship system, in accordance with the Purposes of the United Nations laid down in Article 1 of the present Charter, shall be:

(a) to further international peace and security;
(b) to promote the political, economic, social, and educational advancement of the inhabitants of the trust territories, and their progressive development towards self-government or independence as may be appropriate to the particular circumstances of each territory and its people and the freely expressed wishes of the peoples concerned, and as may be provided by the terms of each trusteeship agreement;
(c) to encourage respect for human rights and for fundamental freedoms for all without distinction as to race, sex, language, or religion, and to encourage recognition of the interdependence of the peoples of the world; and
(d) to ensure equal treatment in social, economic, and commercial matters for all Members of the United Nations and their nationals, and also equal treatment for the latter in the administration of justice, without prejudice to the attainment of the foregoing objectives and subject to the provisions of Article 80.

Article 77

1. The trusteeship system shall apply to such territories in the following categories as may be placed thereunder by means of trusteeship agreements:

(a) territories now held under mandate;
(b) territories which may be detached from enemy states as a result of the Second World War; and
(c) territories voluntarily placed under the system by states responsible for their administration.

2. It will be a matter for subsequent agreement as to which territories in the foregoing categories will be brought under the trusteeship system and upon what terms.

Article 78

The trusteeship system shall not apply to territories which have become Members of the United Nations, relationship among which shall be based on respect for the principle of sovereign equality.

Article 79

The terms of trusteeship for each territory to be placed under the trusteeship system, including any alteration or amendment, shall be agreed upon by the states directly concerned, including the mandatory power in the case of territories held under mandate by a Member of the United Nations, and shall be approved as provided for in Articles 83 and 85.

Article 80

1. Except as may be agreed upon in individual trusteeship agreements, made under Articles 77, 79, and 81, placing each territory under the trusteeship system, and until such agreements have been concluded, nothing in this Chapter shall be construed in or of itself to alter in any manner the rights whatsoever of any states or any peoples or the terms of existing international instruments to which Members of the United Nations may respectively be parties.

2. Paragraph 1 of this Article shall not be interpreted as giving grounds for delay or postponement of the negotiation and conclusion of agreements for placing mandated and other territories under the trusteeship system as provided for in Article 77.

Article 81

The trusteeship agreement shall in each case include the terms under which the trust territory will be administered and designate the authority which will exercise the administration of the trust territory. Such authority, hereinafter called the administering authority, may be one or more states or the Organization itself.

Article 82

There may be designated, in any trusteeship agreement, a strategic area or areas which may include part or all of the trust territory to which the agreement applies, without prejudice to any special agreement or agreements made under Article 43.

Article 83

1. All functions of the United Nations relating to strategic areas, including the approval of the terms of the trusteeship agreements and of their alteration or amendments, shall be exercised by the Security Council.
2. The basic objectives set forth in Article 76 shall be applicable to the people of each strategic area.
3. The Security Council shall, subject to the provisions of the trusteeship agreements and without prejudice to security considerations, avail itself of the assistance of the Trusteeship Council to perform those functions of the United Nations under the trusteeship system relating to political, economic, social, and educational matters in the strategic areas.

Article 84

It shall be the duty of the administering authority to ensure that the trust territory shall play its part in the maintenance of international peace and security. To this end the administering authority may make use of volunteer forces, facilities, and assistance from the trust territory in carrying out the obligations towards the Security Council undertaken in this regard by the administering authority, as well as for local defence and the maintenance of law and order within the trust territory.

Article 85

1. The functions of the United Nations with regard to trusteeship agreements for all areas not designated as strategic, including the approval of the terms of the trusteeship agreements and of their alteration or amendment, shall be exercised by the General Assembly.

2. The Trusteeship Council, operating under the authority of the General Assembly, shall assist the General Assembly in carrying out these functions.

Chapter XIII
THE TRUSTEESHIP COUNCIL

Composition

Article 86

1. The Trusteeship Council shall consist of the following Members of the United Nations:

   (a) those Members administering trust territories;
   (b) such of those Members mentioned by name in Article 23 as are not administering trust territories; and
   (c) as many other Members elected for three-year terms by the General Assembly as may be necessary to ensure that the total number of members of the Trusteeship Council is equally divided between those Members of the United Nations which administer trust territories and those which do not.

2. Each member of the Trusteeship Council shall designate one specially qualified person to represent it therein.

Functions and powers

Article 87

The General Assembly and, under its authority, the Trusteeship Council, in carrying out their functions, may:

(a) consider reports submitted by the administering authority;
(b) accept petitions and examine them in consultation with the administering authority;
(c) provide for periodic visits to the respective trust territories at times agreed upon with the administering authority; and
(d) take these and other actions in conformity with the terms of the trusteeship agreements.

Article 88

The Trusteeship Council shall formulate a questionnaire on the political, economic, social, and educational advancement of the inhabitants of each trust territory, and the administering authority for each trust territory within the competence of the General Assembly shall make an annual report to the General Assembly upon the basis of such questionnaire.

Voting

Article 89

1. Each member of the Trusteeship Council shall have one vote.
2. Decisions of the Trusteeship Council shall be made by a majority of the members present and voting.

Procedure

Article 90

1. The Trusteeship Council shall adopt its own rules of procedure, including the method of selecting its President.

2. The Trusteeship Council shall meet as required in accordance with its rules, which shall include provision for the convening of meetings on the request of a majority of its members.

Article 91

The Trusteeship Council shall, when appropriate, avail itself of the assistance of the Economic and Social Council and of the specialized agencies in regard to matters with which they are respectively concerned.

Chapter XIV
THE INTERNATIONAL COURT OF JUSTICE

Article 92

The International Court of Justice shall be the principal judicial organ of the United Nations. It shall function in accordance with the annexed Statute, which is based upon the Statute of the Permanent Court of International Justice and forms an integral part of the present Charter.

Article 93

1. All Members of the United Nations are ipso facto parties to the Statute of the International Court of Justice.

2. A state which is not a Member of the United Nations may become a party to the Statute of the International Court of Justice on conditions to be determined in each case by the General Assembly upon the recommendation of the Security Council.

Article 94

1. Each Member of the United Nations undertakes to comply with the decision of the International Court of Justice in any case to which it is a party.

2. If any party to a case fails to perform the obligations incumbent upon it under a judgment rendered by the Court, the other party may have recourse to the Security Council, which may, if it deems necessary, make recommendations or decide upon measures to be taken to give effect to the judgment.

Article 95

Nothing in the present Charter shall prevent Members of the United Nations from entrusting the solution of their differences to other tribunals by virtue of agreements already in existence or which may be concluded in the future.

Article 96

1. The General Assembly or the Security Council may request the International Court of Justice to give an advisory opinion on any legal question.
2. Other organs of the United Nations and specialized agencies, which may at any time be so authorized by the General Assembly, may also request advisory opinions of the Court on legal questions arising within the scope of their activities.

Chapter XV
THE SECRETARIAT

Article 97

The Secretariat shall comprise a Secretary-General and such staff as the Organization may require. The Secretary-General shall be appointed by the General Assembly upon the recommendation of the Security Council. He shall be the chief administrative officer of the Organization.

Article 98

The Secretary-General shall act in that capacity in all meetings of the General Assembly, of the Security Council, of the Economic and Social Council, and of the Trusteeship Council, and shall perform such other functions as are entrusted to him by these organs. The Secretary-General shall make an annual report to the General Assembly on the work of the Organization.

Article 99

The Secretary-General may bring to the attention of the Security Council any matter which in his opinion may threaten the maintenance of international peace and security.

Article 100

1. In the performance of their duties the Secretary-General and the staff shall not seek or receive instructions from any government or from any other authority external to the Organization. They shall refrain from any action which might reflect on their position as international officials responsible only to the Organization.

2. Each Member of the United Nations undertakes to respect the exclusively international character of the responsibilities of the Secretary-General and the staff and not to seek to influence them in the discharge of their responsibilities.

Article 101

1. The staff shall be appointed by the Secretary-General under regulations established by the General Assembly.

2. Appropriate staffs shall be permanently assigned to the Economic and Social Council, the Trusteeship Council, and, as required, to other organs of the United Nations. These staffs shall form a part of the Secretariat.

3. The paramount consideration in the employment of the staff and in the determination of the conditions of service shall be the necessity of securing the highest standards of efficiency, competence, and integrity. Due

regard shall be paid to the importance of recruiting the staff on as wide a geographical basis as possible.

Chapter XVI
MISCELLANEOUS PROVISIONS

Article 102

1. Every treaty and every international agreement entered into by any Member of the United Nations after the present Charter comes into force shall as soon as possible be registered with the Secretariat and published by it.

2. No party to any such treaty or international agreement which has not been registered in accordance with the provisions of paragraph 1 of this Article may invoke that treaty or agreement before any organ of the United Nations.

Article 103

In the event of a conflict between the obligations of the Members of the United Nations under the present Charter and their obligations under any other international agreement, their obligations under the present Charter shall prevail.

Article 104

The Organization shall enjoy in the territory of each of its Members such legal capacity as may be necessary for the exercise of its functions and the fulfilment of its purposes.

Article 105

1. The Organization shall enjoy in the territory of each of its Members such privileges and immunities as are necessary for the fulfillment of its purposes.

2. Representatives of the Members of the United Nations and officials of the Organization shall similarly enjoy such privileges and immunities as are necessary for the independent exercise of their functions in connection with the Organization.

3. The General Assembly may make recommendations with a view to determining the details of the application of paragraphs 1 and 2 of this Article or may propose conventions to the Members of the United Nations for this purpose.

Chapter XVII
TRANSITIONAL SECURITY ARRANGEMENTS

Article 106

Pending the coming into force of such special agreements referred to in Article 43 as in the opinion of the Security Council enable it to begin the exercise of its responsibilities under Article 42, the parties to the Four-Nation Declaration, signed at Moscow, 30 October 1943, and France, shall, in accordance with the provisions of paragraph 5 of that Declaration, consult with one another and as occasion requires with other Members of the United Nations with a view to such joint action on behalf of the Organization as may be necessary for the purpose of maintaining international peace and security.

Article 107

Nothing in the present Charter shall invalidate or preclude action, in relation to any state which during the Second World War has been an enemy of any signatory to the present Charter, taken or authorized as a result of that war by the Governments having responsibility for such action.

Chapter XVIII
AMENDMENTS

Article 108

Amendments to the present Charter shall come into force for all Members of the United Nations when they have been adopted by a vote of two thirds of the members of the General Assembly and ratified in accordance with their respective constitutional processes by two thirds of the Members of the United Nations, including all the permanent members of the Security Council.

Article 109[4]

1. A General Conference of the Members of the United Nations for the purpose of reviewing the present Charter may be held at a date and place to be fixed by a two-thirds vote of the members of the General Assembly and by a vote of any nine members of the Security Council. Each Member of the United Nations shall have one vote in the conference.
2. Any alteration of the present Charter recommended by a two-thirds vote of the conference shall take effect when ratified in accordance with their respective constitutional processes by two-thirds of the Members of the United Nations including all the permanent members of the Security Council.
3. If such a conference has not been held before the tenth annual session of the General Assembly following the coming into force of the present Charter, the proposal to call such a conference shall be placed on the agenda of that session of the General Assembly, and the conference shall be held if so decided by a majority vote of the members of the General Assembly and by a vote of any seven members of the Security Council.

Chapter XIX
RATIFICATION AND SIGNATURE

Article 110

1. The present Charter shall be ratified by the signatory states in accordance with their respective constitutional processes.

2. The ratifications shall be deposited with the Government of the United States of America, which shall notify all the signatory states of each deposit as well as the Secretary-General of the Organization when he has been appointed.

3. The present Charter shall come into force upon the deposit of ratifications by the Republic of China, France, the Union of Soviet Socialist Republics, the United Kingdom of Great Britain and Northern Ireland, and the United States of America, and by a majority of the other signatory states. A protocol of the ratifications deposited shall thereupon be drawn up by the Government of the United States of America which shall communicate copies thereof to all the signatory states.

4. The states signatory to the present Charter which ratify it after it has come into force will become original Members of the United Nations on the date of the deposit of their respective ratifications.

Article 111

The present Charter, of which the Chinese, French, Russian, English, and Spanish texts are equally authentic, shall remain deposited in the archives of the Government of the United States of America. Duly certified copies thereof shall be transmitted by that Government to the Governments of the other signatory states.

IN FAITH WHEREOF the representatives of the Governments of the United Nations have signed the present Charter.

DONE at the city of San Francisco the twenty-sixth day of June, one thousand nine hundred and forty-five.

NOTES

1. Amended text of Article 23 which came into force on 31 August 1965. The text of Article 23 before it was amended read as follows:

    1. The Security Council shall consist of eleven Members of the United Nations. The Republic of China, France, the Union of Soviet Socialist Republics, the United Kingdom of Great Britain and Northern Ireland, and the United States of America shall be permanent members of the Security Council. The General Assembly shall elect six other Members of the United Nations to be non-permanent members of the Security Council, due regard being specially paid, in the first instance to the contribution of Members of the United Nations to the maintenance of international peace and security and to the other purposes of the Organization, and also to equitable geographical distribution.
    2. The non-permanent members of the Security Council shall be elected for a term of two years. In the first election of non-permanent members, however, three shall be chosen for a term of one year. A retiring member shall not be eligible for immediate re-election.
    3. Each member of the Security Council shall have one representative.

2. Amended text of Article 27 which came into force on 31 August 1965. The text of Article 27 before it was amended read as follows:

    1. Each member of the Security Council shall have one vote.
    2. Decisions of the Security Council on procedural matters shall be made by an affirmative vote of seven members.
    3. Decisions of the Security Council on all other matters shall be made by an affirmative vote of seven members including the concurring votes of the permanent members; provided that, in decisions under Chapter VI, and under paragraph 3 of Article 52, a party to a dispute shall abstain from voting.

3. Amended text of Article 61, which came into force on 24 September 1973. The text of Article 61 as previously amended on 31 August 1965 read as follows:

    1. The Economic and Social Council shall consist of twenty-seven Members of the United Nations elected by the General Assembly.
    2. Subject to the provisions of paragraph 3, nine members of the Economic and Social Council shall be elected each year for a term of three years. A retiring member shall be eligible for immediate action.
    3. At the first election after the increase in the membership of the Economic and Social Council from eighteen to twenty-seven members, in addition to the members elected in place of the six members whose term of office expires at the end of that year, nine additional members shall be elected in place of the six members whose term of office expires at the end of that year, nine additional members shall be elected. Of these nine additional members, the term of office of three members so elected shall expire at the end of one year, and of three other members at the end of two years, in accordance with arrangements made by the General Assembly.

4. Each member of the Economic and Social Council shall have one representative.

4. Amended text of Article 109 which came into force on 12 June 1968. The text of Article 109 before it was amended read as follows:

1. A General Conference of the Members of the United Nations for the purpose of reviewing the present Charter may be held at a date and place to be fixed by a two-thirds vote of the members of the General Assembly and by a vote of any seven members of the Security Council. Each Member of the United Nations shall have one vote in the conference.

2. Any alteration of the present Charter recommended by a two-thirds vote of the conference shall take effect when ratified in accordance with their respective constitutional processes by two thirds of the Members of the United Nations including all the permanent members of the Security Council.

3. If such a conference has not been held before the tenth annual session of the General Assembly following the coming into force of the present Charter, the proposal to call such a conference shall be placed on the agenda of that session of the General Assembly, and the conference shall be held if so decided by a majority vote of the members of the General Assembly and by a vote of any seven members of the Security Council.

Notes

Notes to Chapter 1: Roots

1. Britain (Lloyd George, Balfour, Bonar Law, Barnes); Canada (Borden, Foster, Doherty); Newfoundland (Lloyd); Australia (Hughes, Cook); South Africa (Botha, Smuts); New Zealand (Massey, Ward); India (Montague, Maharajah of Bikaner, Sinha, Grant); United States (Wilson, Lansing, House, White, Bliss); France (Clemenceau, Pichon, Klotz, Tardieu, Cambon, Bourgeois); Italy (Orlando, Sonnino, Salandra, Robilant, Salvago-Ruggi, Baralai); Japan (Saionji, Makino, Chinda); Belgium (Hymans, Vandervelde, Van Der Heuvel); Greece (Venizelos, Politis); Romania (Bratiano); Portugal (Moniz); Serbia (Paschitch); Poland (Dmowski); and Czechoslovakia (Kramarzh). This list of delegates is not exhaustive but it includes the principals.
2. These various ideas are discussed in F. P. Walters, *A History of the League of Nations* (London: Oxford University Press, 1952) Ch. 4.
3. Detailed discussions of the Covenant of the League of Nations are included in Walters, *History of the League of Nations*; J. L. Brierly, *The Law of Nations: An Introduction to the International Law of Peace* (London: Oxford University Press, 1963); F. S. Northedge, *The League of Nations: Its Life and Times, 1920–1946* (Leicester: Leicester University Press, 1988).
4. These bodies and their work are described in Brierly, *Law of Nations*, ch. 16.
5. See James Barros, *Office Without Power: Secretary-General Sir Eric Drummond, 1919–1933* (London: Oxford University Press, 1979).
6. George Scott, *The Rise and Fall of the League of Nations* (London: Hutchinson, 1973) p. 39.
7. Wilson, Edith, *Memoirs of Mrs Woodrow Wilson* (London: Putnam, 1939) pp. 278–9.
8. Gene Smith, *When the Cheering Stopped* (London: Hutchinson, 1964) pp. 54–5.
9. Daniel Yergin, *Shattered Peace: The Origins of the Cold War and the National Security* (Harmondsworth, Middx: Penguin, 1980) p. 44.
10. Hugh Brogan, *History of the United States of America* (London: Longman, 1985) p. 593.
11. Northedge, *League of Nations*, p. 194.
12. A criticism of South Africa's handling of its mandate in South West Africa is given in Ruth First, *South West Africa* (Harmondsworth, Middx: Penguin, 1963) pp. 169–74.
13. E. E. Reynolds, *The League Experiment* (London: Nelson, 1939) p. 106.
14. Walters, *History of the League of Nations*, pp. 404–11, describes the working of the minorities system.
15. Emilio de Bono, *Anno XIII: The Conquest of an Empire* (London: Cresset Press, 1937) pp. 13–17.
16. The Earl of Avon, *The Eden Memoirs: Facing the Dictators* (London, 1962) p. 227.
17. Hugh Thomas, *The Spanish Civil War* (Harmondsworth, Middx: Penguin, 1965) p. 338.
18. Walters, *History of the League of Nations*, p. 721.
19. Brogan, *History of the USA*, p. 498.

Notes to Chapter 2: Genesis

1. See Clive Ponting, *1940: Myth and Reality* (London: Hamish Hamilton, 1990) ch. 10.
2. US Department of State, *Postwar Foreign Policy Preparation, 1939–1945*, Department of State Publication 3580 (Washington, D.C.: Government Printing Office, 1949).
3. T. R. Fehrenbach, *This Kind of Peace* (London: Frewin, 1967) p. 25.
4. J. K. Horsefield *et al.*, *The International Monetary Fund, 1945–1965: Twenty Years of International Monetary Co-operation*, vol. III (Washington, D.C.: International Monetary Fund, 1965).
5. Fehrenbach, *This Kind of Peace*, p. 20.
6. Anjali V Patil, *The UN Veto in World Affairs, 1946–1990: A Complete Record and Case Histories of the Security Council's Veto* (Sarasota, Fl: UNIFO/ Mansell, 1992).
7. Ted Morgan, *FDR: A Biography* (London: Collins, 1987) p. 762.
8. Merle Miller, *Plain Speaking: An Oral Biography of Harry S. Truman* (New York: Berkley Publishing Corporation, 1974) p. 199.
9. Fehrenbach, *This Kind of Peace*, p. 68.
10. Ibid., p. 75.
11. Ernst B. Haas, *The Web of Interdependence: The United States and International Organisations* (New Jersey, 1970) p. 3.
12. Trygve Lie, *In the Cause of Peace* (New York: Macmillan, 1954) p. 55.
13. Ibid., p. 58.
14. Ibid., p. 59.

Notes to Chapter 3: Profile

1. Conor Cruise O'Brien, 'Saving faces, and maybe the world', *The Independent* (London), 30 April 1993.
2. Michael Akehurst, *A Modern Introduction to International Law*, 6th edn (London: HarperCollins Academic, 1991) p. 207.
3. The English text states that the 'concurrence' of Permanent Members on the Security Council is a necessary condition for the passing of a resolution, a requirement that is taken as consistent with abstention. The French text demands '*un vote affirmatif*', suggesting that an abstention would defeat a resolution. Such differences of interpretation have been crucial to important decisions, such as the Security Council decisions to use force in Korea and in Iraq.
4. These and other subsequent details are taken from Edmund Jan Osmanczyk, *Encyclopedia of the United Nations and International Agreements*, 2nd edn (New York: Taylor and Taylor, 1990).
5. Evan Luard, *The United Nations. How it Works and What it Does* (London: Macmillan, 1979).
6. Akehurst, *Modern Introduction to International Law*, p. 212.
7. See, for example, 'Provisional Rules of Procedure in the Security Council', in Anjali V. Patil, *The UN Veto in World Affairs, 1946–1990: A Complete Record and Case Histories of the Security Council's Veto* (Sarasota, Fla: UNIFO/ Mansell, 1992) pp. 545–54.
8. This is not unlike the situation of British government ministers, authorised to

legislate and to mobilise state power but individually, through 'Crown immunity', in effect above the law.

9. Trygve Lie, *In the Cause of Peace* (New York: Macmillan, 1954) p. 42.
10. Ibid.
11. Dag Hammarskjöld, UN Doc. A/2404, 21 July 1953, p. xi.
12. Ernest Gross, *Dag Hammarskjöld as Secretary-General*, Oral History Project (New York: Columbia University, 1964) p. 36a.
13. Luard, *United Nations*, pp. 82–5, considers Court cases involving damage to British ships in 1946 following mining of the Corfu Channel, a 1951 dispute between Britain and Norway regarding fishing rights, a method of dividing the Continental shelf, territorial disputes, aircraft incidents, and South African obligations to South West Africa. (In this latter case the Court ruled in 1966 that Liberia and Ethiopia had no legal right to bring such a contentious case. In 1970 the Court ruled that South African occupation of South West Africa was illegal.)
14. See Peter Körner, Gero Maass, Thomas Siebold and Rainer Tetzlaff, *The IMF and the Debt Crisis* (London: Zed Books, 1992) pp. 42–73.
15. Richard Dowden, 'Nairobi halts IMF and World Bank reforms', *The Independent* (London), 24 March 1993.
16. Peter Pringle, 'IMF deal means trouble in store for Yeltsin', *The Independent* (London), 15 July 1992.
17. Hugh O'Shaughnessy, 'UN's World Bank condemned for 'immoral' profits', *The Observer* (London), 22 April 11990. Michael Irwin joined the World Bank as director of the health services department after a distinguished 32-year career with the UN Development Programme (UNDP) and the UN Children's Fund (UNICEF). See also Ken Ringle, 'The man who broke open the World Bank', *The Sunday Times* (London), 30 September 1990.
18. Julius Nyerere, 'Foreword' to Chakravarthi Raghavan, *Recolonization: GATT, the Uruguay Round and the Third World* (London: Zed Books, 1990).
19. For an insider's view of UNESCO, see Richard Hoggart, *An Idea and its Servants: UNESCO from Within* (London: Chatto & Windus, 1978); see also *In the Minds of Men: Unesco 1946 to 1971* (Paris: Unesco, 1972).
20. Leonard Doyle, 'Sick tactics in battle for health chief's job', *The Independent on Sunday* (London), 10 January 1993.
21. Michael Sheridan, 'World health chief faces fraud enquiry', '*The Independent on Sunday* (London), 28 February 1993; James Adams, 'Critics battle to oust "disastrous" WHO chief', *The Sunday Times* (London), 18 April 1993.
22. See Seymour Hersh, *The Samson Option* (London: Faber & Faber, 1991).
23. Nick Rufford, David Leppard and Ian Burrell, 'North Koreans build secret A-bomb plant', *The Sunday Times* (London), 4 April 1993.

Notes to Chapter 4: Cold War

1. I owe this detail and much of what follows to Clive Ponting, *1940: Myth and Reality* (London: Hamish Hamilton, 1990).
2. Ibid., p. 203.
3. H. C. Allen, *Great Britain and the United States* (London: Odhams Press, 1954) p. 904.

4. Q. J. C. Campbell (ed.), *The United States in World Affairs, 1945–7* (London: Council on Foreign Relations, 1947) p. 359.
5. Herbert Feis, *Churchill, Roosevelt and Stalin* (Oxford: Oxford University Press, 1957) p. 596.
6. William F. Leahy, *I Was There* (London: Victor Gollancz, 1950) pp. 351–2.
7. D. F. Fleming, *The Cold War and its Origins, 1917–1960* (New York: Doubleday, 1961) p. 270.
8. Ibid.
9. David Horowitz, *From Yalta to Vietnam: American Foreign Policy in the Cold War* (Harmondsworth, Middx: Penguin, 1967) p. 33n.
10. Cited in Fleming, *Cold War and its Origins*, p. 207.
11. Cordell Hull, *Memoirs* (New York: Macmillan, 1948) pp. 1405, 1409.
12. Ibid., p. 1722.
13. E. Gross, Foreign Policy Bulletin, 15 September 1954. During the UN's first decade the United States could rely on the support of many dictatorships: for example, Nicaragua, Haiti, Paraguay, Honduras, Thailand, Taiwan, Venezuela, the Dominican Republic, Turkey, Greece and Peru.
14. Arthur Krock, *The New York Times*, 2 May 1945.
15. James Reston, *The New York Times*, 12 June 1945.
16. Steven E. Ambrose, *Rise to Globalism: American Foreign Policy since 1938*, 5th edn (Harmondsworth, Middx: Penguin, 1988) p. 62.
17. Ibid., p. 69.
18. According to the Russians, between 15 and 20 million Soviet citizens had been killed; the Germans had destroyed completely on partially 15 large cities, 1710 towns and 70,000 villages; they burned or demolished 6 million buildings and deprived 25 million people of shelter; they demolished 31,850 industrial enterprises, 65,000 kilometres of railway track, 4100 railway stations, 36,000 postal, telegraph and telephone offices, 56,000 miles of main highway, 90,000 bridges and 10,000 power stations; they ruined 1135 coal-mines and 3000 oil wells, carried off to Germany 14,000 steam boilers, 1400 turbines and 11,300 electric generators; they sacked 98,000 collective farms and 2890 machine and tractor stations and slaughtered or carried off 7 million horses, 17 million cattle, 20 million hogs, 27 million sheep and goats, 1110 million poultry; they looted and destroyed 40,000 hospitals and medical centres, 84,000 schools and colleges and 43,000 public libraries with 110 million volumes; they destroyed 44,000 theatres, 427 museums and 2800 churches (Official Statement of the Extraordinary State Committee (USSR), and cited in Fleming, *Cold War and its Origins,* p. 923).
19. T. R. Fehrenbach, *This Kind of Peace* (London: Frewin, 1967) p. 139.
20. Howard K. Smith, *The State of Europe* (New York: Alfred A. Knopf, 1949) pp. 232–4.
21. Trygve Lie, *In the Cause of Peace* (New York: Macmillan, 1954) p. 89.
22. Ibid., p. 98.
23. *Foreign Relations of the United States (FRUS)* (Washington, D.C.: US Government Printing Office, 1950) vol. 1, pp. 234–92; made public in 1975; discussed in detail by Noam Chomsky, *Deterring Democracy* (London and New York: Verso, 1991) pp. 10–13.
24. The character of the US-defined Cold War is described in detail in Chomsky, *Deterring Democracy*, pp. 9–68.

25. 'The World Assembly at San Francisco', *Political Affairs*, April 1945, pp. 293, 295.
26. Mohan Kumaramangalam, *The United Nations* (Bombay: People's Publishing House, India: 1945) pp. 3–14.
27. Testimony of Jan Bukar before the House Committee on Un-American Activities, 13 May 1953, committee report, *Soviet Schedule for War – 1955* (Washington, D.C.: US Government Printing Office, 1953) p. 15.
28. Hearings before House Committee on Un-American Activities, 24 September 1953 (Washington, D.C.: US Government Printing Office, 1953) pp. 2596, 2607.
29. G. Edward Griffin, *The Fearful Master: A Second Look at the United Nations* (Belmont, Mass.: Western Islands, 1964) p. 72.
30. Ibid., pp. 73–4.
31. Nicholas von Hoffman, *Citizen Cohn* (London: Harrap, 1988) p. 115.
32. Lie, *In the Cause of Peace*, p. 388.
33. Ibid., p. 397.
34. Ibid., p. 405.
35. Griffin, *Fearful Master*, p. 88.
36. *Time*, 16 April 1945, international section.
37. *Interlocking Subversion in Government Departments*, SISS Report, 30 July 1953, pp. 8–10.
38. Richard Gid Powers, *Secrecy and Power: The Life of J. Edgar Hoover* (London: Arrow, 1989) p. 299.
39. Allen Weinstein, *Perjury: The Hiss–Chambers Case* (New York: Knopf, 1978) p. 15.
40. Ibid., pp. 507, 513.
41. Walter Goodman, *The Committee* (London: Secker & Warburg, 1964) p. 267.
42. Mark Tran, 'Joyful Hiss claims Russian files clear him of spying', *The Guardian* (London), 30 October 1992.
43. Laurence H. Smith, in *Congressional Record*, 18 April 1955.
44. Joseph Z. Kornfeder, 'The Communist Pattern in the UN', speech before the Congress of Freedom, Veteran's War Memorial Auditorium, San Francisco, April 1955.
45. Griffin, *Fearful Master*, pp. 139–50.
46. Congressmen John Ashbrook, William Ayres, Donald C. Bruce, Edgar Hiestand and David Martin, *Minority Report of the House Committee on Education and Labour* (Washington, D.C.: US Government Printing Office, 11 July 1961).
47. James Byrnes, quoted in Joseph M. Jones, *The Fifteen Weeks* (New York: 1964) p. 54.
48. George F. Kennan, telegram to James Byrnes, 22 February 1946, in *Foreign Relations of the United States (FRUS)* (Washington, D.C.: US Government Printing Office, 1946) vol. 6, pp. 697–706.
49. *Time*, 1 April 1946.
50. Wilfried Loth, *The Division of the World, 1941–1955* (London: Routledge, 1988) p. 111.
51. Ambrose, *Rise to Globalism*, p. 93; Loth, *Division of the World*, pp. 134, 147.
52. Sallie Pisani, *The CIA and the Marshall Plan* (Edinburgh: Edinburgh University Press, 1991) p. 81.
53. Ibid., p. 82.

54. See William Blum, *The CIA: A Forgotten History* (London: Zed Books, 1986). It is interesting that Harry S. Truman came to regret his part in the creation of the CIA: 'I think it was a mistake. And if I'd known what was going to happen, I never would have done it . . . it got out of hand . . . they've got an organization over there in Virginia now that is practically the equal of the Pentagon in many ways . . . those fellows in the CIA don't just report on wars and the like, they go out and make their own . . . it's become a government all of its own and all secret . . . That's a very dangerous thing in a democratic society' (Merle Miller, *Plain Speaking: An Oral Biography of Harry S. Truman* (New York: Berkley Publishing, 1973) pp. 391–92.
55. Thomas Bodenheimer and Robert Gould, *Rollback!: Rightwing Power in US Foreign Policy* (Boston, Mass.: South-End Press, 1989).
56. Ibid., p. 21.
57. Christopher Simpson, *Blowback: America's Recruitment of Nazis and its Effects on the Cold War* (London: Weidenfeld & Nicolson, 1988).
58. Frank Wisner, correspondence, reproduced in John Loftus, *The Balarus Secret* (New York: Alfred A. Knopf, 1982) pp. 102–3.
59. Simpson, *Blowback*, p. 245.

Notes to Chapter 5: Issues – I

1. Today we often tend to focus on the Muslim-inspired hostility to Jews, but we should also remember the traditional Christian anti-Semitism, from the time of the early Church Fathers to the modern age. Thus St John Chrysostom stated that all Jews 'are drunkards, whoremongers and criminals'; in 1205 Pope Innocent III declared that Jews should be treated as 'damned slaves'; and the Nazi Julius Streicher, defending himself at Nuremberg, praised Martin Luther's 'On the Jews and their Lies' (in which people are urged to burn the synagogues, to deny Jews safe conduct and permission to use the streets, to reduce them to penury, and so on).
2. Bernard Postal and Henry W. Levy, *And the Hills Shouted for Joy* (New York: David McKay, 1973) p. 4.
3. Trygve Lie, *In the Cause of Peace* (New York: Macmillan, 1954) p. 162.
4. Postal and Leny, *And the Hills Shouted*, p. 4.
5. Peter Mansfield, *A History of the Middle East* (Harmondsworth, Middx: Penguin, 1991) p. 235.
6. Barnet Litvinoff, *The Burning Bush* (London: Collins, 1988) p. 393.
7. Andrew and Leslie Cockburn, *Dangerous Liaison* (London: Bodley Head, 1992) p. 27.
8. Michael C. Sandusky, *America's Parallel* (Alexandria: Old Dominion Press, 1983) p. 145.
9. E. Grant Meade, *American Military Government in Korea* (Oxford: Oxford University Press, 1951) pp. 59–62.
10. George M. McCune, *Korea Today* (Cambridge, Mass.: Harvard University Press, 1950) pp. 51–2, 201–7.
11. A. Wigfall Green, *Epic of Korea* (Washington, D.C.: Public Affairs Press, 1950) p. 95.
12. W. Douglas Reeve, *The Republic of Korea* (Oxford: Oxford University Press, 1963) pp. 31–2.

13. See, for example, David Horowitz, *From Yalta to Vietnam: American Foreign Policy in the Cold War* (Harmondsworth, Middx: Penguin, 1967) pp. 117–23; I. F. Stone, *The Hidden History of the Korean War* (New York: Monthly Review Press, 1952); William Blum, *The CIA: A Forgotten History* (London: Zed Books, 1991) pp. 45–7.
14. D. F. Fleming, *The Cold War and its Origins* (New York: Doubleday, 1961) pp. 603–4.
15. Blum, *The CIA*, p. 48.
16. Robert Leckie, *The Korean War* (New York: Putnam, 1962).
17. Fleming, *The Cold War*, p. 656.
18. William Manchester, *American Caesar* (London: Hutchinson, 1979) p. 610.
19. Lie, *In the Cause of Peace*, p. 273.
20. Ibid., p. 274.
21. Inis L. Claude, *Swords into Plowshares* (London: University of London Press, 1964) p. 91.
22. Kurt Waldheim, *In the Eye of the Storm* (London: Weidenfeld & Nicolson, 1985) p. 51.
23. George Rosie, *The British in Vietnam* (London: Panther, 1970) p. 135.
24. *The Times*, 18 August 1945.
25. Dwight D. Eisenhower, *Mandate for Change: The White House Years, 1953–1956* (London, 1963) p. 372.
26. Anjali V. Patil, *The UN Veto in World Affairs, 1946–1990: A Complete Record and Case Histories of the Security Council's Veto* (Sarasota, Fla: UNIFO/Marshall, 1992) p. 48.
27. George McT. Kahin, *Intervention: How America Became Involved in Vietnam* (New York: Anchor Books, Doubleday, 1987) p. 41.
28. Ibid., pp. 62, 65.
29. Andrew Boyd, *Fifteen Men on a Powder Keg: A History of the UN Security Council* (London: Methuen, 1971) p. 154.
30. *New York Times*, 8 March 1965.
31. See the accounts in Boyd, *Fifteen Men*, pp. 1159–63; Kahin, *Intervention*, pp. 243–5.
32. Kahin, *Intervention*, p. 389.
33. Patil, *The UN Veto*, p. 52.
34. Lie, *In the Cause of Peace*, pp. 445–6.
35. Waldheim, *In the Eye of the Storm*, p. 98; and see subsequent discussion, pp. 98–110.
36. In 1899 Lord Milner declared that the 'ultimate end' of British policy in the area 'is a self-governing white community supported by well-treated and justly-governed black labour'. King Edward VII signed the South Africa Act in September 1909, enshrining white racism. In 1911 the Mine and Works Act was passed by the Union Parliament, blocking the access of black workers to skilled jobs. Western strategic and economic interests were well prepared to support South African racism: witness the 1957 Simonstown Agreement, the ravages of the Oppenheimer Anglo-American Corporation, and the massive British and American investment to secure gold, iron, coal, diamonds and uranium – all mined by racially exploited native labour.
37. Richard Lamb, *The Failure of the Eden Government* (London: Sidgwick & Jackson, 1987) p. 221.

38. After an extension of Trygve Lie's term of office by three years, he resigned on 10 November 1952. He had incurred the hostility of the Soviet Union over Korea, and right-wing Americans thought him 'soft' on Communism. He noted that his successor, Dag Hammarskjöld, was supported by all five Permanent Members of the Security Council, and that 'the door of the office of the Secretary-General' had been 'reopened'.
39. T. R. Fehrenbach, *This Kind of Peace* (London: Frewin, 1967) p. 257.
40. Ibid., p. 266.
41. One representing the Atlantic military alliance, one representing the Communist world, and one representing the uncommitted nations. It was obvious to most observers that such a scheme would lead to a paralysis of the UN, and it was never seriously discussed.
42. G. Edward Griffin, *The Fearful Master: A Second Look at the United Nations* (Belmont, Mass.: Western Islands, 1972) chs 1–6.
43. Blum, *The CIA*, pp. 174–81.
44. Deryck Thorpe, *Hammarskjöld, Man of Peace* (Ilfracombe, Devon: Stockwell, 1969) chs 6–11.
45. Fehrenbach, *This Kind of Peace*, p. 340.
46. Norodom Sihanouk, *My War with the CIA* (Harmondsworth, Middx: Penguin, 1974) pp. 75–6.
47. Ibid.
48. William Shawcross, *Sideshow: Kissinger, Nixon and the Destruction of Cambodia* (London: Hogarth Press and Chatto & Windus, 1986) p. 54.
49. Seymour M. Hersh, *Kissinger: The Price of Power* (New York: Summit Books, 1983) ch 5, pp. 54–65.
50. Blum, *The CIA*, pp. 152–3.
51. See Geoff Simons, *Iraq: From Sumer to Saddam* (London: Macmillan, 1994).
52. Waldheim, *In the Eye of the Storm*, p. 174.
53. BBC World Service, 20 July 1988; *The Independent* (London), 21 July 1988; quoted by Dilip Hiro, *The Longest War* (London: Paladin, 1990) p. 243.
54. Dozens of 'human rights instruments' – Codes, Conventions, Protocols, Declarations, and so on – have been developed by the United Nations, covering such areas as genocide, torture, slavery, employment, race, sexual equality, punishment, child protection, national independence, education, treatment of the disabled, medical ethics, religious freedom, and the rest.
55. Examples are given in the present chapter: the illegal seating of Formosa as Permanent Member of the Security Council for two decades; presenting the Council with a *fait accompli* military invasion in Korea; ignoring the 1986 World Court ruling over Nicaragua, and so on. Many other cases could be instanced; for example: the US insistence in 1954 that its sponsored invasion of Guatemala was no business of the Security Council; and the US invasions of Grenada (1983) and Panama (1989) against the UN Charter, Article 2(4): 'All Members shall refrain . . . from the threat or use of force against the territorial integrity or political independence of any state . . . .'
56. J. William Fulbright, *The Price of Empire* (London: Fourth Estate, 1989) p. 21.

Notes to Chapter 6: Towards the New World Order

1. See, for example, Steven White, *Gorbachev and After* (Cambridge: Cambridge University Press, 1992); Angus Roxburgh, *The Second Russian Revolution* (London: BBC Books, 1991); Dusko Doder, *Shadows and Whispers* (London: Harrap, 1987).
2. Will Hutton, 'Even an omnipotent United States may find it hard to fill the post-war power vacuum', *The Guardian* (London), 23 January 1991.
3. David Marquand, 'How to help America police the universe', *The Guardian* (London), 8 March 1991.
4. J. K. Galbraith, 'The call of arms and the poor man', *The Guardian* (London), 27 March 1991; see also his *The Culture of Contentment* (Sinclair-Stevenson, 1992).
5. Theo Sommer, 'A world beyond order and control', *The Guardian* (London), 13 April 1993.
6. Patrick Brogan, 'Unrivalled Bush set to police the planet', *The Observer* (London), 25 April 1991.
7. Peter Jenkins, 'Shape of a new world disorder', *The Independent* (London), 15 October 1991.
8. Martin Woollacott, 'The New World what?', *The Guardian* (London), 20 August 1992.
9. Alasdair Burnet, 'Has anyone told Clinton that he has to run the world?', *The Sunday Times* (London), 24 January 1993.
10. Will Hutton, 'Cold war thaw leaves Britain high and dry', *The Guardian* (London), 8 March 1993.
11. Lester Thurow, *Head to Head: The Coming Economic Battle among Japan, Europe and America* (London: Nicholas Brearley, 1993) p. 65.
12. Godfrey Hodgson, 'World voice or US puppet?', *The Independent* (London), 18 June 1991.
13. Leonard Doyle, 'Moscow may lose seat at UN top table', *The Independent* (London), 10 December 1991.

Notes to Chapter 7: Issues – II

1. See Geoff Simons, *Iraq: From Sumer to Saddam* (London: Macmillan, 1994).
2. In the late 1980s Saddam Hussein commissioned a study from the Washington Center for Strategic and International Studies, a foundation that had links with Iraq. Henry Schuler, the Center's energy security programme director, has provided an insight into the secret commissioned study (see Schuler, 'The oil exporters are leaving money on the table', *Arab Oil and Gas Journal*, 1 March 1990). In essence, Arab oil producers were urged to adopt an aggressive oil price policy. It is worth remembering that here Saddam followed American advice.
3. Evidence for the US 'green light' is US ambassador April Glaspie's words to Saddam just prior to the invasion: 'We have no opinion on Arab–Arab conflicts like your border disagreement with Kuwait'; and US Assistant Secretary of State John Kelly's comments, just prior to the invasion, that the US, in the absence of a relevant treaty, would have no obligation to act to defend Kuwait.
4. Bob Woodward, *The Commanders* (New York: Simon & Schuster, 1991) p. 334.

5. *The Independent*, London, 12 February 1991.
6. Mohamed Heikal, *Illusions of Triumph* (London: HarperCollins, 1992).
7. Simons, *Iraq*, ch. 1.
8. Ibid.
9. Leonard Doyle, 'UN chief rebukes arms inspectors', *The Independent*, (London), 1 October 1991.
10. 'UN Troops to Leave Kurdistan', *The Guardian* (London), 12 May 1993.
11. See Geoff Simons, *Libya: The Struggle for Survival* (London: Macmillan, 1993).
12. Adrian Porter and Con Coughlin, 'US planes in dry run to bomb Libya', *The Sunday Telegraph* (London), 1 December 1991.
13. Leonard Doyle, 'Ghali finds merit in Tripoli shift', *The Independent* (London), 5 March 1992.
14. Marc Weller, 'The Lockerbie case: a premature end to the "New World Order"?', *African Journal of International and Comparative Law*, no. 4 (1992) pp. 1–15.
15. John A. Marcum, *The Angolan Revolution, vol. 1: 1950–1962* Cambridge, Mass.: MIT Press, 1969) pp. 229–30.
16. Hearings before the House Select Committee on Intelligence (the Pike Committee) published in *CIA: The Pike Report* (Nottingham, 1977) p. 199.
17. 'SA "still in Angola" ', *Portugal Hoje*, 30 September 1981.
18. Karl Maier, 'Violence hits run-up to Angolan poll', *The Independent* (London), 23 September 1992.
19. Victoria Brittain, 'MPLA takes lead in Angolan elections', *The Guardian* (London), 2 October 1992.
20. Karl Maier, 'Savimbi threat of civil war', *The Independent on Sunday* (London), 4 October 1992.
21. Chris McGreal, 'Angola teaches lesson to UN', *The Guardian* (London), 11 December 1992; Victoria Brittain, 'Weak UN abandons democratic cause in warring Angola', *The Guardian* (London), 28 December 1992.
22. Victoria Brittain, 'Rebels wreak trail of terror and despair across Angola', *The Guardian* (London), 2 February 1993.
23. John Carlin, 'Pretoria came close to dropping nuclear bomb on Luanda', *The Independent* (London), 30 March 1993.
24. Tom Gibb, 'End of a headache for US policy-makers', *The Independent* (London), 2 January 1992.
25. E/CN.4/1993/11 (9 February 1993). Report of the Independent Expert on El Salvador, Mr Pedro Nikken, appointed by the Secretary-General in accordance with Commission on Human Rights resolution 1992/62 of 3 March 1992.
26. A summary of the Truth Commission report is appended to the statement (SC/5570, 18 March 1993) of the Secretary-General. The report demonstrates culpability, naming names and providing circumstancial detail. See Michael Reid, 'Truth Commission points finger at Salvador military', *The Guardian* (London), 16 March 1993; Douglas Farah, 'Salvador army challenges civilian rule', *The Guardian* (London), 27 March 1993.
27. Defence Minister, General Rene Emilio Ponce; Vice-Minister General Orlando Zepeda; former Vice-Minister of Public Security, Colonel Inocente Montano; Chief of Staff, General Gilberto Rubio; former Air Force commander, General Juan Rafael Bustillo; Colonel Francisco Elena Fuentes; Colonel Guillermo Alfredo Benavides; the former commander of the Atlacatl battalion, Colonel

Oscar Alberto Leon Linares; Rodolfo Antonio Parker Soto; former commander of the Atlacatl battalion, Colonel Domingo Monterrosa Barrios; Colonel Natividad de Jesus Caceres Cabrera; Supreme Court President Mauricio Gutierrez Castro; Major Robert D'Aubuisson; Army Captain Eduardo Avila; Captain Alvaro Saravia; and Fernando Segrera. The report also names five commanders of the ERP (the People's Revolutionary Army of the FMLN) as responsible for the killing of mayors.

28. Harold Pinter, 'Archbishop Romero's ghost can be avenged', *The Observer* (London), 28 March 1993.
29. CNN Super Channel television broadcast, 24 May 1993; cites memorandum from the US embassy in El Salvador expressing knowledge of how Archbishop Romero's assassination was planned and knowledge also of the El Mozote massacre (200 men, women and children killed in 1980). See also Noam Chomsky, *Deterring Democracy* (London: Verso, 1991).
30. Annika Savill, 'UN set to condemn Palestinian expulsions', *The Independent* (London), 19 December 1992.
31. Ian Black and Mark Tran, 'UN chief calls for sanctions and Israeli expulsions', *The Guardian* (London), 27 January 1993.
32. Anton La Guardia, 'Israel backs down over Palestinians', *The Daily Telegraph* (London), 2 February 1993.
33. Richard Dowden, 'UN under attack for Somalia "bungling" ', *The Independent* (London), 16 January 1992.
34. Michael Simmons, 'Aid agencies condemn UN as raiders seize convoy', *The Guardian* (London), 14 November 1992.
35. Richard Dowden, 'Somali faction warns of US "colonisation" ', *The Independent* (London), 7 December 1992.
36. Mark Huband, 'US marines met by television crews', *The Guardian* (London), 9 December 1992.
37. Richard Dowden, 'US and UN at odds over Somalia', *The Independent* (London), 15 December 1992.
38. Karl Maier, 'Mogadishu protesters lay siege to UN', *The Independent* (London), 4 January 1993.
39. Bernard Morris, 'US seeks way out of the Somali bloodbath', *The Sunday Times* (London), 28 February 1993.
40. Mark Huband, 'US envoy admits failure to control Somali crime', *The Guardian* (London), 3 March 1993.
41. Peter Hillmore, 'They came, they fed – and now they're getting the hell out', *The Observer* (London), 7 March 1993.
42. UN document SC/5573, 26 March 1993.
43. Mark Huband, 'Doubts cloud UN rebuilding of Somalia', *The Guardian* (London), 3 May 1993.
44. Gerald Burke and Jonathan Ewing, 'UN "to blame" for Somalia deaths', *The Guardian* (London), 7 June 1993.
45. Mark Huband, 'Enter the terminator: US takes its revenge for massacre of the peacemakers', *The Sunday Times* (London), 13 June 1993; Peter Hillmore, 'UN deals out a sharp, short shock', *The Observer* (London), 13 June 1993.
46. Karl Maier ('20 demonstrators shot dead in Pakistan "revenge" ') and Jonathan Ewing ('Foreigners are rapidly becoming the enemy'), 'UN killings inflame Somali crisis', *The Independent* (London), 14 June 1993.

47. Martin Walker, 'First sign of new US role', *The Guardian* (London), 14 June 1993.
48. Rakiya Omaar, 'For mercy read murder', *The Guardian* (London), 15 June 1993.
49. Robert Block, 'Former envoy criticises UN actions in Somalia', *The Independent* (London), 16 June 1993.
50. Peter Hillmore, 'The peacemakers at odds', *The Observer* (London), 27 June 1993.
51. Karl Maier, 'Three Italian soldiers die in shoot-out', *The Independent* (London), 3 July 1993.
52. *Somalia: Human Rights Abuses by the United Nations Forces* (11 Marshalsea Road, London: African Rights, July 1993).
53. Mark Huband, 'UN Somalia action comes under fire', *The Guardian* (London), 5 August 1993.
54. Patrick Cockburn, 'Raid fiasco focuses US doubts over rule in Somalia', *The Independent* (London), 31 August 1993; Martin Walker, 'Mission impossible', *The Guardian (*London), 31 August 1993; Martin Walker, 'Pentagon says botched raid was not a mistake', *The Guardian* (London), 31 August 1993; Richard Ellis, 'Can "Delta farce" now get it right?', *The Sunday Times* (London), 5 September 1993.
55. Massimo Alberizzi, 'US helicopters strafe Somalis', *The Independent* (London), 10 September 1993.
56. In articles and broadcasts the investigative journalist John Pilger has worked to expose Western support for Pol Pot's Khmer Rouge: 'Asia's Nazis must not return', *The Independent* (London), 6 July 1990; 'Britain secretly giving military Aid to Khmer Rouge', *The Independent* (London), 8 October 1990; 'In the service of a murderer', *The Guardian* (London), 16 October 1993.
57. Terry McCarthy, 'Cambodia stands on verge of anarchy', *The Independent* (London), 9 November 1992; David Watts, 'Collapse of talks bring Cambodia close to war', *The Times*, London, 10 November 1992; Nicholas Cumming-Bruce, 'Cambodia peace pact "unworkable" ', *The Guardian* (London), 11 November 1992.
58. Jon Swain, 'UN losing battle for Cambodia in the brothels of Phnom Penh', *The Sunday Times* (London), 27 December 1992.
59. Jon Swain, 'UN digs in as Khmer Rouge fear stalks the voting fields', *The Sunday Times* (London), 16 May 1993.
60. Raymond Whitaker, 'UN celebrates rare good news from Cambodia', *The Independent* (London), 29 May 1993.
61. Robert Fisk, ' "Cleansing" Bosnia at a camp called Jasenovac', *The Independent* (London), 15 August 1992.
62. Leonard Doyle, 'UN split over aid for Bosnians', *The Independent* (London), 26 May 1992.
63. Leonard Doyle and Helen Womack, 'Sanctions will be too little, too late', *The Independent* (London), 29 May 1992.
64. Leonard Doyle, 'UN turns deaf ear to plight of besieged cities', *The Independent* (London), 15 July 1993.
65. Ian Traynor, 'UN relief for Bosnia almost exhausted', *The Guardian* (London), 13 April 1993; Ian Traynor, John Palmer and Paul Webster, 'Thousands face starvation as UN food supplies run out', *The Guardian* (London), 14 April 1993.

66. Annika Savill, 'US may boycott UN meeting over Bosnia', *The Independent* (London), 18 May 1993.
67. Peter Pringle, Christopher Bellamy and Annika Savill, 'UN forced to delay Bosnia talks as West fails to agree', *The Independent* (London), 19 May 1993.
68. Text summaries are given in *The Guardian* (London), and *The Independent* (London), 24 May 1993.
69. Christopher Hitchens, *Hostage to History* (New York: The Noonday Press, 1989) pp. 121–30.
70. Ian Black and John Bierman, 'West urges Russia to lift Cyprus veto', *The Guardian* (London), 13 May 1993.
71. Leonard Doyle, 'UN officials "worked against Polisario" ', *The Independent* (London), 15 November 1991.
72. John Hooper, 'Polisario warns of resumed warfare', *The Guardian* (London), 22 February 1993.
73. Inis L. Claude, *Swords into Plowshares* (London: University of London Press, 1965) p. 218.
74. Tim McGirk, 'Kashmiri student tells of torture', *The Independent* (London), 25 May 1993.
75. CIA Memorandum, 18 June 1962, *Declassified Documents Reference System* (Arlington, V, 1975) Document 240A.
76. *The New York Times*, 12 March 1966, p. 6.
77. Noam Chomsky, 'East Timor', in *The Chomsky Reader* (London: Serpent's Tail, 1988); see also William Blum, *The CIA: A Forgotten History* (London: Zed Books, 1991) pp. 217–22.
78. Daniel Patrick Moynihan, *A Dangerous Place* (New York: Little, Brown, 1978).
79. Editorial, *The New York Times*, 13 December 1975, p. 26.
80. It was reported that the killings had put paid to the chances of Indonesian foreign minister Ali Alatas becoming Secretary-General, what would have been in any case an eccentric appointment.
81. Mark Curtis, 'The executioner's charter', *The Guardian* (London), 25 November 1991; John Gittings, 'East Timorese accuse Britain of blocking action on Indonesia', *The Guardian* (London), 17 June 1992.
82. Margaret Coles, 'UN concern at E. Timor trial', *The Guardian* (London), 11 May 1993.
83. Quoted by Susan George, associate director of the Transnational Institute, Amsterdam, 'The billion-dollar men', *The Guardian* (London), 22 May 1992.
84. Carlo Ripa di Meana, EC environment commissioner, 'Why I will stay away from the Earth Summit', *The Guardian* (London), 30 May 1992.
85. David Lascelles, 'Vast agenda but thin on action', *The Financial Times* (London), 2 June 1992.
86. Martin Walker, Paul Brown, Jan Rocha and John Vidal, 'Rio summit crumbling', *The Guardian* (London), 1 June 1992.
87. Nicholas Schoon, 'The Earth's wretched win few favours', *The Independent* (London), 15 June 1992.
88. Nicholas Schoon, 'Japan and EC fail to fulfil their promises', *The Independent* (London), 15 June 1992.

Notes to Chapter 8: Time for Change

1. The systems interpretation of life is classically described in James Grier Miller, *Living Systems* (New York: McGraw-Hill, 1978). This is a magisterial work (1100 pages to two-column text) carrying many references to the United Nations.
2. Boutros Boutros-Ghali, *Report of the Work of the Organisation from the Forty-sixth to the Forty-seventh Session of the General Assembly* (New York: United Nations, September 1992).
3. *Beyond the Nation State: Liberal Democrat Policies for International Institutions*, Federal Green Paper no. 25 (London: Liberal Democrats, July 1992) p. 9.
4. The Proceedings of CAMDUN-1, held 13–15 October 1990 in New York, published as Frank Barnaby (ed.), *Building a More Democratic United Nations* (London: Frank Cass, 1991); CAMDUN-2 was held in Vienna in September 1991, and subsequent meetings held in later years.
5. Leonard Doyle, 'Washington opposes spy role for UN', *The Independent* (London), 20 April 1992.
6. Anthony Bevins, 'Hurd urges UN to take "imperial" role', *The Independent* (London), 19 September 1992.
7. Alex de Waal and Rakiya Omaar, 'Steps toward an accountable UN' (letter), *The Independent* (London), 13 November 1992.
8. Boutros-Ghali, *Report*, p. 9.
9. Simon Jones, 'Gen. MacKenzie slams UN's nine-to-fivers', *The Independent on Sunday* (London), 31 January 1993.
10. Mark Huband, 'Canteen politics tops UN agenda', *The Guardian* (London), 26 July 1993.
11. Ibid.
12. 'Talk poor by day; live rich by night', 'The corrupt heart of the UN bureaucracy', *The Sunday Times* (London), 15 August 1993; 'Inept UN is devastating the poor, says Oxfam', *The Sunday Times* (London), 22 August 1993; 'UN acts on report of waste and fraud', *The Sunday Times* (London), 29 August 1993; Peter Hillmore, 'British officer blows whistle on UN corruption', *The Observer* (London), 29 August 1993.
13. 'UN investigates corruption', *The Guardian* (London), 25 August 1993; Maggie O'Kane, Edward Luce, Ian Black and Edward Pilkington, 'UN promises to stamp out corruption among troops in Bosnia', *The Guardian* (London), 27 August 1993.
14. Norman Stone, 'The soldiers of misfortune', *The Guardian* (London), 27 August 1993; Conor Cruise O'Brien, *The Independent* (London), 27 August 1993.
15. *The UN and The Sunday Times* (London: United Nations Information Centre, 9 September 1993).
16. David Bryer, 'Oxfam puts its case against the UN' (letter), *The Sunday Times* (London), 12 September 1993.
17. Boutros-Ghali, *Report*, pp. 16–17.
18. Hella Pick and Mark Huband, 'Members begrudge UN the cost of policing conflict', *The Guardian* (London), 29 May 1993; Hella Pick, 'Good intentions suffer under the burden of bad debts', *The Guardian* (London), 4 August 1993.

19. Peter Pringle, 'Overload for peace-keepers', *The Guardian* (London), 16 June 1993.
20. The text of the letter is given in *The Guardian* (London), 5 August 1993.
21. Annika Savill, 'UK finds a way to hold on to the mother of all seats', *The Independent* (London), 7 January 1992.
22. *UN Peacekeeping and Intervention Forces*, Defence Committee, fourth report, House of Commons paper 188/369 (London: Her Majesty's Stationery Office, 1993).
23. Annika Savill, 'Britain starts to bow towards the inevitable', *The Independent* (London), 9 July 1993.
24. Richard Gott, 'Nations divided by a lost vision', *The Guardian* (London), 28 August 1993.
25. Leonard Doyle, 'UN starts process of electing a leader', *The Independent* (London), 11 October 1991; Leonard Doyle, 'How Cairo's man finally won the day', *The Independent* (London), 23 November 1991.
26. Barnaby (ed.), *Building a More Democratic UN*. This comprehensive book discusses radical UN reform from many different perspectives.
27. This important proposal cannot be explored here. Interested readers should refer to ibid., especially pp. 83–148; see also Jeffrey J. Segall and Harry H. Lerner (eds), *CAMDUN-2: The United Nations and a New World Order for Peace and Justice*, Report of the Second International Conference on A More Democratic United Nations (Vienna 1991) (London: CAMDUN Project, 1992).
28. Conor Cruise O'Brien, 'Ritual humiliation at the UN', *The Independent* (London), 4 June 1993.
29. Louis Mountbatten, 10 August 1947, Broadlands Archives, D1, quoted in Philip Ziegler, *Mountbatten* (London: Collins, 1985) p. 450.
30. Jon Holliday, 'Secret war of the top guns', *The Observer* (London), 5 July 1992.
31. Conor Cruise O'Brien, *To Katanga and Back: A UN case history* (New York: Universal Library, 1962) p. 63.
32. Ibid., p. 64.
33. Leonard Doyle, 'UN's dream leader heads for disaster', *The Independent* (London), 27 July 1992; Mark Tran, 'Question mark over future of Boutros-Ghali', *The Guardian* (London) 27 July 1992; 'The order of the boot for Boutros?' (editorial), *The Guardian* (London), 28 July 1992; Patrick E. Tyler, 'UN Chief's dispute with Council boils over', *The New York Times*, 3 August 1992.
34. Leonard Doyle, 'Boutros-Ghali's "harsh" style under fire again', *The Independent* (London), 30 October 1992.
35. Cameron Duodo, 'The West is to blame, not Boutros-Ghali', *The Observer* (London), 9 August 1992.
36. 'US cash threat over WHO head', *The Guardian* (London), 5 May 1993; Ian Black, 'West fails to block Japanese chief of world health body', *The Guardian* (London), 6 May 1993.
37. As with the World Court ruling in favour of Nicaragua in 1984; and against the US-supported Morocco, intent on occupying Western Sahara, in 1975.
38. Lynne Wallis, 'Cuba's hunger feeds an epidemic of pain', *The Observer* (London), 23 May 1993.

39. H. J. Morgenthou, *Politics among Nations* (New York: Alfred A. Knopf, 1960).
40. *FAO/WFP Crop and Food Assessment Mission to Iraq*, Special Alert no. 237 (Rome: Food and Agriculture Organisation of the United Nations and World Food Programme, July 1993).
41. Richard Dowden, 'Why the food just stopped', *The Independent on Sunday* (London), 6 June 1993.
42. Richard Dowden, 'Liberia lives at risk as UN blocks food aid', *The Independent* (London), 2 September 1993.
43. Conor Cruise O'Brien, 'Disorder between war and peace', *The Independent* (London), 18 June 1993.
44. Edward Heath, 'UNdone', *The Guardian* (London), 10 July 1993.
45. Hugh Muir, 'Britain lags in battle to beat racism, says the UN', *The Daily Telegraph* (London), 21 August 1993.
46. Boutros Boutros-Ghali, 'UN multilateralism: a cure for ugly new nationalisms', *International Herald Tribune*, 21–2 August 1993.

Bibliography

Three types of publications have been consulted in the preparation of the present work:

(1) books about the United Nations (its character, history, personnel and so on) that are not UN publications. Such books are sometimes written by current or former UN employees;
(2) books not specifically about the United Nations but which provide crucial historical or political background information;
(3) books published by the United Nations or its Specialised Agencies.

The present Bibliography lists items from the first two categories but not from the third. The current UN *Publications Catalogue* includes thousands of items listed in 149 pages. Interested readers should refer to this *Catalogue*.

Akehurst, Michael, *A Modern Introduction to International Law* (London: HarperCollins Academic, 1991).

Allen, H. G., *Great Britain and the United States* (London: Odhams Press, 1954).

Ambrose, Stephen E., *Rise to Globalism: American Foreign Policy since 1938*, 5th edn (Harmondsworth, Middx: Penguin, 1988).

Ash, Timothy Garton, *We the People: The Revolution of '89* (Cambridge: Granta, 1990).

Baehr, P. R. and Gordenker, L., *The United Nations: Reality and Ideal* (London: 1984).

Baer, George W., *The Coming of the Italian–Ethiopian War* (Cambridge, Mass.: 1967).

Bailey, Sydney D., *The Procedure of the UN Security Council* (Oxford: Clarendon Press, 1988).

Bailey, Thomas A., *Woodrow Wilson and the Lost Peace* (New York: Macmillan, 1944).

Baldev, *China, UNO and World Peace* (Delhi: International Reporter Publications, 1971).

Barnaby, Frank (ed.), *Building a More Democratic United Nations: Proceedings of the First International Conference on a More Democratic UN* (London: Frank Cass, 1991).

Barnet, Richard J., *Intervention and Revolution* (London: MacGibbon & Kee, 1970).

Barros, James, *Office Without Power: Secretary-General Sir Eric Drummond, 1919–1933* (Oxford: Oxford University Press, 1979).

Bassett, Richard, *Waldheim and Austria* (Harmondsworth, Middx: Viking Penguin, 1988).

Bennis, Phyllis and Moushabeck, Michel, *Beyond the Storm: A Gulf Crisis Reader* (Edinburgh: Cannongate Press, 1992).

Bergamini, David, *Japan's Imperial Conspiracy* (London: Heinemann, 1971).

Blum, William, *The CIA: A Forgotten History* (London: Zed Books, 1986).

Bodenheimer, Thomas and Gould, Robert, *Rollback!: Right-wing Power in US Foreign Policy* (Boston, Mass.: South End Press, 1989).
Boyd, Andrew, *Fifteen Men on a Powder Keg: A History of the UN Security Council* (London: Methuen, 1971).
Branford, Sue and Kucinski, Bernardo, *The US, the Banks and Latin America* (London: Zed Books, 1990).
Brierly, J. L., *The Law of Nations: An Introduction to the International Law of Peace* (London: Oxford University Press, 1963).
Brogan, Hugh, *History of the United States of America* (London: Longman, 1985).
Bryce, James, *International Relations* (New York: Macmillan, 1923).
Castberg, Frede, *The Voting Procedure in the League of Nations and the United Nations* (Oslo: F. Castberg and E. Dons, 1949).
Cecil, Lord Robert, *A Great Experiment* (London: Oxford University Press, 1941).
Choate, J. H., *The Two Hague Conferences* (Princeton, N.J., and London: 1913).
Chomsky, Noam, *Deterring Democracy* (London and New York: Verso, 1991).
Claude, Inis L., *The Changing United Nations* (New York: Random House, 1967).
—— *Swords into Plowshares: The Problems and Progress of International Organization* (New York: Random House, 1951).
Cockburn, Andrew and Leslie, *Dangerous Liaison* (London: Bodley Head, 1992).
Comay, Joan, *The United Nations in Action* (New York: Macmillan, 1965).
Davis, Betty Jane, *Charter for Tomorrow* (Seattle: University of Washington, 1946).
Degler, Carl N., *Out of Our Past* (New York: Harper & Row, 1959).
Devlin, Patrick, *Too Proud to Fight* (London: Oxford University Press, 1974).
Dusen, Henry P. van, *Dag Hammarskjöld: A Biographical Interpretation of Markings* (London: Faber & Faber, 1967).
Eagleton, Clyde, *United Nations and United States* (Dallas, Tx.: Southern Methodist University Press, 1951).
Echelberger, Clark M., *United Nations – The First Ten Years* (New York: Harper, 1955).
Egerton, G. W., *Great Britain and the Creation of the League of Nations: Strategy, Politics and International Organisation, 1914–1919* (London: 1979).
Evatt, Herbert Vere, *The United Nations* (Cambridge, Mass.: Harvard University Press, 1948).
Falk, Richard A. (ed.), *The Vietnam War and International Law* (Princeton, N.J.: Princeton University Press, 1968).
Fehrenbach, T. R., *This Kind of Peace* (London: Frewin, 1967).
Feis, Herbert, *Churchill, Roosevelt and Stalin* (Oxford: Oxford University Press, 1957).
Finer, Herman, *Dulles Over Suez: The Theory and Practice of his Diplomacy* (Chicago, Ill.: Quadrangle Books, 1964).
First, Ruth, *South West Africa* (Harmondsworth, Middx: Penguin, 1963).
Fleming, D. F., *The Cold War and its Origins, 1917–1960* (New York: Doubleday, 1961).
Foley, Hamilton, *Woodrow Wilson's Case for the League of Nations* (Princeton, N.J.: Princeton University Press, 1923).
Frankel, Joseph, *International Relations in a Changing World* (London: Oxford University Press, 1964).
Fromkin, David, *A Peace to End All Peace* (London: Deutsch, 1989).
Fulbright, J. William, *The Price of Empire* (London: Fourth Estate, 1989).

Garraty, John A., *Henry Cabot Lodge* (New York: Alfred A. Knopf, 1953).
George, Susan, *The Debt Boomerang: How Third World Debt Harms Us All* (London: Pluto Press, 1992).
—— *How the Other Half Dies: The Real Reasons for World Hunger* (Harmondsworth, Middx: Penguin, 1991).
Gildersleeve, Virginia C., *The Making of the United Nations Charter* (New York: Macmillan, 1954).
Goodman, Walter, *The Committee* (London: Secker & Warburg, 1969).
Goodrich, Leyland and Simmons, Anne P., *United Nations and Maintenance of International Peace and Security* (Washington, D.C.: Brookings Institution, 1955).
Goodwin, Geoffrey L., *Britain and the United Nations* (London: 1957).
Griffin, G. Edward, *The Fearful Master: A Second Look at the United Nations* (Belmont, Mass.: Westward Islands, 1964).
Hammarskjöld, Dag, *Markings* (London: Faber & Faber, 1964).
—— *Servant of Peace* (London: The Bodley Head, 1962).
Hancock, Graham, *Lords of Poverty* (London: Macmillan, 1992).
Hersh, Seymour M., *Kissinger: The Price of Power* (New York: Summit Books, 1983).
—— *The Samson Option: Israel, America and the Bomb* (London: Faber & Faber, 1991).
Herzstein, Robert Edwin, *Walheim: The Missing Years* (London: Grafton Books, 1988).
Hiro, Dilip, *Desert Shield to Desert Storm: The Second Gulf War* (London: Paladin, 1992).
—— *The Longest War: The Iran–Iraq Military Conflict* (London: Paladin, 1990).
Hiscocks, Richard, *The Security Council* (London: Longman, 1973).
Hitchens, Christopher, *Hostage to History* (New York: Noonday Press, 1989).
Hoffman, Nicholas von, *Citizen Cohn* (London: Harrap, 1988).
Hofstadter, Richard, *The American Political Tradition* (London: Jonathan Cape, 1971).
Hoggart, Richard, *An Idea and its Servants: UNESCO from Within* (London: Chatto & Windus, 1978).
Holcombe, Arthur N., *The United Nations and American Foreign Policy* (Urbana, Ill.: University of Illinois Press, 1957).
Horowitz, David, *From Yalta to Vietnam: American Foreign Policy in the Cold War* (Harmondsworth, Middx: Penguin, 1967).
Hovet, Thomas Jr, *Bloc Politics in the United Nations* (Cambridge, Mass.: Harvard University Press, 1960).
Hull, Cordell, *Memoirs* (New York: Macmillan, 1948).
Jatlov, Edwin, *The United Nations – The First Twenty-five Years* (London: Peter Owen, 1970).
Jensen, E. and Fisher, T., *The United Kingdom – The United Nations* (London: Macmillan, 1990).
Kahin, George McT., *Intervention: How America became Involved in Vietnam* (New York: Anchor Books, Doubleday, 1987).
Kelsen, Hans, *Law of the United Nations: A Critical Analysis of its Fundamental Problems* (New York: Praeger, 1950).

Körner, Peter, Maass, Gero, Siebold, Thomas and Tetzlaff, Rainer, *The IMF and the Debt Crisis* (London: Zed Books, 1992).
Lash, Joseph P., *Dag Hammarskjöld* (London: Cassell, 1962).
Levine, I. E., *Dag Hammarskjöld, Champion of World Peace* (London: Blackie, 1962).
Lie, Trygve, *In the Cause of Peace* (New York: Macmillan, 1954).
Litvinoff, Barnet, *The Burning Bush* (London: Collins, 1988).
Loftus, John, *The Balarus Secret* (New York: Alfred A. Knopf, 1982).
Loth, Wilfred, *The Division of the World, 1941–1955* (London: Routledge, 1988).
Luard, Evan, *The United Nations: How it Works and What it Does* (London: Macmillan, 1979).
MacIver, Robert M., *The Nations and the United Nations* (New York: Manhattan Publishing Co., 1959).
Manchester, William, *American Caesar: Douglas MacArthur, 1880–1964* (London: Hutchinson, 1979).
Mansfield, Peter, *A History of the Middle East* (London: Viking, 1991).
Miller, Merle, *Plain Speaking: An Oral Biography of Harry S. Truman* (New York: Berkley Publishing, 1974).
Moore, Raymond A., *United Nations Reconsidered* (Columbia, S.C.: South Carolina University Press, 1963).
Nicholas, H. G., *The United Nations as a Political Institution* (London: Oxford University Press, 1959).
Nogueira, Franco, *The United Nations and Portugal: A Study of Anti-colonialism* (London: Sidgwick & Jackson, 1963).
Northedge, F. S., *The League of Nations: Its Life and Times, 1920–1946* (Leicester: Leicester University Press, 1986).
O'Brien, Conor Cruise, *To Katanga and Back* (New York: Simon & Schuster, 1962).
—— and Topolski, *Felix, The United Nations: Sacred Drama* (London: 1968).
Osmanczyk, Edmund Jan, *Encyclopedia of the United Nations and International Agreements* (New York: Taylor & Francis, 1990).
Padelford, Norman J. and Goodrich, Leyland N., *United Nations in the Balance* (New York: Praeger, 1965).
Patil, Anjali V., *The UN Veto in World Affairs, 1946–1990: A Complete Record and Case Histories of the Security Council's Veto* (Sarasota, Fla: UNIFO/Mansell, 1992).
Payer, Cheryl, *The Debt Trap: The IMF and the Third World* (Harmondsworth, Middx: Penguin, 1974).
Pearce, Jenny, *Under the Eagle: US Intervention in Central America and the Caribbean* (London: Latin American Bureau, 1982).
Pisani, Sallie, *The CIA and the Marshall Plan* (Edinburgh: Edinburgh University Press, 1991).
Postal, Bernard and Levy, Henry W., *And the Hills Shouted for Joy* (New York: McKay, 1973).
Powers, Richard Gid, *Secrecy and Power: The Life of J. Edgar Hoover* (London: Arrow, 1989).
Rae, John B. and Mahoney, Thomas H. D., *The United States in World History* (New York: McGraw-Hill, 1964).

Raghavan, Chakravarthi, *Recolonization: GATT, the Uruguay Round and the Third World* (London: Zed Books, 1990).
Reynolds, E. E., *The League Experiment* (London: Nelson, 1940).
Rikhye, Indar Jit and Skjelsbaek, K., *The United Nations and Peacekeeping* (London: Macmillan, 1990).
Rosenzweig, Luc and Cohen, Bernard, *Waldheim* (London: Robson, 1988).
Rosie, George, *The British in Vietnam* (London: Panther, 1970).
Ross, Alf, *Constitution of the United Nations: Analysis of Structure and Function* (New York: Rinehart, 1950).
Roxburgh, Angus, *The Second Russian Revolution* (London: BBC Books, 1991).
Russel, Ruth B. and Muther, Jeanette, E., *A History of the United Nations Charter: The Role of the United States, 1940–45* (Washington, D.C.: Brookings Institution Press, 1958).
Russell, Bertrand, *Which Way to Peace?* (London: Michael Joseph, 1936).
Russell, Frank M., *Theories of International Relations* (New York and London: 1936).
Sandusky, Michael C., *America's Parallel* (Alexandria, V: Old Dominion Press, 1983).
Schiavone, Giuseppe, *International Organisations: A Dictionary and Directory* (London: Macmillan, 1986).
Schwebel, Stephen M., *A Secretary-General of the United Nations: His Political Powers and Practice* (Cambridge, Mass.: Harvard University Press, 1952).
Scott, George, *The Rise and Fall of the League of Nations* (London: Hutchinson, 1973).
Selbourne, David, *Death of the Dark Hero: Eastern Europe, 1987–90* (London: Jonathan Cape, 1990).
Shawcross, William, *Sideshow: Kissinger, Nixon and the Destruction of Cambodia* (London: Hogarth Press, 1986).
Sihanouk, Norodom, *My War with the CIA* (Harmondsworth, Middx: Penguin, 1974).
Simons, Geoff, *Iraq: From Sumer to Saddam* (London: Macmillan, 1994).
—— *Libya: The Struggle for Survival* (London: Macmillan, 1993).
Simpson, Christopher, *Blowback: America's Recruitment of Nazis and its Effects on the Cold War* (London: Weidenfeld & Nicolson, 1988).
Smith, Gene, *When the Cheering Stopped* (London: Hutchinson, 1964).
Smith, Howard K., *The State of Europe* (New York: Alfred A. Knopf, 1949).
Sohn, Louis B., *United Nations Next Twenty-five Years* (New York: Oceana Publications, 1970).
Stettinius, Edward R., *Roosevelt and the Russians: The Yalta Conference* (New York: Doubleday, 1949).
Thomas, Hugh, *The Spanish Civil War* (Harmondsworth, Middx: Penguin, 1968).
Thorpe, Deryck, *Hammarskjöld, Man of Peace* (Ilfracombe, Devon: Stockwell, 1969).
Twitchett, Kenneth J., *The Evolving United Nations: A Prospect for Peace?* (London: Europa Publications, 1971).
The United Nations Conference on International Organization, San Francisco, California April 25 to June 26, 1945; Selected Documents (Washington, D.C.: US Government Printing Office, 1946).
Waldheim, Kurt, *In the Eye of the Storm* (London: Weidenfeld & Nicolson, 1985).

Walters, F. P., *A History of the League of Nations* (London: Oxford University Press, 1960).
Webster, C. K. and Herbert, Sidney, *The League of Nations in Theory and Practice* (London: 1933).
Weinstein, Allen, *Perjury: The Hiss–Chambers Case* (New York: Alfred A. Knopf, 1978).
White, Stephen, *Gorbachev and After* (Cambridge: Cambridge University Press, 1992).
Wilcox, Francis O. and Marcy, Carl M., *Proposals for Changes in the United Nations* (Washington, D.C.: Brookings Institution, 1955).
Wilson, Edith, *Memoirs of Mrs Woodrow Wilson* (London: Putnam, 1939).
Wilson, Florence, *The Origins of the League Covenant: Documentary History of its Drafting* (London: 1928).
Woodward, Bob, *The Commanders* (London: Simon & Schuster, 1991).
—— *Veil: The Secret Wars of the CIA, 1981–1987* (London: Simon & Schuster 1987).
Woodward, Llewellyn, *Great Britain and the War of 1914–1918* (London: Methuen, 1967).
Wright, Martin, *Power Politics* (Harmondsworth, Middx: Penguin, 1979).
Zacher, Mark W., *Dag Hammarskjöld's United Nations* (New York: Columbia University Press, 1970).
Zimmern, Alfred, *The League of Nations and the Rule of Law, 1918–1935* (London: Macmillan, 1936).

Index